D1593075

RUSSIA AND EUROPE IN THE TWENTY-FIRST CENTURY

Advance Reviews

'This volume is a fulsome examination of that most perplexing of contemporary relationships that of Europe and Russia. In offering an examination of both Russia's perspectives on the West and European perspectives on Russia the contributors have provided a fulsome assessment of the dynamics of relations. The editors and contributors have demonstrated a mastery of the subject that will ensure that the book will find a ready audience for its cogent and insightful analysis.'

Professor Richard G. Whitman, Professor of Politics,
University of Bath and Senior Fellow, Europe, Chatham House

'Drawing on political and historical concepts, this superb collection offers an array of rich variations on one of the central issues of current European international politics. Bringing together the work of a remarkable group of scholars, *Russia and Europe: An Uneasy Partnership*, fully demonstrates an importance of understanding of such different political cultures as European and Russian. Lucid and engaging, this book offers not only a comprehensive picture of the dynamic nature of contemporary Russian/European relations but also a refreshing change from much contemporary writing about international politics.'

Evgeny Dobrenko, University of Sheffield

'Relations developing between the EU and Russia are one of the pillars of the new European, indeed, international order that is arising in this first decade of the 21st century. Given the importance of the subject, the lack of serious scholarship on the various facets of EU-Russia relations is worrying and is a gap that must be filled. This volume by Graham Timmins and Jackie Gower does precisely this. Looking at EU-Russia relations from the vantage points of Brussels and of Moscow and then turning to examine the state of partnership as it now stands, this book performs an invaluable service for all those interested in this question. And we all should be.'

Dov Lynch, Senior Policy Adviser, Office of the Secretary General, OSCE, Vienna

'This is a timely publication: Russia and the European Union are too similar in some ways and all too different in others. Is partnership between them possible? Yes, but surely an uneasy one ... this book paints a colourful but objective picture!'

Konstantin Khudoley, Dean of the School of International
Relations of the St. Petersburg State University

RUSSIA AND EUROPE IN THE TWENTY-FIRST CENTURY

An Uneasy Partnership

Edited by Jackie Gower and Graham Timmins

With a Foreword by The Rt. Hon. Lord Robertson of Port Ellen

ANTHEM PRESS
LONDON · NEW YORK · DELHI

Anthem Press
An imprint of Wimbledon Publishing Company
www.anthempress.com

This edition first published in UK and USA 2007
by ANTHEM PRESS
75-76 Blackfriars Road, London SE1 8HA, UK
or PO Box 9779, London SW19 7ZG, UK and
244 Madison Ave. #116, New York, NY 10016, USA

British Library Cataloguing in Publication Data
A catalogue record for this book is available from the British Library.

Library of Congress Cataloging in Publication Data
A catalog record for this book has been requested.

ISBN-10: 1 84331 220 4 (Hbk)
ISBN-13: 978 1 84331 220 8 (Hbk)

1 3 5 7 9 10 8 6 4 2

Printed in India

Contents

LIST OF CONTRIBUTORS

Derek L. Averre is a Senior Research Fellow in the Centre for Russian and East European Studies (CREES) within the European Research Institute at the University of Birmingham. He has written widely on Russian security and defence policy and is co-editor of *Securing Europe's East: New Security Challenges in Post-communist Europe* (with Andrew Cottey), Manchester University Press, 2002.

Irina Busygina is a Professor in the School of Political Science at the Moscow State Institute of International Relations. Her specialist research area is Russian regionalism.

Thomas Frellesen was until 2006 the Head of the Political Section in the European Commission Delegation in Moscow. He has contributed to several studies on the European Union's external relations.

Marco Fantini has worked in the European Commission since 1994 and during the period 1999–2004 was responsible for Russia, Belarus and Moldova within the Directorate-General for Economic and Financial Affairs. His publications include 'The European Neighbourhood Policy: Implications for Economic Growth and Stability' (with Michaela Dodini) in the *Journal of Common Market Studies*, Vol.44, No.3, 2006.

Jackie Gower is a Visiting Fellow in the Department of War Studies at King's College London. She has published widely on the European Union and is a co-editor of *EU Enlargement: The Way Forward* (with John Redmond), Aldershot: Ashgate, 2000 and editor of *The European Union Handbook*, London and Chicago, Fitzroy Dearborn, 2002.

Mark McGuigan is a Senior Consultant on international security issues with Assynt Associates. He was an RAF Officer during 1983–2004 and undertook two secondments to NATO where he acted as a Political Adviser on NATO-Russia issues.

Hiski Haukkala is a Researcher in the Finnish Institute of International Affairs (FIIA) in Helsinki and a PhD candidate in the Department of Political Science at the University of Turku. He has published several research papers on EU-Russian relations and is co-editor of *The Dynamic Aspects of the Northern*

Dimension (with Sergei Medvedev), Helsinki: FIIA, 1999 and *The EU Common Strategy on Russia: Learning the Grammar of the CFSP* (with Sergei Medvedev), Helsinki: FIIA, 2001.

Kristi Raik is a Researcher in the Finnish Institute of International Affairs (FIIA) in Helsinki. Her main research interests are enlargement and the Eastern neighbourhood policy of the European Union, democratization in Central and Eastern Europe and the foreign and security policy of the Baltic States. Her publications include *Democratic Politics or the Implementation of Inevitabilities? – Estonia's Democracy and Integration into the European Union*, Tartu University Press, 2003.

Margot Light is a Professor Emeritus in the Department of International Relations at the London School of Economics. She has published extensively on Soviet and Post-Soviet foreign policy. Her recent publications include 'Russia and the West: is there a Values Gap?' (with Stephen White and Ian McAllister), *International Politics*, Vol.42, No.3, 2005 and 'In Search of an Identity: Russian Foreign Policy and the End of Ideology', *Journal of Communist Studies and Transition Politics*, Vol.19, No.3, 2003.

Julie M. Newton is an Associate Professor in the Department of International and Comparative Politics at the American University in Paris. Her research interests focus specifically on Franco-Russian relations and she is the author of *Russia, France and the Idea of Europe*, London: Macmillan, 2003.

Dimitry Polikanov is a Senior Account Manager with The PBN Company in Moscow. He is a former Director of International and Public Relations at the All-Russia Public Opinion Research Center (VCIOM) and Deputy Director of the Center for Policy Studies in Russia (PIR). He has published widely on Russian foreign and security policy. His publications include 'NATO-Russia Relations: Present and Future' in *Contemporary Security Policy*, Vol.25, No.3, 2004.

Neil Robinson is a Senior Lecturer and Head of Politics and Public Administration at the University of Limerick. He has published widely on Soviet and Post-Soviet Politics. His publications include *Institutions and Political Change in Russia* (ed.), London: Macmillan, 2000 and *Russia: a State of Uncertainty*, London: Routledge, 2002.

Clelia Rontoyanni was until 2006 a Political Officer in the European Commission Delegation in Moscow. She is a former Research Fellow with the Royal Institute for International Affairs. Her publications include 'So Far, So Good? Russia and the ESDP', *International Affairs*, Vol.78, No.4, 2002.

Richard Sakwa is a Professor and Head of Politics and International Relations at the University of Kent at Canterbury. He has published extensively on Russian politics and his most recent publications include *Russian Politics and Society*, 3rd Edition, London: Routledge, 2002, *Putin: Russia's Choice*, London: Routledge, 2004 and *Chechnya: From Past to Future* (ed.), London: Anthem Press, 2005.

Graham Timmins is a Professor and Head of Politics at the University of Stirling. His research specialisms focus on EU and German politics. His publications include *Building a Bigger Europe: EU and NATO Enlargement in Comparative Perspective* (with Martin A.Smith), London: Ashgate, 2000 and *Uncertain Europe: Building a New European Security Order?* (co-edited with Martin A.Smith), London: Routledge, 2001.

Stephen White is Professor of International Politics in the Department of Politics at the University of Glasgow. He has published widely on Russian politics and his current publications include *Communism and its Collapse*, London: Routledge, 2001 and *Developments in Russian Politics*, 6th Edition (edited with Zvi Gitelman and Richard Sakwa), London: Palgrave, 2005.

Mark Webber is a Senior Lecturer in the Department of Politics and International Relations at the University of Loughborough. He is a specialist on European security governance and his publications include *Russia and Europe: Confrontation or Cooperation?* (ed.), Basingstoke: Macmillan, 2000 and *Foreign Policy in a Transformed World* (with Michael Smith), Harlow: Pearson, 2002.

ACKNOWLEDGEMENTS

This project emerged out of a workshop on Russia and Europe convened at the University of Stirling in June 2004. The editors wish to thank the European Commission, the British Academy and the Department of Politics at the University of Stirling for the financial support provided in support of the workshop. The editors also wish to thank the authors for their contributions to what has been a highly stimulating academic project. Finally, many thanks to Paolo Cabrelli and his colleagues at Anthem Press for the encouragement and support provided in the completion of this edited volume.

Jackie Gower and Graham Timmins
August, 2006

LIST OF ABBREVIATIONS/ACRONYMS

ABM	Anti-Ballistic Missile
AWACS	Airborne Warning and Control Systems
CCQS	Franco-Russian Cooperation Council
CDU	Christian Democratic Union
CEE	Central and Eastern Europe
CEECs	Central and East European Countries
CEES	Common European Economic Space
CEO	Chief Executive Officer
CES	Common Economic Space
CFE	Treaty on Conventional Forces in Europe
CFSP	Common Foreign and Security Policy
CIS	Commonwealth of Independent States
COMECON	Council for Mutual Economic Assistance
CSCE	Conference on Security and Cooperation in Europe
CSTO	Collective Security Treaty Organization
DG	Directorate-General
EAPC	Euro-Atlantic Partnership Council
EC	European Community
EEA	European Economic Area
ENP	European Neighbourhood Policy
EP	European Parliament
EPC	European Political Cooperation
ESDI	European Security and Defence Identity
ESDP	European Security and Defence Policy
EU	European Union
EUJUST Themis	EU Rule of Law Mission in Georgia
FATF	Financial Action Task Force
FDI	Foreign Direct Investment
FRTD	Facilitated Rail Transit Document
FSB	Federal Security Service of the Russian Federation
FSJ	Freedom, Security and Justice
FSU	Former Soviet Union
FTA	Free Trade Area
FTD	Facilitated Transit Document
G8	Group of Eight

GCI	Growth Competitive Index
GDP	Gross Domestic Product
GDR	German Democratic Republic
GLONASS	Global Navigation Satellite System
GUUAM	Georgia, Ukraine, Uzbekistan, Azerbaijan, Moldova
ICISS	International Commission on Intervention and State Sovereignty
IFOR	Implementation Force in Bosnia and Herzegovina
IMEMO	Institute for World Economy and International Relations
IMF	International Monetary Fund
INTERREG	Interregional Cooperation
JHA	Justice and Home Affairs
KFOR	Kosovo Force
KGB	State Security Committee
KLA	Kosovo Liberation Army
MEP	Member of the European Parliament
MFA	(Russian) Ministry of Foreign Affairs
NAC	North Atlantic Council
NACC	North Atlantic Cooperation Council
NATO	North Atlantic Treaty Organization
NGO	Non-Governmental Organization
NIS	Newly Independent States
NRC	NATO-Russia Council
NTA	New Transatlantic Agreement
NTB	Non-Tariff Barrier
OAF	Operation Allied Force
OECD	Organization for Economic Cooperation and Development
OPLAN	Operation Plan
OSCE	Organization for Security and Cooperation in Europe
PCA	Partnership and Cooperation Agreement
PfP	Partnership for Peace
PHARE	Economic Reconstruction Assistance for Poland and Hungary (EU)
PJC	Permanent Joint Council
PPC	Permanent Partnership Council
PSC	Political and Security Committee
QMV	Qualified Majority Voting
RISI	Russian Institute for Strategic Studies
SACEUR	Supreme Allied Commander for Europe
SCO	Shanghai Cooperation Organization
SES	Single Economic Space

SFOR	Stabilization Force in Bosnia and Herzegovina
SHAPE	Supreme Headquarters Allied Powers in Europe
SIS	Schengen Information System
SPD	German Social Democratic Party
START	Strategic Arms Reduction Treaty
SVOP	Council for Foreign and Defence Policy
TACIS	Technical Assistance for the Commonwealth of Independent States
TLE	Treaty Limited Equipment
UK	United Kingdom
UN	United Nations
UNSC	United Nations Security Council
UNSCR	United Nations Security Council Resolution
US	United States (of America)
USSR	Union of Soviet Socialist Republics
WEU	Western European Union
WMD	Weapons of Mass Destruction
WNIS	Western Newly Independent States
WTO	World Trade Organization

FOREWORD

RUSSIA AND EUROPE

There have been few times before when there was such a thirst for knowledge and guidance about Russia. In the year when Russia charied the G8 and the oil price rocketed Russia back to super-power status there were still riddles to be solved about Russia and where it is going.

The shutting off of pipelines to the Ukraine started off 2006 which was to become a remarkable year. In one move, the Russian government claiming it was motivated only by normal market economics, the rest of Western Europe woke up to the issue of energy security. Whether this was another law of unintended consequences or part of some Machiavellian plan has still to be resolved, but it has certainly put Russia back in the headlines.

For even the expert Russia watchers there is a need for help in navigating the currents alive in Russian politics today. That is why this collection of essays is so important. Here a number of perceptive people have turned their minds to describing what is going on – and – more importantly, have combined to give us some conclusions.

A multifaceted approach has always been necessary in understanding this great country and its neighbours. Kremlin watching was once a profession all of its own. Nowadays democratic Russia has still many facets which need explanation and interpretation. It is a fact that in today's complicated world to be ignorant of Russia is to be without a key ingredient in understanding what is happening to our lives.

This book has the enormous strength of being both multifaceted and multidimensional and I heartily recommend it to both the expert and for the simply curious.

The Rt Hon. Lord Robertson of Port Ellen, Secretary General of the North Atlantic Treaty Organization (NATO) (1999–2003).

INTRODUCTION

RUSSIA AND EUROPE: WHAT KIND OF PARTNERSHIP?

Jackie Gower and Graham Timmins

Russia and Europe in the Post-Cold War World

At the opening of the twenty-first century there was widespread optimism that the relationship between Russia and Europe was entering a new era of unprecedented cooperation and constructive engagement. Growing economic interdependence and the recognition of shared political, security and environmental challenges provided a powerful rationale for the development of a genuinely strategic partnership. However, by the summer of 2006 when this research project was completed it was clear that there was deep disappointment on both sides that so little had actually been achieved either in terms of practical outcomes or in developing mutual understanding and trust. As is usually the case when relationships are strained, the reasons are complex and rooted in the legacy of the past as much as in the difficulties of the present.

The sudden implosion of the Soviet-type system in central and eastern Europe (CEE) in 1989 and, ultimately, the Soviet Union two years later in 1991, initiated a traumatic period of socio-economic and political disruption and decline in Russia during the 1990s which was to culminate in the collapse of the rouble in August 1998 and the political humiliation of its impotence in the face of the North Atlantic Treaty Organization (NATO)-led military intervention into Kosovo in 1999. During this decade there was a fundamental transformation of the European political landscape which introduced a situation of extreme uncertainty within the international community. The enlargement of the European Union (EU) and NATO to the East may have provided a 'return to Europe' for the states concerned but in the process Russia found itself increasingly marginalized from an expanding western institutional order and subsequently ambivalent regarding its place in the 'New Europe'. Russia clearly is part of the European continent. It has a significant economic relationship with the western European states stretching back for centuries and has in many respects a shared cultural and intellectual history with the West. Yet in political terms Russia traditionally looks Janus-like towards both Europe and Asia which makes locating it within the contemporary European political debate extremely problematic. It is unlikely at present that Russia would be offered membership of either the EU or NATO or that Russia would seek it. But to imagine a stable European political order without the inclusion of Russia in some sense would be nonsensical. Its size alone dictates a degree of inclusion. Moreover, growing western European reliance on Russian natural energy resources together with Russia's economic dependency on energy exports makes the maintenance of at the very least a cooperative working relationship between Russia and Europe a political necessity. The question is not whether Russia has a contribution to make to the creation and maintenance of European order but rather how Moscow's voice is heard; within which venues, under whose terms and regarding which issues?

When Putin rose to power in 1999, little was known about the man or his policies. His New Year speech in December 1999 set out the broad direction of his agenda which was to prioritize the establishment of internal stability and, in the process, rekindle national pride and identity at home and abroad.[1] By 2006 and approaching the latter part of his second and assumed final presidential term, Vladimir Putin has become one of the most recognized political faces in world politics and has achieved his core objectives. The Russian economy has recovered from the shock of 1998 and living standards have demonstrated consistent improvement albeit from a very low base and not always in a universal manner. Most important, however, Russia has rediscovered its voice and has a place at the table in shaping the international agenda. As President of the Group of Eight (G8) for 2006 and with membership of the World Trade Organization (WTO) pending, Putin has made considerable progress in establishing Russia as a 'normal' state. But Russia's domestic recovery and international influence has been based very much on its energy resources and the much-needed revenue provided rather than broadly based economic growth. Large parts of the Russian economy remain fragile and would be unable to cope with full exposure to global market competition. Moreover, with Putin required by the Russian constitution to stand down at the presidential elections in 2008 and with no obvious successor waiting in the wings, there is growing political uncertainty as Russia looks towards the future.

The European Response to the New Russia

But if the end of the Cold War had required Russia to redefine its international identity, the same was true of its European neighbours to the West and the international organizations to which they belonged. If the key western European institutions e.g. the European Community (EC) as it was known until the signing of the *Treaty on European Union* in 1992 and NATO, were to remain in place beyond the Cold War it was imperative that they too provided credible justification for their continued existence. For the EC the end of the Cold War provided the opportunity to extend its historic mission of forging European peace and stability eastwards, a process which was to lead to ten new members joining in May 2004. In the case of NATO, its future after the Cold War was much less certain. Its rationale at the time of the signing of the Washington Treaty in 1949 was to establish a collective defence mechanism to protect the West against the Soviet Union. Once western Europe no longer needed to live in fear of Soviet aggression, the argument began to develop in the early 1990s that NATO was no longer required and this followed the logic that successful alliances invariably fall apart once they are no longer needed. The *London Declaration on a Transformed North Atlantic Alliance* published in July 1990 and the new strategic concept agreed in Rome in November 1991 successfully argued that NATO remained an essential component of the post-Cold War security architecture in providing a 'stable security environment' within which democratic reform could be nurtured in the East.[2] As with the EU, the logical culmination of this policy was an eastern enlargement leading to the entry of three central and eastern European states in 1999 and a further seven in 2004.

EU and NATO policy towards Russia during the 1990s developed along much the same lines as it had for the central and eastern European states. In January 1994 NATO launched the Partnership for Peace (PfP) initiative with Russia as one of its participants and in June of the same year the EU signed a Partnership and Cooperation Agreement (PCA) with Russia. These moves came soon after the publication of the Russian Foreign Policy Concept in June 1993 which suggested that a stable basis for Russia's relations with its European neighbours was in the process of formation. But the outbreak of hostilities in Chechnya prompted western condemnation of alleged human rights abuses in the region and resulted in a cooling of relations. It was not until 1997 that further movement was made. In May the NATO-Russia Founding Act was signed and in December, following the declaration of a ceasefire in Chechnya, the PCA was finally ratified and implemented. But this proved to be yet another false dawn in Russian-European relations. Although Russia had finally come to terms with NATO enlargement towards the end of the 1990s albeit in a tetchy manner, it was finally waking up to the implications that EU enlargement would have for Russian economic interests. Furthermore, the economic crash in Russia in 1998 and the NATO intervention into Kosovo the following year provoked a rapid deterioration in Russia's relations with the US and seemed at the time to have been a situation from which the EU could profit when the new Foreign Policy Concept produced by the Putin Administration in June 2000 identified the EU as a key partner. But although the end of the 1990s had undoubtedly presented the EU with a window of opportunity, Putin was irritated that the EU had produced a Common Strategy on Russia in June 1999 without any Russian input and was sceptical that the European Security and Defence Policy (ESDP), also agreed in June 1999, would become a credible alternative to NATO. The closing of the 'EU window' accelerated after 9/11. The US looked to Russia to become a partner in the 'war on terror' and this provided Putin with increased scope for manoeuvre in Chechnya. This period coincided with an increase in oil prices which also played into Russian hands in reducing Moscow's reliance on western loans and trade in manufactured goods with the West. In May 2002 Putin made considerable progress in achieving Russia's priority of a place at the table when the EU agreed an Action Plan on the ESDP at the EU-Russia summit in Moscow and NATO established the NATO-Russia Council (NRC) at the Reykjavik summit.

Russia and Europe: What Kind of Partnership?

The central objectives of this book are to investigate the current state of Russia's relations with Europe, how these relations have developed and to consider the future prospects. A basic assumption is that neither Russia nor Europe can be viewed as monolithic polities and there is a need to disaggregate our understanding of both. Contrary to the impression given in the western media, which can lead the reader to believe that little has changed since the end of the Soviet Union, political exchange does take place in Russia and it is therefore essential that the West better understands the Russian foreign policy agenda, how foreign policy is formulated and the actors involved. Likewise, Europe is far from being a cohesive political actor and this book resists the temptation to conflate the concept of Europe with the EU but draws NATO and bilateral relations into the investigation.

Within this evolving relationship it is argued that there are three potential modes of cooperation between Russia and Europe; strategic, normative and pragmatic. A strategic mode of cooperation would suggest that there is fundamental agreement between Russia and Europe on the challenges both face and the means by which this common agenda is to be addressed. A normative mode of cooperation would imply that there is a shared set of norms and values underpinning the relationship which informs and guides behaviour and the pragmatic mode suggests that cooperation will be conducted in accordance with short-term, tactical calculations.

In order to address which mode of partnership best fits the contemporary relationship between Russia and Europe, this study has been divided into three parts. The first part, 'Russia looking West', considers the development of Russian foreign policy since the end of the Cold War and, in specific terms, under the Putin Administration. In the opening two chapters Richard Sakwa and Neil Robinson address the evolution of Russian foreign policy thinking and the interaction between foreign and domestic politics. At the heart of the second chapter is a discussion around the notion of 'normalization' and whether the Russian state is moving towards a more predictable pattern of behaviour. The four chapters from Stephen White and Margot Light, Dmitry Polikanov, Irina Busygina and Derek L.Averre which follow cover various aspects of the internal dialogue on Russian foreign policy with the focus on Russian-European relations.

The second part, 'Europe looking East' considers the development of European policy through the two levels of multilateral relations with the EU and NATO and bilateral relations with Germany, France and the 'New Eastern States'. Jackie Gower and Hiski Haukkala examine EU policy development with the latter of these two chapters focusing on the question of norms and values while Mark McGuigan introduces the transatlantic dimension to Russian-European relations via NATO. The three chapters which follow by Graham Timmins, Julie M.Newton and Kristi Raik address the two key relationships that Russia has with Germany and France and looks at the impact on EU-Russian relations of the 2004 enlargement into CEE.

The third part 'Partnership in Practice' attempts to draw the discussions in the first two parts together to consider the extent to which genuine partnership between Russia and Europe has developed. Thomas Frellesen and Clelia Rontoyanni consider the political relationship between the EU and Russia while Marco Fantini focuses his chapter on the development of economic relations. The final chapter by Mark Webber investigates cooperation in the area of European security governance.

This study does not make any claims towards comprehensive inclusivity. There are a range of issues which could easily have been included in this investigation and there are obvious omissions regarding institutions and actors. But what we as authors hope we have achieved is a modest contribution to the setting out of an agenda which will facilitate and inform further research. It is only by recognizing the complexity of the emerging Russian state and the multifaceted nature of its interaction with Europe and, indeed, the complex nature of European multilateral organizations themselves that we can begin to meet the challenges that face practitioners and analysts alike in understanding and responding to the evolution of this most critical of relationships.

Notes and References

1. Vladimir Putin, Russia at the Turn of the Millennium Speech, 31 December 1999. Available in translation at: http://www.government.gov.ru/english/statVP_engl_1.html (accessed 10.06.03).
2. See NATO, 'Declaration on a transformed North Atlantic Alliance issued by the Heads of State and Government participating in the meeting of the North Atlantic Council (The London Declaration')', 6 July 1990 at: http://www.nato.int/docu/basictxt/ b900706a.htm and 'The Alliance's Strategic Concept agreed by the Heads of State and Government participating in the meeting of the North Atlantic Council', Rome 8 November 1991 at http://www.nato.int/docu/basictxt/b911108a.htm (accessed 15.02.06).

PART 1

RUSSIA LOOKING WEST

1

VLADIMIR PUTIN AND RUSSIAN FOREIGN POLICY TOWARDS THE WEST: TOWARDS A NEW REALISM

Richard Sakwa

Introduction

'The only realistic choice for Russia is the choice to be a strong country, strong and confident in its strength, strong not in spite of the world community, not against other strong states, but together with them.'
Putin, state-of the-federation speech, 8 July 2000[1]

President Vladimir Putin's overriding purpose from the very first days of his presidency from 2000 was the normalization of Russian foreign policy. Russia was to be treated as neither supplicant nor threat, but as just one more 'normal' great power. Through a combination of luck, skill and circumstances Putin achieved this remarkably quickly and effectively. By the time of the second Iraq war of 2003 Russia was treated no differently than any other country. That is to say, the harsh realities of the post-post-Cold War world hit Russia just as hard as any other country. The shedding of exaggerated illusions about Russia's status in the world did not mean that the country could avoid making hard choices and assuming responsibility for some of the world's problems. At the same time, unresolved problems of internal political development, the country's regional role and identity questions affected relations with the West. During Putin's second term, following his re-election in March 2004, the 'regime question' – the condition of Russian democracy – became an ever more salient issue in Russo-Western relations.

Towards a New Realism

McFaul and Goldgeier have argued that post-communist Russian foreign policy does not follow the pattern anticipated by realist thinking. According to them Russia has become a 'joiner', and does not conform to the 'balancing' stance anticipated by classical realist theory.[2] At the same time, American policy towards Russia has been torn between realism and liberalism, with the former focusing on the balance of power between states and paying little attention to the type of regime involved, whereas liberals (in the Wilsonian tradition) are more concerned with regime transformation to create more democracies.[3] Paradoxically, the neo-conservatives adopted elements of this tradition, but now bent to great power purposes. Russia's policy has traditionally been firmly located in the realist tradition, but this is now tempered by awareness that integration with the West can only effectively take place when the country takes its place among the democratic nations of the world. It is for this reason that Russia's foreign policy under Putin can be described as a 'new realism'. The pattern was already established during the presidency of Boris Yeltsin, but as we shall see, Yeltsin's realism became coloured by a specific definition of pragmatism that retained much of the classical competitive approach to realism in foreign policy. It was only under Putin that engagement with the West moved onto a more stable and cooperative basis, although relations continued to be soured by the regime question.[4]

Conceptual Innovation

Under the stewardship of Yevgeny Primakov (foreign minister between January 1996 and September 1998, and then prime minister until May 1999) the concept of 'pragmatism' predominated. Primakov's so-called 'pragmatism' in foreign policy achieved few positive results, alienating Russia's friends and confirming the hostility of those traditionally suspicious of its intentions. Russian foreign policy in the late 1990s was built on fake history and mythopoeic representations of traditional alliances. Foreign policy appeared to operate at two levels: what Russia really wanted (foreign policy A); and what it was forced to do (foreign policy B). The tension led to incoherence and confusing signals. By the time he came to power Putin found himself in a position remarkably reminiscent to that facing Mikhail Gorbachev when he became General Secretary in 1985: associated with sullen allies and opposed by increasingly militant foes. Primakov's pragmatism was rooted in a highly traditional understanding of realism, under-scored by a heavy dose of anti-Western Sovietism and by calls for 'multipolarity'. Primakov's multipolarism sought to use the instruments of multilateralism to sustain and manage a competitive view of the world, a traditional realist approach. This is in contrast to policies that genuinely seek to build on the normative values embedded in multilateral organizations to transcend great power rivalries.

These views and contradictions were reflected in the three major documents adopted in Putin's first year as president. They were designed to clarify the risks and opportunities faced by Russia and identify ways of dealing with them. The significance of these documents should not be exaggerated, and in many ways they reflected the priorities and preoccupations of the earlier period rather than setting a programme for Putin's leadership, but all demonstrated the tensions in Russia's view of the West. The first to be adopted was a new National Security Concept, to replace the 1997 version, which was signed into law on 10 January 2000.[5] The document reflected deep concerns about the external environment. The August 1998 economic meltdown revealed Russia's vulnerability to speculative international financial markets, the use of North Atlantic Treaty Organization (NATO) forces with an unclear UN mandate to bomb Serbia between March and June 1999, NATO's enlargement in March 1999 to encompass Poland, Hungary and the Czech Republic, strategic arms control tensions and renewed war in Chechnya, all provoked a rethinking of the international environment. The Concept expanded the list of external threats to Russia's security, noting in particular the weakening of the Organization for Security and Cooperation in Europe (OSCE), the UN and the Commonwealth of Independent States (CIS). The document described the tension between a multipolar world, in which relations are based on international law and an acceptance of a significant role for Russia, and attempts by the US and its allies to carve out a unipolar world outside of international law. Talk of 'partnership' with the West disappeared, and instead more emphasis was placed on more limited 'cooperation'.[6] To complement the above, a new Military Doctrine (replacing the 2 November 1993 version) was ratified by presidential decree on 21 April 2000. The 'no first use' of nuclear weapons was dropped, and as part of the reassessment of the risks facing the country the document called for the forward deployment of troops outside Russian territory.

The new Foreign Policy Concept of 28 June 2000, replacing Yeltsin's 23 April 1993 document that some have seen to be imbued with excessive idealism,[7] stressed that Russia's policy should be rational and realistic and designed to serve Russian economic and political interests.[8] The link between domestic and foreign policy was reinforced. The Concept insisted that the 'relationship with European states is a traditional priority of Russian foreign policy', although Russia's integration into Europe's political and economic space was no longer mentioned. As with all these documents, contradictory perceptions jostled cheek by jowl, with Russia defined as a great power in one paragraph and as fundamentally pragmatic in the next. The tone however was a realistic one, stressing the need to find a 'reasonable balance between its objectives and possibilities for attaining these objectives'. The document called for Russia to lead the development of a multipolar world, a policy explicitly designed to counter the threat of US global domination under the guise of 'humanitarian intervention' and 'limited sovereignty'. The emphasis in relations with the CIS shifted from multilateralism to bilateralism, a change that Putin adhered to throughout his leadership, above all with Belarus, while at the same time the need to protect Russian ethnic minorities in the former Soviet states was noted. Good relations with Europe, the US and Asia were stressed, in that order, although the openly anti-American tone was noticeable. In the wake of NATO's intervention over Kosovo the tone was bitter; nevertheless the Concept stated that Russia was interested in constructive cooperation with NATO 'in the interests of maintaining security and stability in the continent and is open to constructive interaction'.[9] Commenting on the Concept on 25 April 2002 in a speech devoted to the two hundredth anniversary of the Russian foreign ministry, the foreign minister, Igor Ivanov, stressed that 'Russia has consciously given up the global Messianic ideology that had been intrinsic to the former Union of Soviet Socialist Republics (USSR) and at the end of its existence had come into insurmountable contradiction with the national interests of the country'.[10] The concept broadly set the parameters for policy, but as so often with these documents real life quickly passed it by.

The dual and contradictory position of Russia on the world stage on Putin's accession in 2000 has been characterized as follows:

> On the one hand, it has many of the attributes of a world power – in the club of nuclear powers, a permanent seat in the UN Security Council, participates (although not always on an equal footing) in summits of world leaders. On the other hand, its present economic capacities clearly do not correspond to its still surviving nominal military power and political influence. In many respects Russia has declined to the level of a less developed country.[11]

Russia's economy in 2005 was not much larger than Holland's (about $600 billion), compared to the over $11 trillion each of the US and the European Union (EU), and China's Gross Domestic Product (GDP) of nearly $2 trillion. On a narrow economic base Russia tried to maintain a space programme, advanced strategic rocket development, over a million men in uniform, an extended welfare system and a bureaucracy that is bigger than the Soviet Union's. This mismatch between ambition and capacity imbued Russian foreign policy in the 1990s with a bombastic and ineffectual edge,[12] while Russian statesmen such as Primakov insisted that Russia would continue to play a major role in the international system because of its willingness to assume the responsibilities of a major actor.[13] There was clearly a gulf between the way that the outside world saw Russia and the pretensions of its elites and many of its citizens. This was an explosive situation, with an aggrieved Russia potentially becoming a disruptive force in the world community.

A number of theories were applied to sustain Russia's exaggerated idea of its role in the world, notably various strains of neo-Eurasian thinking drawing on the ideas of the 1920s and 1930s. This was based on the belief that Russia's geopolitical position imbued it with unique geopolitical advantages that effectively forced it to be a great power and to make a bid for world leadership. Time had moved on, however, and Dmitry Trenin argues that China's growing strength in the East and the instability of the Islamic south, means that Russia's only geopolitical future lies with the West, including accelerated integration with the EU and solid relations with the US.[14] This is something that Putin recognized: there is little trace of Eurasianism in his thinking, but much about Russia's position in Eurasia. New strains of geopolitical thinking have emerged, for example the school of critical geopolitics that questions the imperatives of space and geography. Putin has not gone so far, but his thinking is remarkably free of the traditionally static, monolithic and zero sum representations of Russia's role in the world. In short, Putin sought to normalize the debate on Russian foreign policy, stripping it of neo-Eurasianism features rooted in nineteenth century views of competitive advantage while acknowledging twenty-first century realities.

From Periphery to Core

With the fall of commusnism the old East-West bipolar world has given way to a more concentric version that lies at the basis of the post-communist neo-imperial approach. A number of core states enjoy the 'democratic peace'[15] while the periphery remains a zone of conflict and economic hardship.[16] In the zone of peace the normative framework of international relations developed since World War II applies, whereas in the periphery the West asserts a renewed mandate to operate according to traditional great power norms.[17] In practice, the notion of the 'West' here divided, with America under President George W Bush taking a more assertive approach, whereas much of Europe remained committed to consensual international norms. While Europe is forced to rely on diplomacy and other 'soft power' instruments, America can apply the whole armoury of hard and soft tools. Indeed, as Robert Kagan argues, Europe's weakness has forced it to emphasize normative soft power as a way of undermining the legitimacy of American full spectrum hard power predominance.[18] Although 'the West' is far from homogeneous, with Europe struggling to ensure that the concept does not become a synonym for America, there remains a dividing line somewhere across Eurasia beyond which there is a non-West. The EU itself is not quite sure where the line should be drawn, hence continuing debates over the eligibility of Turkey and Ukraine as EU members. As far as Russia is concerned, fear that it would be relegated to the periphery and treated as such provoked a range of defensive reactions, in particular at the time of the NATO intervention into Kosovo, as well as in trying to reassert its traditional influence in the former Soviet space. The lands between Russia and the EU became a sphere of competing 'near abroads'. The collision was particularly vivid at the time of Ukraine's 'orange revolution' in late 2004, when Putin ill-advisedly and rather too demonstratively supported the official candidate to replace President Leonid Kuchma, Viktor Yanukovich, against the outsider candidate, Viktor Yushchenko, who in the event won the extraordinary third round ballot.

Russia sought to move from the periphery to the core in international politics. Neo-realists would argue that this is simply a function of Russia's recognition of the actual distribution of power in the international system, while liberal realists like John Ikenberry would go further and argue that liberal values have a positive attraction, especially when the US exercises its hegemony in a consensual way.[19] From an international political economy perspective, growing policy convergence reflected the failure of state-led semi-autarchic modernization programmes and the changed opportunity structure offered by economic globalization.[20] In practice Russia's move from outsider to a core member of the leading group of nations would prove traumatic for all concerned, especially at the time of the partial default of August 1998, yet ultimately the scale of the achievement should be recognized. Under Yeltsin the country appeared to enter a twilight zone of semi-acceptance, but the strategic direction had been established, and it was on this that Putin built.[21] In various and uneven ways the West tried to devise strategies to make integration possible. Relations improved with bodies such as NATO and the EU, although accession was ruled out in the near to medium term. Structural impediments remained, and Russia's own problems, above all economic weakness, criminality, corruption and political divisions, inhibited integration processes. There remains a fundamental contradiction in Russo-Western relations captured by the traditional terms to describe nationality politics in the Soviet Union: while *sblizhenie* (coming together) is accepted by all, there remain fundamental reservations about *sliyanie* (merging). In the early 2000s, as Dov Lynch puts it, Russia still faced the same problems as in the 1990s, the attempt to gain 'an equal voice on major security developments in and around Europe without incurring the costs of membership, which is seen to impose restraints on Russia's domestic room for manoeuvre'.[22]

The legacy of Cold War suspicion only slowly dissipated, and on the Russian side indeed was occasionally replenished by Russia's halting acceptance of the sovereignty of former Soviet states, heavy handed 'peace keeping' operations in the breakaway Transdniestria territory in Moldova and Abkhazia in Georgia, brutal war in Chechnya, unsophisticated rhetorical support for the Serbian strongman, Slobodan Milošević until his overthrow in October 2000, and crude attempts by Primakov to play the Chinese 'card' against the West. These policies reflected a traditional concept of power, where the ultimate sanction was coercion and war. It appeared that although rhetorically Russia favoured good relations with the West, it would insist on remaining part of an alternative pole of world politics and advance a different ideology of international affairs. We shall argue below that this is a misinterpretation of Russian thinking, since Russia's broad aim was not to set itself up as an alternative but as the champion of the autonomy of sovereign states. Residual elements of alternativity were in tension with the striving for autonomy, especially when America set itself up as the champion of 'geopolitical pluralism' in the post-Soviet sphere over which Russia claimed a *droit de regard*. It is for this reason that so much of Russian policy since the early 1990s had a dual character, with Russia becoming both an insider and an outsider.[23]

In the post-Cold War era traditional 'hard power' approaches have to a degree been delegitimated by the normative values associated with 'soft power', where the emphasis shifts to 'the ability to set the political agenda in a way that shapes the preferences of others'.[24] Putin, like the EU, no doubt appreciated the value of soft power in proportion to the absence of effective instruments of hard power. However, as we argue, he was deeply committed to a new realism that rejected much of the zero-sum logic of traditional views of international politics. There was an underlying normalization both in the goals of foreign policy and in the manner in which it was conducted.

Features of the New Realism

According to Article 86 of Russia's 1993 constitution, foreign policy is a presidential prerogative, and hence in institutional terms the priorities of the incumbent are decisive, especially in policy areas that are of high priority for them. There is no doubt that Putin is a pragmatist, but he has decisively rejected the pragmatism of the weak of the earlier period. Putin's pragmatism lacks Primakov's double-edged characteristic and instead inhabits the real world of opportunities, risks and agency. Under Putin foreign policy completed its trajectory from the alleged idealism of the early 1990s, through a period of 'pragmatism' in the second half of the decade, towards a 'new realism'. Most of the elements were already visible under Primakov and even earlier, in particular his predecessor, Andrei Kozyrev, who had shaped Russia's foreign policies as it emerged as an independent state from 1990 until his resignation in January 1996. Kozyrev had long been criticized for his idealism (dubbed 'romanticism') and uncritical Westernism. In the 'new realism' there was a much sharper recognition of the limits of Russian power, grounded above all in economic weakness, accompanied by a recognition that more could be gained through partnership with the West than through competition. This did not mean giving up aspirations to global influence, but it did mean the pursuit of a far more conscious attempt to match ambitions to resources accompanied by modifications to the type of influence that the country sought. The new realism has not given up the notion of Russia as a 'great power', but the definition of what it means to be a great power has changed as well as the way it should behave. Russia would be a power acting as part of the status quo rather than as a putative revisionist power setting itself up as a competitor to the global hegemony. The style and priorities of policy were also to change. According to the foreign minister, Igor Ivanov, 'Russian foreign policy will be independent, predictable and transparent'.[25] Putin devoted considerable attention to Russia's image abroad, exhorting the diplomatic corps on numerous occasions, notably when addressing them at the foreign ministry building on 12 July 2002 and again on 12 July 2004, to improve Russia's international prestige. Particular attention was to be paid to the preservation of Russia's leadership role in the CIS.[26]

The new realism is characterized by a number of key features. The first is the *economisation* of Russian foreign policy. In many public statements Putin insisted that the country's foreign policy had to be subordinated to domestic economic interests.[27] In a keynote speech at the foreign ministry on 26 January 2001 Putin stressed that Russia's strategic aim was 'integration into the world community', and for this the priority task of Russian diplomacy was the promotion of Russia's economic interests abroad.[28] In a speech to the staff of the (Russian) Ministry of Foreign Affairs (MFA) in September 2002 Putin insisted that advancing Russia's business interests was equal to traditional political reporting.[29] Putin remained consistent in his desire to see Russia join the World Trade Organization (WTO), although numerous domestic constituencies (for example, motor manufacturing) were opposed. Similarly, despite domestic hostility, including from his outspoken economic advisor Andrei Illarionov, Putin steered Russia towards ratification of the Kyoto protocol, making possible the adoption of a watered-down version of its CO_2 emission-reduction targets.

On numerous occasions Putin stressed another key feature of his foreign policy, its *Europeanisation*. Already in the early period of Russian independence Yeltsin's policy advisor Gennady Burbulis argued that none of the problems facing the country could be 'solved without learning from the European experience'.[30] In the book of interviews published in his first months in office Putin insisted that 'we are a part of Western European culture. In fact, we derive our worth precisely from this. Wherever our people might happen to live – in the Far East or in the South – we are Europeans'.[31] At his first EU-Russia summit in May 2000 Putin stressed his affinity with Europe, insisting that Russia 'was, is and will be a European country by its location, its culture, and its attitude toward economic integration'.[32] He repeated the idea in the 26 January 2001 speech, arguing that the 'European direction is traditionally the most important for us'.[33] In the same vein, addressing the conference of Russia's ambassadors in July 2002 he argued that economic ties with the EU, especially in the energy sphere, remained the top priority. He did not ignore Russia's other concerns, including accession to the WTO, without which he insisted Russia could not realize its potential.[34] Thus Russia pursues a 'greater Europe' policy, in which it sees itself as part of a single bloc stretching from the Atlantic to the Pacific (the traditional pan-European ideal). However, this is a pan-Europeanism that meshes uneasily with integrationist agendas into the institutions of 'official Europe' (above all the EU).

Some commentators have identified a third leg to Putin's policy, namely its *securitisation*.[35] For authors in the tradition of the Copenhagen school of international relations, security in the post-Cold War era is less about direct threats than about the perception of risk, with the concept of risk defined rather more strongly than general threats or problems.[36] Against the background of the second Chechen war and the impact of the terrorist assault against the US in September 2001, Putin insisted that Russia's policy in Chechnya and cooperation with the 'coalition of the willing' were part of the same problem of dealing with the global security threat. While sovereignty questions were not absent in Putin's approach to the Chechen war (the struggle to maintain the territorial integrity of Russia), the security motif became the predominant one. The West's reluctance to subsume the Chechen conflict into international security management left Russian diplomacy perplexed.

The shift from alternativity to *autonomy* can be seen as a fourth strand in thinking. The discourse of multipolar globalism under Primakov was based on the notion of Russia as an alternative pole balancing that of the West, and indeed working as a competitive actor in the international system. A notable example of this was the attempt to establish a troika consisting of Russia, France and Germany at the meeting of the heads of government of the Council of Europe in October 1997. Elements of troika-thinking have periodically resurfaced during Putin's presidency, notably on the eve of the second Iraq war, but Putin resolutely refused to be trapped into taking sides with one wing of the West against another. Although all denied any anti-American intent, it was clear that the troika approach was seen as a way of counterbalancing American power. Under Putin this approach has been modified based on the view of Russia as an *autonomous* actor but not necessarily in competition with the West. As Igor Ivanov stressed, Russia would defend the idea of 'a democratic, multi-polar system of international relations', but stressed that 'Russia is by no means looking for a pretext for rivalry'.[37]

The shift from alternativity to autonomy had important practical outcomes. The end of the Cold War had been followed by the supremacy, indeed triumphalism, of 'the West', and Russian and Chinese calls for the restoration of a multipolar world reflected concern about the unbalanced world system that had emerged as a result of the disintegration of the USSR and the end of bipolarity and superpower balance. In the event, in the post-Cold War world the Eastern pole could find no satisfactory political form or ideological rationale. Under Putin grand geopolitical schemes of world order, favoured by Primakov, moved down the list of Russian priorities. In particular the idea of a 'strategic partnership' with China was swiftly de-emphasized, although arms sales and the deepening of economic ties continued. The concepts of 'East' and 'West' were rethought. There would be no distinctive third way between, on the one hand, the traditional Cold War confrontation between East and West, and on the other hand, the unabashed reduction of modernization into Westernization.

A fifth aspect of Putin's approach to foreign policy should also be stressed, namely its emphasis on *bilateralism*. Although Russia in the 2000s sought a qualitative improvement of its relationship with multilateral bodies such as the EU and NATO, and policy remained committed rhetorically to broader international multilateralism based, above all, on the UN, Putin clearly felt most comfortable with state to state relations, often based on personal ties. The world from Moscow's perspective remains one of sovereign states, although tempered by a constrained multilateralism. Multilateral bodies were supported to the degree that they amplified Moscow's view of the world, but were marginalized, as in Russia's increasingly difficult relations with the OSCE and even ultimately with the CIS, when they did not. The OSCE proved a thorn in Putin's side, insisting that Russia fulfilled its commitment given at the OSCE's Istanbul summit in November 1999 to withdraw its forces from Transdniestria and Georgia, criticizing Russia's conduct of the Chechen war, and issuing a ringing denunciation of the December 2003 parliamentary elections. As for the CIS, a host of smaller groupings undermined the organisation's work as a broad multilateral body.[38] Following the 'rose revolution' in Georgia in November 2003 and the orange revolution in Ukraine in late 2004, by 2005 there was serious talk about disbanding the organization in its entirety, and there was a marked shift towards the 'economisation' of relations within the bloc. In particular, Russia sought to impose world market prices on energy exports to Ukraine. Faced with the struggle to maintain its position in Eurasia, Putin assiduously nurtured good relations with European leaders. As the former foreign minister Igor Ivanov put it, 'One of the fundamental tenets of Russia's European policy is the expansion of bilateral relations with individual countries... Over the past decade, Russia's relations with virtually all these countries have been taken to a qualitatively new level. We have become privileged partners in our cooperation efforts with such countries as Germany, Great Britain, France, Spain and others. We feel this is exceptionally valuable'.[39]

The concept of 'privileged partner', clearly, was used rather broadly, and in some respects relations with certain countries were especially privileged – notably in the case of Germany. As Putin noted at the Yekaterinburg summit with Germany of October 2003, he had met Schröder 20 times since 2000, arguing that 'such intensive contacts fully reflect the dynamics of Russo-German interaction'.[40] The notion of a 'strategic partnership' between the two countries has even been mentioned,[41] but as we know from previous experience with such rhetoric (notably Primakov's talk of a strategic partnership between Russia and China), reality does not always meet expectations. Bilateral relations offer the opportunity for the stronger partner to act as the advocate of the weaker. Thus Germany championed Russia's membership of the Paris Club of sovereign creditors, and both France and Germany at the beginning of Putin's second term sought to blunt the wave of criticism addressed against Russia. Condemnation of Russia's alleged authoritarian turn was marked following the Beslan school siege in September 2004, when Putin announced a raft of measures including the appointment of governors and a purely proportional parliamentary electoral system, and was intensified after the Ukrainian debacle.

It is this that gives rise to a sixth element of the new realism, namely its *constrained great powerism (derzhavnost')*. This is an approach that takes Russia's status as a major international power for granted, accepts Russia's need to join the West and to enter or develop robust relationships with its political, security and economic institutions, but at the same time has become rather more secure in its own worth and thus more controlled. This is conditioned by the shift from alternativity to autonomy mentioned above. This new confidence allowed Putin to view the American security presence in Central Asia and the South Caucasus with equanimity, and in general to view relations with the West rather more as a positive-sum game.

A seventh element in the new realism is, quite simply, Putin's attempts to '*normalize*' relations with the West. On coming to power Putin sought to devise policies to overcome Russia's isolation and to establish good relations with the West in general and Europe in particular. Russia would do this by applying the principles of the new realism. One key aspect was the rejection of traditional Russian *Sonderweg* illusions. Putin rejected the idea of a special path for Russia, arguing that for the first time in centuries Russia was not seeking any unique path of development.[42] Putin sought to find the golden mean (no longer defined as a third way) between what had been perceived as humiliating subservience to the West since the late 1980s, and the bombastic assertion of great power status that predominated in the late 1990s. Russia's traditionally idealized view of the world now recognized a few hard realities: the economy could no longer maintain aspirations to superpower status; the EU was enlarging and its sphere of concerns was casting an ever deeper shadow in the East; NATO was here to stay and increasing numbers of Russia's neighbours wanted to join, including (perhaps most humiliatingly for 'pragmatists' of Primakov's ilk), Ukraine; and the CIS could not be used as an instrument for Russian aggrandisement but would have to be based on genuine partnerships or it would wither away.

The New Realism in Practice

The gulf between rhetoric and reality typical of Russian foreign policy in the 1990s prompted Putin to tailor Russia's ambitions to feasibility while not losing sight of what made Russia distinctive. These two poles have structured Russian foreign policy in the Putin era: conformity to the realities of power relations in the international system while at the same time redefining what constitutes Russia's national interests. This is a type of constrained adaptation to the international system in which the strategic direction is clear – integration without accession (although in the long-term accession is not excluded) – but the pace and forms of integration would remain at Russia's discretion. Constrained adaptation is the counterpart of constrained *derzhavnost'*, and complements the policy of autonomy without alternativity. Domestic reconstruction became the priority, but at the same time external ambitions in Eurasia and the world are not abandoned.

In the first period of Putin's presidency there appeared to be a shift from an American-centred foreign policy towards a greater European orientation. In part this was a response to America focusing on its own elections, and the more critical approach adopted by the new president, George W Bush, in contrast to President Bill Clinton's wager on Yeltsin.[43] However, at their meeting in Ljubljana, Slovenia, on 16 June 2001 Bush and Putin established a remarkable personal rapport. Although the Bush camp had earlier repudiated Clinton's politics of charm, Bush now outdid his predecessor: 'I looked into that man's eyes and saw that he is direct and trustworthy. We had a very good dialogue. And I saw his soul'.[44]

Russia's dramatic choice to join the 'coalition against terror' after the events of 11 September 2001, therefore, built on earlier developments. Nevertheless, Putin's personal role in that fateful decision was decisive, and rode against the advice of the military and the uncertainty of public opinion. Putin was the first to telephone Bush after the al-Qaeda attack, and he offered not only sympathy but stressed that Russia would stand full-square with the US in the struggle against international terrorism. Putin gave concrete form to the new alliance in a television broadcast on 24 September in which he outlined five areas of cooperation with the West. Russia would provide information at its disposal about terrorist bases and its secret services would cooperate with Western counterparts; Russia would open its airspace to planes carrying humanitarian provisions to areas where antiterrorist operations were taking place; air bases in Central Asia would be made available to Western planes; Russia in case of necessity would participate in search and rescue operations; and Russia would support the internationally-recognized government in Afghanistan with military and other supplies.[45] This policy of close cooperation was the logical conclusion of Putin's earlier approach.

Although there has been much commentary about the strength of popular anti-American feeling, a number of commentators after 9/11 noted, in the light of the outpouring of genuine popular sympathy for those who had suffered, that this had probably always been exaggerated.[46] Although at times of international tension, as during the Kosovo crisis in 1999, the number of Russian citizens who considered America a potential enemy peaked at 48 per cent, by 2001 this had fallen to 13 per cent.[47] For most citizens of St Petersburg, Russia's European identity is not questioned and Putin, too, has no doubts about the matter. After 11 September Putin made a calculated decision (although this choice was in keeping with his intuition and Yeltsin's precedent) that Russia's security and broader interests lay in alliance with the West. At a stroke, Russian ambiguities and doubts about its civilizational identity, whether it was part of the West or an alternative to it, found a framework in which to be resolved. We should, however, keep this in perspective and reject some of the overblown rhetoric prompted by Putin's actions at this time. Putin's courageous stance following 11 September did not mark a fundamental repudiation of long-standing Russian concerns or interests. Putin's choice in favour of normalizing relations with the West had been taken long before; and afterwards, as seen by his stance during the second Iraq war, it was clear that good relations with the West did not mean becoming America's junior partner.

Following 9/11 the Kremlin cooperated with the US on a number of key issues: the Afghan war; the deployment of US forces in Central Asia and, later, in Georgia; arms control and passive acceptance in December 2001 of America's unilateral abrogation of the 1972 Anti-Ballistic Missile (ABM) treaty. Although no formal deal was struck in return for Russia's support for the allied intervention in Afghanistan in late 2001, Russia made no fuss about the placing of US troops in Central Asia, but expected US-Russia trade restrictions to be lifted, in particular the repeal of the Jackson-Vanik amendment of 1975 that tied trade relations to Jewish emigration. The restrictions still remain in place, and other possible benefits for Russia were also slow to materialize. In February 2002 Russian public opinion was incensed at what Putin called 'non-objective judges' at the Winter Olympic Games in Salt Lake City, and soon afterwards the bitter trade war over punitive American tariffs on Russian steel imports and Russia's reciprocal ban on 'Bush chicken legs' revealed how fragile (or perhaps just how 'normal') the relationship between the two countries was. It appeared that Russian policy had once again entered a period of unilateral concessions. NATO enlargement to include the Baltic republics, the stationing of American troops in Central Asia and even in Georgia was considered by Putin as 'no tragedy', while Putin considered America's withdrawal from the ABM treaty 'no threat to Russian security'. In March 2004 NATO enlarged to encompass seven new countries that had earlier been part of the Soviet bloc. Although 40 per cent of NATO's 26 member states are now former communist states, Russia's response was remarkably muted, and even included renewed talk about Russia's possible membership.

Russia's concessions aligned the country as part of the 'coalition against terrorism' but there appeared to be few material gains. Putin had joined the coalition as a matter of principle, so discussion of tangible benefits may be misplaced. Russia did gain two immediate advantages: a muting of Western criticism of its behaviour in Chechnya (and indeed, a partial reclassification of the war as a front in the international struggle against terrorism); and the overthrow of the hated Taliban regime in Afghanistan (that had long threatened Russia's ally Tajikistan) by the Russian-backed Northern Alliance forces. The signing of the Strategic Offensive Reduction Treaty during Bush's visit to Moscow on 24 May 2002, was another positive aspect, with each side pledged to reduce their stockpile to no more than 2200 warheads by 31 December 2012. Although the treaty allowed warheads to be dismantled rather than destroyed and there was no verification procedure, the Duma ratified what became known as the Moscow Treaty on 14 May 2003.

The old Soviet and Primakovian politics of linkage in negotiations and symmetry in concessions gave way to a new understanding of diplomacy that some saw as a new version of Gorbachevian capitulationism In his survey of 'The world after 11 September', Primakov insisted that not much had changed except America's improved geopolitical position in Central Asia and the Caucasus and the increased dangers of American unilateralism.[48] This was a view shared by much of Russia's political elite including the foreign minister, Ivanov, who insisted on an appropriate role for the UN.[49] In this context Russia's stance during the Iraq crisis should not have come as a surprise. On numerous occasions Ivanov's successor as foreign minister, Sergei Lavrov, called for Russia's legitimate interests and concerns to be recognized by the West. In an interview in November 2005, for example, he argued:

> Understanding the lawfulness of our (Western) partners' interests, we expect that they would acknowledge the lawfulness of ours on the territories adjacent to our borders, and which 15 years ago constituted a single country along with Russia and which still have economic, cultural, social ties and sometimes strong family ties. Do not forget that some 25 million ethnic Russians live in the countries bordering Russia.[50]

Even though Putin's European and Western orientation came naturally to him, there was no evidence that he sought to resurrect Soviet-style attempts to drive a wedge between the American and European wings of the Western alliance, and in this respect he was genuinely post-Soviet. In part this may have been recognition that, despite tensions and conflict, the alliance was built on solid foundations of mutual interest, and that any attempt to exploit divisions would be counter-productive. This self-denying ordinance was particularly impressive as the US under Bush entered a period of international activism. Paradoxically, the divisions within the West became most apparent just at the time when Russia renounced attempts to exploit them. For some Europe is emerging from its dependence on America and will in the long-term become a global geopolitical rival to America.[51] In the Iraq crisis Russia sought to act as mediator between Europe and America, a role Britain had traditionally tried to play. Russia, like France, insisted that any war against Iraq should be conducted under the aegis of the UN, and that the legitimate interests of Russia (and France) in the country should be respected in a post-Saddam Iraq. Russia found itself torn between the two faces of the West: the interventionist Anglo-American bloc and the Franco-German 'axis of peace'.[52] In populist terms, these could be dubbed the 'wild West' and the 'normative West'.

Putin's second term in office from 2004 was marked by an increasing superficiality in Russo-American relations. Attention remained focused on traditional areas of cooperation, notably security and non-proliferation of weapons of mass destruction (WMD), although energy supplies became an increasingly important mutual concern. American-Russia bilateral trade in 2003 amounted to only $7.1 billion, making the US Russia's seventh largest trade partner, while Russia ranked in thirty-eighth place among America's trade partners.[53] At the same time, in 2004 the US allocated $880.38 million for various assistance programmes in Russia.[54] Putin's blunt (some would say reckless) support for Bush's re-election in 2004 reflected just how precariously personal the relationship between the two countries had become.[55] Putin clearly preferred Bush's realist approach based on national interests than what he feared would be the Democrat's focus on 'values' (the Wilsonian tradition), and would thus be more critical of Russian domestic policy.[56] In addition, James Richter notes that Bush and Putin shared a psychological profile focused on the order and discipline that was lacking in their youths, and emphasized individual choice rather than the management of problems in consensual and multilateral ways.[57] It was clear at their meeting in Bratislava on 24 February 2004 that both men had invested considerable personal and political capital in ensuring that their relationship remained cordial.

However, there were numerous points of tension in the relationship, notably Russia's supply of technology and materials for Iran's nuclear energy programme, as well as Russia's vigorous arms sale programme, including the supply of anti-aircraft missiles to Syria. The authors of a recent report note, '[T]he gap between glowing rhetoric and thin substance has grown. This shallowness leaves US-Russian ties bereft of constituencies wider than leaders and a few highly placed government officials and increasingly vulnerable to growing choruses of sceptics'.[58] The authors argue that the fashionable distinction drawn between 'interests' and 'values' in foreign policy was a false one, insisting that the way that a state defines its interests reflects its values: hence 'disagreements between Russia and the US reflect differences in how we frame and define our interests'.[59]

Washington's ability to influence Russian policy appeared limited, while Russia, like the rest of the world, had little leverage over Washington. Talk of a 'strategic alliance' between the two countries was redundant, especially since it appeared that there was no common vision or shared set of values. While the neo-conservatives in Washington stressed the imperial and global role that the promotion of democratic values should play, Moscow asserted the sovereign right of each country to define democracy as they saw fit, the new ideology of 'sovereign democracy' that came to the fore after the orange revolution. However, the two countries did share a minimalist view of international integration. As Nikolai Zlobin puts it, 'Bush needs the Kremlin only as an ally in the war against terrorism, which suits Putin perfectly'.[60] The democratic transitions in Georgia and Ukraine placed US-Russian relations under strain and challenged Putin's definition of 'new realism', especially when it came to competition for influence over CIS states. Their relationship appeared based more on rhetoric that the reality of strategic cooperation, with competing goals in the former Soviet space. As Zlobin notes, in Bush's first term 'Washington managed to whittle down bilateral cooperation to its politico-military aspect only ... [while America] went to great lengths to prevent relations from deepening or becoming more strategic ... [and] in no way kept America from squeezing Moscow out of almost every sphere of international authority'.[61] Dmitri Trenin sums this up well:

Western relations with Russia can no longer be described in terms of integration, as it is traditionally understood, that is, gradually drawing Russia into the Western institutional orbit. For that, there is neither particular demand on the part of Russia nor sufficient supply on the part of the United States or the EU. NATO and the EU, which were so successfully used with regard to the countries of Central and Eastern Europe, will have to remain idle in the case of Russia. The famous 'double integration elevator' cannot take Russia aboard because Western institutions simply do not have the capacity to do so.[62]

Relations with the EU are discussed elsewhere in this volume, but a few comments are in order here. The focus of the EU, and with particular intensity following the 2004 enlargement, has been on managing the internal integrative process, and only secondarily has focused on managing external relations with countries with little prospect of membership. The EU's conditionality vis-à-vis Russia, perceived to be selective and instrumental, always irked Russia, considering itself by right a European country and thus resentful of an organization that claimed the prerogative to decide what was and what was not European. Russia deeply resented the EU's claim to be the arbiter of civilizational achievement, and with it the establishment of a binary division: either European or not – especially when Russia suddenly found itself excluded amid allegations that there was no democracy there.[63] According to Sergei Yastrzhembsky, the deterioration in Russo-EU relations had been provoked by the accession of the former communist countries, who had allegedly 'brought the spirit of primitive Russophobia' to the EU.[64] Under Putin's leadership, however, these concerns would not take populist or aggressive forms, despite worries of the orange revolution spreading to Russia. His successor, however, could well use Russia's grievances (as in the dropping of conditionality conditions concerning the Russian minorities on Estonia and Latvia before their accession to the EU), and indeed, deep sense of betrayal by the West, to pursue a more xenophobic policy.

Russia's traditional *Realpolitik* approach to foreign policy found it difficult to grasp that the EU could speak with one voice on behalf of all of its members, and that its normative dynamic was more than an instrument of policy but a genuine commitment to a shared set of values. Russia's doubts on this count were exacerbated by the EU's apparent failure to address Russia's concerns over the status of Russian minorities in Estonia and Latvia. The introduction of the Schengen visa requirements placed restrictions on cross-border transit, especially across the border between Poland and Kaliningrad. It appeared that the West in the guise of the EU was intent on reinforcing Russia's traditional view of itself as an alternative, and competitive, geopolitical subject, and thus attempts by post-communist Russia to find a way of adapting to Western norms and to become part of the West while affirming its own identity, however contradictorily these goals were pursued, were rebuffed. As Yuri Lotman argued, the dualistic opposition between Russia and the West, played out in various guises such as the struggle between Orthodoxy and Catholicism, had long acted as the deep structure of Russian development, providing long-term continuity in Russian culture.[65] As Morozov puts it, 'the West has indeed played the role of constitutive outside for Russian political community, an absolute negation which allows the Russian Self to be constituted'.[66] Putin did not see the world in this way, but his successor may.

Conclusion

Under Putin Russia turned decisively to the West, hoping to establish a realistic and mutually beneficial relationship. The debate over Russian foreign policy in the 1990s tended to focus on a single stark polarity, Atlanticism versus Eurasianism, but under Putin this was transcended. The new realism also represented a move beyond the Eurasian 'bridge' metaphor of Russia linking East and West and an affirmation that Russia was a destination in itself. However, although Russian foreign policy under Putin lost its illusions about Russia's status, this did not mean that Russia could become part of the West. As the authors of the report quoted above note, 'Formally, Russia will not become "part of the West" in the short term: It will stay outside of Euro-Atlantic structures'.[67] They reiterate the points about autonomy and integration made earlier in this chapter: 'Russia will pursue a non-antagonistic, but essentially independent policy vis-à-vis the United States. Russia will not be subsumed within a wider Europe or institutionally integrated into the US system of alliances'. [68] As far as they were concerned, Russia possessed certain 'niche capabilities' (such as membership of the UN Security Council (UNSC), nuclear weapons, and energy resources), and not much else.

Policy under Putin entered a period of new realism in which the view of Russia as an alternative pole to the West gave way to a struggle for Russian autonomy within the framework of a positive-sum view of the world. The West of course did not always reciprocate. There remained the danger that if Putin's new realism did not find a receptive response in the West, then Russian policy was liable to return to the competitive pragmatism typical of Primakov's stewardship of Russian policy. At the same time, Putin built his foreign policy on a tenuous and narrow institutional and social base, and the new realism was very much his own policy and it is far from certain his policy of positive engagement with the West would be continued by his successors. Putin's aim was to find a way to transform Russia's potential into reality, and he believed that this could only be done in partnership with the West. However, if faced by the choice of either moving ever closer to the 'Western world' or to cherish the dream of restoring the country's status as a great power, it was not clear which way Russia would go.

Notes and References

1. http://www.president.kremlin.ru/events/42.html
2. James M. Goldgeier and Michael McFaul, 'Russians as Joiners: Realist and Liberal Conceptions of Postcommunist Europe' in Michael McFaul and Kathryn Stoner-Weiss (eds.), *After the Collapse of Communism: Comparative Lessons of Transition* (New York, Cambridge University Press, 2004), pp. 232–56.
3. James Goldgeier and Michael McFaul, *Power and Purpose: American Policy Towards Russia after the Cold War* (Washington, DC, Brookings Institution Press, 2003).
4. For an overview, see Alexander J Motyl, Blair A Ruble and Lilia Shevtsova (eds.), *Russia's Engagement with the West: Transformation and Integration in the Twenty-First Century* (New York, M E Sharpe, 2003).
5. http://www.scrf.gov.ru/Documents.Decree/2002/24-1.html; *Nezavisimoe voennoe obozrenie*, 14 January 2000.
6. See Jakub M Godzimirski, 'Russian National Security Concepts 1997 and 2000: A Comparative Analysis', *European Security*, 9: 4 (2000), pp. 73–91.
7. Vladislav Chernov in *Nezavisimaya gazeta*, 29 April 1993.
8. *Nezavisimaya gazeta*, 11 July 2000, pp. 1 and 6.
9. 'The Foreign Policy Concept of the Russian Federation', at http://www.mid.ru/mid/eng/econcept.htm
10. Russian Embassy, London, press release, 17 May 2002.
11. V. A. Kolosov (ed.), *Mir glazami rossiyan: mify i vneshnyaya politika* (Moscow, Institut fonda 'Obshchestvennoe mnenie', 2003), p. 11.
12. For the gulf between rhetoric and reality in the 1990s, see Sherman Garnett, 'Russia's Illusory Ambitions', *Foreign Affairs*, 72: 2 (1997), pp. 61–76.
13. Yevgeny Primakov, *A World Challenged: Fighting Terrorism in the Twenty-First Century* (Washington, DC, Brookings Institution Press, 2004).
14. Dmitri Trenin, *The End of Eurasia: Russia on the Border Between Geopolitics and Globalization* (Moscow, Carnegie Moscow Center, 2001).
15. For a discussion of the 'democratic peace' proposition – that democracies rarely if ever fight each other and that democracies in general are more peaceable than non-democracies – see Michael Brown, Sean Lynn-Jones and Steven Miller (eds.), *Debating the Democratic Peace* (Cambridge, MA, MIT Press, 1996); and Michael W Doyle, *Ways of War and Peace* (New York, W W Norton, 1997). For a critique of the democratic peace idea, Errol A Henderson, *Democracy and War: The End of an Illusion?* (Boulder, CO, Lynne Rienner Publishers, 2002).
16. For an early discussion of the idea of core and periphery, see Barry Buzan, 'New Patterns

of Global Security in the Twenty-first Century', *International Affairs*, 67:3 (1991), pp. 431–51. This model is developed by Goldgeier and McFaul, 'Russians as Joiners'.

17. Robert Cooper, *The Breaking of Nations: Order and Chaos in the Twenty-first Century* (London, Atlantic Books, 2003).

18. Robert Kagan, *Paradise and Power: America and Europe in the New World Order* (New York, Knopf, 2003), pp. 113–21.

19. John G Ikenberry, *After Victory: Institutions, Strategic Restraint and the Rebuilding of Order after Major War* (Princeton, Princeton University Press, 2001).

20. John Williamson (ed.), *The Political Economy of Policy Reform* (Washington DC, Institute for International Economics, 1994); Martin Wolf, *Why Globalization Works* (New Haven, Yale University Press, 2004).

21. The strategy of integration was outlined by Yeltsin's last foreign minister and Putin's first, Igor Ivanov, 'Russia, Europe at the Turn of the Century', *International Affairs* (Moscow), 46:2 (2000), pp. 1–11.

22. Dov Lynch, 'Misperceptions and Divergences', in Dov Lynch (ed.), *What Russia Sees*, Chaillot Paper 74 (Paris, Institute for European Studies, January 2005), p. 9.

23. This is explored by Vladimir Baranovsky, 'Russia: Insider or Outsider?', *International Affairs* (Moscow), 46:3 (2000), pp. 443–59.

24. Joseph Nye, 'Hard and Soft Power in a Global Information Age', in Mark Leonard (ed.), *Re-Ordering the World* (London, The Foreign Policy Centre, 2002), pp. 2–10, at p. 5. For a more extended discussion of the various cultural and other ways in which 'soft power' is exercised by the US, see Joseph S. Nye Jr., *Bound to Lead: The Changing Nature of American Power* (New York, Basic Books, 1990), Chapter 2.

25. I. Ivanov, 'The New Russian Identity: Innovation and Continuity in Russian Foreign Policy', *The Washington Quarterly*, 24:3 (2001), p. 3.

26. See Igor Torbakov, 'Putin Urges Russian Diplomats to be More Active in the Post-Soviet States', The Jamestown Foundation, *Eurasia Daily Monitor*, 19 July 2004.

27. Bobo Lo, *Vladimir Putin and the Evolution of Russian Foreign Policy* (Blackwell, Royal Institute of International Affairs, 2003), Chapter 4.

28. http://www.president.kremlin.ru/events/XXX.html.

29. Vladimir Putin, 'We Should Look for Partners Everywhere', *Diplomat*, September 2002; www.diplomat-cd.ru.

30. Cited in Hannes Adomeit, 'Russia as a "Great Power" in World Affairs: Images and Reality', *International Affairs*, 71:1 (1995), p. 43.

31. Vladimir Putin, *Ot pervogo litsa: Razgovory s Vladimirom Putinym*, with Nataliya Gevorkyan, Natal'ya Timakova and Andrei Kolesnikov (Moscow, Vagrius, 2000), pp. 155–6.

32. 'Putin Opens EU-Russia Summit', RFE/RL, *Newsline*, 29 May 2000.

33. http://www.president.kremlin.ru/events/145.html; strana.ru, 26 January 2001.

34. *Newsline*, 12 July 2002.

35. Bobo Lo stresses the interplay between economization and securitization in Putin's foreign policy, 'The Securitization of Russian Foreign Policy under Putin', in Gabriel Gorodetsky (ed.), *Russia Between East and West: Russian Foreign Policy on the Threshold of the Twenty-First Century* (London, Frank Cass Publishers, 2003), Chapter 2, pp. 12–32.

36. See Richard Ullman, 'Redefining Security', *International Security*, 8:1 (1983); Barry Buzan, *People, States, Fear: An Agenda for International Security Studies in the Post-Cold war Era* (Hertfordshire, Harvester Wheatsheaf, 1991); Barry Buzan, Ole Waever and J de Wilde, *Security: A New Framework for Analysis* (Boulder, Co. and London, Lynne Rienner, 1998).

37. 'New Priorities in Russian Foreign Policy', *Internationale Politik: Transatlantic Edition*,

1:3 (2000), pp. 2–3.

38. The institutions include the Collective Security Treaty Organisation (CSTO) which unites Armenia, Belarus, Russia, Kyrgyzstan, Kazakhstan and Tajikistan; the Shanghai Cooperation Organisation (SCO) encompassing China, Russia, Kazakhstan, Kyrgyzstan, Tajikistan and Uzbekistan; and the Common Economic Space (CES) bringing together the more advanced economies of Russia, Ukraine, Belarus and Kazakhstan. It should be noted that bilateral trade between Russia and Ukraine reached $16 billion in 2004, an increase of 40 per cent over that attained in 2003, and made Ukraine Russia's third largest trade partner after Belarus and Germany. Putin sought to legitimise the CSTO by establishing direct contacts with NATO, Putin's speech to the Security Council, 29 January 2005, Kremlin.ru, in *Johnson's Russia List* (henceforth *JRL*), 9040/8.

39. Igor S. Ivanov, *The New Russian Diplomacy* (Washington, DC, Brookings Institution Press, 2002), p. 95.

40. Itar Tass, 9 October 2003.

41. Igor Bratchikov and Dmitrii Lyubinskii, 'Germany: the Mechanism of Strategic Partnership', *International Affairs*, 48:3 (2002), pp. 149–56.

42. B. Volkhonskii and G. Sysoev, 'Vladimir Putin Turns his Back on Lukashenko', *Kommersant*, 14 June 2002; in *JRL*, #6308.

43. Stephen F. Cohen, *Failed Crusade: America and the Tragedy of Post-Communist Russia* (New York, W. W. Norton, 2000).

44. Lilia Shevtsova, *Putin's Russia* (Washington, DC, Carnegie Endowment for International Peace, 2003), p. 203.

45. Roi Medvedev, *Vladimir Putin - Deistvuyushchii Prezident* (Moscow, Vremya, 2002), p. 345.

46. G. G. Diligenskii, '"Zapad" i rossiiskoe obshchestvo', (Moscow, FOM, 2001), pp. 205–14; http://usa.fom.ru/razdel/mbi/382/936/3090.html

47. Kolosov (ed.), *Mir glazami rossiyan*, p. 243.

48. Yevgeny Primakov, *Mir posle 11 sentyabrya* (Moscow, Mysl', 2002).

49. Igor Ivanov, *Vneshnyaya politika rossii v epokhu globalizatsii* (Moscow, Olma-Press, 2002).

50. Published on the BBC's Russian-language service website, in *JRL*, 9293/14.

51. For example, Stephen Haseler, *Super-State: The New Europe and its Challenge to America* (London, I. B. Tauris, 2004).

52. On the long-standing concerns of the Europeans, see Evgenii Grigor'ev, '"Bunt" evropeitsev: Politiki starogo kontinenta ne khotyat igrat' role' satellitov SShA', *Nezavisimaya gazeta*, 15 February 2002, p. 6.

53. Andrew Kuchins, Vyacheslav Nikonov and Dmitri Trenin, *U.S.-Russian Relations: The Case for An Upgrade* (Moscow, Moscow Carnegie Centre, 2005), p. 13.

54. Of this, $45.43 million were for Democracy Programmes, $51.43 million for Economic and Social Reform, $5.60 million for Humanitarian Assistance, and $5.79 for Cross-Sectoral Initiatives, US Department of State, Bureau of European and Eurasian Affairs, Fact Sheet, 15 September 2004, in *JRL*, 8370/25.

55. Mikhail Rykhtik argues that Putin welcomed a Republican victory because of shared concerns over WMD non-proliferation and the fight against terrorism, and the view that Bush would be less concerned about the 'democracy question' in Russia than a Democratic president, *Why Did Russia Welcome a Republican Victory?* PONARS Policy Memo 330, November 2004.

56. For a review of the reasons for support for Bush, see Igor Torbakov, 'Russia's Political Elites Want Bush Re-Elected', *Eurasia Daily Monitor*, 2 November 2004.

57. James Richter, *"A Sense of His Soul": The Relations Between Presidents Putin and Bush*, PONARS

Policy Memo 329, November 2004.
58. Kuchins et al, *U.S.-Russian Relations*, p. 2.
59. Kuchins et al, *U.S.-Russian Relations*, p. 2.
60. Nikolai Zlobin, 'Limited Possibilities and Possible Limitations: Russia and the US – What's Next?', *Russia in Global Affairs*, 3:1(2005).
61. Nikolai Zlobin, *Izvestiya*, 15 November 2004.
62. Dmitri Trenin, *Reading Russia Right*, Carnegie Endowment for International Peace, Policy Brief, Special Edition 42, October 2005, p. 8.
63. Viatcheslav Morozov, *The Forced Choice Between Russia and the West: The Geopolitics of Alienation* PONARS Policy Memo 327, November 2004.
64. *Nezavisimaya gazeta*, 17 November 2004.
65. Yuri Lotman, 'Rol' dual'nykh modelei v dinamike russkoi kul'tury', in *Istoriya i tipologiya russkoi kul'tury* (St Petersburg, Iskusstvo –SPB, 2002), pp. 89–90.
66. Viatcheslav Morozov, *Inside/Outside: Europe and the Boundaries of Russian Political Community*, PONARS Working Paper, October 2004.
67. Kuchins et al, *U.S.-Russian Relations*, p. 6.
68. Kuchins et al, *U.S.-Russian Relations*, p. 6.

2

THE 'NORMALIZATION' OF RUSSIAN POLITICS AND EUROPE

Neil Robinson

Introduction

Russia's relations with Europe depend on more than the diplomatic and the foreign policy positions adopted by contemporary governments. Over the longer term, Russia's relations with Europe depend on two factors: the development of Russia's socio-economic system and political regime, and the way that the development of Russian society and polity relate to the changes that are being wrought in Europe by processes of integration within the European Union (EU).[1] The relationship between these two factors and how they impact on European-Russian relations is both complex and indeterminate; quite simply, relations could go in a variety of directions.

The complexity of the relationship between Russia's development and Europe's is understandable; many other factors and forces, not least domestic pressures in Russia and European states and the continued evolution of the post-Cold War global order and the wider 'Western' interaction with Russia mediate the influence of each on the other.

The indeterminate nature of relations is harder to understand. Developments in Russia and in Europe would seem to be leading to a steady improvement of relations between the two and to the creation of conditions that should guarantee continued incremental improvement. Despite setbacks to further integration (such as delays to the adoption of an EU Constitution) or disagreements over how to deal with extra-European foreign policy issues (such as the Iraq war), Europe as the EU is arguably developing as a civilian superpower, different from state actors in the international system because of its commitment to peace, democracy, human rights and foreign relations based on responsibility rather than self-interest.[2] At the same time, Russia under Vladimir Putin has become a more predictable power, more 'normal', or at least undergoing a process of 'normalization'. It is generally asserted that part of this normalization is a new accommodation with Europe. Putin has certainly made many pro-European statements from early on in his presidency, and has argued that Russia's development should be seen as a part of European experience, different, but sharing common values and aspirations.[3] Putin's pro-European stance and the greater predictability of Russian foreign policy have created hopes that at last Russia may be becoming more of a partner to Europe than a rival to it. This prospect is often presented as inevitable. There would seem, as one prominent Russian foreign policy analyst has put it, to be no other sensible choice for Russia but to draw closer to Europe.[4] The Russian 'Medium-term strategy for development of relations between the Russian Federation and the European Union (2000–2010)' set out the grounds on which Russia believed a 'strategic partnership' should be developed between Russia and Europe.[5] Finally, the Russian Foreign Policy Concept of 2000 emphasized the importance of the EU and Western Europe to Russia as a 'vital resource for Russia's efforts to maintain its national interests in European and global affairs and for the stabilisation and growth of the Russian economy'.[6]

Permanent, stable and sustainable concord between Russia and Europe would be very agreeable. There may, in time, be some such relationship between them. However, this chapter argues that Russia's relations with Europe have not been put on something approaching a permanently stable footing because of normalization; there are still potentially plenty of twists and turns in the developing relationship between Russia and Europe. The chapter looks at this from the Russian side of the relationship by questioning the novelty and meaning of normalization in Russia. It starts by looking at the grounds on which arguments are made about normalization and Russia's relations with Europe, arguing that differences between the Putin and Yeltsin periods should not be overstated. This is particularly true of foreign policy, where Russia has actually been relatively consistent in practice if not in rhetoric. This is explained using some of the arguments made by Goldgeier and McFaul about why Russia's reaction to European Union enlargement and integration has been so measured.[7] It is argued that Russia's relatively measured response to enlargement has been a product of chance in the past, rather than the result of deep-seated changes in present-day Russian politics. Consequently, there is no basis for seeing Russia's relations with Europe as having reached a stable state of equilibrium and there are many factors that could make relations worse in the foreseeable future.

Normalization and Russian Politics

There is no official, 'Putin' definition of what constitutes normalization in Russian domestic or foreign policy, but advisors and commentators close to Putin have used the term. For example, Gleb Pavlovsky, a political analyst close to the Presidential Administration, has talked of a Putin project of 'managed normalization ... bringing the political, economic and public game into the framework of the Constitution, and at the same time into the framework of everyday human life'.[8] In common with other 'semi-official' definitions of normalization, Pavlovsky's usage is vague. The call for the conduct of public life to be based on legal principles is in line with Putin's promise during the 2000 election campaign to create a 'dictatorship of law'.[9] Beyond that, what normalization may be is unclear and would depend on what the 'framework of everyday human life' might be; what that might be is a question of metaphysics rather than concrete politics, and leaves plenty of room for official manoeuvre.

Since 'semi-official' definitions of normalization have been so vague there has been a tendency to read things into the idea of normalization. In particular, the term is often used as a form of short-hand to encapsulate things that are perceived to be different under Putin to the Yeltsin period: incremental management of politics rather than crisis management, the concentration of political power to reconstitute the state and economy, and the regularization of international affairs. The idea of normalization does not deny that there are still problems in Russian political life, nor does it suggest that Russia is necessarily becoming a democratic country. However, it does tend to put forward the notion that politics have become more settled and will henceforth take place within a predictable, regular framework. Hence, Russia under Putin has been described as having become a 'normal' country, a middle income democracy, comparable to other countries with purchasing power parity per capita Gross Domestic Product (GDP) of around $8,000.[10] Such countries – for example, Mexico, Brazil, Malaysia – are not socially just, having high levels of inequality, and have democratic political structures that are lacking in respect of liberal rights in some dimension. Nevertheless they have been relatively stable as incomplete democracies in recent times and have developed their political systems incrementally and without large and whole scale changes of political institutions and elites. In this sense Putin's normalization signifies that the dramatic changes of the 1990s are over and Russia has experienced a move from 'system transformation to system management', even if it is management of an imperfect democratic system.[11]

The idea that there has been a shift from 'system transformation to system management' under Putin rests on the belief that there is a fundamental difference between Yeltsin and Putin as leaders. After all, the tasks of system transformation do not just end overnight, but how they are dealt with can change. At the time of Putin's accession there was little expectation that he would actually be able to change anything in Russia. Yeltsin's successor was supposedly going to be constrained to follow the lead of his patrons because of the power of business and regional elites.[12] The discovery that Putin had 'an agenda of his own and "saving Russia" … from itself … was a part of it' made it possible to conceive of Putin's emergent regime as different to Yeltsin's.[13] However, defining the nature of this difference – normalization rather than another round of system transformation – depended on something else: there have (arguably) been fewer crises in Russian politics under Putin than under Yeltsin and this ability to avoid crisis creates the possibility for management and normal politics. There was not a year of the Yeltsin period that was not marked by crisis or trenchant political conflict. Between 1991 and 1993 there was a struggle over the basic constitutional order and economic principles. A rouble crisis in October 1994 followed the removal of economic liberals from government at the start of that year and was followed by the tragedy of Chechnya entering its military phase. There were votes of no confidence in the government after the invasion of Chechnya in 1995 and great uncertainty about the future due to the electoral strength of the Communist Party of the Russian Federation at the end of 1995. Yeltsin's re-election in 1996 was followed by uncertainty over his health and caustic infighting amongst Russia's elite over policy toward Chechnya and then, in 1997, over the gains of privatization. This infighting led to the 'parade of prime ministers' that stretched from early 1998 to 1999 and Putin's emergence. All this took place against a backdrop of economic collapse. Debates about the nature of Russia's national interest were a perennial feature of Russian politics throughout the 1990s as Russia struggled to achieve a domestic consensus about its international role. This debate, along with institutional change and unclear lines of decision-making and policy enactment, meant that foreign policy was often confused and seemed to be arbitrary in the early 1990s. As a result, Russia appeared to swing between cooperation and belligerence in its relations with the outside world, achieving foreign policy success, in the main, only when compromise suited the interests of other states, and then not being able to capitalise on that success for the most part.

Under Putin, on the other hand, there has been no major economic crisis and only one significant change of government just before Putin's re-election in 2004. Moreover, and leaving aside crises that have been caused by the conflict in Chechnya, what crises there have been in Moscow have often been seen as legitimate extreme action, at least by some commentators and large sections of the Russian public. Hence the arrest and subsequent prosecution of Mikhail Khodorkovsky and other Yukos' executives, or moves against other 'oligarchs', have been seen as justified corrections of abuses left over from the Yeltsin period; they are thus a part of 'normalization', rather than the sort of arbitrary political changes that occurred under Yeltsin. What are really exceptional changes in politics – such as the changes to electoral laws and the powers of regional governors – have not involved changes to the Constitution and therefore fit under the rubric of 'normal' politics, even though they are significant alterations to the fabric of Russian political life. In foreign policy, Putin has appeared to be less demanding than his predecessor, who seemed concerned to foster the idea that Russia had some special status as a great power. Putin believes that Russia should be 'treated as just another country' and should develop its foreign policy to 'serve the country's economic interests' rather than to promote its political leverage in world affairs.[14] Indeed, foreign policy under Putin was initially described as 'commercialized' or 'economized' as much as it was 'normalized'.[15] This shift, whether commercialization or normalization, has been termed the development of a 'pragmatic nationalism' or a 'new realism' in Russian foreign policy, and has been taken as the basis for strategic partnership.[16]

However, whilst there are differences between Putin's style of rule and Yeltsin's, it is very difficult to say that normalization has actually changed anything, or at least to say confidently that any changes that have occurred are due to a policy of normalization rather than something else. This is particularly true for foreign affairs. Part of the change that has occurred in foreign policy since Putin came to power has nothing to do with changes in the Kremlin. Putin has not had to deal with problems as intractable and emotive as the conflict in former Yugoslavia, an issue that in its various incarnations (break-up, Bosnia, Kosovo) mobilized parts of both Russia's elite and people to criticise the West, and strained diplomatic relations. Other issues such as North Atlantic Treaty Organization (NATO) and European enlargement have not been live issues for Putin as they were for Yeltsin since they were settled diplomatically in the main before he came to power or just after.[17] There has therefore been room for Putin to look at Europe, rather than toward the US, in a way that Yeltsin, who was concerned with policy issues where the US played the lead part or had the final say, could not.

Moreover, to argue that there has been a successful normalization in Russian foreign policy under Putin paints too bleak a picture of foreign policy under Yeltsin as aggressive and confrontational and ignores the political foundations – domestic and international – on which policy was made.[18] Accepting that normalization has occurred supposes that Russia under Yeltsin acted in the way that realist theories of international relations assumed it should have after the Cold War. Realist theories see changes in the structure of global politics, such as the end of the bipolar East/West conflict in the Cold War, as automatically stimulating a response in states that have lost power. States will, as rational, unitary actors in international politics, strive to achieve stability in the anarchic international system by building up their power so as to even out the initial gains made by winners from systemic change. Russia has suffered a massive and ongoing loss of power in international politics since the collapse of the Union of Soviet Socialist Republics (USSR) and the end of the Cold War. These losses, as Goldgeier and McFaul have pointed out, have been widely predicted by many scholars and politicians as foreshadowing a period of Russian recalcitrance and hostility toward those states that have gained whilst it has lost.[19] From this perspective, Russia should be belligerent toward Europe specifically and the 'West' generally, and should be opposed to any further loss of power such as the expansion of NATO or the EU. This opposition to Europe and the West has, however, been more rhetorical than anything else, and linked to specific condemnation of certain Western actions, such as bombing campaigns in the former Yugoslavia in the 1990s. And it has even been matched by a strong and consistent counter-rhetoric since the late 1980s: by Gorbachev's desire for the USSR to rejoin the 'common European home', by the aspiration of Russian officials in the early 1990s to join European economic institutions or promote reform as an 'avenue to European civilization'.[20] Despite rhetorical wavering on specifics, in general, argue Goldgeier and McFaul, Russia has 'pursued a policy of integration with the West since the late Soviet period'.[21] Normalization, in other words, has not really brought anything new to the table, and has not served as the basis for good relations between Russia and Europe except that Putin is more congenial to European tastes than Yeltsin.

If not Normalization, what are the Basis and Prospects for Russo-European Relations?

If Russian foreign policy has not been that aggressive in the past and was not dependent on normalization to improve relations, the key questions that arise are, what is the basis on which integration has taken place, are these foundations solid, and is what is happening under Putin making these foundations any more stable? Goldgeier and McFaul argue that there are both pull and push factors that have led Russia to be more interested in integration with Europe than belligerent. The pull factors come from the international system, which is not totally anarchic. It has a liberal core of democratic states that are not competitive in security terms and have developed cooperation both because they are democratic and because they had to cooperate during the Cold War. Although they may disagree with one another over policy specifics − such as policy on climate change − the states of the liberal core are so intermeshed by trade, mutual security commitments, and norms and values, that they are in effect bound to one another and deal with one another institutionally. This liberal core is made up of Western Europe, North America and Japan. The rest of the world is peripheral to this liberal core. In the periphery, security is not guaranteed by institutional arrangements or economic overlap, but is a matter of seeking advantage and balancing out the power of rivals.[22] The relationship between the liberal core and the periphery is uneven, and in general after the Cold War, the core has no direct security interest in the periphery. It only intervenes when it has some vital strategic interest (like oil in Iraq), is geographically threatened by a spillover from conflict (like former Yugoslavia), or is actually attacked (Afghanistan). The one qualification to this is that the core will export its values and institutions to areas that are both contiguous to it territorially and have some inclination to join the core.[23]

Russia falls into the category of states that the liberal core wishes to co-opt. It is not as simply or as fully within this category as central European states since it has not been as inclined towards the core and the cost of expanding the liberal core to include it is higher than in central Europe. Still, Goldgeier and McFaul argue, the liberal core has extended policies and institutional mechanisms to Russia: it has had support from the EU, the World Bank (WB), and International Monetary Fund (IMF), with membership in the latter as well as in European bodies like the Council of Europe; it has been given a special role in organizations like NATO through such mechanisms as the NATO-Russia Founding Act of 1997.

The pull factor of Western desire for Russia to become a part of the liberal core, albeit slowly, are matched by a push factor from within Russia itself: domestic constituencies that are pro-Western and their access to power. Goldgeier and McFaul argue that constituencies of 'liberals', that is actors who are pro-market and for a constitutional polity, have been very successful in Russian politics in maintaining a general drift toward economic reform and democratization and counterbalancing more nationalist or aggressive foreign policy positions.[24] This success has not been based on electoral strength, but push and pull factors have combined to create resources for liberal constituencies in Russian politics so that they have had access to power even when they have not had mass popular support.

This argument is an attractive one in many ways and is correct in certain respects. Russia's liberal constituencies have punched above their weight politically because they have access to external resources, both material and intellectual. When they have lost some access to power – generally after the electorate has signalled their dissatisfaction with liberal policies as they did by voting for Zhirinovsky's Liberal Democratic Party in 1993 or for the Communist Party of the Russian Federation in 1995 – they have been brought back very quickly to balance nationalist forces that seem more in line with electoral opinion. Moreover, the idea of a liberal core engaging erratically with the periphery, being activist in places like central Europe and less committed to supporting change elsewhere, is an attractive one that seems to explain why

Western policy seems to the rest of the world so haphazard and cynical, supporting some humanitarian interventions and not others regardless of the scale of humanitarian crisis, and being selective in its criticisms of such things as human rights abuses across the globe. It also explains the West's engagement with Russia but its greater engagement with central Europe. It also, of course, indicates that the basis for a good relationship between Russia and Europe has been in place since before Putin's administration and normalization. The problem is that it may not be as secure as Goldgeier and McFaul's argument suggests, and that the good relationship may itself be self-defeating.

First, there are other, equally plausible reasons for Russia's relative acquiescence to European enlargement in the past and for the access to power for Russia's liberal constituencies. The latter have helped pull Russia toward Europe and the West but their access to power and ability to influence policy is not a sign that Russia's rulers have bought into liberal ideas unambiguously. There are other factors that have guaranteed Russian liberals some role in government over the course of the Yeltsin and Putin years, specifically, the nature of the Russian presidency and the fiscal weakness of the Russian state. These have sometimes independently and sometimes jointly worked to ensure Russia's liberals a place in government. Securing and sustaining presidential power often required the inclusion of liberals in government as a counterweight to other forces; this enabled Yeltsin to manoeuvre between competing groups and maintain his power, albeit at a cost to governmental order and policy coherence.[25] In the early 1990s, liberals dominated economic policy because of the need to reconstruct Russia's economy after the collapse of the USSR and Yeltsin's need to shore up his position as president. Arguments for economic reform and their validation by external powers and agencies did this better than any other policy option available to Yeltsin. Consequently, liberals dominated the government (although not the Presidential Administration) and had control over economic and foreign policy. This hold was worn away for reasons of political expediency over 1992 and 1993, and broken completely after the December 1993 elections. It was then only slowly and partially rebuilt after the financial crisis in the autumn of 1994 as Yeltsin sort to restore some control over government finances.[26] Subsequently, the power of liberals in government grew when state financing required Russia to reassure international lenders – public and private – of its commitment to tax collection and fiscal probity.[27] Liberals were also particularly useful for Yeltsin to include in government because after 1993 they had no domestic constituency. They were therefore dependent on him and no challenge to him. In his last years as president and as he tried to control the emergence of a successor, Yeltsin's problems came from groups and individuals with domestic constituencies in industry or in regional government, not from liberals. They could be picked up, used and discarded as needed. A place in central administration could be a revolving door for a Russian liberal as the careers of officials like Anatoly Chubais, Boris Nemtsov and Sergei Kiriyenko showed.

The factor pushing Russia towards Europe, the survival in government of a liberal tendency, does exist then, and it has balanced political groups that would be more confrontational in foreign policy. However, the survival of liberalism within government has been largely down to expediency, the usefulness of liberals to Russian leaders, and exogenous factors, such as the fact that they have been the best link to Western financial institutions. In other words, the pull factor, in particular the availability of Western aid and loan capital tied to certain economic policies, helped sustain a push factor that would otherwise be relatively weak politically.[28] Without this sustenance the fate of Russia's liberals would have been even worse than it is since they would have been politically as well as socially isolated. Russia, for reasons of historical development and unlike some central European states, has not seen its liberal groupings link up with social interests domestically.[29] Economic interests have not been there consistently to support liberal constituencies in Russia and give them some force independent of presidential favour. Where there was an effort to support liberalism by a key economic actor, Mikhail Khodorkovsky and the Yukos group, the result was the state suppression of that concern.[30] There has been little in Russia's post-Soviet development to correct the historical and structural legacies of Soviet economic development since there has not been very much foreign investment into Russia.[31] Nor has there been economic diversification; growth in the economy has been centred on mineral extraction and exportation, which in 2003 provided over half of export income, 40 per cent of budget income, and half of industrial investment.[32]

One pillar of the relationship between Russia and Europe is not, therefore, stable due to any immanent property of its own; a liberal element in Russia's government is not there by virtue of its own strength. The position of liberals within the government might be worsening as Russia's economy has recovered under Putin. As the economy has improved since 1999, the political leverage that liberals have enjoyed because of their ability to link to international financial institutions has diminished. Consequently, their place in government has been totally dependent on Putin's support for economic reform to continue and bring about structural change in the Russian economy. This continued support is not, however, guaranteed and may change if Putin changes his mind for reasons of political expediency. There is pressure, for example, to use the Stabilisation Fund, which sets aside some of the income derived from high oil prices as a hedge against fiscal losses caused by lower energy prices in the future, for social welfare expenditure and to fund industrial investment. This might reduce liberal influence over economic policy by shifting the focus from structural reform, the outcomes of which are long-term so their delivery of benefits to the population does not easily or quickly translate into political advantage, to state intervention and the easy political advantage gained through resource transfers. Nor can it be assumed that falling energy prices would lock liberals into government by strengthening the leverage that they have through their international connections. Instead of a fiscally more stringent economic policy to cope with declining revenues in the event of energy price falls and to attract foreign loans, Putin may choose to stabilise falling revenues by increasing state control over the energy industry to ensure a higher state share of declining revenues. The model for this course of action is the Yukos affair and the transfer of that firm's resources back into what are essentially the hands of the state using the legal system and tax authorities. Such a course of action may be popular both with the general population, since it would be another attack on the oligarchs, and with those branches of the state whose personnel Putin has most assiduously promoted in the past, the security services.[33] Finally, it cannot be guaranteed that Putin's successor (and 2008 is not that far away) will keep faith with the rhetoric of economic reform as he has done. Putin may, of course, engineer a situation that enables him to guide Russian political development from behind the scenes, but this is far from certain.

The insecure position of liberals within the Russian establishment means that structural factors pulling Russia to Europe and the West are important if a good relationship is to continue on an even keel over time and as the influence of liberals within the Russian government wanes as well as waxes. The existence of a liberal core in global politics, as Goldgeier and McFaul argue, would seem to indicate that there is a permanent and consistent force in world politics seeking a good relationship with Russia. Consequently, and structurally, good Western intentions and pressure to integrate should help keep things on track even if the relative importance of liberal values in Russian policy circles diminishes. However, the existence of this core does not preclude the existence of other structural factors that might work against a reconciliation of Russia with the liberal core and the possibility of their increased salience in Russian politics, nor does it mean that the core's good intentions toward Russia will always be read as such and met with a sympathetic or positive response.

The structural factors that might work against the pull of the liberal core are twofold. First, there are structural problems of transition in Russia that still have to be faced. Russia has not as yet dealt with some of the most intractable problems of developing a stable post-Soviet political economy. So far, Russia's transformation from communism has been predominantly concerned with reform of political institutions and with the creation of a form of market exchange to underpin a form of capitalist economy. This has meant that certain kinds of developmental problem have not been dealt with. These problems are primarily concerned with the creation of an 'effective national territory', that is the consolidation of Russia's population and economic production sufficient to produce an economic surplus that can support the secure occupation of the whole of the geographic territory of the Russian Federation.[34] The problems that are involved in the construction of 'an effective national territory' are chiefly the result of Soviet developmental practices and legacies of the collapse of the USSR. They include such things as the economically and environmentally costly development of Siberia that serves as a drag on economic performance as a whole and is a burden to state finances; the under- and mis-development of Russia's urban areas so that they cannot sustain economic development independently of booming energy prices; extreme and growing poverty in areas of Russia like the Caucasus that have become border regions since the collapse of the USSR, which are ethnically distinct and where Russia is faced with hard security problems; and the fragmentation of economic space in Russia so that the social and geographical basis of economic development is high.[35]

Obviously, and through integration, Europe – and the West more generally – could play a role in solving some of these problems. However, this would not be a simple process. Historically, the Russian state has resolved these kinds of problems by the coercion of development (which has been the only way of overcoming the high costs of development), by suppressing any problems that remain through the development of a patrimonial, authoritarian system, and through the militarization of the economy to overcome perceived security threats and at the cost of social welfare and market development.[36] Overcoming this historical pattern of development would require a massive Western and European effort, and may anyway backfire. Integration, particularly where it is driven by private concerns through economic globalization rather than by governments, focuses not on Russia's problem areas like the Caucasus, but on developing those zones of Russia where there may be an economic return on investment. These areas are few and far between – Moscow and the energy producing regions, with limited industrial development in places like Samara – and have accounted for the bulk of foreign inward investment and aid.[37] The problem with this is that it exacerbates tensions that have to be managed in the national economy between demands for more openness from successful regions and the demand for redistribution of economic wealth from poorer regions. It also imperils the ability of the central state to manage as rich regions with international connections may attempt to limit its policy options by using their international connections to rein it in. The latter does not appear to have happened as yet, but managing tensions between internationalized regions and economic sectors and those that produce solely for the national economy has been a source of anti-democratic political development elsewhere in the world.[38] *Sub rosa* denationalization of the Yukos variety fits this pattern of development:

a state that is struggling to develop a market economy and at the same time distribute resources to all that make demands of it, and particularly to domestic constituencies that are not able to link up with the international economy, sequesters key resources; this is administratively simpler than building a market economy and enables it to directly redistribute resources for the political advantage of its rulers.

Integration, particularly integration driven by private concerns, may thus actually create pressures that would undermine the political basis of reconciliation between Russia and Europe. In terms of economic administration at least, Europe has tried to forestall this with the insistence in the 1994 Partnership and Cooperation Agreement (PCA) that Russia develop its legislation in line with that of the EU. Russia endorsed this idea in its 1999 'Medium-term strategy for development of relations between the Russian Federation and the European Union (2000–2010)' and in the 2001 joint EU-Russia statement on the creation of a 'common European economic space'.[39] In theory, this should create a bulwark against backsliding on reform by creating a policy anchor for Russia that it can use to hold reform on course. In practice, no Russian legislation appears to have been developed in line with EU norms despite Putin's approval of the notion of such a policy anchor, and anyway such external policy anchors from bodies like the IMF have had little purchase in Russia in the past.[40] The literature frequently asserts that growing Russian trade with the EU-25 will work to bring Russia and Europe together. The impression created is that since the EU-25 takes about 50 per cent of Russia's exports this will give the EU some sort of leverage. Given that the bulk of these exports are oil and gas and given that world oil production has little spare capacity and there is rising demand for oil, this seems unlikely for the immediate future; leverage could cut both ways where trade involves scarce strategic goods. Moreover, Russia's ability to gain from trade further depends on internal reform.[41] Consequently, European leverage in the long run probably depends on Russian political development facilitating reform and this reform then creating economic diversification and the conditions for European influence.

The second structural factor that might work against the pull of the liberal core is that the geo-political context in which the pull works has changed as European integration has developed. The relationship of the liberal core is not just to Russia itself, but also to states that surround it. When the focus of integration was central Europe this was a manageable problem. The integration of central Europe into the liberal core did cause some diplomatic difficulties, but it could be accepted by Russia as inevitable and as irresistible. As former Prime Minister and Minister for Foreign Affairs Yevgenii Primakov put it, Russia did nothing substantive to deflect central Europe's integration with Europe in terms of threats or offering an alternative since 'we put our relations with

[Central Europe] on the back burner. It was not wilful neglect; it was simply that our attention was focused exclusively on our own problems'.[42]

Whether this will be the case as and when further integration begins to affect former Soviet states other than the Baltic nations is questionable. Relations with the other former Soviet states have never been on the back burner for Moscow, even if its own integration project, the Commonwealth of Independent States (CIS), has not been successful. The range of problems that Russia faces if other post-Soviet states are pulled closer to Europe and the liberal core is far greater and more fundamental. It involves questions of identity and diaspora politics, and economic links that have, unlike links with central Europe, been maintained and in some cases extended privately since 1991. In short, Russians, both in the elite and on the street, have emotive links to the post-Soviet space that they did not have to central Europe.[43] Unlike European and NATO expansion into central Europe the further integration of states like Ukraine into European and transnational structures would be seen as a direct assault on Russian power and geo-political leverage. The problem is not just one of Europe or of the post-Soviet states that are in its immediate orbit. Russia seems to equate loss of influence in any post-Soviet state with a threat to its interests in all post-Soviet states. Hence, the democratic 'revolutions' in Georgia, Ukraine, Moldova and Kyrgyzstan were all looked on negatively by Moscow, and all were accompanied by warnings against unwarranted (i.e. non-Russian) outside involvement in the affairs of the area. European involvement and willingness to extend its influence in these states, or in the post-Soviet area more broadly may be slight. There was no great European involvement with Ukraine before the events of late 2004 for example.[44] But those events showed that Russian-European relations could easily become hostage to fortune and the actions and wishes of other players in the area who may want to push their relationship with Europe and the West beyond what Russia finds acceptable.

Conclusion

The idea that Russian politics have been undergoing a process of normalization, or that Russia has become a normal country, captures something of the change that has occurred under Putin. It does not, however, explain very much about how Russian politics will develop, or what the nature and basis of its relations with Europe and the West are or have been. Putin has put more rhetorical emphasis on Europe than Yeltsin did, but he cannot talk Russia into developing a political and economic system that is stable and capable of steady partnership with Europe. Liberal forces that might have an interest in improving relations with Europe on the basis of shared values are still in the Russian government, but their position has never been a strong one. If Putin or his successor's priorities change liberals may find they are excluded from office. The conditions to hold Russia in a steady relationship with Europe are therefore very weak, and have had little to do with normalization. Moreover, structural factors may also not help the development of Russian-European relations. There are still significant problems to be addressed by Russia as it continues to develop a post-communist system. These problems may be solved by policies that would draw Russia away from Europe or at least away from it on the grounds that normalization has supposedly been established. There is little that Europe can do about this. Although the diplomatic framework for European influence is in place through the various agreements that have been made between Russia and Europe, European leverage, indeed any Western leverage, over Russian domestic development is small if not non-existent in practice.

This does not mean that Russia's relations with Europe will be bad. It is most likely that there will be continuity, rather than radical change, that Putin will make statements about how much he thinks Russia should develop toward Europe, and European leaders will make statements about the need to engage with Russia and their hopes for partnership with it. In the meantime, there will be diplomatic traffic between Moscow, Brussels and the capitals of Europe and positive progress may be made on issues of mutual concern. If this diplomatic traffic goes on for long enough it might in time cover enough policy areas and in enough depth to produce a qualitatively new relationship, the strategic partnership that both sides are rhetorically committed to developing. But whilst we await this development we should not assume that good relations are guaranteed and should be mindful of the dangers to relations that still exist in Russia itself and as Russia deals with a world that is changing quicker than it is.

Notes and References

1. K. Khudoley, 'Otnosheniya Rossii i Evropeiskogo soyuza: noviye vozmozhnosti, noviye problemy', in *Rossiya i Evropeiskii soyuz: pereosmyslivaya strateggiyu vzaimootnoshenii*, (Moscow, Carnegie Endowment for International Peace, 2003), pp. 13–34; D. Trenin, 'From pragmatism to strategic choice: is Russia's security policy becoming realistic?', in A. Kuchins (ed.) *Russia after the Fall*, (New York, Carnegie Endowment for International Peace, 2002), p. 203.
2. cf. F. Duchêne, 'Europe's role in world peace', in R. Mayne (ed.) *Europe Tomorrow: Sixteen Europeans Look Ahead*, (London, Fontana, 1972), pp. 32–47; L. Feldman, 'Reconciliation and legitimacy: foreign relations and the enlargement of the European Union', in T. Banchoff and M. Smith (eds) *Legitimacy and the European Union*, (London, Routledge, 1999), pp. 66–92.
3. In his annual 'state of the nation' address to parliament in 2005, for example, Putin placed Russia firmly within Europe, stating that it 'has always been and of course will remain the largest European nation', and argued that Russia's historical experience of

political development both mirrors Europe's and needs to converge with 'all-European standards'. V. Putin, 'Poslanie Federal'nomu Sobraniyu Rossisskoi Federatsii', available at http://president.kremlin.ru/appears/2005/04/25/1223_type63372type 82634_87049.shtml. Translation from BBC Monitoring, in *Johnson's Russia List*, 9130, 25 April 2005, available at www.cdi.org

4. S. Karaganov, 'XXI vek i interesy Rossii', *Sovermennaya Evropa*, 3, 2004, pp. 5–21.
5. 'Medium-term strategy for development of relations between the Russian Federation and the European Union (2000–2010)', 1999, available at http://europa.eu.int/comm/ external_relations/russia/russian_medium_term_strategy/
6. *Nezavisimaya gazeta*, 11 July, 2000.
7. J. Goldgeier and M. McFaul, 'Russians as joiners: realist and liberal conceptions of postcommunist Europe', in M. McFaul and K. Stoner-Weiss (eds.) *After the collapse. Comparative lessons of transition*, (Cambridge, Cambridge University Press, 2004), pp. 232–56.
8. *Vremya novostei*, 30 March, 2004.
9. R. Sakwa, *Putin. Russia's Choice*, (London, Routledge, 2004), pp. 90–1.
10. A. Shleifer and D. Treisman, 'A normal country', *Foreign Affairs*, 83:2 (2004), pp. 20–38; A. Shleifer and D. Treisman, 'A normal country', *Journal of Economic Perspectives*, 19:1 (2005), pp. 151–74.
11. R. Sakwa, 'Regime change from Yeltsin to Putin: normality, normalcy or normalization?', in C. Ross (ed.) *Russian Politics under Putin*, Manchester, Manchester University Press, 2004), p. 19. Whether or not Russia is a 'normal' country and what this might mean is a matter of acrimonious debate, see S. Rosefielde, *An abnormal country*, *The European Journal of Comparative Economics*, Vol 2, No. 1, 2005.
12. D. Treisman, 'After Yeltsin comes ... Yeltsin', *Foreign Policy*, 117 (1999), pp. 74–86.
13. J. Black, *Vladimir Putin and the New World Order. Looking East, Looking West?*, (Lanham, MD, Rowman and Littlefield, 2004), p. 345.
14. Sakwa, 'Regime change from Yeltsin to Putin, *op. cit.*, p. 21.
15. B. Lo, *Vladimir Putin and the Evolution of Russian Foreign Policy*, (Oxford, Blackwell, 2003).
16. Sakwa, *Putin. Russia's Choice, op. cit.*, pp. 208–33; J. Gower, 'Russian foreign policy toward the European Union', in C. Ross (ed.) *Russian Politics under Putin*, (Manchester, Manchester University Press, 2004), pp. 236–54; R. Puglisi, 'The normalization of Russian foreign policy', in G. Herd and J. Moroney (eds.) *Security Dynamics in the Former Soviet Bloc*, (London, Routledge, 2003), pp. 63–79.
17. Trenin, *op. cit.*, p. 193.
18. J. Surovell, 'Yevgenii Primakov: "hard-liner" or casualty of the conventional wisdom?', *Journal of Communist Studies and Transitional Politics*, 21:2 (2005), pp. 223–47.
19. Goldgeier and McFaul, 'Russians as joiners', *op. cit.*
20. M. Gorbachev, *Perestroika i novoe myshlenie dlya nashei strany i dlya vsego mira*, (Moscow, Politizat, 1987), p. 203; I.B. Neumann, *Russia and the Idea of Europe. A Study in Identity and International Relations*, (London, Routledge, 1996); N. Robinson, 'The global economy, reform and crisis in Russia', *Review of International Political Economy*, 6: 4 (1999), p. 533.
21. Goldgeier and McFaul, 'Russians as joiners', *op. cit.*, pp. 233–4.
22. J. Goldgeier and M. McFaul, 'A tale of two worlds: core and periphery in the post-Cold War era', *International Organization*, 46:2 (1992), pp. 467–92.
23. Goldgeier and McFaul, 'Russians as joiners', *op. cit.*, pp. 238–9.
24. *Ibid*, pp. 248–51.
25. N. Robinson, 'The presidency: the politics of institutional chaos', in N. Robinson (ed.) *Institutions and Political Change in Russia*, (Basingstoke, Macmillan, 2000), pp. 11–40.

26. R.W. Stone, *Lending credibility. The International Monetary Fund and the Post-Communist Transition*, (Princeton, Princeton University Press, 2002), p. 165.
27. Robinson, 'The global economy, reform and crisis in Russia', *op. cit.*
28. J. Wedel, *Collision and Collusion. The strange case of Western aid to Eastern Europe 1989–1998*, (New York, St Martin's Press, 1998); S. Mendelson, 'Democracy assistance and political transitions in Russia: between success and failure', *International Security*, 25:4 (2001), pp. 68–106.
29. The Soviet economy, and the Russian economy at the heart of it, was not as open or as diverse in its dealings with the global economy as some central European states since foreign trade was highly centralized and energy dependent. Economic diversity in trade and/or integration with global finance through high debt levels before the collapse of communism correlate strongly and positively with ability to sustain economic reform. Where there was little trade diversity and relatively low foreign debt, as in Russia, economic reform stalled. Economic resources were concentrated in the hands of a narrow range of social actors whose interest was in limited change (at best) and who were opposed to economic openness through liberalization. See N. Robinson, 'Path dependency, global economy and post-communist change', in N. Robinson (ed.) *Reforging the weakest link. Global Political Economy and Post-Soviet Change in Russia, Ukraine and Belarus*, (Aldershot, Ashgate, 2004), pp. 106–26.
30. V. Shlapentokh, 'Wealth versus political power: the Russian case', *Communist and Post-Communist Studies*, 35:2 (2004), pp. 135–60.
31. R. Ahrend and W. Tompson, 'Fifteen years of reform in Russia: what has been achieved? What remains to be done?', (Paris, OECD Economics Department Working Papers, No. 17, 2005), p. 29.
32. C. Gaddy, 'Has Russia entered a period of sustainable economic growth?', in A. Kuchins (ed.) *Russia after the Fall*, (New York, Carnegie Endowment for International Peace, 2002), pp. 125–44; P. Hanson, 'The Russian economic recovery: do four years of growth tell us that the fundamentals have changed?', *Europe-Asia Studies*, 55:3 (2003), pp. 365–82; P. Sutela, 'Did Putin's reforms catapult Russia to durable growth?', *BOFIT Online*, 6, 2005 (www.bof.fi/bofit,) p. 24.
33. O. Kryshtanovskaya and S. White, 'Putin's militocracy', *Post-Soviet Affairs*, 19:4 (2003), pp. 289–306.
34. M. Bradshaw and J. Prendergast, 'The Russian heartland revisited: an assessment of Russia's transformation', *Eurasian Geography and Economics*, 46:2 (2005), pp. 83–122.
35. *Ibid*, pp. 115–8.
36. N. Robinson, *Russia: A State of Uncertainty*, (London, Routledge, 2002); A. Lynch, *How Russia is Not Ruled. Reflections on Russian Political Development*, (Cambridge, Cambridge University Press, 2005); S. Rosefielde, *Russia in the 21st Century. The prodigal superpower*, Cambridge, Cambridge University Press, 2005).
37. N. Robinson, 'A fickle benefactor: Russia and the global economy as a resource for change', in N. Robinson (ed.) *Reforging the Weakest Link. op. cit.* p. 29; I. Iwasaki and K. Suganuma, 'Regional distribution of foreign direct investment in Russia', *Post-Communist Economies*, 17:2 (2005), pp. 153–72.
38. N. Robinson, 'The economy and the prospects for anti-democratic development in Russia', *Europe-Asia Studies*, 52:8 (2000), pp. 1391–416.
39. 'Medium-term strategy …', *op. cit.*; J. Gower, 'Russian foreign policy toward the European Union', *op. cit.*, p. 243.
40. P. Sutela, *Rossiya i Evropa. Nekotorie aspekty ekonomicheskikh vzaimootnoshenii*, (Moscow, Carnegie Endowment for International Peace, 2003); Stone, *op. cit.*

41. P. Sutela, 'EU, Russia and Common Economic Space', *BOFIT Online*, 3, 2005, available at www.bof.fi/bofit

42. Y. Primakov, *Russian Crossroads. Toward the New Millennium*, (New Haven, Yale University Press, 2004), p. 131.

43. J. O'Loughlin and P. Talbot 'Where in the world is Russia? Geopolitical perceptions and preferences of ordinary Russians', *Eurasian Geography and Economics*, 46:1 (2005), pp. 23–50.

44. P. Kubicek, 'The European Union and democratization in Ukraine', *Communist and Post-Communist Studies*, 38:2 (2005), pp. 269–92.

3

THE RUSSIAN ELITE PERSPECTIVE ON EUROPEAN RELATIONS[1]

Stephen White and Margot Light

Introduction

When the long-projected enlargement of the European Union (EU) finally took place on 1 May 2004, the Western Newly Independent States (WNIS), as the European Commission calls the former Soviet states of Belarus, Moldova, Russia and Ukraine, became the EU's new eastern neighbourhood. Although they had no prospect of acceding to the EU in the foreseeable future, they were perceived as 'the EU's essential partners'. Indeed, the attainment of security, stability and sustainable development *within* the Union was deemed to require political reform, social cohesion and economic dynamism *outside* it, in particular in the EU's new eastern neighbourhood.[2] The European Commission proposed a European Neighbourhood programme to promote a set of values 'within the fields of the rule of law, good governance, the respect for human rights, including minority rights, the promotion of good neighbourly relations, and the principles of market economy and sustainable development'.[3]

Russians were appalled that the EU's new neighbourhood plans appeared to put Russia in the same category not only as Belarus and Moldova, but also as the states of North Africa. Russia was duly left out of the European Neighbourhood Policy (ENP); instead the EU and Russia decided to develop their strategic partnership through the creation of four common spaces. However, the EU-Russian strategic partnership was already experiencing considerable strain by this time. Following the December 2003 parliamentary election, the Duma was dominated by the pro-presidential United Russia party, with little or no representation of those parties, Yabloko and the Union of Right Forces, which had previously been the most enthusiastic supporters of relations with the EU and of a 'European perspective' more generally. A number of contentious issues had arisen as a result both of domestic developments in Russia, and of the enlargement of the EU.

This chapter explores the reasons for the deterioration in the Russia-EU relationship, based primarily on a series of interviews with the Russian foreign policymaking community between late 2004 and early 2006 (we sought, as far as possible, to represent five key constituencies: the presidential administration; the foreign ministry; the Duma, especially the chairs of relevant committees; defence and security interests; and business). We look first of all at the views foreign policy elites hold about Russia and the EU,[4] and whether they regard Russia as part of Europe. We then turn to views of the EU and of enlargement, considering whether it is still possible to use the terms 'liberal westerniser', 'fundamentalist nationalist' and 'pragmatic nationalist'[5] to classify elite views about the EU and broader foreign policy perspectives; we find that the terms are still applicable, although the size and membership of each of the three groups has changed.

The second section of the chapter examines in more detail some of the border issues that concern foreign policy elites and that have affected the progress of Russian-EU relations. The third section then considers the reasons why Russian-EU relations have not developed more actively in recent years. It suggests that the reasons are the tendency on both sides to adopt broad programmatic schemes which then have to be filled with practical content; the Russian preference for bilateral rather than multilateral relations; the EU's reluctance to compromise or treat Russia as a special case; and Russian resentment at being expected to adopt EU standards and values, and at being treated in the same way as the EU's other new neighbours, as well as a growing hostility to the intrusive nature of EU policy and to the imposition of Western values and norms. The hostage-taking crisis at Beslan in late 2004, and then a series of 'coloured revolutions' in post-Soviet space, notably in Ukraine, had sharpened these differences still further by early 2006.

Elite views about Russia and the EU

To analyse the perceptions of the foreign policy elite we use a combination of published sources and interviews, particularly those expressed during a research visit in March-April 2004, on the eve of EU enlargement and before the hostage-taking crisis in Beslan and the Ukrainian presidential election, both of which caused tension between the EU and Russia. The interviews were certainly sufficient to establish the broad outlines of elite attitudes towards the EU and its impending enlargement. However, foreign policy elites are not, as a rule, well informed about the details of the country's relationship with the EU; they tend to have opinions about the dramatic highlights, rather than the minutiae.[6] In fact, the relationship is highly institutionalized, with a dense network of regular political consultations and economic negotiations, frequently on highly detailed and technical questions. According to Russia's ambassador to the European Communities, 'the Russia-EU partnership is complex; it deals with a variety of important pragmatic tasks'.[7] The media, in Russia as elsewhere, are also more interested in high drama than low-level detail. In order to investigate the substance of the problems that have arisen in the relationship, therefore, we have made some use of the more specialized journals and of the publications of academics and analysts who focus specifically on the EU.

From the time that Mikhail Gorbachev declared the Soviet Union to be part of a 'common European home'[8] to President Vladimir Putin's announcement in St Petersburg on the occasion of the city's 300th anniversary in 2003 that 'Russia is both historically and culturally an integral part of Europe'[9] there are innumerable examples of elite and official statements claiming that Russia has a European identity.[10] Putin's address to the Federal Assembly in April 2005 was especially eloquent in this respect:

> Above all else Russia was, is, and will of course remain a major European nation. The ideals of freedom, human rights, justice and democracy that were achieved with much suffering by European culture have for many centuries been our society's determining values. For three centuries, we, hand in hand with other European peoples, passed through the reforms of the Enlightenment, the difficulties of establishing parliamentarianism, municipal government and a judiciary, and the establishment of similar legal systems. Step by step, we advanced together toward the recognition and expansion of human rights, toward equal and universal suffrage, toward an understanding of the need to look after the poor and the weak, toward the emancipation of women, and toward other social gains. I repeat, we did all of this together, lagging behind in some things, while sometimes exceeding European standards in others.[11]

Whatever their foreign policy views, Russian elites believe that Russia is part of Europe, but differences between sets of attitudes are apparent in the way that they define Russia's identity. For liberal westernisers, Russia is indisputably part of Europe. 'We are in Europe…and always have been', one businessman insisted. Pragmatic nationalists – the most numerous of our interviewees – are also sure that Russia is a European country, but they draw attention to its unique characteristics. A prominent deputy of the Duma told us, for instance, that Russia is 'a unique part of Europe', while a senior Foreign Ministry official asserted that although Russia is geographically and culturally European, 'it has its own mentality'.

Fundamentalist nationalists, on the other hand, believe that Russia's European characteristics are blended with its Eastern and Asian features to produce a distinctive Eurasian identity.[12] One interviewee who was very insistent on Russia's Eurasian identity claimed that the centre of civilization is not Europe but Russia. Another defined Russia as an 'Eastern European-Eurasian Union'. For the more religiously inclined, Russia shares 'a Christian civilisation' with Europe, but it has its own peculiarities, 'which stem from climatic differences and Russia's twentieth century experiences'. According to the historian, Aleksandr Chubaryan, those who insist on Russia's 'uniqueness' distinguish 'Russian' Europeanism from 'classical' Europeanism, decrying the 'lack of spirituality' in the former.[13]

One of our interviewees insisted that Russia is European, but not 'Western'. Morozov argues that the general tendency among Russian intellectuals to distinguish between Europe and the West, and to include Russia in the former but not the latter is a continuation of a long-standing Russian tradition of distinguishing between 'true' and 'false' Europe. The tradition was inherited by the Soviet Union; thus during the Cold War the North Atlantic Treaty Organization (NATO) was perceived as the embodiment of 'false' Europe. The distinction that many Russians tend to make between 'the good West of Europe/ EU' and the 'bad West of America/NATO' appears to be a continuation of this tradition, and it is one that appears to have some popular resonance.[14]

Liberal westernisers and pragmatic nationalists are, by and large, well disposed towards the EU. Indeed, amongst our interviewees, there was a consensus that the EU does not offer any threat to Russia. On the contrary, 'the EU opens opportunities for Russia to solve its internal as well as its external problems', one of our interlocutors declared. On the other hand, in the fundamentalist nationalist press, the EU is often depicted in negative terms. It is 'permeated through and through with hypocrisy and double standards' and, in its relationship with Russia, it is 'a difficult, petty and biased partner'.[15]

Liberal westernisers either do not expect enlargement to cause any particular difficulties in Russia-EU relations, or believe that it is Russia's responsibility to resolve the problems that occur. They argue that market access will be easier because quotas will increase, for example; the problems that arise will be caused not by tariffs but by the fact that Russian goods are not competitive. Even one of our more fundamentalist nationalist interviewees declared that 'it is a good thing that the EU is enlarging…it will make us develop, rethink'. Most fundamentalist nationalists, however, predict that Russia will suffer serious economic consequences as a result of enlargement, ranging from a decline of aluminium and agricultural exports to being deprived of its own energy resources.[16] Pragmatic nationalists are not opposed to enlargement, but they are apprehensive about the consequences for Russia. One pragmatic nationalist predicted despondently that lower tariffs would not help Russia, since 'it has nothing apart from oil, gas, metals and wood to export to Europe'. Another argued that cross-border trade would be affected.

It is clear even from this brief analysis of foreign policy views that attitudes towards the EU range from complete approval and identification with European values (classified here as liberal westerniser), at one end of the spectrum, to suspicion and hostility, together with the conviction that Russia is unique (which we call fundamentalist nationalist), at the other. However, the views that predominate both in the discourse about the EU and in Russian policy lie between these two extremes: generally benignly disposed towards the EU, they are nevertheless deeply concerned about the problems that EU enlargement – to date, and in the future – may cause for Russia. We classify these views as pragmatic nationalist – pragmatic in that they recognize that Russia has no choice but to develop the best possible relationship with the EU, and nationalist in the conviction that Russia is unlike other states and should have a different and more special relationship with the EU than other states in the EU's new neighbourhood. Whereas liberal westernisers have had little influence on Russian policy since the early 1990s, with the success of the Rodina (Motherland) party in the 2003 Duma elections and the consequent composition of the Duma committees, fundamentalist nationalist views appear to have increasing salience.[17]

One of our interviewees produced a list of future problems that would affect Russia's relations with the EU: the Schengen visa regime, Kaliningrad, and tariffs. Many of the pragmatic and fundamentalist nationalists we interviewed were concerned about the Schengen system more generally, and Kaliningrad in particular. Let us examine these border issues in more detail before considering why, despite the predominantly positive views about the EU, the Russia-EU relationship has not been more productive in recent years.

Border Issues

Border issues have been amongst the most contentious in relations between the EU and Russia. We concentrate here on the imposition of the Schengen regime on the accession countries, the status of Kaliningrad, and the effectiveness of the Northern Dimension in alleviating some of these problems.

The Schengen Regime

The Schengen agreement signed by five EU member states in 1985 replaced border and custom controls at internal borders with a unitary system of rules for entry and exit at external borders, the adoption of a unified system of extradition and the establishment of a Schengen Information System (SIS). The intention was to tighten external control of access into the EU so that internal integration could be facilitated by allowing the free movement of persons, goods, capital and services across the Union. By 1996 13 out of 15 EU member states had joined the Schengen zone, and so had Iceland and Norway. Under the terms of the 1999 Amsterdam Treaty, the Schengen *acquis* was included in the legal system of the EU that candidate states had to adopt. This meant that they had to strengthen their external border controls and implement the EU's common visa regime, although they would not formally have to join the Schengen zone immediately upon accession.[18]

Candidate states were not permitted to negotiate opt-outs (such as the UK and Ireland have) because by the turn of the century, the EU was more concerned with tightening its external border controls as a defence against illegal immigration and organized crime than with using Schengen to facilitate internal integration. The argument put forward by many Western experts that visas are not very effective instruments in curbing either criminal activity or illegal immigration did not persuade EU officials and the governments of member states to change their minds. Nor were they embarrassed by the paradox that new members were expected to impose 'hard' Schengen borders on their non-EU neighbours, while the lifting of border controls between old and new EU members, and the freedom of taking up employment, would be delayed for several years after accession.[19]

Russian policymakers and foreign policy elites have been seriously concerned about the loss of the right to visa-free travel to the countries of Central and Eastern Europe (CEE) ever since the enlargement of the EU eastwards was first proposed. Their concerns grew as the candidate countries began to implement the Schengen system: in 2000 the Czech Republic, Slovakia, Estonia and Bulgaria began to require visas from Russian travellers. The EU argued that the Schengen system bestowed certain advantages (for example, one visa gave access to all Schengen countries, and having identical customs rules and specifications for all EU member states would benefit Russian businesses). The Russians argued that the candidate countries were applying the Schengen conditions more strictly than existing EU members, and complained that there were long delays in receiving visas, the number of people refused visas was increasing and the cost of visas themselves was mounting. It was particularly galling to Russians that whereas Russia was included in the list of 130 countries whose citizens require visas, US citizens do not require them if they visit the Schengen zone for less than three months.[20]

When we interviewed foreign policy elites in an earlier exercise of this kind, in 1999 and 2000, the loss of visa-free travel to Eastern Europe was one of the main negative consequences they predicted as a result of EU enlargement. In 2004 and 2006 our interviewees appeared less concerned about the issue. Liberal westernisers argued that the visa regime was a problem for the new members, not for Russians, or that it was not just Russia's problem, but also a problem for the EU. Pragmatic nationalists called the visa regimes 'inconvenient' and only fundamentalist nationalists complained that visa requirements were increasing. The issue was very prominent, however, in the specialist literature and in official statements about Russian-EU relations. It is clear from these sources that the imposition of the Schengen visa regime by the accession states had turned into a serious political issue in the Russia-EU relationship.

There was a great deal of concern that the imposition of the Schengen system symbolized the redivision of Europe. In 2002, for instance, V V Kotyenov, Head of the Consular Department of the Ministry of Foreign Affairs (MFA), warned that the Schengen agreement risked turning 'into a new dividing wall in Europe'.[21] Deputy Foreign Minister Chizhov maintained a year later that 'an ever higher, difficult to traverse "Schengen wall" [had] been constructed, which [was], year by year, becoming more inaccessible' and which was 'already not far from being analogous to the Berlin wall'.[22] Igor Ivanov, then Foreign Minister, argued that 'Schengen contradicts one of the fundamental freedoms enunciated by the founding fathers of a united Europe – the freedom of movement.'[23]

The claim that Schengen violates the fundamental rights of Russians was prevalent across the political spectrum. Vladimir Lukin, a Yabloko deputy who was then deputy speaker of the Duma, complained that simply 'because the EU has its rules', the EU had removed the right of Russian citizens to freedom of movement from one part of its territory to another. The usually very measured expert on the EU at the Institute of Europe of the Academy of Sciences, Yuri Borko, also argued that while the EU was right to criticize Russia at times for failing to respect human rights, the EU itself was preventing Russians from exercising their fundamental right to move freely across their own territory.[24] Ironically, the fundamentalist nationalist press did not, on the whole, invoke the issue, not because it approved of Schengen, but because human rights are not, in general, part of the fundamentalist nationalist discourse.

Since the EU insisted that the Schengen system could not be modified, President Putin proposed a reciprocal Russian-EU visa-free agreement to the heads of EU member-states in August 2002. The Commission responded by insisting that Russia would first have to conclude a readmission treaty with the EU which would enable the EU to return illegal immigrants who entered the EU from Russia. The Commission also insisted that Russia should strengthen its passport control procedures, issue passports to all its citizens, and make its external borders more effective.[25] These seemingly elementary conditions are, in fact, extremely difficult for Russia to fulfil. In effect, what the EU requires of Russia is very similar to what it imposed upon the new member states: in order to achieve visa-free movement between Russia and the EU, Russia would have to control external access to Russia from the Commonwealth of Independent States. Although the two sides agreed to study the possibility of visa-free travel at the Russia-EU summit in Saint Petersburg in May 2003, little progress had been made by the time the road map for the Common Space of Freedom, Security and Justice was adopted at the May 2005 summit. The Summit Conclusions noted that negotiations on a readmission agreement had not yet been completed and envisaged visa-free travel only 'as a long-term perspective';[26] this remained the case even though a number of further advances were achieved at the October 2005 summit in London.

Kaliningrad

The visa issue became particularly acute in relation to Kaliningrad and it threatened to create an impasse in Russia-EU relations. Kaliningrad had been ceded to the Soviet Union at the Potsdam Conference in 1945. It was administratively part of the Russian Soviet Federative Socialist Republic although it was physically separated from it by Belarus and Lithuania. When the Soviet Union disintegrated, Kaliningrad remained part of Russia, while Belarus and Lithuania became independent states. Travel by land between Kaliningrad and the rest of the Russian Federation now required the crossing of three borders: either the borders of Lithuania and Latvia, or of Lithuania and Belarus, or of Poland and Belarus. Poland and Lithuania granted visa-free travel to Kaliningrad residents, but residents of the Russian mainland needed visas for Lithuania. When the accession of Poland and Lithuania to the EU was mooted, it became clear that Kaliningrad would turn into a Russian exclave within the EU and that people and goods would only be able to move between it and the rest of the Russian Federation by travelling through EU territory. It was only in 2001, however, that the EU began to pay attention to the potential problems this would create.

According to the Commission, Kaliningrad's poor state of governance, lawlessness, environmental degradation, and lack of economic development were all matters that could threaten an enlarged EU. However, the issues that were identified as the most serious for Kaliningrad were the movement of goods and people to and from Russia, its energy supplies, and fishing. The Commission did not think that special arrangements needed to be made for the movement of people in and out of the Kaliningrad Region apart from increasing the number of border crossing points and improving their physical infrastructure and information systems. The Commission seemed unaware that the freedom of Russians to move to and from Kaliningrad was a highly sensitive issue for Russians.[27]

The probability that the already wide socio-economic gap between Kaliningrad and its neighbours would widen was a matter of concern to Russians too. But the issue of the freedom of movement of Russians between Kaliningrad and the rest of the Russian Federation was considered far more serious and it dominated the Russian-EU agenda in 2001 and 2002. President Putin politicized the issue by personally calling for visa-free travel and by appointing Dmitry Rogozin, a fundamentalist nationalist, as his special envoy on Kaliningrad; this made it more difficult for either side to compromise.[28] An agreement was finally reached in November 2002: from 1 July 2003 Russians could transit Lithuania to travel to and from Kaliningrad under a Facilitated Rail Transit Document (FRTD) (a single trip by rail) and Facilitated Transit Document (FTD) (multiple trips by car) scheme which would be free of charge to all Russians. Russians could use internal passports as a basis for applying for both types of FTD until the end of 2004. Thereafter, they would require an international passport to obtain a FTD or FRTD.[29] Poland introduced visas for all Russians on 1 October 2003, but they are free of charge for Kaliningrad residents.

A diplomatic interpretation of the November 2002 agreement saw it as a valuable compromise that had 'removed one of the main obstacles to the rapid and multi-faceted development of cooperation between the EU and Russia' and 'created the conditions for further work with the aim of achieving visa-free movement for Russian and EU citizens throughout the European space'.[30] Experts took a different view, however. One Western analyst calls FTDs 'visas by another name'; to a Russian analyst the agreement demonstrates the incompetence of Russian negotiators. It represents 'a total loss for the Russian side' since Russians now have to obtain 'de-facto visas to move from one part of their country to another'.[31] It should be added that although the agreement produced a compromise solution for one of the problems afflicting Kaliningrad, it was only in April 2004 that an interim agreement on cargo transit was reached.[32]

The Northern Dimension

The Northern Dimension, adopted by the EU in 1998, aimed to promote economic development, stability and security in Northern Europe, address cross-border issues, contribute to narrowing disparities in living standards, ward off threats originating in the region, and contribute to reducing environmental and nuclear threats. The EU and the northern European countries would co-operate in dealing with these problems by drawing on existing regional policies and financial instruments and specifically reinforcing 'positive interdependence between Russia and the Baltic Sea region and the European Union'.[33]

Apart from alleviating the many difficulties afflicting Northern Russia since the collapse of the Union of Soviet Socialist Republics (USSR), the Northern Dimension would have been an excellent means to deal with the economic, ecological and governance problems of Kaliningrad. Despite the adoption of two action plans, however, its potential to coordinate cross-border cooperation has never really been fulfilled. According to the independent liberal deputy Vladimir Ryzhkov, 'it has turned increasingly into a declaratory programme, and today, as before, it is difficult to discern any concrete results'.[34]

One serious problem is that the Northern Dimension does not have a specific budget but is intended to serve as an umbrella to ensure complementarity and coordination between existing regional initiatives. It was also intended to involve other regional organisations, yet the EU does not have regularized channels of communication or well developed relationships with the other regional actors and financial institutions that were envisaged to participate in and fund its activities (for example, the Council of the Baltic Sea States, the Nordic Council of Ministers).[35] A second problem is the revolving presidency of the EU as the Northern Dimension receives more attention when a North European member state holds the EU presidency and less when the presidency moves on after six months.

But the Russian side has contributed to the ineffectiveness of the Northern Dimension. The election of Vladimir Putin to the Russian presidency and his campaign to strengthen the federal government coincided with the adoption of the first action plan. Regional interdependence and cross-border cooperation are not compatible with strengthening the power vertical. Moreover, Russia's traditional concept of national sovereignty cannot easily accommodate the cross-border cooperation envisaged by the Northern Dimension. As Sergounin points out, the regionalisation explicitly fostered by the Northern Dimension contravenes the geopolitical realism that currently predominates in Russian thinking about security. Nor is geopolitical realism sympathetic to the soft security concerns that are the primary focus of the Northern Dimension. Finally, there is very little reciprocal funding on the Russian side. Indeed, there is a tendency to see the Northern Dimension as a means of extracting further funds from the EU to develop Russian infrastructure, or as providing additional room for diplomatic manoeuvring.[36]

The Northern Dimension has not managed to deal with the problems of Kaliningrad or to mitigate the broader border problems that have affected Russian-EU relations. Let us turn now to other reasons why the relationship has not been more productive in recent years.

Obstacles to Russian-EU Relations

Russia has more agreements with the EU than with any other multilateral organization, and the intensity of contacts between Russia and the EU is greater than the regular contacts Russia has with any other organization. Yet policy progress is extremely slow. Some Russian analysts go so far as to call the slowdown in relations 'a systemic crisis'.[37] The border issues that became more acute as enlargement grew closer provide part of the explanation for the deterioration in the relationship since 2000. There are also a number of specific issues that have retarded progress in the EU-Russian relationship in recent years. The wars in Chechnya are one obvious example; Russia's extension of the Partnership and Cooperation Agreement (PCA) to the ten accession states is another. But there are other, broader obstacles on both sides. Some are structural; others derive from the contradictory principles on which the EU and the Russian state operate. Internal and external political developments have also affected the relationship.

One structural factor is the complexity and inflexibility of the Brussels bureaucracy, on the one hand, and the absence in Russia of suitably qualified administrative support or coordinating mechanism to deal with the EU, on the other. It is by now conventional for EU members themselves to complain about the Eurocracy. Russians cannot understand the inflexibility of the Eurocracy and its reluctance to compromise. They also complain about 'the rather woolly decision-making procedure that takes place in Brussels'.[38] The EU Commission, in turn, regularly complains about the inadequacies of the Russian bureaucracy and the lack of coordination within the Russian government. Russian experts have themselves taken up the complaint. They argue that 'Russian official bodies engaged in routine interaction with the EU need to seriously improve their work' and they suggest that either an existing institution should be assigned the role of coordinating Russian policy, or that a special agency should be established to 'coordinate efforts to work out and advance a single Russian position on all aspects of relations with the European Union'.[39]

Apart from not really understanding how the EU works, there is also a marked preference in Russia for bilateral rather than multilateral relations. This preference is compounded by the tendency of President Putin to depend upon the personal relations he establishes with European leaders (for example, Schröder, Berlusconi and Chirac). European leaders themselves cultivate these personal relationships, but in the process they sometimes undermine EU policy.

A further obstacle to deepening relations is the growing hostility in Russia to the intrusive nature of EU policy and to the imposition of Western values and norms. Russia's resentment of the EU's reaction towards Russian policy in Chechnya and the belief that the EU and some of its member states have double standards with regard to international terrorism and the status of those who Russians regard as terrorists provides evidence of this hostility. More generally, however, there is increasing irritation with the EU's 'constant striving to impose its own legislation and standards on third countries as a condition for cooperation'.[40]

Linked to the resentment that the EU expects Russia to adopt EU norms and values is umbrage about the EU's reluctance to compromise or treat Russia as a special case. The Communication from the EU Commission to the Council and the European Parliament (EP), 'Wider Europe— Neighbourhood', which did not distinguish between Russia and other EU neighbours, was particularly galling.[41] The inflexibility of the EU (as for instance in its insistence that the Schengen system cannot be modified in any respect) also hinders the creative development of the relationship. The tendency on both sides to adopt broad programmatic schemes which then have to be filled with practical content is not conducive to a steady incremental growth in the relationship. The Northern Dimension was an early example; the roadmaps to the four Common Spaces are the most recent.

Conclusion: A Values Gap?

Underlying these differences in specific policy arenas was a larger issue: whether Russia was a fully fledged member of the European family now that it had shed its communist system of government. Initially, nothing had seemed more obvious than that Russia should join her 'natural allies' in the developed West, as Yeltsin's foreign minister, Andrei Kozyrev, explained, on the basis of their common commitment to democracy, human rights and the market.[42] But under Vladimir Putin, the perceptions gap began to widen. A series of moves against the independent media, particularly the takeover of the NTV television station by a state-controlled company in the spring of 2001, suggested at best a qualified commitment to freedom of speech. The continuing offensive in Chechnya suggested a still more qualified commitment to human rights, and indeed life itself. Putin had also called for the 'liquidation of the oligarchs as a class', and the moves that were taken against Yukos head Mikhail Khodorkovsky – for what appeared to be no more than his legitimate political ambitions – suggested that the Russian authorities were only prepared to allow private ownership if it was demonstrably 'loyal'.

The Beslan hostage-taking crisis in September 2004 led to a further series of measures, evidently prepared in advance, that further constricted the scope for a genuinely autonomous citizen politics. The governors in Russia's eighty-odd republics and regions would no longer be directly elected; the President would nominate the candidates and local parliaments would make the final selection. There would be no more constituency seats in elections to the State Duma; from 2007 onwards all the seats would be allocated to nationally organized political parties, themselves heavily influenced by the Kremlin. In late 2004 the minimum number of members that a party would require to obtain official registration was increased from 10,000 to 50,000. And from late 2005 there were moves against non-governmental organisations (NGOs), especially those that had Western backing, in what was evidently an attempt to prevent any use being made of them to carry out the Russian equivalent of a coloured revolution.

Policies of this kind reflected – if they were not the inevitable result of – the increasing presence of hard-line figures with a military or security background in the top leadership. According to the most careful analysis that has so far been conducted, those with a force-ministry background (*siloviki*) accounted for no more than 4 per cent of the Soviet leadership in the late 1980s, but more than a quarter (25.1 per cent) in the Putin leadership of the early years of the new century.[43] The *siloviki* had distinctive views on foreign policy, as on other matters. Their 'national project' has been defined as including the following elements: patriotism; anti-westernism; imperialism; Orthodox clericalism; militarism; authoritarianism; cultural uniformity; xenophobia; economic dirigisme; and demographic pessimism.[44] Issues of this kind were taken up by Vladislav Surkov, deputy head of the presidential administration, in a newspaper interview in September 2004. There was a 'good' West and a 'bad' West, Surkov suggested; the first wanted a Russia that was a 'good neighbour and reliable ally', the second wanted to 'destroy Russia and fill its enormous geographical space with numerous unviable quasi-state entities', using a 'fifth column' of domestic oppositionists.[45]

Statements of this kind, and the developments with which they were associated, made it less easy to believe that Russia was indeed a natural part of the European family, and opened the way to an increasingly frank discussion of the 'values gap' that still appeared to exist between the two sides. '[S]ympathy and understanding', as former EU Commissioner Chris Patten has written, 'can only stretch so far'. Putin's regime, he suggests, rests on 'pillars that would have been familiar to the last tsar before the revolution – the army, the secret service, the Kremlin bureaucracy and nationalism'. The security service has tightened its grip on political life; journalists are harassed and even poisoned; governors are hand-picked by the Kremlin rather than being elected; foreign policy is 'tsarist in intent'. The entry into the EU of the Baltic republics, in Patten's view, had 'firmed up our policy', and now Russia had European partners that were prepared to stand up for the democratic values to which they were all supposedly committed.[46]

A decade and a half after the end of communist rule, perhaps the clearest conclusion was that Russia and its European neighbours were finding it difficult to base their relationship on the assumption of a common set of values of this kind. Russian diplomats, from Gorbachev onwards, had liked to quote Palmerston's speech in the House of Commons in 1848, that the state he represented had no eternal allies and no eternal enemies, but only eternal interests. If this was the case, it was likely to be more productive if a greater effort was invested in the development of institutions through which Russians could seek to reconcile their interests with those of other nations, and less productive if they continued to seek an illusory community.

Notes and References

1. This chapter is based on research for the project 'Inclusion without Membership? Bringing Russia, Ukraine and Belarus closer to 'Europe'', which is funded by the UK Economic and Social Research Council under grant RES-00-23-0146 to Stephen White, Margot Light and Roy Allison.

2. Commission of the European Communities, Communication from the Commission to the Council and the European Parliament, 'Wider Europe – Neighbourhood: A New Framework for Relations with our Eastern and Southern Neighbours', COM (2003) 104, Brussels, 11.3.2003, p. 3.

3. Commission of the European Communities, Communication from the Commission, 'European Neighbourhood Policy Strategy Paper', COM (2004) 373, Brussels, 2004, p. 3.

4. We define foreign policy elites as people who have an active interest in foreign policy and who occupy positions in which they either influence, or attempt to influence Russia's foreign policy choices, or are affected by those choices.

5. These are the terms, first proposed in Neil Malcolm, Alex Pravda, Roy Allison and Margot Light, *Internal Factors in Russian Foreign Policy* (Oxford: Oxford University Press, 1996), that we used in an earlier project (*The Outsiders: Russia, Ukraine, Belarus, Moldova and the New Europe,* Project Grant L213252007, part of the ESRC's 'One Europe or Several?' Programme) to characterize three groups of views about Russian foreign policy. See Margot Light, Stephen White and John Löwenhardt, 'A Wider Europe: The View from Moscow and Kyiv', *International Affairs,* 76:1, (2000), pp. 77–88.

6. This is not unique to Russia, of course, as a cursory glance at the quality press in EU member states demonstrates.

7. V. Likhachev, 'Rossiya i Evropeiskii Soyuz', *Mezhdunarodnaya zhizn'*, 12 (2002), p. 30.

8. Mikhail Gorbachev, *Perestroika. Novoe myshleniye dlya nashi strany i dlya vsego mira* (Moscow: Politizdat, 1987), p. 200.

9. http://www.kremlin.ru/eng/text/speeches/2003/05/31/1949_46509.shtml, accessed 3 March 2005.

10. See, for example, the statements quoted by the historian and political scientist, Vyacheslav Morozov, in his article 'V poiskakh Evropy: rossiiskii politicheskii diskurs i okhruzhayushchii mir', *Nepriskosnovennyi zapas,*.4 (2003), pp. 3–4.

11. *Rossiiskaya gazeta*, 26 April 2005, p. 3.

12. Aleksandr Dugin, 'Rossiya – evropeiskaya strana?', *Izvestiya*, 22 April 2005.

13. Aleksandr Chubar'yan, 'Evropa edinaya, no delimaya', *Rossiya v global'noi politike*, April-June 2003, pp. 22–30 (p. 27).

14. *Ibid.*, pp. 5–8, and see Iver B. Neumann, *Russia and the Idea of Europe* (London, Routledge, 1996). For the more recent distinction, see Dmitri Trenin, 'Russia-EU Partnership: Grand Vision and Practical Steps', *Russians on Russia*, Moscow School of Political Studies, February 2000.

15. *Zavtra*, 17 September 2003, and *Sovetskaya Rossiya*, 14 September 2004.

16. *Zavtra*, 17 September 2003.

17. Roy Allison, in an unpublished paper, has identified rising *hard-line or authoritarian westernism* in the debate about Russian security, which perhaps corresponds to this trend.

18. It was predicted that it would take from two to four years for new members to acquire the equipment necessary to join the Schengen zone.

19. Joanna Apap et al., 'Friendly Schengen Borderland Policy on the New Borders of an Enlarged EU and its Neighbours', CEPS Policy Brief, 7, November 2001, p. 2.

20. Vladimir Ryzhkov, 'Introduction', in *Schengen: New Barrier between Russia and Europe?* Russia in a United Europe Committee (RUE), Moscow, 2002.

21. V. V. Kotyenov, 'Schengen: Dividing Line or Search for a Mutually Acceptable Solution?', in ibid., p. 26.

22. Vladimir Chizhov, 'Bezvizovyi rezhim mezhdu Rossiei i Evropeiskim Soyuzom: ot utopii k real'nosti', Moscow: RUE, 2003, p. 20.

23. Igor Ivanov, *Diplomaticheskii Vestnik*, February 2003.

24. Discussion in *Schengen: New Barrier Between Russia and Europe?*, pp. 36, 43.

25. Richard Wright, 'Bezvizovyi rezhim mezhdu Rossiei i Evropeiskim Soyuzom. Vzglyad iz EC', in *Bezvizovyi rezhim mezhdu Rossiei i Evropeskim Soyuzom: ot utopii k real'nosti*, Moscow: RUE, pp. 8–14.

26. EU-Russia Summit, Moscow, 10 May 2005, Conclusions, Annex 2, Road Map for the Common Space on Freedom, Security and Justice, p. 21, http://europa.eu.int/comm/external_relations/russia/summit_05_05/finalroadmaps.pdf#fsj accessed 20 July 2005.

27. Communication from the Commission to the Council, 'The EU and Kaliningrad', COM (2001) 26 final, Brussels, 17 January 2001. http://europa.eu.int/comm/external_relations/north_dim/doc/com2001_0026en01.pdf, accessed March 2005.

28. Philip Hanson, 'Making a Good Entrance', in *Russia's Engagement with the West: Transformation and Integration in the Twenty-First Century*, edited by Alexander J. Motyl, A. Blair, A. Ruble and Lilia Shevtsova (Armonk NY, Sharpe, 2005), pp. 142–3.

29. Communication from the Commission to the Council, 'Kaliningrad Transport', COM(2002) 510 Final, Brussels, 18 September 2002; 'Joint Statement on Transit between the Kaliningrad Region and the Rest of the Russian Federation,' Brussels, 11 November 2002, www.europa.eu.int/comm/external_relations/russia/summit_11_02/js_kalin.htm (accessed 16 December 2003).

30. Likhachev, 'Rossiya i Evropeiskii Soyuz', p. 36.

31. Hanson, 'Making a Good Entrance', and Sergei Karaganov, *Rossiiskaya gazeta*, 2 April 2005.

32. Aleksei Likhachev, 'Russia's Economic Interests in a United Europe, *International Affairs* (Moscow), 5, 2004, p. 77.

33. 'A Northern Dimension for the Policies of the Union', Communication from the Commission to the Council, COM/98/0589, 25 November 1998, http://europa.eu.int/comm/external_relations/north_dim/doc/com1998_0589en.pdf, accessed 1 July 2005.

34. Vladimir Ryzhkov, Introduction, in *'Severnoye izmereniye': ideya i real'nost'* (Moscow: Russia in a United Europe Committee, 2002).

35. Hiski Haukkala, 'The Northern Dimension of EU Foreign Policy', in *Russia and the European Union*, edited by Oksana Antonenko and Kathryn Pinnick (London: Routledge, 2005), pp. 35–50.

36. Alexander Sergounin, 'Regionalisation around the Baltic Sea Rim: Perceptions of Russian Elites', in *The Regional Dimension of the Russian-Baltic Relations*, The Centre for Integration Research and Projects, St Petersburg 2004, pp. 119–33.

37. *Conclusions, Russia and the Enlarged European Union: The Arduous Path Toward Rapprochement*, Moscow: RUE, 2004.

38. Vladimir Lukin, 'In 2004, Russian foreign policy moved ahead cementing its achievements and never losing initiative', *International Affairs* (Moscow), 1 (2005), p. 58.

39. *Otnosheniya Rossii i Yevropeiskogo Soyuza: sovremennaya situatsiya i perspektivy*. Situatsionnyi analiz pod rukovodstvom S. A. Karaganova. Moscow, 2005, pp. 21–2.

40. *Ibid.*, p. 19.

41. Commission of the European Communities, Communication from the Commission to the Council and the European Parliament, 'Wider Europe – Neighbourhood: A New Framework for Relations with our Eastern and Southern Neighbours", *op cit.*

42. *Izvestiya*, 2 January 1992, p. 3.

43. Olga Kryshtanovskaya and Stephen White, 'Putin's militocracy', *Post-Soviet Affairs* 19: 4 (2003), p. 294.

44. T. Polyannikov, 'Logika avtoritarizma', *Svobodnaya mysl'*, 1 (2005), pp. 59–60.

45. *Komsomol'skaya pravda*, 29 September 2004, p. 4.

46. Chris Patten, *Not Quite the Diplomat. Home Truths about World Affairs* (London: Allen Lane, 2005), pp. 199–206. The empirical evidence of a 'values gap' is considered in Stephen White, Margot Light and Ian McAllister, 'Russia and the West: is there a values gap?', *International Politics*, 42:3 (2005), pp. 314–33.

4

DOMESTIC POLITICS AND FOREIGN POLICY FORMULATION

Dmitry Polikanov

Introduction

As at many times in its history, Russia has approached a certain turning point, when it has to decide once again about its true identity and actual role in the world. The era of stability during President Putin's first term and the reforms initiated during that period have created the prerequisites for rethinking the future development of the country. Russia is hesitating between modernization and accelerated qualitative growth and the desire to maintain the long-awaited stability and ensure gradual evolution, which is more appropriate for the public and the bureaucratic staff.

Domestic Policy Developments Affecting Russia's External Course

The President seems to support the first model and is prepared to sacrifice his unprecedented rating (around 60 per cent of approval even during the wave of protests in early 2005) to ensure his place in Russian history. As a prudent politician, he is attempting to make compromises in line with reality, but as a lame-duck President, who has to leave in 2008, he recognizes the limited period of time left for substantial achievements. Therefore, the launch of most of the reforms in Russia has been planned for between 2005 and early 2007, in other words, the period when the President can at last convert his incredible popular support into deeds – with the aim of enhancing Russia's 'competitiveness' and ensuring its modernization.

Obviously, to perform this noble mission, including the doubling of Gross Domestic Product (GDP) proclaimed in 2003, there is a need for deep restructuring of the Russian economy and social system. Therefore, the President's policy drifts to the right – by reducing the social commitments of the state and focusing more on the provision of equal opportunities for those 43 per cent of Russians who choose this liberal model[1] and would like to live on their own initiative without extra 'protection' from the state. Even the leftist initiatives of Vladimir Putin declared in September 2005 in the form of 'national priority projects' aimed at improving the living standards and the situation in agriculture, healthcare, housing and education seem to be a cushion against potential public unrest due to some unpopular reforms that are pending (including in three out of four of the aforementioned areas).

The public, however, is more cautious about the future course of the economy and politics. About half of the population (49–51 per cent) believes that the country requires stability and evolutionary reforms.[2] Even the very notion of 'reform' has an a priori negative meaning in the Russian context based on the gloomy experience of the early 1990s, when innovations (such as the liberalization of prices or voucher privatization) resulted in a substantial decrease in the standard of living. Today over 72 per cent believe that reform of the public utilities will have a negative impact on their living standards, 76 per cent are not happy about the need to pay for healthcare, 60 per cent are not ready to pay for education.[3]

The best example in this respect is the reaction of Russians to the so-called monetarization of social benefits approved in summer 2004 and commenced in January 2005. Lack of information, apprehension about the low amount of compensation payments, the absence a unified procedure for all the Russian regions (due to the clause in the legislation enabling the regions to undertake reform at their own pace) and partly psychological reasons (senior citizens feeling abandoned by the state and suffering from a lack of due respect, as the social benefits were regarded as their reward for service to the greatness of the Soviet Union), all led to a counter-revolution in Russia. Nearly one million people in total participated in demonstrations and rallies across the country in protest against the pace of reforms and their substance.

The situation is even worse when it comes to the bureaucratic machine, which is sluggish and corrupt. 'What has been characteristic of the recent period is that an unprincipled part of our bureaucracy – both federal and local – has learned to consume the achieved stability in its own selfish interests and has begun to use the favourable conditions and opportunities that we at last have, for maximizing the growth of its own welfare, not public wealth', said the President in his Address to the Federal Assembly in 2005.[4] The administrative reform announced in early 2004 has brought additional chaos and misunderstanding about the basic features of key government institutions. It will be further aggravated in 2006, when the municipal reforms should become effective. The local self-government bodies will acquire new functions and most probably also new financial problems. In combination with the lack of trained human resources at the communities' level (notably lawyers, accountants, managers[5]), the entire system runs the risk of being paralysed. Furthermore, technical difficulties exacerbate the situation: the monetarization of benefits showed that it was difficult even to create a single database and coordinate the division of labour. The same issues may rise again due to the changes in responsibilities of the municipal and regional levels of power.

All attempts to streamline the bureaucracy have so far not been successful. The new procedure for electing governors announced after Beslan is based on a positive principle – to eliminate the regional opposition by including the former rebels into a single team with the federals. Under this new order the governors eventually get full control of their territory, with responsibility not only for socio-economic but also law enforcement issues. However, all this puts extra strain on the top of the pyramid. People now regard President Putin as the only person responsible for successes and failures on the ground and this limits the ability of the federal authorities to delegate the blame to lower levels. This was the case over monetarization: despite the media and the government's attempts to refocus public dissatisfaction and to use regional and municipal leaders as scapegoats, the peak of the popular protests was targeted against the federal government (54 per cent) and the President (32 per cent).[6]

In addition, there is the ongoing split within the elite and increasing confrontation among various power groupings in the Kremlin. The threat of collapse is recognized,[7] but the problem is not resolved. The situation is aggravated by the lack of clarity about Putin's successor and, hence, continuity of the current policy. Under these circumstances, some parts of the Presidential Administration are interested in staging a 'manageable crisis', in order to ensure the successful re-election of the current rulers, many of whom enjoy little or no public trust. Ratings of potential candidates from the ruling elite are quite low (for instance, about 4 per cent of respondents would vote for Boris Gryzlov and about 1 per cent for Sergey Ivanov[8], who are sometimes referred to as the most probable 'successors' of Vladimir Putin). The same is true with respect to key political and social institutions: 67 per cent disapprove of the work of the Duma, 57 per cent of the Government, 51 per cent of the Federation Council, 40 per cent of the Governors, 63 per cent of political parties, 60 per cent of the law enforcement bodies and 53 per cent of the courts.[9]

Thus, to a certain extent, the virtual reality, in which the Kremlin preferred to live and act during the early years of Putin's presidency, is disappearing like a bubble. The hidden problems of the Russian economy, which is in urgent need of structural reform, impede its economic growth and create the danger of a sudden collapse. The intensification of public activities such as street protests due to the desire to get dividends from high oil prices and the lack of a civilized means to canalize the discontent within legitimate political institutions (such as parties, trade unions, parliament, civil society), adds to the stress of the authorities. And finally, the series of 'democratic revolutions' that have taken place around Russia has resulted in decreasing influence and growing tensions with other major global players – be it the European Union (EU) or the US.

All this makes the regime more aggressive to compensate for its weaknesses and obviously affects Russia's foreign policy. The latter has also to cope with the country's identity crisis, which re-emerged in 2003–04, when it became obvious that Moscow had reached a certain threshold in its rapprochement with the West and could not go further without seriously transforming its political system and value orientations. Russia today is sending conflicting signals to the world and its foreign policy is characterized by substantial dualism, following two axes: declarations and actions in line with the course promoted by the President and uncertainty (westernism vs nationalism) in the minds of the public.

New Identity Crisis: Form and Substance

In fact, there is a certain gap between the declarative aspirations of the President and public sentiments. During his first and second terms in power, Putin has repeatedly emphasized that Russia belongs to the common European legacy. He had already stated in 2001 in the German Bundestag that 'Russia is a friendly European country'.[10] Due to the political will of the President, the majority of the elite was forced to realize that the modernization of the country could not be achieved without access to western investment, management and technological resources. Therefore, despite the slow sabotage they had to pursue the course of rapprochement with the West.

Nonetheless, by late 2003 it became clear that the Russian-Western partnership had reached the point where qualitative changes were required, including the acceptance of European values and the substantial transformation of society. As a result, Russia stopped at the stage of mutually beneficial and pragmatic cooperation and did not want to move further. This was partly due to a typical feature of the current presidential administration – the fear of responsibility and, hence, the desire to avoid additional commitments in any field. This was camouflaged with the proclamation of Russia's 'self-sufficiency' in defence and security issues, as well as the mockery of some European regulations and 'double standards'.

The wave of criticism on the part of the West after the Beslan tragedy of September 2004 and the contentious elections in Ukraine in the autumn of the same year has pushed the President to embark back onto the European course, in order to prevent the emergence of 'new dividing lines' on the continent. In his address to the Federal Assembly in 2005 he was eloquent in pointing out that 'above all else, Russia was, is and will of course remain a major European nation. The ideals of freedom, human rights, justice and democracy that were achieved through much suffering by European culture have for many centuries been our society's determining values.'[11] This idea was further developed during the celebrations of 'Victory Day' and at the Russia-EU summit in May 2005. This does not necessarily mean that Moscow will immediately start deeper integration into the western civilization or that it will not be irritated with the attempts of the West to support 'velvet revolutions' in the countries of the former Soviet Union. But this vector helps Putin to maintain his credo of 'the last liberal in Russia' and suits his rightist cause mentioned above.

But will the population support this idea? Here we can observe a growing split among the Russians. While 40 per cent of respondents are ready to back political forces standing for Russia's quick integration into western civilization, 46 per cent assume that there is no need for speed.[12] Further evidence can be seen in the response of Russians to western criticism after the Beslan attack and after Putin's programme of strengthening the power vertical. One can see nearly the same numbers – 37 per cent believe the criticism to be fair, while 46 per cent do not think it is just.[13]

The Yukos case has also become a watershed for Russia-West relations and for the two camps in Russian society. For many in the West the trial of Mikhail Khodorkovsky meant a dangerous line had been crossed by Moscow in going back on democratic values (freedom of speech, respect for the opposition) and market reforms (guarantees of property rights and transparent rules of the game on the part of the state). Russians seemingly approach the issue from a different perspective: the idea of revisiting the results of the privatization is popular with over two thirds of the population. People are not really interested in the development of the Yukos case and 55 per cent consider western concerns to be a crude interference in Russia's domestic affairs. But when it comes to the affect of the Yukos case on Russia's relations with the developed world, one can witness the same picture. While 37 per cent argue that this will lead to a substantial or temporary cooling down of ties, 43 per cent maintain that there will be no impact on Russia's relations with the West.[14]

All this indicates that the pendulum is swinging and if there is the political will and a readiness to shape public opinion, there could be more supporters of the western vector. The split in opinion correlates with age, education and income. Obviously, 'Russians with prospects' – young people with a higher education and high income – are more inclined to integrate into the 'golden billion'. Thus, it seems that if Russia manages to maintain the current rate of economic growth and improvement of living standards, the identity crisis may be resolved in favour of further rapprochement with the West. After all, there are still about 30 per cent of Russians who share the idea of joining the EU.[15]

On the other hand, there is a more realistic scenario related to the strengthening of the middle class in Russia. The dominating values of this group are stability and manifest conservatism, which get entangled with nationalism and isolationism. The middle-income and middle-aged groups currently form the core of the supporters of the present-day regime in Russia, so it is clear that the President cannot totally neglect their feelings with respect to international affairs. They have already indicated their dissatisfaction with Putin's policy. In January 2004 61 per cent of respondents believed that the President had succeeded in consolidating Russia's position in the world; by January 2005 their number had fallen by 10 per cent.

These people have faith in Russia's 'particularity' and believe it should not be diluted through interaction with the developed world. Nearly one-third assumes that the preservation of such 'particularity' should be one of the nation's priorities. Only 2 per cent of Russians identify themselves as Europeans and 3 per cent as citizens of the world (although the figures are much higher among those who live in Moscow and St. Petersburg), which indicates that presidential appeals based on the 'European nature' of Russia are quite far from reality. The overwhelming majority (68 per cent) is quite happy to emphasize that the large territory and population (despite the reality of the demographic crisis in the country and its decreasing population) assure Russia a special place in the global arena.

These sentiments are encouraged by the 'siloviki' group within the Presidential Administration, who are known for their 'state capitalism' ideals and willingness to enhance the government's and 'national' control over strategically important industries, such as energy, oil and gas sectors, various infrastructure and even some machine-building. Conceptually this idea sometimes turns into the 'special mission' of Russia in history – from defending Europe from the Mongol-Tartar invasion to current efforts to fill the cruel capitalist consumer society model with Russian spirituality[16] and to prevent the establishment of a fundamentalist state. As Putin said to the German media:

How does it relate to the problem of the independence of Chechnya? Those people, who attacked Dagestan, were pursuing totally different goals – to build a new Islamic state, a fundamentalist state from the Caspian to the Black Sea – a caliphate. And this is what we are fighting against. Is

Europe really interested in the emergence of a fundamentalist state in this part of Europe? And the fact that we are fighting it – through this we carry out the all-European mission.[17]

The fertile ground for this feeling that Russia is 'special' is the Great Power syndrome, which Russia has yet to overcome. The attempts to play down these ambitions were not really successful. Even though in 2003 the President set out the idea of Russia as a regional power with a stable neighbourhood and a modest foreign policy aimed at facilitating domestic reforms,[18] the majority of Russians have other goals in mind. For instance, 34 per cent believe that the Russian Federation should regain the superpower status enjoyed by the Union of Soviet Socialist Republics (USSR). Another 35 per cent support the efforts to join the list of the top ten to 15 leading nations of the world in the twenty-first century. Another 16 per cent are ready to limit its status to that of a regional leader – but hope that through the exploitation of integration mechanisms it will again reach the level of the US and the EU. Only 7 per cent of the public do not want to set any global objectives for their country.[19] Under these circumstances and together with the President, who keeps expressing sorrow about the collapse of the Soviet Union,[20] there is an increasing number of people who feel nostalgia for the USSR, a leap to 27 per cent in 2005 from 16-20 per cent in several previous years.

It is obvious that the Russian public understands the difference between ambitions and their implementation. It is noteworthy that the situation is slightly improving in that more and more people are beginning to assess the country's position pragmatically. One can see here the same split, which indicates a certain degree of awakening from the 'grandeur' syndrome: 36 per cent are sceptical about Russia's ability to become a leading nation in the foreseeable future. At the same time, 40 per cent assume that it may happen in 15 to 20 years, while 12 per cent believe that Russia is a Great Power now. If the respondents are offered the milder formula, which had been the elite's slogan in 2004, of 'a competitive country on the world arena in five to ten years', the division is even more evident: 49 per cent assume that this is a realistic goal, while 42 per cent do not share the optimism of the Government.

Such scepticism is based on the evaluation of the Russian economy. The claims for global status imply that the country should have a developed and modern economy (55 per cent), high living standards for its people (32 per cent) and strong armed forces (31 per cent). The majority of Russians regard science and high technology (35 per cent), the export of raw materials (32 per cent) and the military-industrial complex (26 per cent) as the pillars for such an economic revival. Therefore, as Russia becomes more and more economically independent and powerful, the desire for the restoration of its global status can only intensify.

Another aspect of Russia's 'particularity' is the growth of nationalism. So far it remains mostly a latent idea, which cannot serve as a mobilization factor,[21] but it makes a volatile cocktail when combined with other tools – such as the exploitation of the image of an external enemy to consolidate the society and the elite.[22] Nowadays 45 per cent of respondents assume that the slogan 'Russia for the Russians' is acceptable (as such, 16 per cent, or with the reservation that Russians make up the majority of the population – about 78 per cent, according to the 2002 census). They are confronted by the 48 per cent of the population who are internationalists, believing that Russians should not claim any specific rights in the Federation. The split is obvious, but the trend is depressing: within the last six years the first group increased (from 30 per cent in 1998).[23] The only reason for optimism is that the number of pure nationalists, who are ready to support the implementation of the 'Russia for the Russians' agenda, does not exceed 5 per cent.

As a result, the country witnesses inter-ethnic tensions, as noted by nearly half of the population. Even though the majority prefers to demonstrate the socially acceptable pattern of behaviour of tolerance towards other nations (56 per cent), one cannot help emphasizing the widespread dislike of the Caucasians (such as the Chechens and Azerbaijanis – around 30 per cent in total), sporadic outbreaks of anti-Semitism[24] and extremism.[25] Such negative attitudes towards foreigners and particularly migrants, is based not only on economic factors ('they take our jobs and live off us'), but also on cultural stereotypes ('they are different from us'), which is much harder to fight.

All this transforms into the third aspect of the 'particularity pattern' – Russia's retreat to its borders and lack of motivation for integration with other nations. Such an isolationist mood and the besieged fortress syndrome run counter even to some Kremlin initiatives undertaken in the former Soviet Union area. The polls indicate that 51 per cent of respondents would like to live in their own country rather than in any alliance – be it Commonwealth of Independent States (CIS), Single Economic Space (SES), or the EU. Russians are totally indifferent towards major conflicts in the adjacent territories – they prefer a policy of non-interference and certainly not the threat of force, for example towards Abkhazia, South Ossetia, Transdniestria, or any of the 'velvet' republics. They are opposed to most of the economic measures envisaged within the SES of Russia, Ukraine, Belarus and Kazakhstan.[26]

Thus, all this forms a curious concept within the minds of the people, which is the core of what the public actually want in the area of foreign policy. This pattern implies that the Russians would like their country to be great and to have global influence – this is partly accounted for by the fear that a weak country may fall apart and become a lucrative target for any external aggressor/ occupant. This status should be built, in the eyes of the population, on a strong economic basis and only partly on military capabilities, including the bases abroad and extra-territorial activities.[27] However, such global positioning should not lead to any alliances, which would require additional commitments, economic sacrifices or open Russia up to the inflow of migrants.

This model is at variance with the declarative aspects of Putin's foreign policy – notably the rapprochement with Europe and the West – which expect Russia to become a 'normal' power. But this approach coincides with numerous real-life steps of the authorities and is shared by many in Putin's entourage. This concerns at least one aspect of public-elite consensus – the promotion of the interests of large Russian businesses abroad, which has become an underlying strategy for Russia's relations with the Newly Independent States (NIS) and Europe.

Therefore, Russian foreign policy is quite ambiguous and suffers from a lack of logic and strategic vision. It focuses instead on the implementation of short-term tactical missions and remains reactive rather than proactive. Even in the most sensitive area – ties with the countries of the former Soviet Union – Moscow tends to follow the approaches and concepts, which emerged four to five years ago during Putin's first presidency.

Foreign Policymaking: Major Actors

One of the reasons for that is the narrow circle of policymakers, who are thus incapable of inventing new strategies and rarely seek the advice of any external players. The decision-making process is highly personalized and is concentrated in the hands of the President and his close entourage, namely different units within the Presidential Administration. While in the Yeltsin era official policy was the result of a confusing mixture of interests pursued by various 'towers of the Kremlin', nowadays the number of spokespersons has been reduced.

President Putin will most probably leave office in 2008, even though some parts of his clientele would like him to extend his powers regardless of the Constitution. Nonetheless, there is a high probability that he will continue to have an impact on Russian policy either through the party mechanisms (as leader of United Russia or any other megaparty, a sort of Russian version of Den Xiaoping) or as a top manager of a megacorporation (for example, a giant state-run company uniting major Russian oil and gas assets). Therefore, he is concerned about his image and has been doing a lot to improve it during his lame-duck period – the example of the Northern Europe Gas Pipeline speaks for itself. Moreover, Vladimir Putin is still listened to, even though he is in the middle of his second term. On the one hand, this enables him, for instance, to lobby for a new agreement with the EU in 2007, when the Partnership and Cooperation Agreement (PCA) expires, or to promote the realization of the

Russia-EU agenda. On the other hand, being cautious, he will be unlikely to take any really radical steps so as not to spoil his post-presidential career. Nor will he start the process of preparing Russia for accession to the EU or seeking any associate membership – his successor will most probably try to maintain the status quo as well.

The major presidential advisor on foreign policy issues is Sergey Prikhodko, who still guides the work of the Foreign Policy Directorate even after the early 2004 administrative reform. Prikhodko is known for his liberal views and, thanks to his unique position, has managed to keep close ties with the 'old Moscow guard' (previously represented by Alexander Voloshin) and with the 'chekists' (most probably through Deputy Chief of the Presidential Administration Igor Sechin and Sergey Yastrzhembsky, Special Presidential Representative for Relations with the EU). Due to Prikhodko and Voloshin, who were connected with many Russian 'blue chip' companies interested in conquering European and US markets, the country's vector became mainly pro-European after 2001. Prikhodko's position was further strengthened after the resignation of Alexander Voloshin in the autumn of 2003, since the new chief of the Administration – Dmitry Medvedev – was not particularly interested in external relations. By default, he was the one who was responsible for top-level contacts with the US administration, but unlike his predecessor he was not directly involved in resolving problems in the post-Soviet space[28] and mostly dealt with domestic issues. One of the exceptions was the staging of the elections in Ukraine in the autumn of 2004, where Gleb Pavlovsky and Vyacheslav Nikonov – both interlocutors of Medvedev in the expert community – were major aids to Victor Yanukovich. After the replacement of Medvedev by Sergey Sobyanin, ex-governor of Tyumenskaya oblast, in November 2005, the policy functions of the head of the Presidential Administration seem to have been even further reduced.

However, in 2005 after the series of 'velvet revolutions' the Administration established a new directorate – the Directorate for Interregional and Cultural Links with Foreign Countries and the CIS. The new department is headed by Modest Kolerov, an ex-political technologist close to Gleb Pavlovsky and renowned for a number of quite successful public relations and propagandistic projects.[29] The idea behind the unit is to imitate the US scheme of working with civil society and Non-Governmental Organizations (NGOs) around the world. The major mission for Kolerov is to identify pro-Russian forces and to build up a network of 'friends of Russia' by promoting the elite and supporting various civil society entities. Another task is to look after and champion the rights of 'compatriots abroad', which has always been a very sensitive issue for Moscow from the point of view of political dividends and bargaining with Europe and the NIS. Thus, the department may eventually seek a piece of the budgetary pie allocated for the promotion of Russia's image abroad (currently the major bulk of this work is carried out by RIA Novosti News Agency). Nonetheless, Kolerov, as well as many other representatives of the Administration, prefer to place their stakes on the existing elite in the Former Soviet Union (FSU) states, even though this approach has already led to a number of failures for the Kremlin, notably in Ukraine.

Kolerov's directorate is, to a certain extent, a rival for two other major players dealing with CIS policy. One of them is Victor Khristenko, Minister of Industry and Energy, who is responsible for various integration projects in the ex-USSR zone. Khristenko is closely connected with large Russian businesses operating in the NIS and is one of the ideologists of the 'integration cores' model,[30] especially as far as the SES is concerned. The concept implies that Russia with the help of the Eurasian Economic Community and the SES should form around itself a group of countries in order to bargain with the EU and other economic giants (such as the World Trade Organization (WTO)) and claim fairer terms of cooperation.

The other one is Igor Ivanov, Secretary of the RF Security Council and ex-Minister of Foreign Affairs. Ivanov had little impact on Russian foreign policy at his ministerial post and under his leadership the Foreign Ministry turned into a technical office to implement the decisions elaborated and approved in the Kremlin. Unlike his predecessors – Andrey Kozyrev and Yevgeny Primakov, who helped the (Russian) Ministry of Foreign Affairs (MFA) to maintain the status of a strategic centre during Yeltsin's time – Igor Ivanov did not have sufficient 'bureaucratic weight' nor close enough access to the President to determine the Russian course. After his appointment to the Russian Security Council this body should have been transformed into a think tank mostly focusing on the development of strategy and maintaining relations with the NIS.

As far as the first mission is concerned, the Council is still in the process of preparing the National Security Strategy to replace the 2000 document. The instruction to do this was given by the President after the Dubrovka events in Moscow in October 2002,[31] to ensure that Russia's doctrines meet the challenges of the modern world more effectively. However, after nearly three years only the draft of the Strategy is ready and it is now being reviewed by a number of selected experts. The Security Council has also reverted to its role of holding regular sessions to discuss topical issues concerning the country's development. Between 2002 and 2003 this practice had virtually ceased and there were only a few sessions devoted to nuclear weapons, military-technical cooperation and some other matters. Currently 'expanded' Council sessions, involving representatives of different ministries and agencies, are organized roughly on a monthly or bi-monthly basis and are aimed at making the policymaking mechanism more transparent and at initiating debates. Moreover, the 'planning meetings' in the Kremlin every Saturday, where 'various issues of domestic and foreign policy are discussed',[32] are also held under the auspices of the Security Council and its staff take an active part in their preparation.

As for the second mission, the Security Council dealt with the contacts with Abkhazia and South Ossetia and was responsible for links with the Kyrgyz opposition in spring 2005.[33] The events surrounding the elections in Abkhazia in the autumn of 2004, when Moscow exerted harsh pressure in favour of 'its' candidate against the will of the people and despite the Abkhazians' objections to such high-handed behaviour, have demonstrated the inability of the Security Council staff, most of whom are ex- Federal Security Service of the Russian Federation and ex-MFA employees, to handle and forecast the situation even in such small break-away republics.

The MFA remains an implementation body: 'Russia's foreign policy is determined by the President and the Foreign Ministry implements it'.[34] But Sergey Lavrov, who has led it since early 2004, is much more apt and assertive in diplomatic wars than his predecessor. However, even the President is not happy with the current state of affairs and has recently demonstrated his dissatisfaction with the work of the Ministry, urging it to ensure intellectual breakthroughs and to take a more proactive line in promoting Russia's interests, especially in the economic area.[35]

Finally, there are two more people involved in the process, but mostly for their lobbying capabilities. One of them is Defence Minister Sergey Ivanov, who is a close friend of President Putin and is sometimes regarded as his potential successor.[36] Ivanov represents the interests of the military and is responsible for maintaining relations with the North Atlantic Treaty Organization (NATO). He is often used to probe western public opinion on various issues and is notorious for his harsh statements. His views are characterized by a high degree of opportunism and are dependent on the situation. A good example is Ivanov's position on the US bases in Central Asia. In 2001, he was the most prominent opponent of US deployment and did not see even the 'hypothetical possibility' of it; the President came close to having to apologize and to correct his statements which ran contrary to the 'antiterrorist coalition' slogans.[37] In 2004, Ivanov suddenly 'confessed' to a US audience that he was the major initiator and supporter of Russia's agreement on the deployment of US troops in Uzbekistan and Kyrgyzstan.[38] To be fair, one has to recognize Ivanov's positive role in improving Russia's relations with NATO, since one of his major objectives as a 'civilian minister' was to destroy the unwieldy and cumbersome General Staff and to take over the initiative in military decision-making. Dialogue with NATO was one of the elements which helped him to perform this task of fighting 'retrograde' generals.

The other lobbyist was Andrei Illarionov, Presidential Economic Advisor. Illarionov was connected with Alexander Voloshin and represented the interests of some Russian businesses (such as 'Russian Aluminium'), mostly serving as a rostrum for liberal concepts. Illarionov, for instance, was one of the most active opponents of the Kyoto Protocol and did a lot to delay its ratification. However, his position, which became shaky after Voloshin's resignation, weakened further when he lost his position as Putin's representative at the Group of Eight (G8) in early 2005. His distance from the Kremlin team and decision-making has, therefore, decreased his influence to a minimum. The aforementioned important mission was transferred to Igor Shuvalov, Assistant to the President and another liberal economist, who was responsible for preparing along with the MFA for Russia's chairmanship of the G8 in 2006.

As for the role of the legislative bodies in foreign policy, the Duma and the Federation Council to an even greater extent nowadays serve mainly the purposes of parliamentary tourism and providing a 'pressure valve' for ultra-patriotic sentiments. The parliament is mostly satisfied with its role as a 'bad policeman' and performs it with respect to the Council of Europe, the Organization for Security and Cooperation in Europe (OSCE) and other international organizations, which are regarded by the Kremlin as redundant in the current system of global affairs. As a matter of fact, the Duma is notorious for its habit of adopting harsh statements (which have no real effect on policy) as Russia's 'threatening response' to 'unfriendly' actions of other countries, for example Georgia, Moldova and Latvia. Most of these documents are used to exert pressure at negotiations and mobilize public opinion but normally have no practical implications for Russia's course.[39]

Unlike in Yeltsin's times, the Duma is no longer involved in foreign policy-making through the instrument of ratification of international agreements. As an example, one can recall the endless discussion on the START II Treaty in the late 1990s, which was only partly constructive for the executive branch and served as a bargaining chip for the missile defence talks. Nowadays the parliament, which is dominated by the pro-presidential majority, is a disciplined tool of the Presidential Administration to pass the ratifications promptly or to suspend them for tactical reasons. For instance, in the autumn of 2004, the Duma immediately approved Russia's accession to the Kyoto Protocol in order to improve relations with the EU and to mitigate the wave of western criticism after the Beslan attack. At the same time, when it came to the border treaties with the Baltic states, Moscow preferred to withhold consent and to kick the ball into the yard of Tallinn and Riga.

The role of the Duma's Committee for International Affairs has also decreased since the 2003 parliamentary elections. Dmitry Rogozin used this post for substantial self-promotion and, hence, was quite actively performing the aforementioned role of the 'pressure valve' and 'bad policeman', for example with respect to the Kaliningrad region. His successor, Konstantin Kosachev, instead belongs to the expert community and is famous for promoting the idea of Russia as a 'democratic leader' in the post-Soviet space.[40] At the same time, unlike Rogozin, he is less consistent in his statements and more often changes his line in tune with the Kremlin's propagandistic strategy of the moment.[41]

In fact, the expert community as such, despite a certain degree of superficial criticism of the Kremlin, tends to strive for the reputation of being an 'outright supporter of Putin.' Most of the think tanks have no significant impact on foreign policymaking. There are a few exceptions though. One of them is the Council for Foreign and Defence Policy (SVOP), which maintains contacts with the MFA and Sergey Prikhodko, although it is more of a discussion club of experts. The Council's recommendations are normally based on the premises of political realism, notably the need for a tougher policy in the conditions of global competition and for further rapprochement with the US, as a unique world leader.[42] Another body is the Russian Institute for Strategic Studies (RISI), which is affiliated to the Security Council and which provides expertise on hard security matters and the NIS. One of the remnants of the Soviet legacy is the Institute for World Economy and International Relations (IMEMO) of the Russian Academy of Sciences. Its role in advising the country's leadership has substantially diminished in recent years, but it still maintains contacts with the MFA and the Government Staff in making policy analysis. The overwhelming majority of the other institutions do not go beyond academic debate and sporadic preparation of numerous analytical materials and publications for government bodies, which are not necessarily taken into consideration by the Kremlin.

Moreover, the expert community today is divided into two major camps. The first one consists of 'derzhavniki', who quickly revived under President Putin and promote Russia's Great Power status and a more assertive foreign policy. They are competing with the other group – remnants of the liberal tendency, who mostly collaborated with Yeltsin's administration, and tend to support the rapprochement with the west. Thus, they are partly replicating the split already identified in public opinion, although the emphasis is slightly different due to their professional approach to the issues, unlike that of the general public.

The role of Russian businesses in foreign policy could be the subject of a separate study. Nowadays they are not significantly involved in policymaking, since most of them have learned from the presidential strategy of 'equidistance' and from the case of Yukos. In most cases they are used by the Kremlin to promote some of its diplomatic games, notably in the ex-USSR area. The expansionist policy of Gazprom and United Energy Systems in Moldova, Tajikistan, or Armenia fits into the concept of binding the NIS together with infrastructure networks and economic interdependence. These natural monopolies are supported by the state and get substantial concessions. More and more often Russia threatens to use such levers as gas and electricity prices to punish disloyal countries for their 'unfriendly' policy towards Moscow (Georgia, Moldova, or Ukraine). Other giants, such as Lukoil, play a secondary role in carrying out this mission (for example in the Caspian region or in Uzbekistan). Russian businesses are also penetrating the European markets, especially through property acquisition in Southern and Eastern Europe. This facilitates the establishment of a Russian lobby within the EU, while Brussels still lacks such mechanisms on Russian territory.

Conclusion

Under President Putin, Russia's foreign policy has become more than ever tied to domestic developments. While Russia is entering a period of difficult and mostly unpopular social reforms, it becomes more and more sensitive on various external issues, such as its diminishing influence in the former Soviet Union zone and the 'revolutionary pattern' in neighbouring states.

There is a certain gap between the declarative aspirations of the President, who would like his country to be a fully-fledged member of the community of civilized nations, notably Europe, and the public, which tends to back a nationalistic and isolationist agenda. Both parties, however, agree on the need for the restoration of Russia's global status, as well as on more pragmatism and the advisability of promoting influence through the realization of economic interests. The Russians are not happy about integration initiatives based on economic concessions and would rather prefer the Kremlin to use ideological instruments (such as the common historical legacy, Russian language etc) or business expansion as tools. The public and the elite also show no desire to undertake additional responsibility and commitments resulting from membership in any alliances.

The situation is exacerbated by the new round of identity crisis: the Russians are split almost in half into supporters of a pro-western course and followers of the Russian 'particularity' path. All this has only a partial impact on the narrow circle of foreign policymakers, most of whom are not providing adequate strategic vision and coherence. They concentrate instead on tactical issues, notably routine implementation of the Kremlin's decisions, which are often based on expediency and are taken without due consideration of the long-term consequences.

As a result, in order to ensure an unprecedented level of public support for their foreign policy, the President and his entourage have to manoeuvre and find compromises, even if they result in certain failures on the international arena, especially in the eyes of the West. The Russian ruling class, though, has another option: to start shaping public opinion and forcing it to think in a different way, if the pro-western declarations are really going to be put into practice to enhance the modernization of the country. The quality and efficiency of Russian foreign policy will depend on the ability of the Kremlin to resolve this dilemma.

Notes and References

1. All-Russia Public Opinion Research Center (VCIOM), poll results, 5–6 February 2005. All poll results quoted in this text are based on VCIOM's monthly (2003–04) and weekly (2005) surveys conducted with a national representative sample of 1,600 respondents in 40 Russian regions with error not exceeding 3.4 per cent.
2. VCIOM poll results, January 2004 and 26–27 January 2005.
3. VCIOM poll results, 26–27 January 2005.
4. Presidential Address to the Federal Assembly of the Russian Federation, 25 April 2005.
5. Puti sovershenstvovaniya raboty mestnogo samoupravleniya v Rossii (Ways to improve the work of local self-government in Russia). Report of the Center for Political Analysis in Russia (CPKR), Moscow, October 2002.
6. Average from weekly VCIOM polls carried out in late January to mid-February 2005.
7. Valery Fadeev, 'Sokhranit effektivnoe gosudarstvo v sushchestvuyushchikh granitsakh' (Preserve the efficient state within the existing borders). Interview with Head of the Presidential Administration Dmitry Medvedev. *Expert*, April 4 2005.
8. VCIOM poll results, 30 April – 1 May 2005.
9. *Ibid.*
10. Vladimir Putin, speech to the German Parliament on 25 September 2001. Available at: http://www.pegmusic.com/putin-in-germany.html
11. Presidential Address to the Federal Assembly of the Russian Federation, 25 April 2005. Available at http://www.kremlin.ru/eng/speeches/2005/04/25/2031_type 70029_87086.shtml
12. VCIOM poll results, March 2004.
13. VCIOM poll results, October 2004.
14. VCIOM poll results, November 2003.
15. Evraziiski monitor: Osnovnye rezultaty vtorogo etapa issledovaniya (Eurasian monitor: Key results of the second stage of the study). *Monitoring obshchestvennogo mneniya*, 4, October–December 2004.
16. In fact, this is very close to the Chinese concept of the 1990s. See Alexander Lomanov, 'Kak uvyadali sto tsvetov' (How hundreds of flowers were fading). *Rossiya v globalnoi politike* (Russia in Global Affairs), 3:2 (2005), p. 87.
17. 'Putin: govorit o Chechne – eto prosto' (It's easy to speak about Chechnya). *Grani.ru*, 6 May, 2005.
18. *Foreign Policy Concept of the Russian Federation, 2000.* Available in translation at: http://www.bits.de/EURA/EURAMAIN.htm#RFpoldoc
19. VCIOM poll results, October 2003.
20. Appeal of the President of Russia Vladimir Putin, 4 September 2004.
21. Leontiy Byzov, 'Zhdet li Rossiyu vsplesk russkogo natsionalisma?' (Is Russia awaiting the splash of Russian nationalism?). *Monitoring obzhestvennogo mneniya: ekonomicheskiye i sotsialnye peremeny* (Russian Public Opinion Monitoring), 4 (72), October–December 2004, p. 21.

22. Elena Ovcharenko, 'Zamestitel glavy administratsii presidenta RF Vladislav Surkov: Putin ukreplyaet gosudarstvo, a ne sebya' (Deputy Chief of the Presidential Administration Vladislav Surkov: Putin strengthens the state, not his personal power). *Komsomolskaya Pravda*, 29 September 2004.
23. Leontiy Byzov, *opt. cit.*, p. 22.
24. One can recall the notorious letter of the Duma deputies aimed against Jewish organizations in January 2005, or several attacks against synagogues. However, only 2.5 per cent of Russians admit that they feel some sort of antipathy towards the Jews.
25. One of the cities suffering most from the activities of the skinheads and other extremist organizations is St. Petersburg. Attacks against foreigners there have already led to a certain degree of panic, for example among Arab students who have had to cease their studies. This does not necessarily mean that the Russians support such an approach. Over 70 per cent believe that tough measures should be taken against such xenophobia and radical and racist actions.
26. According to the third wave of the Eurasian Monitor (April 2005) conducted by VCIOM jointly with Ukraine, Belarus and Kazakhstan, the Russian public seems to be most opposed to steps to liberalise the movement of goods, labour and capital within the Single Economic Space. The rate of negative answers is about 43 to 45 per cent when it concerns movement of goods and investments from Russia and into Russia, 55 per cent are not happy to see workers from the four states and 71 per cent do not want the businesses from these neighboring countries to buy land and property in Russia.
27. As of April 2005, only 6 per cent do not think it is necessary to keep Russian bases in the NIS, while the majority assumes that they should ensure Russia's security at distant ranges (55 per cent), defend Russian national interests in these countries (20 per cent) and enhance the security of Russian citizens there (18 per cent). As for the physical elimination of terrorists and their bases abroad, 79 per cent of respondents support this idea of 'preemptive strikes'.
28. For instance, Alexander Voloshin was known for his shuttle diplomacy, when there was a need to unblock the withdrawal of Russian munitions from Transdniestria, or when it was necessary to monitor the situation in Azerbaijan, in order to ensure the smooth transfer of power from Heydar Aliyev to his son.
29. Tatiana Vitebskaya, 'Naznachen otvetstvenny za lyubov k Rossii' (Appointed a person responsible for love to Russia). *Izvestia*, 23 March 2005.
30. Victor Khristenko, 'Nuzhna li nam integratzia?' *Polit.ru*, 25 February 2004.
31. Statement of the President at the meeting of the supreme commanders of the Russian Armed Forces, 26 November 2002.
32. This cliché is used for every Saturday meeting. See for instance, 'Vladimir Putin obsudil s chlenami Soveta Bezopasnosti RF ryad voprosov vnutrennei i vneshnei politiki Rossii' (Vladimir Putin discussed with the Security Council members some issues of domestic and foreign policy of Russia). *ITAR-TASS*, 5 March 2005.
33. The Kyrgyz opposition leaders also met the heads of the foreign relations committees of the Federation Council and the State Duma Mikhail Margelov and Konstantin Kosachev in February 2005.
34. 'Lavrov: MID RF budet stroit otnosheniya s Kremlem v sootvetstvii s Konstitutsiei' (Lavrov – the Russian Foreign Ministry will build relations with the Kremlin in accordance with the Constitution). *RIA-Novosti*, 17 March 2004.
35. 'I am sure that the initiative, independent role of the embassies is extremely important here… Who, if not you, has to do this work, to make timely proposals and to look for mutually acceptable formulas?… It is not the first time we speak about the need to give it

[information coming from the embassies] a more business-like, practical character... Many issues should be solved on the spot. Your information-analytical work should not lag behind the requirements of the time as far as its quality and timeliness are concerned... Heads of embassies and permanent missions should not exclusively play the role of postmen and simply mechanically translate the requests of the partners to the center. Each piece of information should be regarded through the prism of Russian interests and accompanied with analysis and proposals'. Statement of the President at the plenary session of the meeting of ambassadors and permanent representatives of Russia, 12 July 2004.

36. Igor Plugatarev, Andrei Terekhov, 'Ivanov pokazal zuby i chelovecheskoe litso' (Ivanov showed teeth and human face). *Nezavisimaya Gazeta*, 3 March 2005.

37. 'Sergey Ivanov: NATO ne budet bombit Afganistan s territorii SNG' (Sergey Ivanov: NATO will not bomb Afghanistan from the CIS territory', *Lenta.ru*, 14 September 2001.

38. Svetlana Babaeva, 'Otvetsvenny, zdravomyslyashchii, bez ispugannogo litsa' (Responsible, rational-minded, without feared face). *Izvestia*, 9 April 2004.

39. See for example, the response of the Russian MFA to the parliamentary request concerning Moldova and the suggested set of measures against it. 'Pravitelstvo RF razrabatyvaet predlozheniya po vozmozhnomu vvedeniyu ekonomicheskikh sanktsii v otnoshenii Moldavii' (Russian Government develops proposals on the possible introduction of economic sanctions against Moldova). *ITAR-TASS*, 18 March 2005.

40. Konstantin Kosachev, 'Rossiya dolzhna stat exporterom demokratii' (Russia should become the exporter of democracy). *Izvestia*, 25 June 2004.

41. Konstantin Kosachev, 'V ozhidanii orangevoi revolutsii v Brussele' (Expecting the orange revolution in Brussels). *Nezavisimaya Gazeta*, 29 April 2005.

42. Vneshnyaya politika: rossiiskie interesy i zadachi novogo etapa (Foreign Policy: Russian Interests and Tasks for the New Stage). Report to the 12th Assembly of the Council for Foreign and Defense Policy, Moscow, April 2004.

RUSSIA'S REGIONS IN SHAPING NATIONAL FOREIGN POLICY

Irina Busygina

Introduction

One of the main trends shaping the character of the contemporary international relations system is the increasing role of sub-national territorial units (regions). Nation states tend to take into account the opinions of their territorial units when elaborating their national external relations policy while from the other side their decisions are evaluated from the perspective of their consequences for regional development.

Direct involvement of the sub-national territorial actors in the realm of international relations represents one of the distinctive features of the so-called 'new regionalism.' This is especially true for federative political systems that involve at least two meaningful levels of government and each level has its own institutionally designed policymaking responsibilities. Any discussion of the policymaking process must consider the degree to which the country's authority is centralized. Such discussions about the distribution of political authority usually focus on a single constitutional feature: does a country have a unitary or a federal political system?

Nowadays the desire of the regions to increase their autonomy in the international arena represents a constituent element of more general processes of intrastate regionalization and federalization. In turn, these very processes stimulate further activation of the regions when they try to influence the agenda in the external relations sphere. It is important to stress that the degree and character of the regions' involvement in the national decision-making process in the field of external relations represent a significant feature of a national model of federalism; the very character of centre-regional relations in a state determines the degree of possible involvement of the regions in shaping external relations at the national level.

The aim of this chapter is to evaluate the international activities and participation in interregional cooperation of Russia's regions. It consists of two parts. The first part seeks to analyse the contribution the regions make to the federal decision-making process in the sphere of foreign policy before and after President Putin's reforms; to achieve this goal a brief overview of the current state of federative relations in Russia will be presented. The second part is devoted to the European dimension of Russia's foreign policy and to the divergence of current federal and regional priorities.

The federal order in Russia was created at the beginning of the 1990s by a process of 'unconscious design'. It was 'designed' in the sense that its main institutions have been constructed 'from above', artificially; they did not grow out of already existing political practices. However, this design was unconscious because the actual functioning of these institutions and the rules of the game were determined not by a systemic approach and a clear vision of the strategic goals they were meant to achieve but primarily by force of circumstances, based on what politicians would argue was 'politically advisable.'

In spite of the fact that federative relations in Russia in the 1990s had to some extent taken shape in institutions and legislation, they still remained unstable and lacked clear mechanisms. Instability showed itself in three main aspects: the extremely complicated structure of the federation and its asymmetric character; the gigantic disproportions between the regions in terms of per capita regional product, the size of the territory, population and economic profile;[1] and finally, the weakness of the federal centre, which by 1999 had almost totally lost the capacity to influence the situation in the regions. The policy of the federal centre towards the regions was generally *ad hoc*, determined by short-term factors of a political, economic, ethnic or even (and often) personal character. The Yeltsin federation thus had 'weak legs': its transformation towards a more centralized union or a loose confederation was only a question of time.

President Yeltsin had tried to build his relations with the regions on a system of exclusivity, the development of political favouritism and personal bargaining. Informal institutions and rules of the game either began to replace new formal institutions, or to fill an existing institutional vacuum. Unfortunately federalism in Russia did not acquire value as a 'public good'; it was still federalism 'from above', its design dependent on the political situation. Not only does the population not value the federation, it does not understand the rationale and need for federalism. It is true that William Riker wrote that federalism was a 'rational bargain' between political elites,[2] Daniel Elazar stressed that federalism was something more than a structural construction: it was a special mode of political and social behaviour, including a commitment to partnership and active cooperation from individuals and institutions.[3] In other words, federalism defends private interest and at the same time proceeds from it. The people of Russia lack this self-interest in federalism.

Channels of Influence of the Regions upon National Foreign Policy

The representation of regional interests through federal institutions represents the most significant form of regional influence upon the decision-making process and conduct of national foreign and external policy. The participation of the regional elites in the working process of the legislative and executive federal authorities as well as formal and informal interaction between regional representatives and the federal authorities afford the regions opportunities to influence federal decision-making.

The key federal institutions that need to be considered are first of all the Federation Council (Council), the State Duma (Duma) and the Ministry of Foreign Affairs (MFA). In the Russian institutional system the Federation Council and the State Duma – the upper and lower chambers of the country's Federal Assembly (federal parliament) – are the most useful sites for lobbying regional interests.

During the rather short history of the Federation Council, the principle of its formation has been changed three times. This was possible as Art.95 of the Federal Constitution does not specify how the representatives are to be chosen. Thus, in December 1993 the Members of the Federation Council were elected by direct popular vote (two from every 'subject of the federation' or constituent territory); in 1995 after long discussions the principle was changed and the heads of the regional legislative and executive branches of power were given mandates without elections. Finally, in July 2000 a new federal law was adopted according to which the Federation Council is composed of two representatives from each constituent territory – one from the regional legislature and one from the executive. The representative of the legislature is elected by the regional deputies, while the representative from the executive branch is nominated by the governor unless opposed by two-thirds of the legislature.

This is not the place to examine the role of the Federation Council in Russia's political system in detail. However, it should be said that since 1995 the Federation Council has shown a lot of pragmatism, being more inclined towards consensus with the President than confrontation. Ryzhkov has called it a 'political stabiliser.'[4] Besides that, the Federation Council turned out to be a kind of political school for regional leaders and the springboard from which they could move to the national level.

The Council includes a special committee on international relations, which consists of 13 members. Some heads of the regions successfully used this body to put forward new initiatives; in particular it was due to the efforts of the St Petersburg delegation that the Council proposed to establish in the city a Petersburg Economic Forum. As a result, from 1997 the Forum turned into a significant instrument of national foreign policy. Another example is connected to the attraction of foreign investments: the governor of the Novgorod region, M.Prussak, worked in the 1990s as the head of the Committee on International Relations and this position helped him to create effective guaranties and attract foreign investors. Yuri Luzhkov, the mayor of Moscow, was probably the most active of the regional leaders in pushing his own foreign policy initiatives through the Federation Council, for example in relation to the situation of the Russian-speaking population in the Baltic states (1998) and the status of Sebastopol. The Council adopted a declaration and created a special commission to prepare a legislative act concerning the status of Sebastopol. However, the ambitious plans of Luzhkov were not realized as on 31 May 1997 the Russian Federation and Ukraine signed the Treaty on Friendship, Cooperation and Partnership as well as other agreements, which confirmed that Sebastopol and the Crimea belong to Ukraine.[5] As for the Russian-speaking population in the Baltics, Luzhkov together with some other governors who supported him initiated several declarations that the Council sent to President Yeltsin.

Moreover, through the Council the regional leaders not only had the opportunity to lobby their interests but also to conduct Russia's foreign policy directly – in the framework of the Parliamentary Assembly of the Council of Europe and other international organizations.

The State Duma also played an important role in lobbying regional interests. The largest parliamentary groups formed on a regional basis were the factions 'New Regional Policy' (1993–1995), 'Russia's Regions' (1995–1999), 'Regions of Russia' and 'Motherland – All Russia' (1999–2003) and the deputy group 'North of Russia' formed in 2000 that represented the interests of regions of the North and North-West of the country. Taking part in the work of the committees of the Duma, the deputies from the regions could directly exert influence upon the adoption of decisions in the fields of foreign policy and international relations. The Committee on International Relations was active in discussing questions like the status of the Caspian Sea, the situation in the Kaliningrad region, trans-border cooperation between Russia and China, and the problems of Russian-American cooperation.[6]

Interaction with the MFA represents another channel for lobbying by the regions. In 1994 President Yeltsin had issued a decree creating a Consultative Council in the Ministry on international and external economic cooperation of the constituent territories of the Federation; the Ministry thus became the main institution for coordinating federal and regional interests in the field of foreign policy. During the mid 1990s, one of the tasks of the Consultative Council was to collect the opinions of the regions and then to inform the MFA so that it could take them into account in the preparation of decisions. In 1996 Evgeni Primakov said that the regions should participate in the process of the preparation of Russia's international treaties.[7] In fact, in some cases the regional elites really could contribute to the elaboration of the concepts – for example concerning Russia's participation in the Black Sea Economic Council. It should be added here that from the beginning the MFA's position was ambivalent: on the one hand, it proposed formal support to the regions in expanding their international contacts, but on the other, the Ministry was concerned about the scale of regional initiatives which could directly or indirectly contradict the general (federal) foreign policy priorities of Russia.

The second half of the 1990s was the period when regionalization in the country reached its peak and the political autonomy of the regions was very extensive. During this time the heads of the regions tried not only to expand their international contacts and to further their interests through lobbying the federal authorities but also to influence national foreign policy directly – 'to make' Russia's foreign policy themselves. The regional leaders were not afraid to put forward initiatives that sometimes contradicted directly the official line and thus encroached on the sphere of federal competences. Such regional activity was primarily concentrated in the following areas:

1. *The demarcation of the state border.* For several years the governors of Primorski and Khabarovski regions situated in the Far East of Russia were opposed to the implementation of the Russian-Chinese treaty demarcating the border between the two states. They perceived the treaty as an unfair document on the basis of which Russia (and also these regions as they lay on the border) would lose part of its historical lands. The legislature of the Primorski region shared this view and in February 1995 adopted a resolution on halting all demarcation work on the Chinese border and demanding that Moscow should review the conditions of demarcation.[8]

2. *Relations with Commonwealth of Independent States (CIS) countries.* This concerns first of all relations with Belarus; in August 1997 the governors of Yaroslav and Lipetzk regions had invited the President of the country, Alexander Lukashenko, to visit their regions which at the time directly contradicted the federal line as relations between Moscow and Minsk were rather tense. Yuri Luzhkov, the mayor of Moscow, has also supported Lukashenko, in particular at the time of the constitutional crises in Belarus (1995–1996). The development of contacts with CIS countries especially with Belarus and Ukraine became one of the most important priorities in Luzhkov's foreign policy.

3. *Support of compatriots abroad.* The mayor of Moscow was the most active also in this direction supporting publicly the Russian-speaking population abroad and undertaking negotiations about the fate of the Russians in the Baltic states, Transdniestria and Gagauz-Yeri (Moldova) and Northern Kazakhstan. Luzhkov has also provided the Russian-speaking population of Crimea with political and economic assistance as well as supported the wish of the

population of the peninsula to gain more political autonomy from Kiev. The mayor persisted in his objection to the status of Sebastopol as a Ukrainian city.

President Putin's Reforms and the Role of the Regions

Putin's Russia is a different country. The basic features of the new political regime began to form even before 2000, when Vladimir Putin was elected as the President of the Russian Federation. The regime had started to take shape when the prime-ministers were for the first time nominated by Boris Yelsin from the military and security power bloc, the so-called *siloviki*. First it was E Stepashin and then V Putin and the power base of this bloc – the Ministry of Interior, the Federal Security Service, the Army and the Security Council – was generally strengthened. Another trend that took place was the appointment of people with a military background (primarily ex-army or ex-KGB generals) to head the regions. Such developments were the response of the ruling coalition to the wish of the majority of the population for a 'strong hand' and an 'effective state'.

The only opposition that tried to resist the concentration of political power by the main actor (the President) was a regional coalition embodied in the political movement *Otechestvo – Vsya Rossiya* (Motherland – All Russia) headed by the Mayor of Moscow, Yuri Luzhkov, and the President of Tatarstan, Mintimer Shaimiev. The other regional leaders who joined the coalition represented only rich and advanced regions of the country – and that meant that the base of the coalition was rather narrow as most of Russia's regions are heavily dependent upon financial aid from the federal centre.

The regional coalition had to capitulate and after his election President Putin concentrated his attack in this direction – against the regional leaders. First the governors and later the oligarchs have been excluded from the ruling coalition. So the federal government, the force ministries (*siloviki*) as well as the State Duma where the party *Edinaya Rossiya* (One Russia) has got a constitutional majority, all became part of Putin's 'political machine'. The President started the reform process with the creation of a new institution – the federal district – that has separated the President from the regional authorities, the governors. The aim of creating the new institution was to take federal agencies working in the regions out of the control of governors. In general the coordination of various federal agencies in the regions was really very weak and they often depended upon the regional executive authorities and were *de facto* 'privatised' by them. Thus, in many regions federal structures had acted not in the interests of the federal centre, but in the interests of the regional establishment.[9] The Presidential Decree represented an attempt to separate the federal structures in the regions from the regional executives in order to increase massively the presence of the Federal President in the regions. Vladimir Putin has broken with the previous tradition of President Yeltsin whose support in the regions had been built on the personal loyalty of the governors and personalized relations with them.

One finds some very polarized opinions concerning the meaning of the new institution among experts and analysts. Some of them are inclined to see it as a very serious political innovation, a sort of 'unitarian superstructure over the federation',[10] while others regard the federal districts as 'pure technological rationalisation'.[11]

At the moment the role of the presidential representatives (the heads of the federal districts) in representing regional interests at the federal centre, in particular in foreign policy, remains rather insignificant. During their first years the representatives tried not only to head the international contacts of the regions but also to coordinate their various international initiatives, in such a way that they would correspond with the national foreign policy course. Some of the experts considered that by doing this the representatives could contribute significantly to 'the realisation of the foreign policy line of Russia, in strengthening the positions of our country in the international arena'.[12] However, the reality turned out to be different. The only real form of interaction between the presidential representatives and the federal bodies in the field of foreign policy is the organization of presentations of federal districts abroad which is done by the MFA. During these presentations diplomatic and business circles of a foreign country have the opportunity to get comprehensive information concerning the potential and characteristics of the federal districts. Such presentations were organized in Berlin (Northern Western District), London and Brussels (Central District), London, Vienna and Frankfurt am Main (Urals District).

In general, we can state that the creation of federal districts did not give the regions an additional channel for lobbying their interests at the federal level. The system – regional leaders, presidential representatives, federal executive authority – has an asymmetrical character because the representatives serve only as federal agents. They inform the regions about the opinions and priorities of the federal authorities and see to it that the regions follow federal guidelines, but they do not represent and defend the collective interest of the regions that compose the federal district at the federal centre.

The reform of the Federation Council changed the very nature of the institution. The Council, being composed from the regional representatives, does not correspond to the constitutional competences of these bodies as the deputies have no political weight and are unknown as political figures. Moreover, the introduction of the new principle means the weakening of parliamentarism in Russia, decreasing the role of parliament in the country's political system.

Now we observe not only the atomization of the Council but also its transformation into a lobbying body where the deputies have been turned into political managers employed by regional executives and legislators. In general the reform of the Federation Council has decreased the democratic legitimacy of the institution. Now the Council attracts professional lobbyists who use this channel to further the interests of their corporations. Thus, the Federation Council in its new manifestation cannot be seen as a regional tribune, as a channel through which the regions could transform the national agenda in their own interest, in particular in the sphere of foreign policy.

In the framework of the reforms the President has created a new institution – the State Council, as a kind of compensation for the regional leaders for the loss of their political weight. The institution is composed of seven governors nominated by Putin – one from each federal district. Every six months they are replaced by others according to the rotation principle. According to numerous declarations of the President, the Council should be a 'political body of strategic importance' and could play a significant role in shaping Russia's internal and external policies. However, the State Council has only advisory status; it is not a constitutional institution, it can be seen as more a façade institution than a real channel for regional interests.

The same has happened to the Consultative Council working in the framework of the MFA. The last session of this institution (26 April 2005) showed that it has slowly lost its substance and turned into a façade institution where the representatives from regional administrations produce reports on the current conditions of their international activities with almost no reaction from the Ministry.

After the regional leaders were excluded from the ruling coalition, foreign policy was for a short period 'privatised' by the oligarchs and the so-called natural monopolies. However they were soon excluded as well and the decision-making process in the foreign policy field was concentrated in the hands of the federal bureaucracy.

Russia and the European Union: Federal and Regional Priorities

Relations between the EU and Russia have already passed several stages and today it is obvious that the previous approach based on common values and the transfer of democratic institutions has proved to be ineffective. During the first half of the 1990s European rhetoric and declarations by President Yeltsin about the 'Europeanisation of Russia' served as a 'democratic façade' for real politics. Moreover, Yeltsin did not have a clear foreign policy course; he used various popular slogans together, without thinking that they might be contradictory. For the President the European vector – closer relations with the EU – meant primarily an additional source of legitimation (primarily in the eyes of democratically-oriented intellectuals) and an additional source of finance through TACIS (Technical Assistance for the Commonwealth of Independent States).

The EU, on the other hand, did not (and probably could not) evaluate Russia's political transformation correctly. The Union saw the restoration of communist rule as the main danger; under these conditions Yeltsin was the only political actor who could guarantee that this danger would not materialize. He was also perceived in the West as a *'rynochnik'* – a champion of the market economy. Liberalization of the economy to make Russian economic institutions compatible with Western markets and open this huge zone to Western products and investments was the goal of the Union's financial aid to Russia; officially it was termed 'transition to a market economy'. The EU was interested first of all in deliveries of energy resources from Russia; the second important thing was security. Apart from that, the Union proceeded from a certain abstract model – that democratic institutions and values could be mechanically copied in Russia and could start effectively working in the country in quite a short period of time. Declarations and/or imitations of democratic practices in Russia proved to be enough for the Union; under these conditions the existence of democratic institutions that really functioned was not that important.

From the regional perspective it is evident that during the first years the resources from the EU were concentrated in Moscow, although in the Partnership and Cooperation Agreement (PCA) cooperation forms between Russia and the EU included the development of infrastructure and regional development. However in the North-West of Russia trans-border cooperation developed quite quickly; during the 1990s the leaders of these regions signed numerous agreements with neighbouring regions in Norway, Finland, Poland and Lithuania. For example, in Karelia the specific nature of its geographical position – having a border with Finland which is also the EU border – has meant that international contacts are a priority of its regional strategy. The main goal of the trans-border and interregional projects that Karelia was undertaking with Finland was the equalization of the standards of the border infrastructure, as well as the stimulation of trans-border economic, cultural and tourist contacts. The creation of the Euroregion 'Karelia' in February 2000 became an interesting and forward-looking form of interregional cooperation.

The regions of the north-west (Kaliningrad, Leningrad, Novgorod regions, the Republic of Karelia and St Petersburg) take part in international sub-regional organizations: the Council of the Baltic States and the Council of Barents Euro-Arctic Region. In 1998 St Petersburg became a member of the Northern Council – an international non-governmental organization (NGO) of the Northern regions created in 1991. The EU programmes and initiatives – TACIS and INTERREG (Interregional Cooperation) – played an important role in stimulating regional development. For several years TACIS was the main financial instrument of the EU in helping the development of the Russian North-West; the majority of the projects were concentrated in the spheres of ecology, trans-border and interregional cooperation. In 1995 the north-western region of Russia became a priority in the framework of the TACIS programme. The EU initiative INTERREG embraced two regions of the Russian North-West: INTERREG Barents that geographically includes Norwegian, Finnish, and Swedish regions and the Murmansk region, and INTERREG Karelia that includes Finnish Karelia and the Republic of Karelia within the Russian Federation.

The Northern Dimension concept also played an important role in stimulating trans-border cooperation in the North-West. On Russia's side it includes the Republics of Karelia and Komi; the regions of Arkhangel, Vologda, Kaliningrad, Pskov, Novgorod, Murmansk and Leningrad; St Petersburg and the autonomous district of Nenets. The Northern Dimension concept covers the activities of various non-governmental and regional and local actors and has become an effective instrument in attracting foreign investments to the north-western region.[13]

During the 1990s, the new trend in Russia's regional development was the problem of growing competition between the regions for Western financial resources and programmes. However, this trend shows that Russia is entering the process of globalization which increases drastically the competition between regions for investments, human capital, political and economic influence, international contacts and external financial resources. In general we can conclude that during the 1990s the regions of Russia's North-West suddenly found themselves in a more favourable geographical position in relation to the EU. It gave them the opportunity to develop trans-border and interregional cooperation and they were able to develop various, and in many cases effective, forms of cooperation. The federal centre did not formulate a spatial strategy of development for the north-west; its role was rather passive during this period. However, it did not prevent the regions from developing their own international contacts.

In many cases TACIS resources were used by regional and local elites to strengthen their position in the regions; the projects and contacts have been controlled by regional authorities. However, direct investments and the presence of European firms in the regions produce new demands in relation to the standards of management and administration: they should be at least to a certain extent compatible with Western standards A significant number of the projects were devoted to increasing the effectiveness of the administration and governance at regional and local level. In some regions (Karelia would be the best example here) projects supporting NGOs proved to be very effective as they contributed to the development of 'private-public partnerships' (between regional authorities, business communities and the NGO sector) within the regions.

From 2000 onwards the European policy of Russia as well as the EU approach towards Russia have changed. In 1999 the Union adopted its 'Common Strategy for Russia', where the Union stressed stability, democracy, the rule of law and the social market economy in Russia as its strategic goals. The list of concrete proposals for cooperation included regional and trans-border cooperation. However, the sense and rhetoric of the Russian document – 'Strategy for the development of relations between the Russian Federation and the European Union for the medium-term perspective (2000–2010)' – is completely different; the main goals of the Strategy are preserving national interests and increasing the role and authority of Russia in Europe and in the world. The content of the document is shaped by the perception of Russia as a 'world power located at two continents' which should preserve the freedom to determine and realize her internal and external policies, her status and advantages as a Euro-Asiatic state and the largest country within the CIS, and the independence of her positions and activities in international organizations.

From a practical perspective, the EU remains dependant upon Russian deliveries of oil and gas and thus is objectively interested in stable relations and long-term contracts. This dependency plus Russia's economic growth and his own high rating among the population gave Putin the freedom to shape relations with the EU while for the Union the room for manoeuvre is relatively narrow even when it is not possible any more to ignore the changing character of the political regime in Russia. Putin does not need an additional source of legitimation and financial aid from the Union is not that important.

The concept 'Wider Europe – Neighbourhood' proposed by the European Commission in March 2003 became the next document in the series of agreements, strategies, programmes and initiatives of the EU towards Russia. This concept caused a negative reaction in Russia as according to the document Russia was treated merely as one of the EU's neighbours. Russia did not want to be the object of the Union's neighbourhood policy as the status of 'neighbour' is obviously lower than the status of 'partner'. The Union realized that Russia's position was not going to change and therefore proposed a new vision of partnership through the concept of the four spaces that was adopted at the EU-Russia Summit in May 2003. In 2004 in the EU Strategy Paper Russia was not mentioned among the countries covered by the new neighbourhood policy but objectively still remains a country neighbouring the EU. Thus it is obvious that 'neighbouring country' and a country that has the status of an EU 'neighbour' are different things. This status refers not to geographical proximity but to the strategic perspective of a country in developing its relations with the EU. The status of a neighbour means recognition and adaptation to the

European norms and rules in all spheres apart from participation in the political institutions and decision-making process in the EU. Instead, Russia's federal elite has accepted the four spaces concept as the basis for the strategic partnership between Russia and the EU. At the EU-Russia Summit in May 2005 the 'road maps' for these four spaces were adopted.

During this complicated period the divergence between federal and regional priorities in Russia were becoming more and more open. Federal priorities in developing relations with the EU became clearer and much more disciplined in comparison with the Yeltsin period. Russia seeks to consolidate her position as the central power in the post-soviet space; she refuses to adapt her internal policy to European norms and values. Regional priorities have a much more practical character: they are interested in participation in the TACIS and INTERREG programmes on trans-border cooperation in order to use the financial resources proposed by the Union. However, the MFA does not take into account the grievances of the regions and will not approve these regional initiatives while relations between Russia and the EU are not officially determined.

Conclusions

From the beginning of the 1990s, the regions of Russia for the first time in history entered the international arena and became part of the processes of globalization and internationalization. During this period there were sufficient institutions through which the regions could lobby, in particular in the field of external relations. However, the regions did not succeed in shaping their position and lobbying their interests as a consolidated actor, which is hardly surprising considering the interregional differences and disparities existing in Russia. From 2000, the consolidation of the new monocentric political regime, the new type of centre- periphery relations and a general re-centralization have also heavily influenced the spectrum of regional channels through which they can participate in the decision-making process at the federal level. The regions did not get additional channels for lobbying, on the contrary, they lost some of the existing channels while others lost their substance and became useless.

Analysis of the federal and regional (Russia's North-West) priorities regarding the EU shows similar trends. During the 1990s the contacts of the regions with their European neighbours were much more effective, practically oriented and diverse than the relations between Russia and the Union which remained rather abstract and reflected more aspirations than practice. Regional strategies were in many cases different from those declared by the federal centre. Now the situation is fundamentally different: relations between the EU and Russia lack a conceptual basis, they have to be re-thought, and the regions have proved to be the main victims of this delay at federal level.

Notes and References

1. Let us compare, for example, Moscow and Kalmykia: they are not at different levels of socio-economic development, but at different historical stages.
2. W. Riker, *Federalism: Origin, Operation, Significance* (Boston, little Brown, 1964).
3. D. Elazar, *Exploring Federalism* (Tuscaloosa, The University of Alabama Press, 1987), p. 479.
4. V. Ryzhkov, *The Fourth Republic: Essay on the Political History of Contemporary Russia* (Moscow, MSHPI, 2000), pp. 98–9.
5. See *Vneshnya politika I besopasnost sovremennoi Rossii* (Foreign Policy and Security of Contemporary Russia), (Moscow, MONF, 1999).
6. See O. Aleksandrov, *The role of the regions in Russia's foreign policy (example of the regions of North-Western federal district – 1991–2002)*, Moscow, 2003), pp. 143–7.
7. See A. Makarychev, 'Foreign Policies of Sub-National Units – the Case of the Russian Regions' in A Makarychev (ed) *New and Old Actors in Russian Foreign Policy* (Oslo, NUPI, 2000).
8. V. L. Larin, 'Russia and China on the eve of the third millennium: who will defend our national interests?' *Problems of the Far East*, No.1, 1997, pp. 15–26.
9. See L. Smirnyagin, 'Wonderful Seven', *Russian Regional Bulletin*, 2/10, May 2000, p. 22.
10. See V. Zubov, 'Unitarianism or Federalism (To the Question of Future Organization of Russia's State Expanse)', *Polis*, No 5, 2000, p. 32.
11. See S. Kaspe 'To Construct a Federation – *Renovatio Imperii* as a Method of Social Engineering', *Polis*, No 5, 2000, p. 67.
12. See O. N. Barabanov, 'Presidential representatives and international contacts: new opportunities for Russia'. in *International relations in the XXI century: new actors, institutions and processes*, Nizhnij Novgorod, 2001.
13. C. E. Stalvant, 'The Northern Dimension: A Policy in Need of an Institution', *The Baltic Area Studies*, Gdansk-Berlin, No 1, 2001.

6

THE RUSSIAN MILITARY AND EUROPEAN SECURITY COOPERATION

Derek L. Averre

Introduction

The period since the end of the Cold War has witnessed a transformation of the European security map and – as a necessary precondition of this – of political-military relations between Russia and Europe. The withdrawal of former Soviet forces from Central and Eastern Europe (CEE), the conclusion of arms control arrangements – in particular the Treaty on Conventional Forces in Europe (CFE) treaty, CFE-1A agreement and Open Skies treaty – verbal agreements on non-deployment of tactical nuclear weapons, cooperative threat reduction programmes and establishment of confidence and security building measures were designed to end the period of confrontation and usher in a new era of security cooperation while preserving, at least in formal terms, a balance of military power. This has been complemented by the institutionalization of security arrangements with the North Atlantic Treaty Organization (NATO) and the European Union (EU) and active Russian involvement in regional security organizations. Since Europe needed Moscow's acquiescence to carry out the dual NATO/EU enlargements and stabilize the continent, and Russia needed access to 'Western' institutions, these developments have often been presented positively in diplomatic terms, not least in commentaries on the supposedly 'pro-Western shift' in foreign and security policy initiated by Putin in his first term.

The pressure of internal developments has often tended to push political-military relations between Russia and Europe into the background. In Europe, the enlargement and transformation of NATO, the management of conflicts in the Balkans, EU enlargement and the launch of the European Security and Defence Policy (ESDP), as well as defence reviews in European states, have involved a huge amount of time and effort. In Russia, military restructuring and reform, the conflicts in Chechnya and the Union of Soviet Socialist

Republics (USSR) successor states and attempts to re-establish security cooperation among the latter through the Collective Security Treaty Organization (CSTO) have, similarly, presented a considerable challenge to the Russian leadership. The emergence of new security challenges facing Europe and Russia alike, not least the dramatic impact of international terrorism, and ideational and institutional strains in the transatlantic relationship as a result of unilateralist US actions have created a fluid international environment which has also absorbed the attention of policymakers.

In fact the legacy of the Cold War has repeatedly resurfaced to provide a reminder of the potential for political-military confrontation between Russia and Europe. The 1997 decision on NATO enlargement into CEE, Moscow's embittered reaction to the Alliance's intervention in Kosovo without a UN Security Council (UNSC) mandate (the fifth anniversary of which was even commemorated in a Russian foreign ministry statement on 24 March 2004), disputes over the adaptation of the CFE treaty and – albeit less controversial – the geopolitical and international legal implications of ESDP have been watched with concern, especially by the Russian military. Further NATO enlargement to include the Baltic states has brought a powerful and, in the eyes of Russia's defence establishment, only partially reconstructed Alliance to Russia's borders and left a gaping hole in CFE arrangements. The signing of the NATO-Ukraine memorandum formalizing Kiev's agreement to the movement of NATO troops and armaments on Ukrainian territory (despite Ukraine's 'non-bloc status' enshrined in its 1990 Declaration of State Sovereignty), the Alliance's closer relationship with the other USSR successor states and continuing concern over NATO's military-technical superiority and ability to effect out-of-area operations, including the potential for deployment on Russia's periphery, generate suspicion and resentment among defence planners in Moscow who discern Russia's growing strategic vulnerability.

The situation described above should be kept in context. Substantial progress, albeit incremental, has been made in establishing mechanisms for consultation with NATO and the EU and, on less controversial issues, for joint decision-making with the Alliance. Official Russian reactions to the latest wave of NATO enlargement have been 'calm but negative', in contrast to the previous round when there was much talk of 'red lines' and influential figures in the defence establishment pondered a military response. Moscow is committed to maintaining cooperation with European states and organizations on shared security challenges. Nevertheless evidence – examined in more detail below – suggests that what is still perceived as a potentially hostile NATO remains a central concern in its defence planning. In the recent period greater emphasis has been laid by Moscow on reinforcing the CSTO and reasserting influence in the CIS, accompanied by renewed plans to reform and reequip the military.

Put simply, relations with NATO are by no means crisis-proof. This prompts a central question: does the residual mistrust described above simply represent the unfinished business of the Cold War or – with due regard for the changes in relations prompted by new security challenges – does it demonstrate that there is still potential for a more assertive long-term Russian strategy which might translate into doctrinal and operational choices and limit security cooperation, perhaps laying the foundations for a renewed adversarial relationship with Europe?

Much has been written about Russia's relations with NATO and the EU and about security governance in Europe, and indeed other chapters in this volume contribute to the debate. There has been much less analysis in the recent period of the attitudes of the Russian military and defence establishment to arms control and security cooperation with Europe. This chapter first examines debates within the Russian defence establishment on political-military cooperation with European states and organizations, outlining the impact of threat perceptions on its thinking and the conflicting views of the civilian and military leadership. It goes on to consider the achievements and limitations of political-military cooperation with NATO and the EU, including military-technical cooperation, in the context of the changing military roles of these organizations, and analyses the continuing dispute over the CFE treaty. The conclusions attempt to highlight how and to what extent the defence establishment's views influence Russia's security relations with Europe.

Threat Perceptions and Military Responses

Political-military relations between Russia and Europe still centre largely on the former's relations with NATO. The position of the Putin administration is that NATO does not represent a military threat and that a strategy for long-term relations with the Alliance is a central component of Russia's security policy. Moscow recognizes that NATO is reviewing its strategic and operational plans, reducing troops and armaments to levels even lower than those stipulated in the CFE treaty, and that a substantial percentage of tactical nuclear missiles have been withdrawn from Europe; military cooperation in the NATO-Russia Council (NRC) is increasing, especially in important areas such as developing a concept for joint peacekeeping operations and principles of military compatibility in joint operations, which is already being translated into joint exercises and training. Two key issues for Russia are transparency in military policymaking and planning, and establishing a basis for joint rather than NATO-led operations. As defence minister Sergei Ivanov has stated, alongside its collective defence function the Alliance is acquiring a 'consultative' role for member states seeking policy responses to new security challenges, particularly the threat of terrorism and Weapons of Mass Destruction (WMD) proliferation.[1] Although cooperation is taking time to develop from political negotiations to practical joint actions, the fundamentals of political-military relations appear to be solid.

The same officials emphasize, however, that in many respects the concerns over NATO's military capabilities and strategic doctrine which engendered confrontation in the 1990s still hold good. The spectre of Kosovo, and the avoidance in NATO's 1999 Strategic Concept of a commitment to seek a UNSC mandate for the use of force in out-of-area operations, has prompted Ivanov to warn against this kind of action even to fight terrorism and argue that NATO should act exclusively in accordance with traditional international law.[2] Key Russian concerns arising from the 2004 round of NATO enlargement also need to be addressed. The Alliance is perceived to be operating in Russia's 'zone of vitally important interests'; Moscow has warned that deployment of NATO forces near Russian borders could contravene the Alliance's undertaking to refrain from additional permanent stationing of substantial military forces in Eastern Europe under the 1997 Founding Act and threaten the balance of forces established under the CFE treaty restrictions, to which the Baltic states were not party. One authoritative commentator concludes that, although the new member states are concerned primarily with strengthening their defence as part of NATO's integrated military structure rather than providing forward bases for Alliance deployments and in fact are concentrating their capabilities on combating new security challenges, traditional threat perceptions are prompting defence officials to plan for 'NATO's physical, if not geopolitical, movement eastwards'.[3]

The view in Moscow is thus that, even though the Alliance's article 5 defence commitment is now secondary, its functional transformation is lagging behind geographical enlargement and is hampered by Cold War-era thinking. One experienced foreign policy official sums up the equivocal attitude of the political establishment as a whole to the Alliance:

> There are no grounds for conflict. Russia has partnership relations with NATO... At the same time the impression is that NATO prefers to keep powder dry, while the Cold War era functions – to maintain combat readiness for armed confrontation with a major adversary – are still in place... The [Alliance's] military leadership, however, still takes guidance not so much from the practical assessment of the situation in the European region, where direct security threats have been eliminated, not least as a result of unprecedented arms reduction efforts, as from outdated internal NATO regulations concerning the defense of the [Alliance's] members. This compels Russia to react appropriately.[4]

In terms of formulating a response Russian officials in charge of European policy have spoken in the conditional mood, stating that, if NATO increases its force deployments in CEE, measures will be taken by the military, including reconfiguring Russian forces in the north-west region and, *in extremis*, pulling out of CFE Treaty negotiations.[5] This may represent, on the one hand, an attempt to establish a bargaining position in CFE negotiations – the same officials recognize that ratification of an adapted CFE treaty would minimize their concerns – and, on the other, an attempt to placate the defence establishment. In such a situation, however, relatively innocuous events – such as the transfer in 2004 of four F-16 fighter aircraft to patrol Baltic air space, together with components of an anti-missile system, in a move to bring the Baltic states' air defences under NATO command – have been interpreted by Moscow as a 'provocation' contrary to the spirit of cooperation. Similarly, the visit of a senior NATO military official to Tbilisi in June 2003 to discuss Georgia's readiness to allow Airborne Warning and Control Systems (AWACS) aircraft to patrol its territory prompted a report by the General Staff (channelled through the defence and other ministries) warning that Russian bases in Abkhazia, Armenia, the North Caucasus and the Black Sea could be spied upon and that the Russian military reserved the right to take harsh measures.[6]

These disputes should be seen against wider strategic concerns in the Russian defence establishment. Despite the retirement of prominent figures openly hostile to NATO such as General Leonid Ivashov, former head of the Defence Ministry's Main Administration for International Military Cooperation (who has ironically proposed renaming the Russian defence ministry 'the Federal Agency for Friendship with NATO'[7]), views among some sections of the military appear to have changed little since the mid 1990s. With Kaliningrad now surrounded by NATO allies and 'mainland' Russia outflanked around the Black Sea with the accession of Romania and Bulgaria alongside Turkey, and with Ukraine aiming for NATO membership – throwing into doubt the long-term future of Russia's Black Sea fleet – Russia is perceived as even more vulnerable, both militarily and in terms of the possibility of further erosion of Moscow's influence in the CIS. This has led Ivanov to warn that Moscow will review its defence and security relations with Ukraine and Georgia if they join the Alliance.[8] Commentators on defence issues have even speculated that, although Russia needs cooperation with NATO, the collapse of the CFE treaty might allow Moscow 'greater freedom if the need arises to take countermeasures to guarantee security' on its flanks.[9] One reports that the idea of stationing tactical nuclear weapons in Kaliningrad is again being discussed in defence circles and that, although this does not form part of official policy, these weapons are being maintained in Russian force structures as a potential deterrent.[10]

The most recent detailed exposition of the military's views appeared in a Russian defence ministry paper which was presented at a conference attended by Putin and Ivanov in October 2003.[11] This document, a lengthy review of current defence policy and reform to which the General Staff presumably made a substantial contribution, generally presents a positive assessment of 'partner relations' between Russia and NATO and the reduced likelihood of large-scale conflict. Nevertheless, it goes on to refer directly to the Alliance and the 'anti-Russian elements' at work there, stating that doctrinal and operational changes – including in nuclear strategy – will be taken in Russia's military planning 'if NATO remains a military alliance with the offensive military doctrine it has at present'. It also emphasizes the danger of an air-space attack against Russian territory – currently possible only from the West – and speaks of preventive strikes to defend Russian interests, including in CIS states. As Aleksei Arbatov points out, the defence ministry paper's characterization of future conflicts and wars focuses largely on responses to the kind of threat that NATO represents[12] – very much at odds with the positive rhetoric of cooperation with the Alliance.

Part of the problem in assessing the dynamic of Russia's political-military relations with Europe lies in the conflicting signals regarding threat perceptions, naturally a major factor in formulating defence policy, given out by the political leadership. In the wake of the Nord-Ost theatre siege in Moscow in October 2002, Putin instructed the defence ministry and General Staff to make changes in Russia's national security concept – and indeed to consider other changes to the whole system of security planning – to place greater emphasis on the terrorist threat.[13] Yet, as one commentator notes, by attending the abovementioned conference Putin and Ivanov appeared to associate themselves with a possible review of military planning to counter NATO's offensive military doctrine – easily interpreted as an attempt by a more assertive leadership to demonstrate readiness to defend Russia's national interests.[14] Also, the Russian military has reportedly criticized calls to reform the Armed Forces to combat terrorism, implicitly contradicting Putin's instructions following the theatre siege. The then head of the General Staff, General Anatoli Kvashnin, made it clear that Russia's geostrategic position, its perception of actual and potential threats and the defence of national interests demand an independent policy:

'For deeper, partner, brotherly relations with world centres such as the US, Europe and China we should have both sufficient strategic defensive and strategic offensive forces, proceeding from forecasts as to the development of the situation, including the military-political situation'... the strategic credo of the RF Armed Forces General Staff is clear: while the US and NATO retain forces and means of waging a major nuclear war, Russia will strive to maintain corresponding parity...and as far as terrorism is concerned – let the politicians and special services fight it.[15]

It has even been suggested that defence minister Ivanov himself has expressed scepticism about reorienting Russia's defence priorities to combat terrorism.[16]

Divisions between the defence ministry and the General Staff reflect this ambivalence and have influenced cooperation with Europe. A positive response by the defence ministry to an invitation to take part in large-scale NATO air and naval exercises in the North Atlantic in 2004 was reportedly undercut by the then deputy chief – and current chief – of the General Staff, General Yuri Baluevsky, and Russia's chief military representative to NATO, Vice-Admiral Valentin Kuznetsov, who wanted to postpone them. Baluevsky is quoted as stating that the military still has urgent questions about why NATO and the US are developing high-precision weapons, as well as systems for protection against and use of WMD, and concluding that the US still has designs – albeit unspecified – on Russian territory for which it continues to assign forces.[17] Russian defence analysts have also pointed to the practice of sending officers to NATO for joint training and then sacking them on their return or recalling to Moscow those who have established good working relations in Brussels.[18]

There is thus a 'persisting deterrence-cooperation dichotomy in Russia-NATO relations'[19]: a clear differentiation between the traditional strategic threat of an attack by large-scale forces, leading to an emphasis on the need for defence sufficiency, and cooperation over new security threats in responses by the Russian military. While NATO's changing role, with greater emphasis on collective security, has drawn a positive response from the Putin administration, its collective defence commitment – still seen by the defence establishment as underpinned by US global strategy and military-technical superiority – continues to cast a long shadow over favourable political-military relations between Russia and Europe.

Military reform in Russia is a crucial factor in assessing how political-military cooperation with Europe will develop. Leading analysts have argued that presidential control of the military in Russia is purely an imitation of contemporary notions of civilian political control, and is based on the loyalty of the military in return for its exclusive responsibility for strategic planning, direction and control. This is reflected in the defence ministry paper described above: 'Real control on the part of the civilian minister and the political leadership in general over the General Staff and the military bureaucracy has still not been established. And it is this which determines the contradictory nature of the document which is mooted as Russia's new military doctrine'.[20] Effective legislative and expert control over military budgets – information on which is severely restricted – is impossible. Indeed, Sergei Ivanov has publicly deplored the fact that the defence ministry has remained a 'dwarf' compared to the 'giant' General Staff. [21]

This situation was addressed by measures introduced in 2004 to remove operational control over the Armed Forces from the General Staff, which left the defence ministry as the primary decision-making body for military affairs and responsible for military reform.[22] The longer-term implications of this development are yet to emerge. However, while the defence ministry has drawn up extensive plans for thoroughgoing military reform, a long and painful period of modernization to introduce the kind of military organization and culture which has evolved in Western armed forces in response to new security challenges – with the participation of democratic institutions – is in prospect.[23] Again, this may well continue to make political-military cooperation with Europe problematic.

Political-Military and Military-Technical Cooperation: Achievements and Limitations

In spite of the problems outlined above, the Putin leadership has consistently emphasized that there is no alternative to far-reaching political-military interaction between Russia and Europe. Moscow's pragmatic objectives – to ensure that new NATO member states observe agreements reached in the NRC on military restraint and on the CFE statutes – underpin a strategic political aim; foreign minister Sergei Lavrov, after the first informal meeting of foreign ministers in the expanded NRC format of 27 members, spoke of a single European security space based on the continued transformation of NATO and establishment of the EU's military component in parallel with the deepening of partnership between Moscow and both organizations.[24] While this is inevitably a gradual process, relations have developed from purely formal consultations to Russia's practical involvement in NATO activity, underpinned by more than 20 working groups set up under the auspices of the NRC, and joint efforts to address specific security challenges in Europe.

A key focus of the NRC is to promote military interoperability between NATO and Russian forces. A political-military framework for enhanced interoperability has been established; Russian military branch offices have been set up at NATO's two top military command headquarters, and a military liaison mission is helping to improve transparency on military doctrine and activities, aiming to create a cadre of professionals versed in each other's strategy and tactics and thereby increase the capacity for cooperation in multinational operations. Efforts are concentrating on clarifying specific military procedures for joint operations, drawing on existing dialogue on operational control, interoperability of communications and information, exchange of training experience, compatibility of armed forces and logistical support for peacekeeping.[25] There has also been cooperation on nuclear doctrine and strategy, including exchanges of experiences in NRC seminars and the holding of nuclear weapons accident response field exercises.

Political modalities for future joint peacekeeping operations constitute an important area of cooperation. The 'Political Aspects of the Basic Concept of Russia-NATO Joint Peacekeeping Operations' have been agreed, providing for political control and strategic governance of joint peacekeeping. Joint training and exercises have been carried out and discussions held about Russian support for the NATO-led International Security Assistance Force in Afghanistan through logistical support, heavy airlift and intelligence. A Russian unit, the 15th Motorised Rifle Brigade, has been prepared for participation in international peacekeeping operations.[26] Though the establishment of extensive joint capabilities remains a long way off, Moscow signed in April 2005 the Partnership for Peace Status of Forces Agreement which regulates the legal status for movements of troops between partner countries, thereby facilitating NATO-Russia exercises on Russian territory.

Interaction on defence reform, including force planning and protection, improving communications capabilities and retraining discharged military and associated personnel, has also been assessed positively. Cooperation between naval forces is dealt with by several NRC working groups. Reciprocal naval visits have been initiated; Russia is a member of the NATO-led Submarine Escape and Rescue Working Group and Russian units participated in the NATO 'Sorbet Royal 2005' submarine search-and-rescue exercise in June 2005. Russian industry has been invited to collaborate in research into the international interoperability of search-and-rescue systems.

Combating terrorism has emerged as an important area of cooperation. Joint intelligence assessments of terrorist threats in the Euroatlantic area are being developed and ideas exchanged via the NRC ad hoc working group on military-military interaction in dealing with these threats. The NRC Action Plan on Terrorism was adopted in December 2004; a Russian contribution to NATO's Operation Active Endeavour in the Mediterranean, aimed at deterring and defending against terrorist attacks, has been agreed and NATO representatives have observed the *Avariya*-2004 Russian military exercises aimed at protecting nuclear weapons convoys and responding to terrorist attacks. Joint naval patrols in the Mediterranean are planned for 2006 onwards. Progress in several other areas – notably work on a common assessment of WMD proliferation dangers, cooperation in counter-narcotics training, developing a road map to interoperability of theatre missile defence systems, civil emergency planning exercises and a feasibility study for a reciprocal exchange of civil and military air traffic data under the Cooperative Airspace Initiative – has also been made.

While the above constitutes an impressive register of cooperative activities, key questions remain for the NRC, such as when and under what circumstances it should meet in crisis situations, which issues involving the use of force it should decide upon, what role there might be for a Russian military component in NATO commands, including Combined Joint Task Forces, and what the Russian role in multilateral forces and operations will consist of. Progress in agreeing the parameters of joint military activities has been slow and incremental and remains very much at an early stage, with Moscow insisting on joint decision-making and conceptual design of joint peacekeeping operations. Sustained political support in Moscow for deeper military engagement with NATO will depend to a large extent on developing common perceptions of security problems.

As Russian officials readily admit, despite efforts to further cooperation with the EU's military structures, political-military interaction with the EU is lagging behind cooperation with NATO. The initial positive response by Moscow to the ESDP was reflected in the Joint Declaration on Strengthening Dialogue and Cooperation on Political and Security Matters in Europe adopted at the October 2000 summit, which promised to institute specific consultations on security and defence matters, develop strategic dialogue, including on disarmament, arms control and non-proliferation, and promote cooperation in operational crisis management.[27] The Russian defence ministry followed this up with proposals for joint work on crisis management with the EU, including joint planning and multinational peace support units. The Russian Ministry for Emergency Situations also submitted a concept for civilian crisis management. EU member states responded by elaborating modalities for the participation of Russian forces in EU-led crisis management operations, opening up the possibility of Russian force contributions and Moscow's participation in the Committee of Contributors, the main body carrying out day-today operational management.[28]

Although dialogue on crisis management cooperation continues there has been minimal Russian involvement in ESDP to date, however. One authoritative Russian commentator argues for a more flexible approach by the EU, complaining that Moscow has for several years now been 'knocking on the door of the EU with a proposal for practical interaction' in security and crisis management issues but that Brussels appears to lack the political will to respond.[29] Direct contact between Russian defence ministry and General Staff officials and their counterparts on the EU's Military Committee and Military Staff has been limited. Moscow, which is pressing for shared decision-making, has refused – other than making an unsubstantial contribution of five officers to the EU Police Mission in Bosnia and Herzegovina – to take part in other peacekeeping and police missions; officials have warned that other proposals are likely to be turned down unless an appropriate format is agreed.[30]

More extensive commitments are unlikely in the immediate future, due primarily to the complex nature of the decision-making process in the EU itself – which is likely to exclude any part for Moscow – and Brussels' cautious approach to involving non-member states, as well as uncertainty about the scope of ESDP missions and the general ambiguity of EU policy on its Eastern periphery. The road map for the EU-Russia common space of external security agreed in May 2005, while mentioning a framework agreement on legal and financial aspects of cooperation in crisis management operations, states only that the two sides will 'strengthen EU-Russian dialogue… [and] improve mutual understanding of respective procedures and concepts… [which] could lead to the development of principles and modalities for joint approaches in crisis management'.[31] The road map lacks any reference to ESDP and there appears to be little immediate prospect of moving from consultation to practical initiatives and some kind of joint decision-making arrangements in this area. The widening technical gap in command, control and intelligence and the 'single information space' with real-time information processing, as well as in high-precision armaments, also means that Russia would not be ready to join operations carried out by the European Rapid Reaction Force, or indeed the NATO Response Force.

In many respects the 'informed pessimism' voiced by the experienced former NATO military representative Manfred Diehl over the limited progress achieved on military reform in Russia, which leads to doubts about its ability to contribute to cooperative activities with NATO, the EU and their member states, still holds good.[32] Despite good tactical and operational cooperation in the field during the Balkans conflicts and exchanges of experience on defence reform, resistance to military interaction still exists. Diehl has argued that Baluevsky was appointed as Russia's representative in negotiations with NATO on military and defence reform when a civilian figure might have generated more positive exchanges. Further development of a common understanding of democratic reform and control of the armed forces along European lines, and of common approaches to contemporary security challenges, entail high benchmarks which Russian defence officials – who interpret concepts of democracy and reform in different ways – struggle to meet. Whether joint efforts in the struggle against terrorism will do much to further political-military cooperation, given the differing perceptions of the threat and the baleful legacy of Russian operations in Chechnya, is also open to doubt.

In a recent speech delivered in Moscow, NATO Secretary General de Hoop Scheffer appealed for greater trust as the basis for 'a shared vision of a common future'.[33] Incremental progress has been achieved, but a far-reaching partnership presupposes both the political will to cooperate and a genuine spirit of cooperation between militaries – preconditions for a common security culture

– which are currently lacking. Moscow appears no less resentful over the tendency of both NATO and the EU still to take unilateral decisions over key security matters and no less wary about extensive involvement of these organizations in the CIS. Sustained dialogue is needed on developing NATO-Russia joint decision-making mechanisms to cover a wider range of security matters than is currently the case, as well as on activating the EU-Russia relationship, in particular on mutually acceptable preconditions for military action and modalities for cooperation for conflict prevention/crisis management purposes in their shared neighbourhood.

The potential for military-technical cooperation between Russia and European countries, including through NATO and EU programmes, has been explored as a means of furthering relations by integrating Russian technologies into European markets to the benefit of European defence economies and in terms of modernizing Russia's defence industrial base. Russia is technologically competitive in aviation – heavy-lift air transport and advanced tactical fighter aircraft – real-time satellite reconnaissance, some areas of communications and intelligence technology, anti-aircraft/anti-missile defence systems and rocket and space technology. There have been a few examples of successful cooperation, notably with France on the MIG-AT training fighter aircraft and with the French company Dassault on pilotless aircraft; Russia has signed several protocols with Dassault and the European Aeronautic Defence and Space company for collaboration on developing military aircraft. The European Space Agency has also established cooperation with the Russian Federal Space Agency to exploit the Soyuz launcher and to research and develop future launchers, and is currently considering employing the Russian Kliper reusable orbiter to replace the Soyuz spacecraft. The common external security space road map refers to promoting contacts between Russia and the recently created European Defence Agency.[34]

However, recent analysis suggests that, due to the absence of political will in Europe to cooperate and the desire of Europeans to use their own technologies, as well as inadequate Russian government support for its domestic defence industry and poor project management and infrastructure in Russia – only partly compensated for by Russian R & D expertise in some areas of military-related science and technology – Russia and Europe are not ready for extensive military-technical cooperation.[35] High-level cooperative decision-making mechanisms are still lacking; potential major projects, for example involving the use of Antonov military transport aircraft and the Russian dual-use space navigation system GLONASS, have not materialized. Several analysts have also expressed doubt about Europe's interest in missile defence – mooted as one potential area for cooperation in which Russia has comprehensive technological expertise – given its numerous other defence priorities. The thrust of Russia's military-technical cooperation is thus likely to remain with China and India for the foreseeable future.

The CFE Treaty

In many respects ongoing disagreements over the adapted CFE treaty – despite what would appear to be a relatively minor problem compared with the original settlement, which codified the end of the Cold War in terms of conventional arms control – are a distillation of the lasting mistrust between Russia and NATO. The CFE treaty is seen by Moscow as central to political-military relations between the major powers, a 'corner-stone' of European security and a guarantee that Russia cannot in future be faced with a potentially hostile alliance of powerful states to the West. For the NATO allies, the continuing presence of Russian troops in Moldova and Georgia has cast doubt on Moscow's readiness to eliminate residual sources of conflict in Europe.

The current *impasse* is due to the refusal of most NATO member states to ratify the adapted CFE treaty, agreed at the November 1999 OSCE summit in Istanbul, on the grounds that Moscow has not fulfilled political commitments made at the summit by withdrawing its troops from Moldova and Georgia. Under the terms of the adapted treaty NATO's political commitment not to deploy on a permanent basis substantial combat forces on the territory of new member states was matched by Russia assuming political obligations to exercise 'restraint' in force deployment in the Kaliningrad and Pskov regions, as well as pulling out surplus treaty-limited equipment (TLE) from Georgia and its entire TLE from Moldova. Moscow is arguing that it has fulfilled the agreement on flank limitations and has done much to make its withdrawal of TLE transparent, and that a false link is being made between the treaty itself and the political commitments made at Istanbul; it insists that the settlement of military issues with Moldova and Georgia is a subject for bilateral relations. Also, in Moscow's view the admission of the Baltic states into NATO without their formal accession to the CFE treaty constitutes a potential threat to the flank limitation regime and could make Russia question its restraint on its north-west flank, despite NATO's political commitments and the fact that the CFE Treaty is designed to restrict the movement of armaments within the Treaty zone and thereby eliminate the possibility of a rapid scale-up of offensive capabilities.[36]

Moscow's reluctance to implement its Istanbul commitments stems from the argument that the frozen conflicts in these countries threaten Russia's security and that complete withdrawal could further destabilize the situation. Cool relations with the Georgian leadership, which has attempted to engage international involvement and minimise Russia's role in settling its internal conflicts in Abkhazia and South Ossetia, and Moscow's resentment over Europe's blocking in 2003 of Russian proposals for a political settlement of the Moldova-Transdniestria conflict, have engendered a difficult political environment. There have recently been signs of progress; compromise was reached with Georgia in May 2005 over the withdrawal of Russian bases by 2008 and the EU now has a small monitoring presence in the Georgia-Russia border region, while Moscow has reacted favourably to a Ukraine-sponsored framework for a settlement of the Transdniestria problem – involving the phasing out of Russia's military presence – as well as accepting a role for the EU there.[37] However, much more extensive cooperation between Europe and Russia over the frozen conflicts is needed to help forestall the prospect of a renewed escalation.

Ultimately, the CFE Treaty dispute goes beyond technical arms control, which forms only a small part of the wider relationship between Russia and Europe. Moscow's concerns over the military potential of a powerful alliance, of which it does not form part, at its borders and over loss of influence in neighbouring states hinder the transition to a deeper political-military partnership. Russian officials closely linked with the CFE Treaty negotiations have unambiguously expressed the doubts of Moscow's defence planners:

> Arms control took a back seat and came to be used solely as a means to advance NATO's geopolitical interests in the post-Soviet space... we regard the arms control regime as the basis for relationships with our Western partners in the military-political area. If there is a reliable system of limitations, transparency, and predictability we in Russia would be happy to switch our attention to other areas of cooperation, including a radical refocusing of the Armed Forces to counter new challenges and security threats in cooperation with NATO and the EU, without the fear that the next day we would be compelled to revert... to old defensive patterns.[38]

Conclusions

While the relatively smooth post-Cold War transition from confrontation to cooperation, and indeed Russia's key role in the transition, is beyond dispute, perceptions of political-military relations between Russia and Europe differ. At one extreme, concerns about the potential for new crises remain. In Europe these concerns focus on the lack of substantive change in Russia's military doctrine, excesses in Chechnya, hostility to NATO enlargement and a more assertive CIS policy. Influential sections of the Russian elite point to the continuation of the NATO defence alliance, intervention in Kosovo, successive waves of NATO and EU enlargement and attempts to circumscribe Russia's influence in its immediate neighbourhood as proof of Western hostility. At the other extreme, it is argued – and European diplomats are very much at pains to emphasize – that the Putin administration's policy of pragmatic engagement is leading to Russia's institutional adaptation to the new European order. Through extensive political-military cooperation, Russia and Europe have moved on from a relationship based on constraining confrontation to one where major conflict or a new cold war is becoming unthinkable, one of the preconditions for a security community.

Even if one accepts that the Cold War is buried, the instability and fluidity of the current international environment, generating uncertainty both in terms of security governance and of how to define and combat new and diffuse security threats – failed states, terrorism, WMD proliferation – is troubling both Russia and Europe, in the shape of NATO and the EU, alike.[39] Sergei Karaganov has argued that 'the paradox lies in the fact that the system of European security is directed towards solving not new but old problems, problems that have already been solved' and points to the lack of a clear agenda – whereby Russia is offered cooperation on peacekeeping or joint military operations but without defining their scope and modalities, and without being accorded a decision-making role in conflict prevention and crisis management – and of a clear conceptual vision among leading policymakers in a disorientated Europe where trust and confidence are still limited.[40] The old security dilemma is receding (although greater clarity and transparency in force structures, military planning and doctrine is still needed) but uncertainty over the extent of Russia's inclusion in European security governance magnifies the importance of arms control and military planning to deal with potential threats from the West. Even the transformation of NATO from a predominantly military alliance into an organization dealing with common security in the fragmented post-Soviet space generates problems as, without deeper partnership with the Alliance, Moscow's difficulty in sustaining political-military relations with the CIS countries leaves it feeling more and more isolated.

The process of adaptation is especially painful for Russia; its internal development and shifting political currents in the CIS are engendering domestic debates which produce an uneven effect on Russian political-military decision-making. Military reform – the functional, organizational and psychological adaptation to new challenges in a changed security environment and the establishment of professional and accountable military, security and intelligence agencies underpinned by democratic control and the rule of law – is proving particularly troublesome. Internal factors thus still have the potential to trigger crises in external relations with Europe, as Russia's mistrust feeds back into uncertainty over how its policies should be interpreted and how far Russian interests should be accommodated.

Herd and Akerman have argued persuasively that the conservative pro-military lobby has largely failed to articulate viable alternatives to pro-Western engagement and overcome more influential groups in favour of stable relations with Europe.[41] The Russian military today plays a lesser role in political decision-making than under Yelstin, who ignored problems relating to reform and civilian control and thus became hostage to conflicts within a politicized high military command. As outlined above, these conflicts have not disappeared completely but Ivanov is attempting through the defence ministry to impose the policy of the Putin leadership on the General Staff.

However, Moscow's more assertive position on political-military issues in the CIS, an attempt by the Putin administration to lend coherence to a foreign and security policy which drifted badly in the 1990s, inevitably draws on concerns in the wider political establishment over perceived threats to Russia's national security. One prominent commentator voices the views of a substantial part of this establishment: 'Russia needs a harsher policy. Enough of being hyper-compliant… Our relations with Europe will not be so pleasant but we don't need pleasant relations. We need relations where we will be respected and reckoned with. I'm not calling for confrontation, but for us to defend our positions clearly and definitely'.[42] While it might be going too far to suggest that an authoritarian government could in future be captured by a nationalist pro-military lobby in favour of a more aggressive foreign policy, such views might be exploited to manipulate public perceptions against attempts to deepen partnership with Europe and to obstruct military reform. Offering Russia a more inclusive role in European security governance, with a greater degree of military cooperation, would allow it more scope to defend its interests and prevent a return to a 'mobilisation regime' which greater assertiveness in its immediate security environment might entail. Without it, the prospects for favourable development, particularly under a post-Putin regime, are far less certain.

A dual dynamic has emerged in Russia's political-military relations with Europe: engagement with European institutions, with elements of both strategic partnership and cooperative security, alongside greater emphasis on strengthening sovereignty and pursuing an independent foreign and security policy. This is most visible in attempts to integrate the CIS – what Putin has called a 'civilising mission'[43] – and establish a Russian 'pole' of influence aimed at denying other external powers a leading role there. Sergei Ivanov has stressed the importance of the military to Russia's future strategy: 'Nobody has put it better than [tsar] Alexander III. As before we have two allies – the army and navy. We live today in a cruel world… And the reliable defence of our sovereignty can be guaranteed only by a strong army and navy and an efficient economy'.[44] Russia's ruling elite 'has formed the strong opinion that international relations is the field of *Realpolitik*… "real politics" in the 21st century is a combination of geopolitics and geoeconomics with a substantial role for military power preserved', with policy based on 'limited partnership and local rivalry' in Russia's immediate neighbourhood.[45] The implications of this for Russia's future defence orientation are yet fully to emerge; might they delay further cooperation with NATO and the EU and make Europe's military planners wary of too extensive involvement of Russia in European security arrangements? One thing appears certain: the search for durable political-military relations between Moscow and Europe's key security organizations has only just begun.

Notes and References

1. Interview with Ivanov in *Komsomol'skaya Pravda*, 26 October 2004.
2. Speech at Munich Conference on Security Policy, 7 February 2004, at http://www.securityconference.de/konferenzen/rede.php?menu_2004=&menu_konferenzen=&sprache=en&id=126& (accessed 20 February 2004).
3. D. Danilov, 'Russia and European Security', in D. Lynch (ed.), *What Russia sees*, Chaillot Paper No 74, EU Institute for Security Studies, January 2005, p. 83.
4. A. Kelin, 'Russia-NATO: A new era of cooperation?', *International Affairs (Moscow)*, 51:1 (2005), pp. 36–7.
5. Interfax interview with deputy foreign minister V.A.Chizhov, 31 March 2004, at http://www.ln.mid.ru/ (accessed 11 May 2004).
6. I. Korotchenko, 'Moscow awaits explanations from NATO', *Nezavisimoe voennoe obozrenie*, 18 July 2003.
7. 'Whom does Sergei Ivanov serve?', *Sovetskaya Rossiya*, 8 April 2004.
8. A. Roze, A. Terekhov, 'Sergei Ivanov "said nothing dramatic"', *Nezavisimaya gazeta*, 15 September 2005, p. 5.
9. E. Grigor'ev, 'Russia in NATO's strong grip', *Nezavisimoe voennoe obozrenie*, 26 March 2004.
10. N. Poroskov, 'A nuclear outpost', *Vremya novostei*, 7 July 2004.
11. 'Current tasks in the development of the Russian Federation Armed Forces', *Krasnaya zvezda*, 11 October 2003.
12. A. Arbatov, 'A matrix. Overload', *Profil'*, 13 October 2003, at http://www.arbatov.ru/news/upload/Profil.13.10.03-Web-1.htm (accessed 23 August 2005).
13. *Introduction to Security Council session*, Moscow, 31 October 2002, at http://www.kremlin.ru/text/appears/2002/10/29537.shtml (accessed 29 November 2005).
14. V. Mukhin, 'Russia defines its new defence orientation', *Nezavisimoe voennoe obozrenie*, 10 October 2003.
15. V. Solov'ev,' Our General Staff responds to NATO', *Nezavisimoe voennoe obozrenie*, 24 January 2003.
16. A.M. Golts and T.L. Putnam, 'State Militarism and Its Legacies', *International Security*, 29:2 (2004), pp. 128–9.
17. V. Solov'ev, V. Ivanov, 'General Staff again in dispute with defence ministry', *Nezavisimoe voennoe obozrenie*, 5 December 2003.
18. P. Zolotarev, 'Moscow plus NATO', *Nezavisimoe voennoe obozrenie*, 23 January 2004.
19. Danilov, 'Russia and European Security', p. 84.

20. Arbatov, 'A matrix. Overload'.
21. D. Trenin, 'Defence: the army and society', *Vedomosti*, 25 February 2004. See also V. Dvorkin, 'The impact of new global security challenges on the reform of the Russian Armed Forces', in A. Kaliadine and A. Arbatov (eds.), *Russia: Arms Control, Disarmament and International Security*, IMEMO supplement to the Russian edition of the SIPRI Yearbook 2004, Moscow, IMEMO 2005, p. 101, 103–4.
22. D.R. Hersping, 'Vladimir Putin and Military Reform in Russia', *European Security*, 14:1 (2005), p. 150.
23. See D. David, 'The cultural gap as a security problem', *Nezavisimaya gazeta*, 7 February 2004.
24. Press conference, 2 April 2004, at www.ln.mid.ru (accessed 11 May 2004).
25. Speech by Sergei Ivanov at the International Institute for Strategic Studies, London, 13 July 2004, at http://www.iiss.org/showdocument.php?docID=402 (accessed 10 September 2004).
26. 'NATO and Russia move forward on interoperability', *NATO Update*, 10 June 2005, at http://www.nato.int/docu/update/2005/06-june/e0610a.htm (accessed 7 July 2005).
27. Text at http://europa.eu.int/comm/external_relations/russia/summit_30_10_00/stat_secu_en.htm (accessed 22 June 2004).
28. D. Lynch, *Russia faces Europe*, Chaillot Paper No. 60, EU Institute for Security Studies, May 2003, p. 68.
29. D. Danilov, 'The Russia-EU common external security space: ambitions and reality', *Mirovaya ekonomika i mezhdunarodnye otnosheniya*, 2 (2005), p. 40.
30. V. Chizhov, 'Russia-EU Cooperation: The Foreign Policy Dimension', *International Affairs (Moscow)*, 51:5 (2005), p. 137.
31. 'Road map for the common space of external security', pp. 42–3, at http://www.europa.eu.int/comm/external_relations/russia/summit_05_05/finalroadmaps.pdf#es (accessed 6 June 2005).
32. M. Diehl, 'The Importance of Domestic Reform and Control of the Russian Armed Forces for the Successful Development of Military Cooperation with NATO/EU and NATO/EU Members ', *European Security*, 12:2 (2003), pp. 77–84.
33. Speech on 24 June 2005, at http://www.nato.int/docu/speech/2005/s050624a.htm (accessed 23 September 2005).
34. 'Road map for the common space of external security', p. 37.
35. See *Russia and the EU: Brothers in arms?*, Committee 'Russia in a United Europe', Moscow 2003, at http://www.rue.ru/Bratja.pdf (accessed 1 May 2004); V. Rubanov, 'Outlook for Cooperation Between the Defense and Industrial Complexes of Russia and the NATO Countries', in R.E.Hunter, S.M.Rogov (eds.), *Engaging Russia as Partner and Participant*, RAND National Security Research Division, 2004, pp. 51–66.
36. See S. Oznobishchev, 'NATO enlargement and the prospects for the CFE Treaty', in *Russia: Arms Control, Disarmament and International Security*, pp. 76–81.
37. See D. Trenin, *Russia, the EU and the common neighbourhood*, Centre for European Reform essay, September 2005, p. 6.
38. V. Chernov, A. Mazur, 'CFE Treaty: Russia Has Travelled Its Part of the Road', *International Affairs (Moscow)*, 51:1 (2005), pp. 82–3.
39. See H. Riecke, 'The Need for Change', *NATO Review*, Spring 2005.
40. *European security: does it include a place for Russia?*, Committee 'Russia in a United Europe', Moscow 2002, at http://www.rue.ru/6.pdf, p. 19 (accessed 21 October 2003).
41. G. Herd and E. Akerman, 'Russian Strategic Realignment in the Post-Post Cold War Era?', Security Dialogue, 33:3 (2002), pp. 219–34.

42. Yu. Dolinskii, 'Aleksei Pushkov: Only a strong Russia will be reckoned with', *Trud*, 12 May 2005, p. 2.

43. 'Address to the Federal Assembly of the Russian Federation', Moscow, 25 April 2005, at http://president.kremlin.ru/text/appears/2005/04/87049.shtml (accessed 23 May 2005).

44. 'Russian defence minister Sergei Ivanov: If necessary we will carry out preventive strikes', *Komsomol'skaya Pravda*, 26 October 2004.

45. 'Moscow's *Realpolitik*: Moscow withdraws into the post-Soviet space', *Nezavisimaya gazeta*, 9 February 2004.

PART 2

EUROPE LOOKING EAST

7

THE EUROPEAN UNION'S POLICY ON RUSSIA: RHETORIC OR REALITY?

Jackie Gower

Introduction

In 1999 Javier Solana, the European Union (EU)'s newly appointed High Representative for the Common Foreign and Security Policy (CFSP), described developing a partnership with Russia as 'the most important, the most urgent and the most challenging task that the European Union faces at the beginning of the 21st Century'.[1] It has also proved the greatest test of its credibility as a foreign policy actor, raising critical questions about its capacity for coherent and effective action. Although it has aspirations to play a global role, it is in Europe that the EU's most immediate interests and ambitions lie and Russia is recognized as the other key player on the continent. It is the EU's largest neighbour both in terms of population and territory and has immense reserves of natural resources, including oil and gas. Despite its loss of 'superpower' status, it is still a major military power in both conventional and nuclear terms and remains a key actor at the global level with a permanent seat on the UN Security Council (UNSC) and membership of the Group of Eight (G8). It has strong interests and significant influence in regions central to the EU's security, such as eastern Europe, the Middle East, the Balkans and Central Asia. The long common border means that cooperation with Russia is extremely important in tackling soft security threats such as illegal immigration, international crime, terrorism, nuclear accidents and environmental pollution. Russia is also an increasingly important trading partner with a potentially large and growing market (see Chapter 14). Although in statistical terms the trading relationship might seem more important for Russia than for the EU, accounting for over 50 per cent of its trade in 2004 compared to only 6.3 per cent of the EU's external trade,[2] the preponderance of oil and gas in the EU's imports from Russia make it absolutely central to its strategy to achieve security of energy supplies.[3] Russia is the single most important external supplier of natural gas, accounting for 50 per cent of total imports into the EU25. It also accounts for 25 per cent of the EU's imports of crude oil which represents a steady increase since 2000 in both absolute terms and market share.[4] Energy alone would ensure that good relations with Russia was a key priority for the EU and for some member states it is probably the overriding consideration. But the EU has ambitions to establish more than just a stable trading regime with Russia: it recognizes for the reasons that have been discussed above, that Russia is an important potential partner in a much broader policy agenda.

For over a decade it has actively pursued an ambitious policy aimed at establishing a 'strategic partnership' with Russia based on shared values but there has been disappointingly little in the way of concrete results. In 2004 all the EU institutions (Council, Commission and Parliament) were involved in a comprehensive and refreshingly self-critical review of both the content and conduct of EU policy towards Russia.[5] The European Parliament (EP) concluded that 'the gap between the rhetoric and reality has widened.'[6] It is clear that one of the problems is that Russia has not gone through the kind of transition, namely towards a stable liberal democracy and market economy, which had been the key assumption on which the EU's strategy had been based.[7] One of the most disappointing conclusions is that the EU has had very little influence over domestic developments in Russia, in marked contrast to the leverage it has exerted in relation to the countries of central and eastern Europe (CEE), and indeed Turkey. The essential difference, of course, is that Russia is one of the very few European states that has no aspiration for EU accession and the limitations that fact places on the EU's capacity to pursue its normative agenda are only slowly being appreciated in Brussels. But it is not only the policy strategy that is being reassessed. It is also widely conceded by those who have been most intimately involved in the conduct of EU-Russian relations that the EU has often failed to coordinate its policy effectively or to speak with one voice in its dealings with Russia.[8] The reasons for this failure lie in the unique characteristics of the EU's foreign policy system involving a complex interrelationship not only between the three institutions that constitute 'Brussels' (Council, Commission and Parliament) but also the 25 member states which continue to conduct bilateral relations with Russia. This results in a complex multilevel game with at least the possibility for member states to pursue different priorities if not different objectives depending on whether they are conducting policy at the bilateral or EU level. It is also clear that there can be significant differences within the EU's institutions as well as between them. In analysing the EU's relations with Russia it would therefore be misleading to present the EU as a unitary actor. As White has argued, it is more appropriate to analyse the EU as a 'non-unitary or disaggregated entity in world politics.'[9] This chapter will therefore first outline briefly the institutional and political characteristics of the EU foreign policy system and attempt to 'disaggregate' the EU by identifying the main foreign policy actors. The evolution of EU policy towards Russia will then be traced and the prospects for the future assessed.

The EU's Foreign Policy System

One of the reasons that the relationship with Russia is so complex is that it spans all three of the 'pillars' which constitute the EU created by the Maastricht Treaty. Under the second pillar, the common foreign and security policy (CFSP) covers general political relations, dialogue on a wide range of international issues and some limited but potentially increasingly important cooperation in relation to security and defence (ESDP). However, if analysis of the EU's interaction with Russia was restricted to this rather narrow concept of 'foreign policy', many of the most intensive and potentially productive areas of cooperation would be missed. Trade, economic cooperation, aid and technical assistance, the single market, the environment, energy, transport and trans-European networks, research and development, education and culture and visas all come under the first pillar, the European Community (EC) established by the Treaty of Rome. These are all areas where both Russia and the EU are likely to perceive at least a degree of interdependence and where cooperation can bring tangible rewards. The same is true of the increasingly important cooperation between the EU and Russia's police and judicial authorities on issues such as cross-border crime and international terrorism which fall under the third pillar. However, in most of these policy areas the treaties do not give the EU exclusive competence and member states therefore may legitimately pursue bilateral initiatives and continue to conduct their 'own' policies towards Russia. Karen Smith's definition of the EU as 'a foreign policy system, composed of the three pillars as well as the member states' foreign policies'[10] is therefore the most useful for analysing the rich mosaic of EU-Russia relations. It also means that the 'foreign policy system' is as much to do with negotiations within and between the EU institutions as it is with direct dealings with third parties.

The significance of the pillar system is that it means that different decision-making procedures apply in different policy areas, with the 'community method' used in the first pillar while intergovernmentalism prevails in the second and third pillars. One of the most important consequences is that different EU institutions take the lead in the formulation, articulation and implementation of different aspects of EU policy towards Russia. So in Brussels responsibility is divided between the Council Secretariat headed by the High Representative for the CFSP, Javier Solana, working closely with the rotating Council Presidency, and several Commission directorates-general (DGs) loosely coordinated by the Commissioner for External Relations, Benita Ferrero-Waldner. The Council Presidency and the High Representative for the CFSP take the lead on political dialogue and ESDP issues while the President of the Commission and the relevant Commissioners lead on first pillar matters. At EU-Russia summits this is graphically illustrated by the fact that the EU is represented by the Prime Minister of the member state holding the Council Presidency, the High Representative for the CFSP and the President of the Commission. There is no 'opposite number' for Putin to relate to and establish an ongoing working relationship, let alone the close personal friendships that have been the hallmark of bilateral relations with the leaders of some member states. The system of the rotating Council Presidency means that at every EU-Russia summit, there is a different head of government leading the EU delegation.

A further recognized weakness of the diffusion of policy responsibility among the different EU institutions is the difficulty of ensuring effective coordination and 'speaking with one voice' in negotiations with Russia across a wide range of policy areas. In a House of Lords Select Committee inquiry on EU-Russia relations it was noted that 'different aspects of the relationship tended to be dealt with in separate compartments within the EU' and 'the division of views and competences between the Council of Ministers and the Commission, and differing responsibilities within creates problems for EU/Russian relations.'[11] It strongly recommended the creation of a Russia Office within the Commission headed by an official at a sufficiently high level to act as a 'progress chaser' and give EU policy greater clarity and consistency.[12] If the Constitutional Treaty is ever adopted, the appointment of an EU Foreign Minister who is also a Commission vice-president might go some way to resolving the problem, which is by no means unique to the EU-Russia policy area. However, although institutional reform might improve the coordination of policy presentation and implementation, the fundamental problems of a policymaking process involving continuous negotiation between so many distinct actors would remain. This not only undermines the EU's effectiveness and ability 'to interact strategically with Moscow'[13]; it may also make it vulnerable to Russian tactics of 'divide and rule.' Although there have been frequent claims that the Russian authorities find the EU system complex and confusing, Lynch reports that some EU officials believe that in recent years they have become adroit at exploiting it for their own purposes, 'playing various levels of the organisation off against each other − the Commission and the Council, the Presidency foreign ministry and EU bodies.'[14] It is therefore important to identify the various actors and the levels at which they operate in order to understand how the EU foreign policy system works.

The Main Foreign Policy Actors

The Commission

The Commission is actively engaged in all aspects of EU-Russia relations both in Brussels and in Moscow where it has a sizeable delegation. This is true not only in relation to first pillar policy areas where it has the exclusive right of initiative and direct responsibility for policy implementation, but also the CFSP where it participates at all levels of policy planning and is closely associated with the Presidency Troika.[15] Indeed, it is important to note that almost all of the policy instruments available to the Council for pursuing CFSP objectives are actually exercised through the Commission directorates-general (DGs) and the delegation in Russia, for example, trade agreements and sanctions, democracy promotion projects, technical assistance, educational and cultural exchanges and cross-border cooperation initiatives. This not only means the Commission has a great deal of 'on the ground' information and experience which it can contribute to the internal EU policymaking process but also from Russia's perspective is most often the 'face' presented by the Union in its bilateral contacts.

Although DG External Relations takes the lead in terms of overall strategy and coordination, many other DGs also have significant responsibilities in relation to Russia, including Economic and Financial Affairs; Trade; Internal Market; Transport and Energy; Freedom, Security and Justice; Environment; Education and Culture. There are therefore a significant number of Commissioners and their staff who have a stake in EU-Russia relations and have regular contact with Russian officials although only a few of them work on Russia exclusively. Inevitably there have been suggestions that at times different agendas or at least different priorities have been pursued by individual DGs and the coordinating role assigned to External Relations has not always worked effectively.[16] In some cases the staff involved in detailed negotiations with their Russian counterparts have adopted a problem-solving approach to what they regard as technical issues and been frustrated by what they see as their 'politicisation' by other actors. Others have regarded the *acquis* as sacrosanct and been unwilling to consider a more 'flexible' approach to meet wider political goals. Furthermore, Commission officials working in Russia itself either at the delegation headquarters in Moscow or at local Technical Assistance for the Commonwealth of Independent States (TACIS) support offices in major centres such as St Petersburg, Kaliningrad, Rostov on Don and Ekaterinburg may have a different perspective from colleagues in Brussels. The conclusion, therefore, is that while the Commission is one of the key actors in the formulation and implementation of policy towards Russia, it would be a mistake to regard it as a homogeneous institution.

The Council

The Council framework is where the representatives of the member states meet together to agree to the overall strategy of EU-Russia policy as well as the details of specific policy briefs. They meet in different formations and at different levels: the European Council with the heads of state and government; the General Affairs and External Relations Council with foreign ministers; sectoral Councils such as Economic and Financial Affairs and Transport, Telecommunications and Energy with the relevant ministers; the Committee of Permanent Representatives, the Eastern Europe and Central Asia Working Group and the Political and Security Committee with senior officials; and dozens of Council working groups involving national civil servants and diplomats. In many of the first pillar policy areas decisions are taken on the basis of a qualified majority vote (QMV) but in CFSP and ESDP areas consensus is generally required. What this means in practice is that representatives of the member states are engaged in a continuous process of negotiations among themselves on a whole range of issues concerning Russia. Once a common position has been agreed, it leaves little room for flexibility in negotiations with Russia itself.

The work of the Council is supported by the *Council Secretariat*, which provides policy advice and expertise, particularly for the CFSP and ESDP aspects of EU-Russia policy. Its Secretary-General is now the *High Representative for the CFSP* who plays a pivotal role in the conduct of the EU's Russia policy as the only permanent member of the Council Troika. The other key actors are the head of government and foreign minister of the member state holding the *Council Presidency* although their level of activism depends on the level of importance Russia is afforded in their Presidency priorities. Most of the key initiatives have been either proposed or taken forward by a Presidency with a particular commitment to the development of the EU's Russia policy, such as the Northern Dimension launched by the Finns in 1999, the Common Strategy under the Germans at Cologne in 1999 and the provisions for Russian participation in ESDP actions under the French in 2000. When a Presidency is not particularly interested in Russia, summits tend to become more 'routine' and there is little sense of momentum. Finland will hold the Presidency again in the second half of 2006, followed by Germany in 2007, which could provide valuable momentum in negotiations on a successor to the Partnership and Cooperation Agreement (PCA).

The European Parliament

The formal powers of the EP in relation to foreign policy are quite modest, although it does have to give its assent to international agreements such as the PCA and can exert some leverage over TACIS through its control over the budget. Furthermore, both the Commission and the Council, through the Presidency, are required to report to the EP and these occasions afford the opportunity for Members of the European Parliament (MEPs) to express their opinion on any aspect of EU-Russia relations. The Committee on Foreign Affairs has also taken a keen interest in EU-Russia relations and produced a number of detailed and highly critical reports on EU policy, which it regards as ineffective and failing to achieve its objectives.[17] It assigns the major part of the blame on those member states who have not upheld the agreed EU line in their bilateral dealings with Russia and is pressing for 'a measure of public and parliamentary control' to be introduced to try to improve the situation.[18] Realistically, though, large member states are not going to worry unduly about negative comments from the EP.

Many MEPs have been very critical of political developments in Russia which they believe are leading her away from democracy, and those from the new member states have been particularly outspoken (see Chapter 12). The influence of these new members is expected to make the EP even more active in trying to press for a tougher line to be taken although there are a number of influential figures from states such as Germany who are urging more circumspection. The EP has also been the institution that has taken the strongest line in condemning Russia's policy in Chechnya, stressing that 'the massive human rights violations taking place there are an insurmountable obstacle to the enhancement of a genuine partnership between the EU and Russia.'[19] However, it is difficult to ascertain whether the EP actually manages to exert much influence. It is certainly taken seriously by the Commission but large member states in particular tend not to take much notice and generally its proceedings receive scant attention in the press.

The Member States

One of the key questions in the literature has always been whether member states regard EU foreign policy as a constraint on their freedom to pursue an independent bilateral policy or an opportunity to achieve national objectives through acting collectively.[20] With respect to the EU's policy on Russia, there is no evidence that any of the large member states have felt it is a constraint and both the EP and the Commission have repeatedly expressed their opposition to the way some of them have undermined agreed EU policy in their bilateral relations. By contrast, and for obvious reasons, many of the smaller member states have seen acting through the EU as an opportunity to exert (they hope) much more influence on Russia and even to achieve national objectives by 'Europeanising' them. This has been particularly true of Finland and the Baltic states who previously were constrained by their geographical proximity to Russia and feel able to be much 'bolder' now they are part of the EU. The importance of the role played by individual member states in determining the overall picture of EU-Russia relations is explicitly recognized by the inclusion of separate chapters in this section of the book on France, Germany and the new member states. So in this chapter, only brief reference to some of the other member states will be made.

The other two large member states –the UK and Italy – continue to pursue active bilateral policies although in the UK's case, it is generally close to the official EU line whereas Italian policy has often seemed at odds with it. Blair worked hard initially to establish a good personal relationship with Putin but his closeness to the US, especially over Iraq, inevitably had a negative impact. In these circumstances, it has been in the UK's interest to support a strong EU policy to try to counter the danger of France and Germany dominating relations with Russia and freezing out the UK. Berlusconi, by contrast, enjoyed a close personal friendship with Putin and was his most loyal defender in EU circles, most spectacularly by expressing his sympathy for his difficulties over the arrest of Mikhail Khodorkovsky, the Yukos affair and Chechnya at the press conference in Rome in 2003 during the Italian EU Presidency. But the Russian-Italian special relationship is much deeper rooted than just personal empathy between their current leaders with extensive and longstanding economic and cultural ties. This makes it highly likely that the special relationship will survive under Berlusconi's successor.

None of the other 'old' member states have a tradition of much interaction with Russia. The main exception is Finland which since its accession in 1995 has been very active in the development of the EU's policy towards its big neighbour. It proposed the concept of the Northern Dimension in 1997 and hopes to negotiate a new Action Plan during its 2006 Presidency. It also made a big contribution to the development of the EU's Common Strategy on Russia and continues to be one of the most active players in the formulation of policy. The new member states are already proving to be particularly vocal on EU-Russia relations both in the EP and in the Council but it remains to be seen how much influence they will be able to exert (see Chapter 12).

There is no reason to believe all 25 member states do not share the EU's policy objectives. Of course everyone would like to see Russia develop into a stable democracy where the rule of law and human rights are respected. It is only in the area of priorities that one may perhaps discern differences in positions and there is evidence that some member states may pursue different priorities depending on which level the 'game' is being played: normative at the EU level but more pragmatic and more driven by concerns about energy supplies or commercial advantages at the bilateral level. Katinka Barysch claims EU member states are 'happy to leave the difficult bits of the EU-Russia relationship to the Commission and other EU institutions, while reassuring Putin that it is ultimately the capitals rather than Brussels that call the shots in foreign policy'.[21] This undoubtedly has undermined the effectiveness of EU policy but may also go some way to explaining the motivation to develop an EU policy at all.

The Evolution of the EU's Policy on Russia

The Cautious Years

When in 1991 Russia became an independent state with a government avowedly committed to democracy and the market economy, the EU was faced with a policy challenge which it clearly had not anticipated and was ill-equipped to meet. Formal relations between the Union of Soviet Socialist Republics (USSR) and the EU had been established for the first time during the Gorbachev period and a modest trade and economic cooperation agreement had been concluded in 1989. Relations were therefore at a very early stage and there were very few people in the Commission with any expertise in relation to Russia. The initial reaction therefore was perhaps understandably rather cautious with an emphasis on the two traditional EC policy instruments: trade and aid.[22] The TACIS programme of technical assistance was established in 1991 and in October 1992 the member states decided to open negotiations with Russia for the conclusion of a PCA.[23] The decision to offer a PCA to Russia rather than an association or 'Europe' agreement like the countries of CEE marked a clear distinction even at this early stage between those states that were envisaged as potential EU members and those that were not. The assumption that Russia will almost certainly never become an EU member has remained the starting point for EU policy and accords with Russia's own objectives so in itself it does not cause any problems in the relationship (see Chapter 1). The same, however, cannot be said for the other core assumption on which the PCA was based: that partnership with Russia must be based explicitly on 'common values', which include democratic principles and human rights. As is discussed by Hiski Haukkala in his chapter, this has been a constant source of tension in the relationship.

Most of the articles of the PCA are concerned with economic and trade issues and are fairly modest in their scope and ambition. However, there is provision for examining 'whether circumstances allow the beginning of negotiations on the establishment of a free trade area'[24] which would represent a significant upgrading of the economic relationship. Apart from this, though, there was clearly no real idea how Russia was going to fit into the 'new Europe' that everyone was talking about in the immediate post-Cold War period. But the PCA did establish a fairly extensive institutional framework through which not only the technical work on the trade and economic agenda could be conducted but also a more general 'political dialogue' at ministerial, official and parliamentary levels.

The PCA did not come into force until December 1997 and the first couple of years of its operation were particularly inauspicious. The Russian government was increasingly unpredictable with President Yeltsin's failing health and a succession of weak Prime Ministers which meant there was no effective coordination or commitment on their side. After the Russian financial crash in August 1998 the idea of a free trade area was clearly not on the foreseeable agenda. The problems though were not seen as entirely caused by Russia. The EU was also acutely conscious that the CFSP initiated by the Maastricht Treaty had failed to live up to the high expectations of the early 1990s. In the Treaty of Amsterdam a new policy instrument, the Common Strategy, was introduced and it was decided that Russia should be the subject of its first use. The document therefore needs to be seen as much as a reflection of the EU's ambition to raise its game in the foreign policy arena as a realistic programme for developing its relationship with its important neighbour. In other words, as a piece of sublime rhetoric which would fail to deliver anything very significant in terms of actual substance.

However, the rhetoric was good and clearly went beyond the rather prosaic PCA with talk of the 'vision of the EU for its partnership with Russia':

A stable, democratic and prosperous Russia, firmly anchored in a united Europe free of new dividing lines, is essential to lasting peace on the continent. The issues that the whole continent faces can only be resolved through ever closer cooperation between Russia and the European Union. The European Union welcomes Russia's return to its rightful place in the European family in a spirit of friendship, cooperation, fair accommodation of interest, and on the foundation of shared values enshrined in the common heritage of European civilization.[25]

The 'vision' was clearly inspired by the 'common European home' paradigm, with Russia, like the prodigal son, renouncing its 'deviance' and becoming more and more like the other members of the 'family'. But what is striking in the Common Strategy is that the EU is not just making partnership with Russia conditional on its adherence to shared values (as is the case in the PCA) but actually sets out as one of its own principal objectives 'the consolidation of democracy, the rule of law and public institutions in Russia'. The other objectives also indicate a much more ambitious and broader agenda of cooperation that crosses all three of the pillars, with proposals for developing 'a permanent policy and security dialogue' not only on Europe but in other parts of the world and 'stepping up their cooperation in the fight against common scourges, such as organised crime, money-laundering, illegal trafficking in human beings and drug trafficking.'[26] The overall tone as well as the content is thus much more political than the economics-dominated PCA but it was not intended to replace it as the framework for the conduct of relations with Russia. Although it was published, its primary purpose was to serve as an internal document to try to improve the coherence and effectiveness of the EU's approach towards Russia.[27] It was hoped that by bringing together in one document, like a kind of 'inventory', all the forms of cooperation and instruments available through both the Union and the member states, it might help to overcome one of the core problems of the EU's foreign policy identified earlier. However, unfortunately, it ended up being a classic example of the difficulty in negotiating a common EU position. Javier Solana, in a confidential report to the Council on the operation of the common strategies, said:

> The wide scope of the Common Strategy and the particular, sometimes detailed concerns of individual Member States resulted in a 'Christmas tree' approach based on the 'lowest common denominator' where Member States and the Commission insisted on covering all possible aspects of relations, including so many different issues in the Common Strategy that in the end it became difficult to distinguish priorities from questions of secondary importance.[28]

The lack of clear priorities was the greatest weakness of the Common Strategy because it allowed it to become the victim of another of the institutional weaknesses of the EU's foreign policy system: the rotating Council Presidency. The main mechanism for the implementation of the Common Strategy was to be a 'work plan' prepared by each incoming Presidency, which meant that the priorities could change every six months. Probably even more damaging, some member states were clearly less interested in Russia and so made it a low priority on their Presidency agenda. Solana complained that they were often 'routine exercises to which little attention is paid'.[29] Enthusiasm for Common Strategies in general quickly dissipated amid a consensus that all they did was to raise high expectations without significantly increasing the EU's capacity for effectiveness. The Common Strategy on Russia expired in 2003, was renewed for one year and then unceremoniously buried. However, one lesson that seems to have been learnt from the experience was that a genuine 'strategic partnership' with Russia needs to be negotiated with her rather than unilaterally proclaimed. It was widely resented in Russian circles that the EU should adopt a strategy 'on' Russia rather than developing one 'with' her. The adoption by Russia of its own Medium Term Strategy in the autumn of 1999 was a positive signal that Russia was beginning to show more interest in developing a more substantial relationship with the EU.[30]

The Optimistic Years

Although the two Strategies in themselves did not lead to a significant upgrading of the relationship between the EU and Russia, they did contribute to raising its profile and generating expectations of further initiatives. Furthermore, a number of other factors helped to make the period 1999–2001 more favourable for the development of the relationship and offered a window of opportunity for real progress to be made. The appointment of Vladimir Putin as Yeltsin's last Prime Minister and his subsequent election as his successor was initially seen as very positive and for reasons discussed in other chapters, there was a qualitative change in Russia's EU policy both in terms of political content and administrative effectiveness.[31] The EU's decision to launch the ESDP opened up new possibilities for EU-Russia cooperation in the security arena (see Chapter 15). The economic recovery of Russia after the 1998 crash was also important in creating an atmosphere of greater confidence on both sides about the viability of Russia's integration into the wider European (and indeed global) economy. Economic interdependence was already a reality and would be increased when the countries of CEE became members of the EU. The prospect of enlargement added a sense of urgency to EU-Russian relations not only because it raised a number of substantial practical issues, but also because both parties were anxious to minimize the extent to which it would 'create new dividing lines across the continent.' Even the launch of the 'global war on terrorism' in September 2001 initially seemed to have a positive impact by offering a powerful incentive to develop more substantial police and judicial cooperation although in the longer term it tended to reinforce Russia's traditional prioritization of the relationship with the US.

Over the next three years, therefore, a number of initiatives were taken which seemed at the time to mark a qualitative leap in the EU-Russia relationship. In 1999 the Finnish Presidency successfully launched the Northern Dimension, which provides the framework for a number of concrete projects for cross-border cooperation in the Baltic region involving Russia. In 2000 the EU-Russia Action Plan on Combating Organised Crime[32] and the Energy Dialogue[33] were initiated. At the Nice European Council in December 2000 the EU member states agreed to the principles for 'stepping up the dialogue' on the arrangements for possible Russian participation in civilian and military crisis management operations under ESDP. [34] At the EU-Russia summit in May in 2001 it was decided to set up a high-level expert group 'to elaborate the concept of a common European economic space'. [35] At the time it was only seen to merit a single sentence in the *Joint Statement* issued at the end of the summit, but after the September 11 terrorist attacks on the US it became one of the main planks for intensifying the EU-Russia partnership. The summit in October 2001 marked a high point in EU-Russia relations with the *Joint Statement* proclaiming 'We are determined that relations between the EU and Russia should be given real impetus…We are resolved to take advantage of the momentum which has built up in order to intensify our cooperation and our strategic partnership. '[36] Commissioner Chris Patten and Deputy Russian Prime Minister Victor Khristenko were appointed to co-chair the high-level group charged with translating the vague concept of the common economic space (CES) into concrete measures to bring the EU and Russian economies closer together. Another high-level committee on energy cooperation was set up to take forward the proposals generated by the energy dialogue to create an energy partnership. There was also a *Joint Declaration on stepping up dialogue and cooperation on political and security matters*, which introduced the regular monthly meetings between the EU Political and Security Committee Troika and the Russian Ambassador to the EU which by all accounts has been one of the most useful forums for building mutual confidence. [37]

The Frustrating Years

Progress in translating these ambitious projects into concrete action was disappointingly slow and the gap between the rhetoric of the summit declarations and real achievements on the ground proved frustrating to both sides. One of the reasons was that as the date of EU enlargement came closer, the agenda at meetings at all levels was dominated by a number of very politically sensitive and difficult issues arising from Russia's concern about its consequences. Foremost was the question of transit of people and goods between the region of Kaliningrad and the rest of the Russian Federation once Lithuania and Estonia became EU members and had to apply the *acquis* in respect of border controls. The Russian negotiators were incensed by what they regarded as the inflexibility of the Commission in respect of the Schengen rules while the Commission complained that some member states were undermining the EU's collective bargaining position in their bilateral contacts with Russia. A compromise was finally agreed in November 2002 for a 'facilitated transport document' to be introduced rather than visas, with greater cooperation between the relevant authorities to try to make the system as straightforward as possible for legitimate travellers.[38] However, the Kaliningrad case only served to reinforce the Russians' resentment that EU enlargement would involve the imposition of new restrictions on their travel throughout CEE. President Putin's call for visa-free travel between Russia and the EU as a mark of their strategic partnership placed the EU on the defensive, sensitive to the charge of resurrecting the cold war divisions with a new 'paper curtain' of visas and border formalities.[39] The implications of the new EU external border for Russia's trade also became a major cause of contention and a large number of specific issues were the subject of detailed negotiations. The treatment of the large Russian-speaking minorities in Estonia and Latvia was also regularly raised by the Russians with accusations that the EU was applying double standards on human rights by not adhering to the Copenhagen criteria for accession. In some respects the quality of the meetings between Russian and EU officials was enhanced by the fact that at last the agenda involved concrete issues amenable to a problem-solving approach rather than endless grandiose declarations with no real impact. However, it was definitely not part of the EU's enlargement strategy for it to cause long-term strains in its relationship with its most important neighbour so there was a renewed sense of urgency to come up with a 'big idea' to reassure Russia that the intention was not to exclude her from Europe.

The Commission's original idea seems to have been to include Russia in its 'Wider Europe – Neighbourhood' initiative alongside not just fellow CIS states like Ukraine, Moldova and Belarus but also the EU's Mediterranean partners such as Algeria and Lebanon.[40] However, Russia made it clear that it regarded such a proposal as totally inappropriate for a state of its size and importance and insisted that it was only interested in a genuine strategic partnership between equals. Nevertheless, both parties had a strong interest in making the summit to be held in St Petersburg in May 2003 a great success: for Russia it was the three hundredth anniversary of the founding of the city as Peter's 'window on the west' and for the EU it was the first summit involving the leaders of all the 25 current and future member states after the signing of the Treaty of Accession the previous month. It was therefore decided to use the occasion to announce their intention to extend the common economic space (CES) concept to the other main areas of EU-Russia cooperation with a commitment to create common spaces in freedom, security and justice, external security and research and education. The 'St Petersburg four common spaces' was subsequently to become the paradigm for the long-term development of EU-Russia relations although precisely what was to fill those spaces was as yet unspecified. An important institutional reform was also agreed to strengthen cooperation; the rather ineffective Cooperation Council which had met annually at Foreign

Minister level would be transformed into a Permanent Partnership Council (PPC) which would meet more frequently and also in different formations such as energy, environment and justice and home affairs.

However, once again the optimism generated by the *Joint Statement* at the conclusion of what was described as the 'very fruitful meeting' was short-lived.[41] It soon became clear that the 'big idea' was still at the gestation stage and there was no agreement on what it really meant in concrete terms. Two more years were to pass before the promised 'road maps' were published and in the meantime EU-Russian relations went through an exceptionally difficult period with a protracted crisis over the extension of the PCA to the new member states only being resolved days before their accession on 1 May 2004.[42] Although not directly linked, this evidently helped to clear the path for the conclusion of the bilateral market access negotiations for Russia's accession to the World Trade Organization (WTO) at the following summit. However, President Putin in his welcoming speech made plain his frustration at the delays in creating the common spaces, which he claimed were 'already holding back joint projects in business, science and culture.'[43]

Negotiations dragged on for the rest of the year at endless working groups but nothing concrete seemed to materialize from them. One of the reasons was the unusually protracted period taken to confirm the appointment of the new EU Commission which led to a certain amount of drift on the EU's side. All hopes of a breakthrough at the autumn summit were dashed by the 'Orange Revolution' unfolding in Ukraine which brought EU- Russian relations to their nadir. The presence of EU representatives in Kiev directly engaged in the mediation of the disputed presidential election brought them into open competition in what Russia continues to consider her legitimate sphere of influence. The prominent role played by the Polish and Lithuanian governments in the Ukrainian crisis also reinforced Russia's fears that EU enlargement was impacting negatively on her geo-political interests. The exceptionally brief joint press release at the summit in The Hague indicated that in the prevailing icy atmosphere nothing substantive could be agreed.[44]

Towards a New Realism?

In the spring of 2005 both parties seem to have decided that the time had come for a fresh start and there was an intensive round of visits to Brussels and Moscow by ministers and senior officials in an attempt to break the deadlock. The reward came at the May summit in Moscow when a comprehensive package of road maps for each of the common spaces was finally agreed.[45] The President of the Commission, José Manuel Barroso, had expressed the hope in a pre-summit briefing that an agreement would 'revitalise the EU-Russia partnership giving it the tools it needs to meet the challenge of a new century.'[46] However, it was clear that all that had actually been achieved was the identification of a long list of possible areas for future cooperation and the challenge remained to turn the rhetoric into reality.

One early success may provide a model for a more realist approach based on identifying areas where there is a strong mutual interest in success. Two long-standing policy objectives in which both parties had a strong interest were explicitly linked: a visa-facilitation agreement which would ease the pain of the post-enlargement border regime and a readmission agreement which the EU regards as essential for its internal security. After a great deal of hard bargaining agreement was reached on both in time for the London summit in October 2005 and was seen as an important concrete achievement which would bring tangible benefits to people in both Russia and the EU. The summit also focused on strengthening cooperation in the energy field, another area where there is clearly strong mutual interests. The first Energy Permanent Partnership Council met the previous day with the objective of 'adding political impetus to EU-Russia energy cooperation.'[47] There was also a significant shift in the approach of both parties to the perennial issue of Chechnya. The Russians indicated a willingness to accept the Commission's offer of 20 million euros for assistance to the socio-economic recovery in the North Caucasus. Potentially, this could pave the way for the EU's active engagement with Russia in the region on a practical, constructive basis which might achieve more than the normative rhetoric of the past decade.

Conclusions: Prospects for the Future

So does the EU now have a clear and realistic policy for developing its relationship with Russia and does it have the capacity to deliver it effectively? Since the adoption of the road maps on the four common spaces it certainly does have a policy agenda. Furthermore, because they were negotiated with Russia and agreed jointly they represent a shared agenda which is a much better basis for developing cooperation than the unilaterally proclaimed objectives of the Common Strategy. They envisage constructive engagement through a process of continuous negotiations on a wide variety of issues which could bring tangible benefits to both Russian and EU citizens. However, the common spaces agenda does not really amount to a strategy: the 'road maps' are not really maps at all as they contain no indication of what the final destination might be nor the specific stages along the route. It would be more accurate to call them à la carte menus from which the EU and Russia could construct a gourmet meal of cooperation if they both had the appetite to do so. Clearly, if steady progress was to be made in creating the four spaces, it would go a long way towards creating the kind of 'greater Europe' to which Russia aspires and the stable and friendly neighbourhood which is the EU's goal. However, speculation as to whether the long-term objective is the creation of something akin to the European Economic Area (EEA) is premature. For Russia to establish as close a relationship with the EU as, say, Norway, will ultimately depend on it becoming a stable liberal democracy with a well-functioning market economy and respect for the rule of law. The recent trend of developments in Russia clearly does not make that a realistic prospect in the medium term and there seems to be evidence that the EU is coming to terms with the fact that it must deal with the Russia it faces rather than base its policy on the false assumption that it can mould it in its own image. Even the President of the Commission, the traditional self-appointed custodian of the EU's values, was prepared to describe the relationship as 'pragmatic and results-orientated' when commenting favourably on the outcome of the London summit in October 2005.[48]

The legal and institutional framework within which the EU-Russia relationship will be conducted in the future is still uncertain. The PCA expires in December 2007 but it has been agreed that it should remain valid until a new agreement enters into force to allow time for what are expected to be protracted and difficult negotiations on what should replace it.[49] It is not clear whether it will be merely revised to incorporate the policy and institutional developments that have been introduced over the past decade or replaced by a totally new agreement. Although the EU view is that the potential of the PCA has still not been fully realized, it is clearly the case that the circumstances today are very different from those in the early 1990s when it was originally drafted. Furthermore, once Russia has acceded to the WTO, a large part of the PCA will become redundant. The Commission is proposing that the agreement 'will adopt ambitious objectives' on political and external security cooperation, effective multilateralism, provisions on the fight against organized crime, WMDs, migration and asylum, and counter-terrorism.[50] It is also proposing that energy cooperation should be a key element in the new agreement based on the principles of 'reciprocity, fair and equal access and a level playing field' which will mean facing head-on the very difficult issues that have soured EU-Russian relations in recent months.[51] Also very difficult will be the negotiations on the 'Preamble' where the issue of common values will need to be addressed and some member states and the EP will want to see political conditionality strengthened. The hope is that the Council will reach agreement on the EU's common negotiating position by the end of 2006 so that negotiations with the Russians can begin in early 2007. However, it is likely to be a difficult and long-drawn out process, especially as any new treaty would need to be agreed and ratified by all the EU member states as well of course as Russia.

It seems almost certain therefore that the PCA will be extended on an annual basis for the foreseeable future, supplemented by the increasingly dense network of ad hoc committees, working groups and dialogues set up as and when the need arises. The system of PPCs is likely to be developed further with an Environment PPC due to be inaugurated in Helsinki in October 2006 and one for transport also planned. The hope is that the PPC might provide a more efficient way of conducting business and make the EU-Russia relationship less 'summit-driven' than in the past.[52] That in itself might reduce the propensity for grand rhetoric and increase the chance of concrete achievements. However, the EU is determined to resist Russian pressures to agree to the meetings being held at twenty-five plus one on the model of the NATO-Russia Council (NRC), insisting that the Troika will continue to represent the EU position. As former Commission President Romano Prodi said, the EU is willing to 'share everything except its institutions'[53] with its neighbours and there is no prospect of Russia being afforded even quasi-insider status.

Finally, has the EU managed to improve its own effectiveness as a foreign policy actor in relation to Russia? The uncertainty over the fate of the Constitutional Treaty has meant that two of the most important envisaged reforms (the appointment of a Union Foreign Minister and creation of an External Action Service) have not yet been implemented. Internal procedures, however, have been introduced to improve inter and intra-institutional coherence. One of the most important is the annual adoption by the General Affairs and External Relations Council of a document setting out the agreed common position or 'line to take' on key outstanding issues which is meant to be binding on all the EU institutions and member states in their relations with Russia. However, in the opinion of the EP's Committee on Foreign Affairs in May 2005 'this has not resulted in sufficient improvement' and there remains frustration at the way the large member states continue to pursue their bilateral agendas. Unfortunately, there seems no prospect of this problem becoming any less serious in the future as two of the issues that are expected to impact most severely on EU-Russian relations – gas and oil pipelines and Ukraine's aspirations for NATO and EU accession – will inevitably throw up into sharp relief divergent national interests. Therefore, although the EU's policy towards Russia does seem more rooted in reality and less prone to rhetoric than in the past, its capacity to deliver it effectively and coherently remains uncertain.

Notes and References

1. 'The EU-Russia Strategic Partnership', speech by Dr Javier Solana, Stockholm 13 October 1999.
2. EUROSTAT (Comext, statistical regime 4) contained in a report by DG Trade *EU Bilateral Trade and Trade with the World*, available at http://trade-info.cec.eu.int/doclib/docs/2005/july/tradoc_113440.pdf, accessed on 21.08.05.
3. A recent report from the Commission saw Russia as 'being in some ways the most promising – and geographically the closest – alternative to the Middle East as energy supplier for Europe', *Communication from the Commission to the Council and the European Parliament: The Energy Dialogue between the European Union and the Russian Federation between 2000 and 2004*, COM(2004) 777, Brussels 13.12.2004.
4. European Commission Staff Working Paper, *Energy Dialogue with Russia: Update on Progress*, SEC)2004)114, Brussels 28.1.2004.
5. *Communication from the Commission to the Council and the European Parliament on relations with Russia*, COM(2004)106, 9 February 2004 and *Report with a proposal for a European Parliament recommendation to the Council on EU-Russia relations*, Final A5-0053/2004, 2 February 2004. There was also a confidential assessment report on relations with Russia prepared for the Council by COEST (Eastern Europe and Central Asia Working Party).
6. *Report with a proposal*, 2004, p. 17.
7. *Ibid* p. 9.
8. This point was made strongly in all the reports cited above and also in the earlier Report of the House of Lords Select Committee on the European Union, *EU Russia Relations*, 17 December 2002.
9. Brian White, *Understanding European Foreign Policy* (Basingstoke, Palgrave, 2001) p. 29.
10. Karen Smith, *European Union Foreign Policy in a Changing World* (Cambridge, Polity, 2003), p. 2.
11. House of Lords, *EU Russia Relations*, paragraph 84.
12. *Ibid*, paragraph 13.
13. Dov Lynch, *Russia faces Europe*, Chaillot Papers No. 60, (Paris, Institute for Security Studies, 2003), p. 81.
14. *Ibid*, p. 78. Katinka Barysch makes a similar point that 'they seem to understand the EU well enough to turn its internal contradictions and complexities to Russia's advantage, through skilful 'divide and rule' tactics.' See her *The EU and Russia: Strategic partners or squabbling neighbours?* (London, Centre for European Reform, 2004) p. 53.
15. Ben Tonra and Thomas Christiansen, *Rethinking European Union Foreign Policy* (Manchester, Manchester University Press, 2004) p. 6.
16. Katinka Barysch claims the different DGs 'have long pursued their own Russia policies'. See *The EU and Russia*, p. 56.
17. European Parliament, *Report on the Implementation of the Common Strategy of the European Union on Russia*, (rapporteur Arie Oostlandr) Final A5-0363/2000, 29 November 2000; *Report with a proposal for a European Parliament recommendation to the Council on EU-Russia relations* (rapporteur Bastiaan Belder) Final A5-0053/2004, 2 February 2004; *Report on EU-Russia relations* (rapporteur Cecilia Malmström) Final A6-0135/2005, 4 May 2005.
18. European Parliament *Report on EU-Russia*, 2005, p. 4.
19. European Parliament *Report with a proposal*, 2004, p. 7.
20. See for example Ian Manners and Richard Whitman (eds.), *The Foreign Policies of European Union Member States* (Manchester, Manchester University Press, 2000)

21. Barysch, *The EU and Russia*, p. 54.
22. For a more detailed discussion of this early period, see Jackie Gower, 'Russia and the European Union' in Mark Webber (ed.) *Russia and Europe: Conflict or Cooperation?*, (Basingstoke, Macmillan, 2000).
23. 'Agreement on Partnership and Cooperation between the European Communities and their Member States and Russia', *Official Journal of the EC*, L327, 28 November 1997
24. *Ibid*, Article 3.
25. 'Common Strategy of the European Union on Russia', *Official Journal of the EC*, L157, 24 June 1999, p. 1.
26. *Ibid.*
27. Javier Solana in a confidential evaluation of the effectiveness of the common strategies lamented the fact that they had been published and recommended that in future they should be strictly internal policy documents. See Council of the European Union, *Common Strategies: Report by the Secretary-General/High Representative*, 14871/00, Brussels, 21 December 2000.
28. *Ibid*, p. 3,
29. *Ibid*, p. 4.
30. *Medium-term Strategy for Development of Relations between the Russian Federation and the European Union (2000–2010)*. An unofficial translation is available at http://europa.eu.int/comm/external_relations/russia/russian_medium_term_strategy/
31. See also Jackie Gower, 'Russian foreign policy towards the European Union' in Cameron Ross (ed.) *Russian Politics under Putin* (Manchester, Manchester University Press, 2004).
32. 'European Union Action Plan on Common Action for the Russian Federation on Combating Organised Crime', *Official Journal of the EC*, C 106, 13 April 2000.
33. EU-Russia Summit *Joint Declaration*, Paris, 30 October 2001.
34. European Council, *Presidency Conclusions*, Nice 7, 8 and 9 December 2000, Annex VI, 'Presidency Report on the European Security and Defence Policy.'
35. Russia-EU Summit *Joint Statement*, Moscow, 17 May 2001.
36. EU-Russia Summit *Joint Statement*, Brussels 3 October 2001
37. *Ibid*, Appendix 4.
38. *Tenth EU-Russia Summit, Joint Statement on Travel between the Kaliningrad Region and the Rest of the Russian Federation*, Brussels 11 November 2002. For further discussion of the Kaliningrad issue, see Jackie Gower 'EU-Russian Relations and the Eastern Enlargement: Integration or Isolation?' in *Perspectives on European Politics and Society*, 1:1, December 2000.
39. See *Through the Paper Curtain: Insiders and Outsiders in the New Europe*, edited by Julie Smith and Charles Jenkins, (London, Royal institute of International Affairs and Oxford, Blackwell Publishing, 2003).
40. Communication from the Commission to the Council and the European Parliament, 'Wider Europe- Neighbourhood: A New Framework for Relations with our Eastern and Southern Neighbours', COM(2003) 104 final, 11 March 2003.
41. EU-Russia Summit: *Joint Statement*, St Petersburg 31 May 2003.
42. It was finally agreed as part of a package of measures to meet Russia's concerns about the impact of enlargement. See *Joint Statement on EU Enlargement and EU-Russian Relations*, Luxembourg 27 April 2004, EU Council 8664/04 (Presse 122).
43. Mission of the Russian Federation to the European Communities, Press Release No 31/04, available at http://www.russiaeu.org, accessed on 22 May 2004.
44. Council of the European Union, *Fourteenth EU-Russia Summit, Joint Press Release*, The Hague, 25 November 2004.
45. The texts are available at http://europa.eu.int/comm/external_relations/russia/summit_05_05/finalroadmaps.pdf#ces

46. DG External Relations, *EU-Russia Relations*, Press Release, IP/05/522, Brussels 3 May 2005.
47. Joint EU Presidency and European Commission Press Release on the EU-Russia Permanent Partnership Council on Energy, 3 October, London, IP/05/1218, Brussels 3 October 2005.
48. *Joint Press Conference at EU-Russia Summit*, London, 5 October 2005, available at http://www.number-10.gov.uk/output/Page8258.asp accessed 8 October 2005.
49. EU-Russia Summit, *Joint Statement*, Sochi, 25 May 2006.
50. 'European Commission approves terms for negotiating new EU-Russia agreement', Press Release, IP/06/910, Brussels, 03 July 2006.
51. *Ibid.*
52. Tuomas Forsberg, 'The EU-Russia Security Partnership: Why the Opportunity was Missed', *European Foreign Affairs Review*,9:2 (2004), p. 254.
53. Romano Prodi, 'A Wider Europe – A Proximity Policy as the Key to Stability', Speech to the Sixth ECSA-World Conference, Brussels, 5–6 December, 2002.

8

THE ROLE OF NORMS AND VALUES IN THE EUROPEAN UNION'S RUSSIA POLICY

Hiski Haukkala

Introduction: Norms, Values, and EU Foreign Policy*

For the European Union (EU), the link between norms, values and foreign policy seems to be an obvious one. For example, the new Constitutional Treaty spells out the set of values on which the Union's external action is based: democracy, the rule of law, the universality and indivisibility of human rights and fundamental freedoms, respect for human dignity, the principles of equality and solidarity, and respect for the principles of the United Nations Charter and international law. In the treaty, the development of relations with third parties is made conditional upon sharing and upholding them.[1]

In its external action the Union thus wants to be seen as an essentially normative power.[2] This emphasis is understandable not only in the light of the EU's own history as a successful economic project based on political reconciliation between former deadly foes, but its current postmodern, or civilian power nature as well. Despite the recent and hectic work on the development of its military crisis-management capabilities, the Union still largely lacks the traditional (military) means of coercion, and is consequently forced to rely on 'softer' means for influence and persuasion instead.[3] Moreover, it needs to be stressed that this choice is not merely practical, reflecting the lack of means, but it also stems from the Union's self-conception (or identity) as a new and qualitatively different international actor that shuns away from traditional modes of 'power politics' and seeks to promote a 'rule-based international order' in its stead.[4]

In order to understand the current strong emphasis on norms and values in EU external action, one needs to keep in mind how the period of rapid development of its external capacities and competences (from 1991 to the present) has coincided with the end of the Cold War and the sea change in the perceptions concerning what are the legitimate building blocks for the emerging 'new world order'. Although the euphoric mood about the end of history has somewhat subsided, the fact remains that strict understandings of sovereignty as the foundation of the international order has lost some of their standing, and sovereignty has been made increasingly conditional upon upholding certain principles that mainly stem from the western/European strands of liberalism. A case in point is the work of the International Commission on Intervention and State Sovereignty (ICISS) whose initiative called 'Responsibility to Protect', although reiterating the centrality of sovereignty in principle, makes a case for making any state's sovereignty conditional upon its ability to protect its own citizens' security and well-being.[5]

Europe and the EU can be considered as laboratories for normative change in world politics. Even before the dissolution of the Soviet Union, steps were taken in Europe to change the 'rules of the game' on the continent. These ideas were expressed in the Charter of Paris for a New Europe in November 1990, which was endorsed by all the members of the Conference on Security and Cooperation in Europe (CSCE), including the already frail Soviet Union. The document – which remains one of the corner stones in the EU's current vision of international relations, especially in Europe – emphasized the role of peace, democracy, human rights, the rule of law and economic liberty as the guiding principles in the building of a 'New Europe.'[6] It also erased the clear distinction between the internal and external – domestic and foreign policies – by obligating all European countries to develop not only their mutual relations but also and primarily their domestic policies in line with these principles. Even if one removes the pompous wording of the document, one is faced with the fact that the Paris Charter represented a drastic break in the bipolar constellation in Europe, which had not merely been a contest of an economic or military kind, but one that had also had a strong normative, or ideological component to it. In short, the Paris Charter discredited the socialist experiment as a credible alternative to western modes of liberalism, the market economy and the democratic rights of individuals and consequently sounded the death-knell to the legitimacy and the very existence of the Soviet Union.

These principles and institutions also bind the Russian Federation as a successor state to the Soviet Union. Thus, and like veritable Gulliver's threads, the Organization for Security and Cooperation in Europe (OSCE), the Council of Europe, and most importantly for the purposes of this chapter, the Partnership and Cooperation Agreement (PCA) between the EU and Russia, form a web of overlapping and intertwining political, legal and moral commitments that act as the guiding principles and parameters for the evolving interaction between Russia and 'Europe'. But to be precise, the Gulliver metaphor is only partially correct, as although Russia is indeed bound by these norms and institutions, it is not so against her own wishes: throughout the 1990s Russia actively sought and promoted this normative entanglement by seeking membership of the Council of Europe and advocating a close 'strategic partnership' based on shared values with the EU.

This chapter focuses on one central factor in Russia's normative entanglement with Europe: its relationship with the EU. This is done mainly from the Union's vantage point. The chapter sets out to achieve two objectives. Firstly, it seeks to examine the normative basis – the role of norms and values – in the EU's Russia policy. The analysis that follows is based on a distinction between them where values are the higher order principles related to the conduct of both international and domestic politics in Europe whereas norms relate to more technical issues, such as pieces of Community legislation or standards and certificates. It is argued that taken together they form a normative framework, which in effect forms the parameters for Russia's interaction and even integration with (although perhaps not into) the European structures and especially the EU. Furthermore it is argued that the function of norms and values as such parameters are a source of increasing friction between the EU and Russia, as Moscow has started to challenge both the appropriateness and the legitimacy of these principles for its own future development.

The Normative Framework of the EU's Russia Policy

Analysing the Union's policy framework on Russia is no simple task. Like the EU's external and foreign policies in general, it, too, is a product of two different processes, reflecting both the internal dynamism of and the external pressures on the Union. Thus on the one hand the internal dynamics of the Union, such as enlargement and the recent drive towards increased competences and capacities in the field of external action, shape the EU's ability to engage itself with third parties in the first place, while also affecting the menu of issues in which the Union is interested.[7] On the other hand, the current framework also reflects the external dynamism of, firstly, the EU–Russia interaction where Russia's own development and policies are a factor in their own right and, secondly, the wider currents of global politics, where events such as the 9/11 attacks and the US war on terror have left their mark on the agenda.

As a consequence, the Union's Russia policy is an intricate mix of different levels and instruments. Firstly, and primarily, it is based on the bilateral PCA that the EU concluded with the Russian Federation in June 1994.[8] Secondly, it is – or has been – based on a host of varying internal documents and mechanisms, such as the EU's Common Strategy on Russia (1999–2004), the

Commission's country strategy papers and indicative national programmes (2002 onwards), the Technical Assistance for the Commonwealth of Independent States (TACIS) programme (since 1991), and the Northern Dimension initiative (1999, still on-going). Thirdly, in recent years we have witnessed the mushrooming of cooperation into new issue-areas not originally envisaged in the PCA. This has been reflected primarily in the so-called high-level dialogues on energy and the common European economic space (CEES) (since 2000 and 2001, respectively) that were combined and elevated into the concept of four common spaces (a common economic space (CES); freedom, justice and security; external security; research and education) at the EU–Russia summit in St. Petersburg in May 2003. These bilateral initiatives form an additional layer of joint EU–Russia mechanisms on top of the institutional framework laid out in the PCA.

This is not, however, what makes the EU unique as any international actor would have its own internal mechanisms as well as the interfaces and legal instruments through which foreign relations are managed on a bi- or multilateral level. By contrast, the EU's *sui generis* character stems from two additional sources: from its civilian, or normative, power nature, which has resulted in a strong emphasis on norms and values in its external relations, and from the intricate multilevel game *within* the Union between 'Brussels' (the Commission, the Council and the European Parliament) and the member states. This is more than bureaucratic politics; it is a mix of intergovernmental bargaining and supranational decision-making that often results in a rather 'messy' policymaking environment and, inevitably, slow, reactive, incoherent, and sub-optimal policies.[9]

It is the first characteristic of the Union – the primacy of norms and values in its Russia policy – that is discussed here in an attempt to throw light on the content of the normative agenda, which has often received surprisingly scant attention even in the civilian power debate.[10] The second level is another, equally important factor in explaining the problems in EU's Russia policy but only a few short comments on that problematic will be given later (see Chapter 7 for a more extensive discussion).

Before proceeding in our analysis, an important conceptual distinction has to be made. By norms we mean a set of fairly technical standards that relate mainly to the realm of economic activities. These norms are mainly derived from the EU's *acquis communautaire* and they are used in varying degrees as both models and yardsticks against which the convergence of third parties with EU legislation and consequently the level and depth of market access is assessed. Being a highly developed legal animal (although not yet an entity), the EU seems to experience grave difficulties in dealing with actors and partners that do not operate under a similar logic to its own. This has resulted in a drive to promote convergence on the level of (Community) norms with third parties.

The clearest example of this approach is of course the accession process but also the recent European Neighbourhood Policy (ENP) is based on the same logic.[11] What is interesting, however, is that the EU seems to be insisting on this objective even in situations when EU accession is not on the cards. In this respect, the Union's Russia policy is no exception but a part of the overall tendency in European foreign policy.

By contrast, values are higher order normative principles that relate to the very foundation and existence of the relationship. For the EU the existence of a set of shared values with its partners in general and in this case with Russia in particular has two functions: on one hand they act as the very foundation and prerequisite on which the relationship rests in the first place but on the other they act, in addition and above the norms just discussed, as the benchmarks against which the future breadth and depth of interaction is measured. It is here, that the primary modus operandi of EU foreign policy and external relations, political conditionality, enters the picture.[12]

Taken together, norms and values form the normative framework of the EU's Russia policy. The relationship between them can be summed up by saying that norms equal the concrete 'rules of the game' *within* the game that is based on the (assumption of) shared values.[13] This basic distinction is reflected in all the present EU external agreements and the PCA with Russia is no exception.[14] The preamble of the treaty makes numerous references to 'common values'.[15] However, the main article in this respect is Article 2, which codifies the primacy of common values as the foundation of the partnership as follows: 'Respect for democratic principles and human rights as defined in particular in the Helsinki Final Act and the Charter of Paris for a New Europe, underpins the internal and external policies of the Parties and constitutes an essential element of partnership and of this Agreement'.[16] The rather cryptic reference to 'essential elements' stems from the fact that previously international law has not considered violations of human rights as grounds for the suspension or termination of treaties. Under the *Vienna Convention on the Law of Treaties* (1969), a treaty can only be suspended or terminated if the treaty so provides, or if 'material breaches' – such as a violation of a provision *essential* to the accomplishment of the object or purpose of the treaty – have taken place.[17] By insisting on establishing democracy and human rights as an 'essential' element of the PCA – as well as practically every other external agreement the EU has concluded since the end of the Cold War[18] – the EU has reserved itself a legal right to consider a breach of certain 'European values' as being sufficient to warrant the termination or suspension of the agreement. The essential clause is also to be found in the joint declaration appended to the PCA, which confirms that respect for human rights constitutes an essential element of the agreement.[19]

The notion of the centrality of norms in the relationship is derived from Article 55 of the PCA. After taking note of the overall importance of approximation of legislation in strengthening the economic links between the Union and Russia, the article unambiguously states, 'Russia shall endeavour to ensure that its legislation will be gradually made compatible with that of the Community'.[20] The article then lists the areas to which the approximation of laws shall extend, in particular: company law; banking law; company accounts and taxes; protection of workers at the workplace; financial services; rules of competition; public procurement; protection of health and life of humans, animals and plants; the environment; consumer protection; indirect taxation; customs law; technical rules and standards; nuclear laws and regulations; and transport.[21] In short, the obligation of legal approximation deals with practically all walks of life even remotely connected with the economy. In principle, however, the obligation is not confined to these issues alone, as the obligation refers to Russia's legislation in general and even the list just enumerated is not exhaustive but only highlights the issue-areas where *in particular* the process should move forward.

The Norms and Values in Practice

Taken together, the values and norms underlying the EU's approach to Russia are part and parcel of wider trends in the recent debate on 'good governance,' or the 'second wave' of political conditionality.[22] It is, however, important to note that these are both concepts that are mainly linked with a set of highly asymmetrical donor-recipient relationships. In fact, the strong emphasis on the export of norms and values and the political conditionality attached to it implies that the EU–Russia relationship – as it is envisaged in 'Brussels,' that is – can be seen not as a traditional international institution based on inter-state bargaining but as an essentially post-sovereign international institution that promotes one-sided transformation, harmonization and gradual integration, even assimilation, with the EU's norms and values, but not with its institutions.[23]

However, the Union's Russia policy does not take place in a vacuum but in intensive day-to-day interaction with the object/partner of the policy, the Russian Federation. It is within this interaction that the problems in the EU's approach have become visible, as the teacher/student roles built into the relationship do not gel well with Russia's own ideas about the relationship.[24] In fact, the Union's well-meant insistence on common values and normative convergence are seen as being overly intrusive and basically demanding Moscow's full capitulation in the face of Europe.

Consequently, politically the EU–Russia relationship has enjoyed a rather rocky ride that has repeatedly succumbed to crises of varying severity. Underlying this negative overall tendency is the fact that Russia has, until recently, perceived the EU as a fairly peripheral entity in political and security issues in Europe. This neglect has been based on a rather narrow and shallow understanding of the Union as primarily an economic bloc.[25] During Vladimir Putin's presidency this basic stance has, however, been significantly altered. A prominent Russian analyst has called this sea change Russia's 'Europe first' policy.[26] It seems clear that Putin has made the decision that the EU is after all a crucial player for Russia's interests, in at least two respects. First, it is a vehicle and partner with whom the rapid modernization and transformation of the Russian economy can take place. The EU is thus seen as an economic power to be reckoned with and one with whom Russia should seek a privileged trade relationship while using it as a channel to acquire foreign direct investments (FDIs), loans on beneficial terms and technical assistance. This would in turn enable Russia to acquire once again the great power status that she still covets.[27] Secondly, the EU is seen as a potential political ally in the re-ordering of the security architecture in Europe. It is seen as an organization with which Russia can, and indeed must, seek a privileged relationship not only in trade, but also, and perhaps increasingly, in political and security matters, too.[28]

The change in Russian perceptions and priorities concerning the EU has gone hand in hand with Russia's growing economic dependence on it. After the 'Big Bang' enlargement in May 2004, the Union represents over 50 per cent of Russia's total trade. The relationship is highly asymmetric with Russia representing a mere fraction of the EU's trade, around 7.8 per cent of imports and 4.7 per cent of exports, respectively.[29] This is, however, ameliorated by the fact that most of Russia's exports to the EU are hydrocarbons – oil and gas – strategic commodities on which the EU is highly dependent, currently satisfying over 20 per cent of its needs in imported fuel from Russia. One might suspect that the change in Russian priorities combined with the Union's growing economic leverage might give grounds for the EU to impose its normative policy more strongly on Russia. The reality has, however, shown things to be otherwise with persistent problems emerging on both sides of the normative agenda.

In terms of values, the biggest source of friction has been the second war in Chechnya. Already the first war (1994–6) dented Russia's image in this respect but since its inception in September 1999 the second campaign has put Russia's commitment to human rights into serious question and soured the overall mood in the EU–Russia relationship. The beginning phase of the campaign witnessed by far the severest EU–Russia crisis, with the Union threatening and even applying some small-scale economic sanctions on Russia during the spring 2000.[30] The Union's policy on Chechnya has, however, been far from consistent.

Already in spring 2000 we witnessed the crumbling of the EU's unified opposition to Russia's conduct. Some EU member states saw Vladimir Putin's rapid ascension to power as a window of opportunity to re-engage Russia and made bilateral overtures in blatant disregard of the commonly agreed political line on Russia and its conduct in Chechnya. In this respect the main culprits were the British Prime Minister, Tony Blair, and Chancellor Schröder of Germany. Since then the failure by especially the larger member states to toe the common line has become a mainstay of the Union's Russia policy with the President of France, Jacques Chirac, and the Prime Minister of Italy, Silvio Berlusconi, following suit.

To be fair, in the case of Chechnya the Union has been caught between a rock and a hard place. On the one hand the end-result of its attempted sanctions in spring 2000 bitterly demonstrated that as still a largely civilian power, the Union basically lacks the coercive instruments to effect change on Russia. Even the economic leverage the EU enjoys over Russia has been made largely redundant by the fact that it could not hit Moscow where it would have hurt it most – its exports – as they mainly consisted of hydrocarbons that the Union itself badly needed and which could have only been replaced with a significant risk and sacrifice on the part of the Union. Also the steadily rising oil prices on the world market have ensured that Russia's own coffers are robust enough so that it cannot be lured into changing its course by offering or withholding the fairly modest sums of technical assistance the EU is channelling into Russia. And finally, there has been a genuine concern on the EU's part that by pushing Russia too harshly over Chechnya the already turbulent country could be nudged towards increasing isolationism, which in turn could have unpredictable consequences for the country's future development and role in Europe.

The other side of the civilian power coin, persuasion and dialogue, has not proven very fruitful, either. This is due to the fact that the Union has been met with a resolve from Moscow and President Putin unknown during the first war and Yeltsin's presidency in general. This is largely due to the fact that the tragic events in Chechnya have formed a part of the overall drive for increased state-capacity-building and centralization of power in Russia during Putin's reign. The creation of a stronger Russian state has been the overriding priority of Putin's presidency. Although such measures were clearly justified at the turn of the millennium, the reining in of independent media, economic oligarchs, regional governors, political parties and to a certain extent even the still nascent civil society and NGOs have raised concerns as to whether Putin's hierarchical concentration of power is the appropriate solution to Russia's present woes and whether a 'values gap' between the country and the Euro-Atlantic community is emerging.[31] Increasingly also the Union's answer to the question seems to be affirmative with the most recent EU documents on Russia having all come to the same conclusion: Russia is no longer on a path of convergence towards European values but has departed along a path of its own.[32]

The role of norms in the EU's Russia policy has not fared much better. Russia's legislative approximation with the Union – an obligation Moscow took upon itself in Article 55 of the PCA – has been painstakingly slow with very little tangible progress in sight. What is more, recently Russia has started increasingly to question the very feasibility and legitimacy of this convergence, especially when one keeps in mind the fact that Russia is not aspiring to become a member of the Union.[33] The adoption of first the CEES and later the road maps for the four common spaces in May 2005 can be seen as attempts at 'operationalising' the rather monolithic and abstract obligation for Russia to harmonize its trade-related laws and rules with those of the EU *acquis*. In essence, they would seem to be attempts at generating a forward momentum in a process that has so far been disappointing, to say the least.

Despite these innovations the process has remained cumbersome. In this respect, the high-level dialogue on the adoption of the CEES between 2001 and 2003 is a telling example. The process was originally initiated in particular to make progress in achieving regulatory approximation and to consider the 'ultimate objectives' of the actual work to be done under the auspices of the CES.[34] In practice this would mean assessing the breadth and depth of the normative convergence and legal approximation between the Union and Russia in more concrete terms: what are the sectors of cooperation and the precise norms that would have to be adopted by Russia? After two years and several high-level meetings, the end result of the preparatory phase was summed up in the CEES concept paper adopted at the EU–Russia summit in Rome in November 2003. The document is remarkable only for its lack of visible progress when compared to the PCA almost a decade earlier: it was only agreed that the process would ultimately lead to the adoption of a CES, or 'an open and integrated market between the EU and Russia, based on the implementation of common or compatible rules and regulations, including compatible administrative practices' that 'shall ultimately cover substantially all sectors of the economy'.[35] For all intents and purposes, this merely reiterates what was already agreed in the PCA.

To be fair, the concept paper does envisage that the CEES will be broader and deeper in its scope compared to the PCA and World Trade Organization (WTO) regulations. Simultaneously, however, it fails to specify in practical terms how this would be achieved. Instead, the paper sets the process fairly strict parameters by insisting that it has to remain compatible with the parties' existing and future commitments within the WTO context.[36] It is, indeed, important to note that for the time being it is not necessarily the CES and the EU that will play the central role in integrating Russia into the system of free trade and global norms and regulations. As also the concept paper points out, for the moment it is the still ongoing and admittedly difficult negotiations for Russia's membership of the WTO that is the most important factor in this respect. One can say that until Russia's WTO membership is clear, the prospects for the CEES and eventual free trade between the EU and Russia are negligible. This is partly due to the fact that it is unlikely that Russia will have enough qualified civil servants to run two parallel processes that include intensive dialogue and negotiations of very technical issues of trade and economic cooperation.[37] Also, the EU has made this clear by arguing that the marching order is WTO membership first, and that only then will other institutional arrangements in the field of the economy be feasible. The EU stance is understandable and natural, as Russia's eventual WTO membership would require the country to make a host of domestic reforms that would automatically make Russia more compatible with EU rules and regulations as well, thus facilitating the creation of a CEES and the possible free trade area, too. For example, two Russian scholars have estimated that Russia has to make changes to about a thousand laws and regulations in order to comply with WTO rules.[38] This is a task that would make the CEES process with the EU much easier in the future.

Conclusions

This chapter has sought to analyse the normative framework of the EU's Russia policy. It has been argued that the European norms and values – as defined by the EU itself – act as a set of parameters against which Russia's post-Cold War rapprochement with 'EU-Europe' has been modelled and as benchmarks against which the progress the country has been able to achieve to date has been measured. From the EU's vantage point these norms and values are not to be negotiated; they are not optional extras but the very fabric of which efficient and modern (European) societies are made.

In essence, the EU is using its economic power and normative clout to build asymmetric post-sovereign institutions and relationships with its partners, Russia included. They are asymmetric in the sense that in exchange for deep-ranging structural, economic and societal reforms as well as adherence to a set of certain principles, the EU is willing to reciprocate by giving certain concessions and other benefits of a mainly economic nature to its partners. The benefits include increased access to the single market as well as loans, economic aid and technical assistance. They are post-sovereign in the sense that the Union is using its leverage to insist on domestic transformation from its partners that goes well beyond the remits of bargaining taking place within more traditional institutional arrangements. Despite this post-sovereign nature of the arrangements, it is important to take note of the fact that the EU itself is guarding its sovereignty and autonomy jealously. The content of the *acquis*, which is often the basis of the cooperation and partnership agreements as well as the new ENP action plans, is non-negotiable, and it is largely the Union that sets the parameters for interaction and integration unilaterally. As such, the EU's policy vis-à-vis Russia is closely reminiscent of the accession process with the important difference that full accession into the Union's institutions is not on the cards.

The Union's approach is Janus-faced, as it includes not only incentives but also the possibility of sanctions in case of non-compliance with the obligations. But despite making norms and values the essential clause in its external agreements, the EU has sought a rather cautious and moderate approach in its application. Usually the EU avoids a negative or punitive approach. Instead it seeks to 'promote dialogue and positive measures... and the prevention of crises through establishment of a consistent and long-term relationship.'[39] The Union's Russia policy is no exception. In fact, the EU has sought to make a virtue out of the necessity: as enforcement through sanctions has proven unrealistic, it has been deemed better to develop the relationship in a pragmatic manner in the hope of achieving some of the normative aims in the process. Vaughne Miller has summed up the approach by saying that the Union's decision to merely 'condemn Russia's actions in Chechnya rather than apply sanctions appears to be based on the aim of engagement through dialogue, rather than disengagement through sanctions.'[40] This approach is consistent with the EU's image as a civilian power: it is better to retain the dialogue and seek progress through positive incentives rather than resort to negative sanctions and punitive measures.[41]

But this 'pragmatic partnership', as Graham Timmins has dubbed it[42], comes with a price tag, and it is one that is equally steep for both parties concerned as well as to the development of their mutual 'strategic partnership'. For the EU, its ability to apply its norms and values consistently in the case of Russia has presented a litmus test for the credibility of its approach on international relations which it has clearly been failing. This has repercussions beyond the Union's Russia policy, especially in the so-called new post-enlargement neighbourhood. It can be asked, what are the Union's chances of promoting the same value-laden agenda through, for example, its ENP, if Russia is largely exempted from these principles and the conditionality they imply?

Although Russia would at first sight seem to be the winner in this process, this is not exactly the case. The gaps in the consistency of the EU's policy line that Russia has so carefully cultivated have undoubtedly enabled her to pocket some short-term tactical gains but by doing so she has also managed to derail the wider process of EU–Russia interaction. As a consequence, the 'strategic partnership' between the EU and Russia has largely failed to live up to the original promise and its potential has remained largely unrealized. This has meant that not only the Union has failed to achieve its original objectives vis-à-vis Russia, but also Russia has failed to reap the kind of economic and political benefits that were on offer at the beginning of the 1990s.

But the damage need not remain beyond repair. The reason for this stems paradoxically from the EU's own multifaceted foreign policy approach. The structured nature of interaction combined with the fairly rigid logic of the Union has resulted in a certain – although largely unintentional – self-correcting mechanism in the relationship: despite Russia's attempts at departing from the normative framework and the damage done by some member states by supporting her, the next EU–Russia summit is always around the corner with a chance for the 'machinery' in Brussels or a more stern Council presidency to re-assert the normative agenda and put the relationship back on track.

As a result, the EU–Russia relationship develops – and regresses – in fits and starts. It can, however, be questioned whether this is the most prudent way of developing a 'strategic' partnership between the two parties. Arguably it is not but the process has its merits as well. For the Union, the detours do not take the process forward, as the only way forward at the EU level is through the implementation of the normative agenda put forward by the Union and – it is worth reiterating – jointly agreed by the parties. As a consequence, there might be delays and deviations but at the end of the day the machinery takes the agenda back to its original course, possibly in new packaging. One needs only to take a brief glance at the evolution of Article 55 of the PCA through the CEES to the present concept of four common spaces in order to realize that they basically represent the same substance in slightly different format.

For Russia the story is different. It cannot be denied that the fact that Russia's adherence to the EU's normative framework is increasingly framed in legal terms speaks volumes about Russia's current lack of commitment to it. It also inadvertently reveals the problematic premises on which the Union's Russia policy is at present based. Yet the Union should be encouraged to stay the course and develop new ways through which it could continue, and even deepen Russia's normative entanglement with Europe. This is so, firstly, because the weight of the already existing normative entanglement with Europe puts Russia under a legal, political and moral obligation to deliver on its own choices and declarations. Secondly, there is more at stake for the Union than its Russia policy alone. The viability of its neighbourhood policy also hangs in the balance. If Russia is allowed to slide from the common principles, norms and values then the EU's credibility vis-à-vis the rest of its eastern neighbourhood could be seriously jeopardized.

Finally, one should also bear in mind that the reverse could be the case as well: If the ENP is made to work, then it is Russia that will increasingly be the odd one out in the Union's eastern neighbourhood. It is possible that in the coming years Russia will witness how Ukraine and Georgia – perhaps even Azerbaijan – will speed by Russia on the road to European integration via the ENP. This is a process that would not only eat away Russia's traditional sphere of influence but it would also slowly erode Russia's chances of resisting the pressure of normative entanglement. The EU seems to be aware of this, too, and it could be that it is simply willing to wait out its recalcitrant partner, relying on its immense and slow gravity to pull the laggard into line. It is thus quite likely that in due time Russia will also have to follow suit, or risk lagging behind and being marginalized in Europe in the future.

Notes and References

*   This article forms a part of ongoing work on a doctoral thesis, which is prepared under the auspices of the Graduate School of Cultural Interactions and Integration and the Baltic Sea Region at the University Turku and 'Russia's European Choice: With or Into the EU?' –project at the Finnish Institute of International Affairs in Helsinki. The project is part of the Finnish Academy's larger 'Russia in Flux' Research Programme 2004–2007. The author wishes to acknowledge the support he has received from all of these institutions.

1. See the *Treaty establishing a constitution for Europe*, Official Journal of the European Union, C310, volume 47, 16 December 2004, Title V, Chapter I, Article III-292.

2. See Ian Manners, 'Normative Power Europe: A Contradiction in Terms?', *Journal of Common Market Studies*, 40:2 (2002), pp. 235–58.

3. The original civilian power Europe argument was made in François Duchêne, 'The European Community and the Uncertainties of Interdependence' in M. Kohnstamm and W. Hager (eds.), *A Nation Writ Large? Foreign-Policy Problems before the European Community* (London and Basingstoke, Macmillan, 1973).

4. For a fuller exposition of this argument see Robert Cooper, *The Breaking of Nations. Order and Chaos in the Twenty-First Century* (London, Atlantic Books, 2003). Also the EU's own Security Strategy betrays this notion. See *A Secure Europe in a Better World. European Security Strategy*, passim, esp. pp. 1 and 10–11.

5. See ICISS, *The Responsibility to Protect. Report of the International Commission on Intervention and State Sovereignty* (Ottawa: International Development Research Center, December 2001), pp. 7–8. See also Gareth Evans and Mohamed Sahnoun, 'The Responsibility to Protect', *Foreign Affairs*, 81:6 (2002), pp. 99–110. About the roots of the concept, see Thomas G. Weiss, 'Governance, good governance and global governance: conceptual and actual challenges', *Third World Quarterly*, 21:5 (2000), pp. 795–814, p. 800. The homepages of ICISS are at http://www.iciss.ca/, accessed 18 April 2005.

6. *Charter of Paris for a New Europe*, CSCE 1990 Summit, Paris, 19–21 November 1990. Available at http://www.osce.org/docs/english/1990-1999/summits/paris90e.htm, accessed 17 March 2005.

7. For overviews concerning the process, see, for example, Roy Ginsberg, 'The Impact of Enlargement on the Role of the European Union in the World' in J. Redmond and G.

G. Rosenthal (eds.), *The Expanding European Union: Past, Present, Future* (Boulder and London, Lynne Rienner, 1998); and Roy Ginsberg, *Foreign Policy Actions of the European Community. The Politics of Scale* (Boulder and London, Lynne Rienner and Adamantine Press, 1989), pp. 151–2.

8. It entered into force for a period of ten years in December 1997.

9. Cf. John Peterson and Michael E. Smith, 'The EU as a Global Actor' in E. Bomberg and A. Stubb (eds.), *The European Union: How Does it Work?* (Oxford and New York, Oxford University Press, 2003); Fritz W. Scharpf, 'The Joint-Decision Trap: Lessons from German Federalism and European Integration', *Public Administration*, 66:3 (1988), pp. 239–78.

10. See, for example, Karen E. Smith, 'The End of Civilian Power EU: A Welcome Demise or Cause for Concern?', *The International Spectator*, XXXV:2 (2000), pp. 11–28; Adrian Treacher, 'From Civilian Power to Military Actor: The EU's Resistible Transformation', *European Foreign Affairs Review*, 9:1 (2004), pp. 49–66.; Richard G. Whitman, *From Civilian Power to Superpower? The International Identity of the European Union* (London and Basingstoke, Macmillan, 1998). Here I essentially agree with Manners who has complained that the 'Civilian Power Europe' debate has centered too much on the nature of that actorness (capabilities and the lack of them) while largely sidelining its (normative) content. Cf. Manners, 'Civilian Power Europe', p. 239.

11. About the logic of accession, see Graham Avery and Fraser Cameron, *The Enlargement of the European Union* (Sheffield, Sheffield Academic Press, 1998), pp. 32–3. About ENP, see Hiski Haukkala, *The EU as a Regional Normative Hegemon: The Case of European Neighbourhood Policy*, unpublished article manuscript under review for publication.

12. For more about conditionality in EU's external relations, see Karen E. Smith, 'The Use of Political Conditionality in the EU's Relations with Third Countries: How Effective?', *European Foreign Affairs Review*, 3:2 (1998), pp. 253–74; and Marcela Szymanski and Michael E. Smith, 'Coherence and Conditionality in European Foreign Policy: Negotiating the EU–Mexico Global Agreement', *Journal of Common Market Studies*, 43:1 (2005), pp. 171–92.

13. It should be stated that neither this article nor the writer assumes that the normative component is the only significant dimension in EU's Russia policy. Traditional (inter-state/actor) bargaining co-exists there as well and should be kept in mind. Inserting that factor into the equation is, however, beyond the aims of this chapter.

14. Richard Youngs, 'European Union Democracy Promotion Policies: Ten Years On', *European Foreign Affairs Review*, 6:3 (2001), pp. 355–73. For a comprehensive survey of EU external agreements and the role of human rights in them, see Vaughne Miller, *The Human Rights Clause in the EU's External Agreements*, House of Commons Research Paper 04/33, 16 April 2004.

15. *The Partnership and Cooperation Agreement* (hereafter PCA). Available at http://europa.eu.int/comm/external_relations/ceeca/pca/pca_russia.pdf, accessed 20 April 2005.

16. PCA, Title I, Article 2.

17. Miller, *The Human Rights Clause*, p. 11.

18. For an overview, see Youngs, 'European Union Democracy Promotion'. For more specific treatments of, for example, EU–Mexico and EU–Africa, Caribbean and Pacific (ACP) elations, see Szymanski and Smith, 'Coherence and Conditionality'; and Soile Kauranen and Henri Vogt, *Piilopoliittisuudesta poliittisuuteen: Afrikan, Karibian ja Tyynenmeren valtioiden ja Euroopan unionin yhteistyön kehitys*, FIIA Report 5/2003 (Helsinki, the Finnish Institute of International Affairs, 2003), respectively.

19. PCA, Joint declaration in relation to articles 2 and 107.

20. PCA, Title VI, Article 55.1.

21. PCA, Title VI, Article 55.2.

22. See Weiss, 'Governance, good governance and global governance'; Olav Stokke, 'Aid and Political Conditionality: Core Issues and State of the Art' in O. Stokke (ed.), *Aid and Political Conditionality* (London and Geneva, Frank Cass in association with the European Association of Development Research and Training Institutes EADI, 1995).

23. About more traditional international institutions, see Robert O. Keohane, *International Institutions and State Power: Essays in International Relations Theory* (Boulder, San Francisco and London, Westview Press, 1989); K. J. Holsti, *Taming the Sovereigns: Institutional Change in International Politics* (Cambridge and New York, Cambridge University Press, 2004). The same logic is to be found from the Union's new neighbourhood policy, which, in the words of the (then) Commission President Romano Prodi, is about sharing 'everything but institutions' with the Union's new neighbourhood. See Haukkala, *The EU as a Regional Normative Hegemon*.

24. About the teacher/student approach and Russia, see Christopher S. Browning, 'The Region-Building Approach Revisited: The Continued Othering of Russia in Discourses of Region-Building in the European North', *Geopolitics*, 8:1 (2003), pp. 45–71.

25. Vladimir Baranovsky, *Russia's Attitudes towards the EU: Foreign and Security Policy Aspects*. Programme on the Northern Dimension of the CFSP, No. 15 (Helsinki and Berlin, the Finnish Institute of International Affairs and Institut für Europäische Politik, 2002).

26. Sergei Karaganov, 'Russia and the international order' in D. Lynch (ed.), *What Russia sees*. Chaillot Paper No 74, January 2005 (Paris, European Union Institute for Security Studies, 2005), p. 34.

27. About Putin's agenda concerning Russia's modernisation, see Richard Sakwa, *Putin – Russia's Choice* (London and New York, Routledge, 2004).

28. Hiski Haukkala, 'A problematic "strategic partnership"' in D. Lynch (ed.), *EU-Russian security dimensions*. Occasional Paper No. 46, July 2003 (Paris, European Union Institute for Security Studies, 2003), p. 10; Timofei V. Bordachev, 'Strategy and Strategies' in A. Moshes (ed.), *Rethinking the Respective Strategies of Russia and the European Union*. Special FIIA–Carnegie Moscow Center Report (Helsinki and Moscow, the Finnish Institute of International Affairs and Carnegie Moscow Center, 2003). Russia's mid-term EU strategy betrays this notion as well, see 'Medium-term Strategy for Development of Relations between the Russian Federation and the European Union (2000–2010)', *Diplomaticheskii Vestnik*, No. 11, November 1999, pp. 20–8.

29. *Russia – EU bilateral trade and trade with the world*. DG Trade, 30 March 2005. Available at http://trade-info.cec.eu.int/doclib/html/113440.htm, accessed 2 May 2005.

30. The beginning phase of the conflict has been reconstructed and analysed in depth in Hiski Haukkala, 'The Making of the European Union's Common Strategy on Russia' in H. Haukkala and S. Medvedev (eds.), *The EU Common Strategy on Russia: Learning the Grammar of the CFSP*. Programme on the Northern Dimension of the CFSP, No. 11 (Helsinki and Berlin, the Finnish Institute of International Affairs and Institut für Europäische Politik, 2001), esp. pp. 51–62. An excellent analysis of EU's policy on Russia and Chechnya is Tuomas Forsberg and Graeme Herd, 'The EU, Human Rights, and the Russo-Chechen Conflict', *Political Science Quarterly*, 120:3 (2005), 455–78.

31. A term coined by the US Ambassador in Moscow, Alexander Vershbow. Quoted in Dov Lynch, 'Misperceptions and divergences' in D. Lynch (ed.), *What Russia sees*, p. 17.

32. See *Report with a proposal for a European Parliament recommendation to the Council on EU-Russia Relations*, Final a5-0053/2004, 2 February 2004; *Communication from the Commission to the Council and the European Parliament on relations with Russia*, COM(2004) 106, 9 February 2004.

33. Karaganov, 'Russia and the international order', p. 32; Bordachev 'Strategy and Strategies'.

34. See *Report of the High-Level Group on the common European economic space*. Tenth EU–Russia summit, Brussels, 11 November 2002. Available at http://www.europa.eu.int/comm/ external_relations/russia/summit_11_02/concl.htm, accessed 1 May 2005.

35. *The Common European Economic Space (CEES) Concept Paper*, III.12. EU–Russia summit, Rome, 6 November 2003, Joint Statement, Annex 1, 13990/03 (Presse 313). Available at http://www.europa.eu.int/comm/external_relations/russia/summit11_03/ 1concl.pdf, accessed 1 May 2005.

36. *Ibid.*, III.14.

37. Hiski Haukkala, 'What Went Right with the EU's Common Strategy on Russia?' in A. Moshes (ed.), *Rethinking the Respective Strategies*, p. 76.

38. S. Prikhodko and A. Pakhomov, *Problems and Prospects of Russia's Accession to WTO*. Russian-European Centre for Economic Policy (RECEP), Policy Paper Series, September 2001, p. 13.

39. *Ibid.* See also p. 29.

40. Miller, *The Human Rights Clause*, p. 47.

41. Karen E. Smith, 'The EU, Human Rights and Relations with Third Countries: "Foreign Policy" with an Ethical Dimension?' in K. E. Smith and M. Light (eds.), *Ethics and Foreign Policy* (Cambridge and New York, Cambridge University Press, 2001); see also Hanns W. Maull, 'German Foreign Policy, Post-Kosovo: Still a "Civilian Power"?', *German Politics*, 9:2 (2000), pp. 1–24.

42. Graham Timmins, 'Strategic or Pragmatic Partnership? The European Union's Policy Towards Russia Since the End of the Cold War', *European Security*, 11:4 (2002), pp. 78–95.

9

NATO AND RUSSIA:
PROGRESS OR PROCESS?

Mark McGuigan

Introduction

As its title implies, this book is concerned with the nature of Russia's relationship with Europe. In that context, the NATO-Russia dimension poses a specific consideration in that the North Atlantic Treaty Organization (NATO) is much larger than European NATO. Consequently, there is a temptation to disaggregate NATO in order to focus upon its 'European-ness' in terms of its interaction with Moscow. The temptation should be resisted, however. It may in theory be possible to disaggregate NATO by separating out its North American and European components, but no meaningful discussion of Europe's security relationship with Russia is possible if it fails to acknowledge the primacy of the US in guiding, if not determining, the existence and persistence of NATO. One may write of the Alliance without specific reference to, say, the views of some of its smaller European members: indeed, in a sense, one may even discuss historical NATO views or positions without reference to France, given its history of autonomy from the military structures. However, any understanding of post-Cold War NATO, including the relationship with the Russian Federation, must contend with the views of Washington and the consequences thereof for its European allies, as will be discussed below. To that extent, nothing much has altered since the Cold War and the US remains, as Richard Holbrooke described it a decade ago, a European power.[1] NATO-Russia interaction as examined here will reflect that fact.

The course of NATO-Russia relations since 1991 indicates not so much a reconciliation of former adversaries as a series of ad hoc accommodations, reflecting a desire to perpetuate the significance of NATO and Russia in Europe's security order. This has included inter alia helping to sustain the status and functioning of the North Atlantic Alliance, and providing recognition of Russia's continued status as a major security player. The current relationship has been arrived at, and is therefore best understood, as a result of the difficult history of post-Cold War NATO-Russia interaction, especially as tempered in the fires of the Balkans in the 1990s. Former Yugoslavia provides a concentration of interaction between post-Cold War NATO's search for a new *raison d'être*, Russia's attempts to establish a foreign policy reconciling great power ambition with greatly constrained post-Soviet circumstances, and the subsequent efforts of both parties to give effect to expressions of partnership and cooperation. Further, the (re-?) emergence of NATO's internal divisions of the recent past can be discerned in transatlantic differences over capabilities and outlook as evidenced in former Yugoslavia, well before the bitter recriminations over Iraq. Today, in what we may describe as the post-Iraq era, certain themes persist, enabling us to identify elements of continuity in the relationship.

In Bosnia the post-Dayton NATO-Russia partnership – at the military if not always at the political level – had appeared to herald a promising future for Alliance relations with Moscow. Such optimism was shattered by the 1999 launch of Operation Allied Force (OAF) over Kosovo, ushering in the lowest point in the relationship and leading to bitterness and stagnation in the Kremlin's dealings with the Alliance. This period of drift came to an end in late 2001 when the events of 11 September (9-11) in the US provided President Vladimir Putin with the diplomatic opportunity to initiate a rapprochement with the West.

The attacks on the American mainland did more than provide a diplomatic opening for the Kremlin, however: to the extent that the US resolved to pursue a war on terror, and to the extent that its NATO allies understood – or failed to understand – the depth and implications of that resolve, 9-11 represents a further milestone on the road to NATO's troubles over Iraq. The advent of the NATO-Russia Council (NRC) boosted the NATO-Russia relationship, breathing life into moribund consultation arrangements, and generating a great deal of work to enhance cooperation in areas such as anti-terrorism, crisis management, non-proliferation, and airspace management. Nevertheless, the overarching issue of NATO enlargement, and the interest in NATO membership evinced by Caucasian and Central Asian states, continue to generate considerable concern in Russia. Against that background the NRC, with its broad agenda, has become the focus of engagement between the parties, and the repository of hopes for the development of their relationship. For different reasons – which we may characterize broadly as Russian expedience, and NATO convenience – it has also come to represent the apparent height of ambition for both parties in terms of their relationship, as the international agenda has moved away from prioritizing European concerns.

For NATO the recurrence of existential angst in 2003, reminiscent of the debates of the early 1990s, has widened the Alliance's latent fissures. While there have always been periodic disagreements in NATO, the Soviet threat ensured that no rift was ever sufficient to undermine the Alliance. With that threat long gone, there is no overriding compulsion for NATO to resist the debilitating effects of internal divisions. Rather, the cumulative effect of crises and campaigns since the end of the Cold War has been to confound the claim to European NATO's solidarity and autonomy of action, and to underline the hegemony of US military and political power as essential to the future vitality of the Alliance. As one commentator has observed,[2] the problem for 'old' Europe is one of balancing its fear of US loss of interest in European security matters with its loathing of the potential excesses of American unilateralism. It is in this context of NATO's fractious harmony that a somewhat impatient US and a somewhat quarrelsome Franco-German link, the latter initially bolstered by Russian support over Iraq, sought and continue to seek an effective accommodation, enabling NATO to continue to present a united front to the world, Moscow included.

Recent NATO-Russia engagement thus maps an uneven terrain, the main signposts along which read Bosnia, Kosovo, 9-11 and Iraq. These are not the only signposts (one might consider partnership efforts, or weapons of mass destruction (WMD) issues, for example) but they indicate the most striking features to appear en route to an understanding of where we find ourselves now. For Russia, the terrain has been clouded continually by the enlargement of NATO, and in particular its encroachment into former Soviet territory. Moscow's concerns about US-led NATO influence in Central Asia and the Caucasus feed the fears of some that NATO remains an expansionist military threat to Russia. It would seem, therefore, that while the formal NRC mechanisms remain busy, there are significant underlying concerns for NATO and Russia, the former needing to strengthen its own cohesion, the latter anxious to exercise a higher degree of influence than its circumstances permit. When considering the relationship as it has developed, and the centrality of the NRC, we may now ask whether we are dealing with progress or process.

Balkan legacy – Russia Resentful, Europe Divided, US Disillusioned

The conflicts in Bosnia and Kosovo, while markedly different in many respects, display a similarity in terms of the NATO-Russia dynamic. NATO interventionism became a decisive feature of the Balkan wars and obliged Moscow to contend with a growing, changing and increasingly militarily active alliance. The end of the Cold War, far from signalling the demise of NATO, provided it with a new rationale for its existence in countering new forms of insecurity in Europe.[3] The former Yugoslavia was also the testing ground for the evolution of the new Russian Federation's foreign policy. Events in Bosnia and Kosovo highlighted a pattern of NATO interventionism, Russian foreign policy motivation (a desire for a place at the decision-making table), Russian reaction to NATO activities (initial opposition, belated concurrence), and a subsequent attempt to reconcile differences and carry on in a spirit of professed cooperation. If the Balkan experience taught Russia to swallow its pride, NATO's leading player also underwent an educational experience regarding the perception of its European allies. These key lessons continue to colour the development of NATO-Russian relations in the Putin era.

Former Yugoslavia provided the first major test of European security arrangements in the changed post-Cold War order. US reluctance to become involved sat well with Europe's desire to demonstrate its maturity as a security provider as well as consumer. This hour of Europe also coincided with Russia's desire to continue to act, and be perceived, as a great power. The dichotomy between NATO Europeans' willingness and ability to act effectively, and that between Russia's self-esteem and reduced circumstances would prove a recurrent theme not just in the Balkans but in the wider NATO-Russian relationship.

The Clinton administration eventually took the view that US involvement in Bosnia was unavoidable if NATO were to be preserved as a credible functioning alliance. Reliance upon NATO's leading European players had revealed their inability to agree among themselves. Driven by differing national interests, lacking an agreed understanding of the desired endgame in Yugoslavia (witness the bitterness engendered by German recognition of Slovenia and Croatia), and lacking the discipline afforded by US involvement, Europe's major states did not prove to be up to the challenge of the troubled Balkans. This did not bode well for European competence to deal unaided with what were essentially local matters.

In Bosnia NATO came to face up to the lack of European unity in foreign policy, the diplomatic and military primacy of Washington, and the futility of courting the Yeltsin regime in Moscow. The latter's very weakness, however, obliged NATO to bolster Moscow's position to sustain the portrayal of an international community united in dealing with the horror of the Balkans. Despite Russian objections, a NATO interventionist template was created in Bosnia – a clear indication of the senior-junior nature of the Alliance's relationship with Moscow. This relationship of unequals became even more apparent in Kosovo, which marked the post-Cold War nadir of NATO-Russian relations.

Writing a year after NATO's launch of Operation Allied Force (OAF), Boris Yeltsin summarized the fears of many Russians that an existing world order, whose rules were widely understood and in which Russia had a significant influence, was being dismantled.[4] In its place was the prospect of a new, arbitrary, Western-dominated system which threatened Moscow with exclusion. Widespread Russian public debate, allied to the outrage caused by NATO's actions, indicates clearly that OAF was not simply a foreign policy issue for the Kremlin, but a domestic one as well. NATO's lack of mandate from the UN, where Russia wielded influence, brought home the dangers for Moscow of bypassing the Security Council. By implication, Russia's status as an influential actor in European security, to say nothing of its great power ambition, was diminished. Finally, the timing of the launch of OAF, so soon after the admission of new members to the Atlantic alliance, was not lost on the Kremlin.

Russian policy had been based upon promotion of the Organization for Security and Cooperation in Europe (OSCE) as the prime mover in Europe's security decision-making. This was complemented by Moscow's view of the Permanent Joint Council (PJC), established by the 1997 Founding Act on Mutual Relations, as a partnership of equals in which matters were debated and joint decisions taken. Sitting above these arrangements was the UN Security Council (UNSC) in which Russia held a permanent seat. In launching OAF NATO bypassed the UN, OSCE and the PJC, shattering any illusion that Russia possessed a guaranteed strong voice in European security decision-making.

The shock to the Russian system was enormous, its foreign policy having been exposed as a complete failure. However, Yeltsin recognized the importance to Moscow of not risking isolation from the West. Consequently, the Russians did not withdraw from the Stabilization Force in Bosnia and Herzegovina (SFOR) or from negotiations on Treaty on Conventional Forces in Europe (CFE) matters. In effect, Russian diplomacy once again underwent a rapprochement with the West at the official level, notwithstanding the variety and strength of feeling of domestic opinion on Kosovo.

Its cooperation with NATO, however, was not entirely smooth. The absence of a detailed peace treaty for Kosovo provided scope for ambiguity and interpretation, a situation of concern to NATO since it permitted Russia to adopt contrary views to the Alliance regarding the provisions of United Nations Security Council Resolution (UNSCR) 1244, the Helsinki Agreements and the functioning of the Kosovo Force (KFOR).[5] NATO's Operation Plan (OPLAN) 10413 detailed the rules of engagement for its peacekeeping forces. It too became the subject of correspondence between Moscow and Brussels at senior political level as Russia sought to create elbow-room for its participation in Kosovo.[6]

This divergence of interpretation translated into changes in the complexion of Russian liaison at Supreme Headquarters Allied Powers in Europe (SHAPE). NATO sources noted a reduction in the decision-making authority of the KFOR Senior Russian Representative, as well as variations in the KFOR delegation reporting line to Moscow. Other variations included a greater emphasis on employing liaison officers who did not have a professional military background, and a perceived change of emphasis in the focus of Russian liaison efforts from tactical level cooperation in SFOR to more Foreign Ministry-directed policy objectives on joint decision-making in KFOR. The overall tenor of these changes suggested that Russian participation in KFOR, apparently analogous to that in the Implementation Force in Bosnia and Herzegovina (IFOR)/SFOR, had in fact a more overtly political emphasis.

If OAF caused enormous difficulties for Russia, it also exposed the transatlantic fault lines in NATO. By any measure, OAF was essentially a US effort with a small amount of European support. The enormous imbalance in military capabilities between the two was starkly exposed. Perhaps more significantly here, the manner in which the campaign was conducted caused Washington, and the Pentagon, to reflect hard upon the value of cooperating with allies who contributed little militarily yet could hamper the conduct of a campaign in terms of political intervention and questioning.

The US military's disenchantment with interference in its conduct of operations was understandable from a professional military viewpoint, but it should be remembered that political control of the campaign rested as much, if not more, with Washington as with the Europeans. It is quite conceivable that the latter could have prevailed in Kosovo, though not in the manner in which the campaign was conducted. Nevertheless, OAF appeared to demonstrate that the Europeans contributed little beyond constraints upon the conduct of an essentially US campaign, something which would cause concern for the future, and colour the outlook of US decision makers.

From Kosovo to NRC – Gradual Rapprochement

In February 2000, amid tentative signs that NATO and Russia might begin to overcome their post-Allied Force difficulties, the then NATO Secretary-General Lord Robertson visited Moscow and spoke reassuringly about the relationship. This was followed a month later by the first meeting of the PJC since the launch of NATO's air campaign in Kosovo. However, differences of outlook persisted over the Kosovo Liberation Army (KLA), treatment of attacks on Serbs, and interpretations of UNSCR 1244. Above all of this loomed the unresolved issue of Kosovo's future status. Nevertheless, by late 2000 NATO and Russia could find some common cause for optimism in the election in Belgrade of Vojislav Kostunica as the successor to Milošević. For NATO, Kostunica's election marked the end of the Milošević era, while for Russia the new President's opposition to a Pax Americana was welcome.[7] On the Russian side too some had been arguing for greater rapprochement in the wider NATO-Russian relationship based upon a mutuality of interests including peacekeeping efforts in the Balkans.[8] Others acknowledged the positive experience of Russian and NATO military cooperation in SFOR and KFOR, but recognized that there needed to be caution as well as optimism in assessing the prospects for future rapprochement.[9]

Resumption of Russian participation in the PJC was characterized by a perceived imperative to cooperate, and by a degree of wariness. Once again, there was a divergence from NATO on fundamental interpretations regarding the role of the PJC. Russian diplomacy centred on a variety of issues including influencing internal NATO decision-making; elevating the PJC's status in Europe's security architecture to convey the impression of Russian influence over Alliance decisions regarding Eastern Europe; promoting the role of the PJC as the mechanism for peacekeeping cooperation in preference to NATO's Partnership for Peace (PfP) programme; and attempting to transform NATO-led military activities into 'joint' activities, playing up the Russian contribution.[10]

By contrast, almost a year and a half after the end of the war in Kosovo NATO still lacked a clear overall strategy for its relationship with Russia. Without such direction NATO would continue to be reactive to Russian input instead of guiding the relationship in a direction favourable to itself.[11] Owing to the deficiencies of the PJC, NATO was limited in its capacity to act as the best mechanism for engaging Russia at the political level; however, it could still provide a lead in promoting Russian military reform. In the absence of a truly strategic plan for its relationship with Moscow, the best chance for genuine progress appeared to lie in military-to-military cooperation at the tactical level, based upon getting things right in KFOR. For NATO, therefore, peacekeeping was seen as the primary means of advancing the relationship. This absence of a NATO strategy beyond military cooperation foreshadows the current arrangements somewhat, whereby tactical cooperation under the auspices of the NRC accounts for the primary means of engagement.

Steady incremental successes throughout 2001 enabled the operational commander of SFOR and KFOR to provide a sober yet upbeat assessment of the situation by March 2002.[12] By the time of this assessment the world had witnessed the attacks of 9-11 in the USA, among the many ramifications of which was the further impetus given to NATO and Russia to improve their relationship. While military-tactical cooperation in SFOR and KFOR was generally accepted as a success, at the level of political strategy Russian Foreign Minister Ivanov could still speak critically of NATO-led operations in Kosovo in July 2001, condemning the province as a hotbed of terrorism and organised crime.[13] However, after 9-11 greater rapprochement became evident, and there were calls for a new partnership as each side began to focus more clearly on how to cultivate their strategic relationship.[14]

Even prior to 9-11 there had been some indications of NATO-Russian rapprochement.[15] Putin, while espousing the standard Kremlin line denying any need for NATO, conceded that it was here to stay and might even include Russia.[16] Immediately after 9-11 others argued for the West to cultivate Russia for inter alia its peacekeeping capabilities in Kosovo should the US withdraw its forces in the event of commitments in the Muslim world.[17] Putin now began repositioning Moscow and set about improving Russia's cooperation with the NATO allies, a bold move given the brief passage of time since the Kosovo campaign.[18]

On the whole, the Kremlin's new line was regarded as a positive development in the West.[19] Putin's motives were variously attributed – economic, geopolitical (justifying Russian conduct in Chechnya), fear of the rise of Islam and its implications for Russia, a desire to improve Russia's international standing.[20] In any event, Russia's westward orientation swiftly generated moves to improve its relationship with NATO[21] despite some initial caution in Brussels.[22]

Momentum having been generated, the new mood was well summed up by Lord Robertson in January 2002.[23] Targeting a Russian audience he stressed the seminal nature of the changes brought about by the attacks of 11 September, and the immediacy of the common threat of terrorism. The message was simple enough – that which divided NATO and Russia was of less consequence than that which united them, namely the threat posed by terrorism.

Robertson's overtures were carefully calculated, but he also made clear that enlargement of the Alliance would proceed, though it would not pose any threat to Russia. This second wave of NATO enlargement in only five years might have been expected to generate considerable official resistance from the Kremlin but Putin appears to have recognized the realpolitik involved.[24] In any event, the new post-9-11 mood of rapprochement was abroad, and officials worked hard on both sides throughout the spring of 2002 to enable the creation of the new NRC in May of that year, marking, perhaps optimistically, 'a new quality' in the relationship.[25]

Towards Iraq – Revealing Transatlantic Fault Lines

The functioning of the NRC is described in greater detail in Chapter 15 of this book. Here, we may observe that perhaps its real significance lies not so much in the substance of its debates as in the symbolism of its creation in the first place. It represents a move away from the bitterness generated in Moscow by the Alliance's actions in Kosovo. It affords a hitherto lacking equality – procedurally, at least – to the Russians. It also marks a considerable improvement in relations in the post-9-11 atmosphere, and a form of recognition of Russian support of the West.

If the NRC helped put NATO-Russia relations on a sounder footing than previously, it enjoyed only a brief opportunity to act as a harmonious representative forum before internal Alliance relations started to fray. As Iraq began to command greater diplomatic attention in 2002 and 2003, European divisions were once again exposed over how to deal with Baghdad and the issue of WMD. So too was a transatlantic divide between the US, UK and their allies from 'new Europe' (largely Spain, Italy and Poland) on the one hand, and 'old Europe' (France and Germany, with Russian support) on the other. These transatlantic divisions, overlaid by intra-European divisions, and public squabbling over whether the Alliance should provide assistance to Turkey in the event of war against Iraq, heralded a period of crisis for the Alliance. Its cohesion was undermined, generating a renewed debate over the future of NATO. Although Iraq was the catalyst for debate, it is of longer standing and can be seen as a consequence of the development of the history of post-Cold War NATO, and in particular a growing American disillusionment with its European allies.

NATO's invocation of Article 5 in the aftermath of the 9-11 attacks was something of a no-win situation for the Alliance. If the invocation had not been made, the fundamental premise upon which NATO was established, that of mutual defence of member states, would have been exposed as meaningless and undermined the credibility of the Alliance. By invoking Article 5, however, one also invoked questions about how it could be enacted. In essence, this was the capabilities issue once again.

The US's cool reaction to European NATO's offers of assistance was a clear indication of the extent of American disenchantment with its European allies. The prosecution of the war on terror would be conducted not by a formally constituted alliance but by coalitions of willing states, or indeed without allies if need be. The strength and depth of US feeling after 9-11, allied to Europe's less than impressive performances in the Balkans, marked this period as a real turning point for NATO. In a sense, if one accepts that NATO *has* suffered a near-death experience, it may be more accurate to attribute it to the autumn of 2001 and the post-9-11 debates than to February 2003 and disagreements over Iraq.

As suggested, NATO's internal divisions are not confined to the spectacular public disagreement over Iraq, nor do they date from early 2003. The Iraq-related issue of WMD, and the future governance of arms control and proliferation issues have long been a source of significant disagreement between the US and some of its allies, as well as the US and Russia.[26] Nevertheless, the Iraq fallout was particularly bitter, polarizing France, Germany, Belgium and Luxembourg on the one hand and the signatories to the letter of eight[27] on the other. As a public example of Europe's discord the letter was spectacular. Jacques Chirac's venomous response underlined the depth of resentment of the protagonists, and gave impetus to the Franco-German axis to pursue greater European security autonomy, independently of NATO, via the European Security and Defence Policy (ESDP). This led to the widely disparaged 'chocolate summit' of late April 2003, hard on the heels of Chirac's reported assessment that NATO was now irrelevant.[28] Needless to say, his assessment was not shared by NATO's accession states, the largest of which, Poland, moved swiftly to distance itself from the Franco-German axis and its Russian support.[29] Rumsfeld's new Europeans were solidly opposed to the Moscow-backed Paris-Berlin link, rendering it less and less influential within NATO circles.

Though nothing came of the April 2003 summit, ESDP remained symbolic of a European divergence from NATO and by extension from the US. Consequently, the UK's Berlin rapprochement with France and Germany in September 2003 was unwelcome in Washington, and led to an extraordinary debate in the North Atlantic Council (NAC).[30] Although Tony Blair was attempting to guide it in a direction compatible with NATO, any attempt to promote ESDP planning was viewed with suspicion by the US, such was the cumulative effect of a rancorous diplomatic atmosphere, and barely restrained US anger with 'old' Europe. Washington's increasing impatience with its allies was fuelled by its perception that, as a global power with global responsibilities, it was encountering obstacles from, at most, a regional power. At a time when its global responsibilities required it to focus on Iraq and the Middle East, the US was having to contend with distractions from a peaceful, prosperous and potentially powerful continent. While Washington may have been the centre of European concerns, Europe was not the priority for the US.

It has been observed that this is only the beginning of an ongoing revolution in US foreign policy, the consequences of which may yet be to undermine NATO, as Washington continues to regard its European allies as less than committed.[31] Iraq merely reinforced this message, given the acrimony between Bush's White House and the French-German-Russian triangle. This entails obvious longer-term consequences for NATO cohesion, if not handled skilfully.

NATO's Lack of Coordination – Agreeing to Disagree

The Alliance's obvious discord since 2003 is symptomatic of a lack of vigour, and somewhat ailing health – and yet NATO is also the physician capable of healing himself. Transatlantic divisions need a forum in which genuine differences of outlook can be discussed and resolved. Such a forum must be recognised as having the good of all concerned parties at heart, and the ability to foster and implement agreement. A demonstrable track record of success in transatlantic relations, a wealth of experience in addressing European security problems, and an instant 'recognition' factor all point to NATO as being the obvious forum within which transatlantic allies can reach agreement on major policy issues. NATO is at once patient and doctor.

In such circumstances it may be reasonable to have expected a more positive response to Gerhard Schröder's suggestion in February 2005 that NATO review the way it conducts its affairs. He had in mind a fundamental reappraisal of the role and place of NATO as the forum for conduct of transatlantic relations. A coordinated transatlantic approach should result in, amongst other things, a coordinated NATO approach to Russia. Schröder's call for NATO to become a medium for the interface of US and European policy was, on the face of it, unexceptional and perhaps even conventional. That has not happened, for a variety of reasons.

Schröder, in suggesting that the Alliance was becoming less relevant as the primary forum for allied engagement in the modern era, was echoing Chirac's sentiment of nearly two years earlier. This signalled that the lines of division of 2003 were still drawn in 2005. He was also clearly positing that European views needed to be given greater weight. US officials regarded this as a clumsy way of relegating NATO in favour of promoting the EU/ESDP in the security sphere, all the while appearing to cleave to good transatlantic credentials. Given Washington's scepticism regarding ESDP, and the criticism which even allies like Blair attracted in September 2003, the German proposal was never going to be well received.

Newly re-elected, Bush launched his own charm offensive by visiting European capitals and NATO HQ in February 2005, significantly the first overseas trip of his new term of office. While playing down his differences with Schröder and others, he nevertheless made it plain that the US continued to regard NATO as the obvious forum for transatlantic issues, signalling no change in structural arrangements. In turn, this implied that in the absence of significant policy changes on either side of the Atlantic, the matters which divided NATO allies were likely to persist, and that agreement to disagree, rather than genuine unity and coordination of views, was to be the order of the day.

The list of significant transatlantic disagreements is a long one, and Bush's brief European visit could hardly be expected to resolve the differences. These included Iraq, Iran's nuclear development programme, the perennial Israel-Palestine problem, European proposals to drop the arms embargo on China, US opposition to the Kyoto treaty and the International Criminal Court, as well as the continued utility or otherwise of NATO as a transatlantic forum. In the circumstances, agreement to disagree may even be considered progress of a sort. Agreement to disagree, however, also meant blocking the French-supported German initiative for reviewing NATO as the forum for conducting transatlantic business. Instead, policy would continue to be the preserve of national capitals, and would therefore continue to reflect a lack of harmony among the NATO member states. In terms of NATO's relationship with Russia, there was no realistic prospect of a coordinated allied policy via the NATO forum.

Other factors too have played their part in the lack of NATO coordination towards Russia, not least a kind of 'Russia fatigue', characterized by reticence on the part of NATO to upset the Putin regime. It seems that there is an ambivalence toward Moscow. The desire to promote the day-to-day work of the NRC goes hand in hand with a tolerance of the Kremlin's increasingly centralist tendencies. Putin's growing authoritarianism, stalled political reforms (if indeed they ever existed) and the depressingly familiar lack of progress in military-security reform all draw surprisingly little focused comment from NATO. The Alliance is not prepared to question the Kremlin on human rights or rule of law issues, for example. This is not the case in other fora, such as the Council of Europe.[32] The contrast in willingness to offer constructive criticism may be explained in part by the differing membership of the organisations, and their different *raisons d'être*. However, given NATO's self-proclaimed purposes in promoting and defending democracy, human rights and the rule of law it is at least curious that the Alliance is so coy in its dealings with the Kremlin. No voices are raised in NATO HQ to challenge the lack of progress in military-security reform, for example, a problem of such long-standing that it almost beggars belief that we are still discussing it.

Military reform (and we are not talking here about bureaucratic tinkering at the margins, but fundamental and wholesale restructuring) has been a staple of any consideration of the problems besetting Moscow since the establishment of the Russian Federation, and indeed before then. It is depressing to find that, in November 2005, one well-placed commentator still felt obliged to call for serious Russian military reform, now to be based in part upon the experience of NATO militaries, and in part upon greater Russia-NATO interoperability.[33]

The call for interoperability was made in the context of Russia's need rather than wish to cooperate with NATO, which is accused indirectly of lacking transparency, and of harbouring expansionist ambitions in Russia's near-abroad. Moscow's cooperation in the military sphere is therefore premised on tactical need rather than strategic vision or harmony of purpose, a reflection of its wider political cooperation with the Alliance. While it may appear harsh to assess NATO-Russian engagement as based solely upon Russian expedience and NATO convenience, it is optimistic to regard the relationship as reflecting mutuality of genuinely held understandings and interests. On a less ambitious level, it is also optimistic to think that military interoperability is achievable in the present circumstances.

The prolonged and continued challenges which NATO militaries have faced in attempting to achieve interoperability – the capabilities question again – are well documented. It is difficult to envisage Russia's under-reformed and under-funded military rising successfully to the same challenge in the near future, notwithstanding the number of cooperative training exercises conducted by NATO and Russian forces under NRC. Nevertheless, the call for military-to-military cooperation echoes the early days of the Founding Act and the success of NATO-Russian military peacekeeping in the Balkans. It is perhaps telling that, for all the undoubted activity of the NRC, we do not seem to have moved much beyond that period. Indeed, we may even have regressed from the optimism of those days, given Russian concerns about ever-encroaching NATO expansionist ambitions.

Influential Russian voices have continued to call for the channelling of Russian diplomatic effort into directions other than NATO, presumably in the belief that the NATO role in European security can be balanced by, or subordinated to, other institutions.[34] This has been a recurring theme in post-Cold War Russian foreign policy. Deputy Foreign Minister Vladimir Chizhov's speech in Potsdam in June 2005, while declaring Russia 'on the whole satisfied' with its cooperation with NATO, made a wider plea for a formal mechanism to coordinate and harmonize Russian and EU foreign policy actions. He also called for the reform and reinvigoration of the OSCE, another favoured institution of the Kremlin. Finally, he sought the creation of a new European security architecture involving the UN, Russia, EU and NATO. This desire to curb NATO indicates a consistent theme in Russian foreign policy thinking, and also reflects the persistence of Russia's self-perception as a great power. NATO, lacking cohesion in its own approach to Moscow, has done nothing to disabuse the Kremlin of its great power illusions, evincing an unwillingness to engage on thorny issues such as Chechnya or human rights.

On the NATO side, the Supreme Allied Commander for Europe (SACEUR) enjoys good personal contacts in Moscow, and started out with high ambitions. He has been unfortunate in that his tenure has coincided with a lack of energy in NATO's approach to the relationship with the Kremlin. This is regrettable but not surprising if we consider that the subject no longer commands the undivided attention of national policymakers preoccupied with Iraq, Iran and Israel. Put simply, in recent years everyone has had, and continues to have, bigger fish to fry.

Quite apart from Iraq and, increasingly, Iran, there are a number of significant factors affecting European NATO members' ability to afford some priority to relations with Moscow. These include, but are not limited to, a European Union (EU) struggling to win a mandate from its own citizens, the expansion of the Alliance itself, major internal NATO transformation, the growing marginalization of Blair (a prime mover in establishing the NRC), and Russia's skilful exploitation of its relationship with Schröder, now a senior executive with a Russian-led gas consortium. These are just some of the factors which have contributed to a situation in which it is difficult to justify giving priority to the faintly quaint topic of NATO-Russian relations. There is only so much energy to be expended, and priorities change.

Real engagement with Moscow seems to revolve around the Iran nuclear issue, in other words, only the top emotive issue of the day. There is little incentive to engage Russia further in any strategic fashion, since officials continue to work busily in the NRC forum, which offers plenty of activity to support the contention that there is genuine engagement between the parties. This is not to denigrate the work done in the NRC, a busy institution. Rather, it is to observe that the NATO-Russia relationship seems to have found a staging post, if not necessarily a direction.

The outlook for NATO is not entirely cloudy, however. The Alliance persists, reforms, and adapts at it has done for the last 15 years, and the bitterness of February 2003 is, slowly, becoming part of the background noise.[35] NATO remains engaged in operations in Europe and beyond. Non-members continue to seek security through membership of the Alliance. Notwithstanding disagreements among the allies, all are publicly committed to the work of the Alliance, though if European members do not improve their military capabilities significantly it may well become less of a hard security provider and more of a political engagement process. This would blunt NATO's edge, or unique utility, in European security affairs. NATO also has its influential supporters in the current US administration, and remains an important institution in US security thinking.[36] It is also the case that NATO has periodically undergone, and survived, internal disagreements in the past.[37] Consequently, it is probably premature to write the Alliance's obituary just yet.[38]

There has, however, been a depth of bitterness in the exchanges of recent times. Thus, while obituaries may be premature, it is clear that Alliance cohesion has been undermined considerably and that NATO today is less important as a going concern to the Bush administration than it was to the Clinton administration in the mid 1990s. In contrast to the immediate post-Cold War situation, the onus now is on NATO to demonstrate its continued relevance to its own members, particularly its leading member, as much as to the outside world. NATO dare not fail in Afghanistan, for example, where a successful performance would bolster its credibility and relevance, and ease US pressure on Europe vis-à-vis Iraq. Recent assessments, however, do not inspire confidence.[39] The reforms of the recent past, such as the introduction of new EU defence planning headquarters and the creation of a Reaction Force, need to bear fruit soon if NATO is not finally to be convicted of the frequently made charge of having outlived its usefulness. There is no immediate sign that these reforms are making any great difference, though it is still early days.

The Alliance's recent and not so private grief is also of great significance for Russia. Despite its opposition to the Iraq war and its temporary alliance with Paris and Berlin, Moscow does not view the war in Iraq as a pivotal event, as was Kosovo or 9-11, in shaping the world order.[40] However, the attack on Iraq is seen as potentially divisive among the anti-terrorism coalition forged after 9-11. In essence, although strongly opposed to the Iraq war, the Kremlin had no real means of preventing it once the matter moved beyond the UN, a situation reminiscent of the Kosovo precedent.[41] Russian diplomacy may continue to call for a UN-centred approach[42] but cannot insist upon it. This epitomises Russia's long-standing dilemma in reconciling its ambition for recognition as a respected and significant security actor with its constrained circumstances. To some extent NATO has fuelled this dilemma. The idea of Russia as a major power has faded fast in the West, but there has been very little Alliance attempt to take Russia to task for its overbearing behaviour towards Moldova, Belarus or pre-Yushchenko Ukraine. Since little has been done to make Moscow *want* to change, its erroneous self-perception persists.

Moscow needs a serious interlocutor in European security issues, given its disappointment with the current functioning of the OSCE, and the difficulties inherent in dealing with the EU as a capable military player.[43] The EU's efforts to give itself credible security capabilities via ESDP are proving protracted. NATO's own engagement with the EU has highlighted the fact that the latter remains properly ambitious but under-resourced in security capabilities, and is not (yet?) a substitute for the former when it comes to providing for Europe's security requirements. Short of an unlikely European willingness to invest heavily in security capabilities, this situation is not going to change in the near or medium-term future. Moscow is therefore obliged to continue to give due consideration to its relations with the Alliance, notwithstanding its preference for subordinating it to the UN or OSCE.

Conclusion

So, we are where we are and the NRC mechanism continues to function busily. If we consider the most pressing security challenges which the Alliance seeks to address, they include terrorism, arms proliferation, regional instability, and trafficking in drugs and people. Russia's geography, history, intelligence capabilities and regional influence make it an essential partner for NATO in those undertakings.[44] This opens up opportunities for further cooperation. Russia's signing of the April 2005 Partnership Status of Forces agreement, while some way short of joint NATO-Russian military structures, hints at future possibilities in that direction. The details would take considerable work, but the Balkan peacekeeping experience shows that both parties are capable of a high degree of successful cooperation at the appropriate level.

Of course it is possible that a great deal could yet disrupt the continued engagement in the NRC. Moscow continues to have considerable reservations concerning NATO's eastward enlargement[45] and the US's increasing focus on the Caucasus and Central Asia. Given that there is likely to be further NATO enlargement in the Balkans and possibly (though less likely) even in the former Soviet territories of Azerbaijan, Georgia and Ukraine, it is reasonable to anticipate further Russian angst, however futile. One of Moscow's chief concerns is the possibility of finding itself increasingly isolated and without influence in areas formerly under the sway of the Kremlin. To that extent, the possibility that Caucasian and Central Asian states may review and reform their military doctrines and equipment, making them more interoperable with NATO members than with Russia, is a real worry for Moscow.[46]

These states include Russia's CIS partners in the Collective Security Treaty Organisation (CSTO), and there is evident potential for that organization to be a counterweight to NATO in areas of immediate strategic interest to Russia. Anything which might interfere with Russian influence within the CSTO is a cause for concern for Russia. Conversely, the opportunity to use CSTO to enhance Russian influence and balance that of NATO is to be welcomed in the Kremlin. Such thinking finds practical expression at the NRC level through the interventions of Russia's Chief of the General Staff, Yuri Baluyevsky, in his call for a united military effort between NATO and the CSTO in the Caucasus and Central Asia.[47] This echoes similar suggestions for the creation of cooperative peacekeeping structures.[48]

The underlying theme here is a Russian desire, shared by political and military elites, to lessen the perceived growth of NATO influence in Russia's neighbouring states. The Director of the Russian General Staff's Centre for Military-Strategic Studies has identified five main priorities for Russian political-military cooperation with the West, all pertaining to the negative consequences for Moscow of NATO's eastward expansion.[49] Consequently, Russia's interests are deemed to be best served by lessening NATO influence, especially in those countries bordering the Russian Federation.

Russia remains engaged in the NRC, claiming parity with all other participants, and promoting the line that there are no pre-cooked positions, only open discussion. That could change should Moscow find its initiatives stalled sufficiently often to throw aside the veil of 'at 27'. Dependent upon how US forces conduct themselves in the Caucasus, Moscow might also come to regard the American presence there as deeply inimical to its own national interests. NATO cohesion may yet come unstuck as US patience with some of its European allies wears thin. Alternatively, a bloated NATO may succumb to organizational inertia as it attempts to integrate its newest members; while reform has been a constant feature of recent years, much remains to be done.[50] Caught between the pressures of NATO's out-of-area commitments and Europe's fledgling autonomous commitments, the European allies may overreach themselves. Afghanistan gives every indication of being problematic for the Europeans, yet NATO cannot afford to fail there. Finally, the absence of final and lasting settlements in Bosnia and Kosovo may yet give rise to renewed conflict.

Nevertheless, with the NRC espousing common cause, NATO determined to continue to demonstrate its relevance, and Russia keen to remain engaged (albeit through the necessity of mitigating its own weakness), there is scope for a more fruitful partnership. Those highlighting Russian concerns over the Caucasus and Central Asia also acknowledge that there are mutual interests linking Russia and NATO.[51] The Balkan wars demonstrated that NATO and Russia had, have and most likely will continue to have their significant differences, but that they can remain engaged and have a proven ability to cooperate even under the most difficult of circumstances. The response to 9-11 ushered in a recognition of the need for NATO and Russia to unite around certain common concerns and to improve their level of cooperation. The NRC continues to offer a mechanism to facilitate that engagement. In uncertain times, as NATO and Russia focus their attention on a wide thematic and geographic agenda, that at least provides some cause for guarded optimism, and supports the contention that the busy NATO-Russia process remains important even if progress has been fitful at best. Further progress will be difficult until such time as NATO can achieve greater internal cohesion, including a willingness to engage Russia on aspects of its domestic politics, and Russia comes to terms with its reduced role in Europe, particularly in its near-abroad. Until then, NATO and Russia appear destined to remain uneasy partners.

Notes and References

1. Richard Holbrooke, 'America, A European Power', *Foreign Affairs*, 74:2 (1995), pp. 38–51.
2. Terry Terriff, 'Fear and loathing in NATO: The Atlantic Alliance after the crisis over Iraq', *Perspectives on European Politics and Society*, 4:3 (2004), pp. 419–46.
3. There is a great deal of literature on this, but for an early articulation see Gregory L Schulte 'The Former Yugoslavia and the New NATO', *Survival*, 39:1(1997), pp. 19–42. For an exposition of the centrality of the Former Yugoslavia in the development of Russian foreign policy see also Michael Andersen 'Russia and the Former Yugoslavia' in M Webber (ed.), *Russia and Europe: Conflict or Cooperation?* (Basingstoke, Macmillan, 2000), pp. 179–209.
4. Extract from Yeltsin's memoirs *Midnight Diaries*, quoted in *The Times*, 10th October 2000.

5. Notes from an address to NATO staff officers at Naples, May 2000. NATO thinking at the time reflected serious concerns that at the political level Russia was seeking to revise the terms of the Helsinki Agreement, and working to return the Yugoslav Army to Kosovo as soon as possible. Russian liaison officials at SHAPE were also promoting the view that UNSCR 1244 did not restrict peacekeeping to NATO-led forces but allowed for a Russian-led peacekeeping force as well.

6. Author's discussions with senior NATO political advisers at SHAPE, September 2000.

7. Voislav Koshtunitsa, 'Serbi i zapad. Novi President Yugoslavia protiv Pax Americana', *Nezavisimaya Gazeta*, 13 October 2000.

8. Dmitri Trenin, 'Russia-NATO relations: Time to pick up the pieces', *NATO Review*, 48:1, (2000).

9. Andrei Zagorski, 'Great Expectations', *NATO Review*, 49:1, (2001), pp. 24–7.

10. Author's meetings at SHAPE, September 2000.

11. This absence of a strategic plan for the end product of the relationship is echoed in Martin A. Smith, 'A Bumpy Road to an Unknown Destination: NATO-Russian Relations 1991–2002', *European Security*, 11:4 (2002), pp. 74–5. However, Smith charges that neither party had a strategic plan, across the course of their post-Cold War relationship. NATO observers in September 2000 were of the opinion that the Russians did indeed have a strategy aimed at influencing, or reducing the effectiveness of, alliance decision-making. This dictated the actions and reactions of the Alliance, so highlighting NATO's own strategic shortcomings.

12. Gregory Johnson, 'The Balkans: Prospects and Challenges One Year Later', *NATO's Nations and Partners for Peace* 1/2002, pp. 110–114. Admiral Johnson was Commander-in-Chief of NATO's Allied Forces South, (AFSOUTH) based in Naples. Headquarters AFSOUTH assumed operational command of the SFOR and KFOR missions in January 2001, hence the title of the article written in spring 2002. For publication in a military in-house journal, Johnson's article is refreshingly candid and measured.

13. Speech delivered by Russian Foreign Minister Igor Ivanov at the first Russian International Studies Association Convention, 20 April 2001, published as 'The formation of new Russian foreign policy completed', *International Affairs* (Moscow) July 2001.

14. Willem Matser, 'Towards a New Strategic Partnership', *NATO Review*, 49:4 (2001).

15. Fareed Zakaria, 'Could Russia Join the West?', *Newsweek*, 25 June 2001.

16. Amelia Gentleman, 'Replace NATO by pan-European pact, Putin says', *The Guardian* 19 July 2001.

17. Anatol Lieven, 'Russia and realpolitik', *Financial Times*, 4 October 2001.

18. Robert Cottrell and Quentin Peel, 'A Stealth Fighter', *Financial Times*, 6–7 October 2001. Also, Ian Black, 'Russia hints at rethink on NATO', *The Guardian*, 4 October 2001.

19. 'Putin's big opportunity', *Jane's Intelligence Digest*, 19 October 2001. Also, Vlad Sobell, 'Russia turns west' *The World Today*, November 2001.

20. Andrew Nagorski, 'America's new friend?' *Newsweek*, 19 November 2001, pp. 40–3.

21. Alexander Nicoll, 'Blair seeks closer NATO ties with the Kremlin', *Financial Times*, 17–18 November 2001. Also, Ian Black, 'NATO pledges to reward Putin', *The Guardian* 24 November 2001.

22. Luke Hill, 'NATO fails to warm to Putin', *Jane's Defence Weekly*, 7 November 2001.

23. George Robertson, 'A New Quality in the NATO-Russia Relationship', *International Affairs*, Moscow, January 2002.

24. Dmitri Trenin, *'Silence of the Bear'*, *NATO Review*, Spring 2002.

25. *NATO-Russia Relations: A New Quality*, Declaration by Heads of State and Government of NATO Member States and the Russian Federation. Available at www.nato.int/docu/basictxt/b020528e.htm

26. See Terry Terriff, '"A train wreck in the making": the proliferation of weapons of mass destruction and transatlantic relations', *Journal of Transatlantic Studies*, 3:1 (2005). Also, Terriff, 'Fear and Loathing', *op cit.*

27. Philip Webster, *The Times*, 30 January 2003.

28. Roger Boyes, *The Times*, 17 April 2003.

29. *Ibid.*

30. 'The United States is not pleased', *Foreign Report*, Jane's Information Group, 23 October 2003.

31. Irwin Stelzer, 'Wake up! America is dreaming of a new order'. *The Times*, 19 July 2004.

32. *Honouring of Obligations and Commitments by the Russian Federation*, Council of Europe Parliamentary Assembly Document 10760 dated 9th December 2005. See http://assembly.coe.int/

33. A.I. Voronin, 'Problemi i perspektivi strategicheskovo partnerskva Rossiya- NATO', *Voennaya Mysl'*, 30 November 2005, pp. 39–44.

34. Vladimir Chizhov, 'Sotrudnichestvo Rosii i Evrsoyuza: Vneshnepoliticheskoe Izmerenie,' *Mezhdunarodnaya Zhizn*, 31 August 2005, pp. 155–60.

35. A word of caution is appropriate here: there remains a lingering aftermath of resentment. In recent (summer 05) debates on whether to extend membership of PfP to a particular Central Asian state, Franco-German objections successfully stalled the US-led initiative. Objections centred on somewhat outdated concerns about out-of-area activities, and the ability of the state in question to pay its dues. US diplomacy proved unable to overcome these seemingly innocuous obstacles. Although a minor example, it illustrates the dangers of complacency regarding the assured cooperative future of NATO, and the persistence of diplomatic division among its leading players.

36. Nicholas Burns, Under Secretary of State for Political Affairs at the State Department, is the former US ambassador to NATO. Speaking at Chatham House on 6 April 2005 he made clear the US's continued commitment to the Alliance (http://www.state.gov/p/us/rm/2005/44378.htm).

37. See, inter alia, Paul Cornish, 'NATO: The practice and politics of transformation', *International Affairs*, 80:1 (2004), pp. 63–74.

38. This view, with caveats and suggestions regarding the future development of the Alliance, is echoed in *The United States, The European Union and NATO: After the Cold War and Beyond Iraq*, Report and Conclusions of a Summit on The Future of US-EU-NATO Relations, Center for Strategic and International Studies. Report dated 15 June 2005, online at http://www.csis.org/europe. CSIS can occasionally evince a somewhat nostalgic transatlanticism. For an arguably more clear-eyed transatlantic agenda see Timothy Garton Ash, *Free World*, London 2004.

39. Discussions with senior NATO official, Cambs, July 2005. See also BBC News website, 12 December 2005, *NATO in a spin over Afghan expansion'.

40. See Mark A. Smith, *'Igor Ivanov on Iraq and the struggle for a new world order*, Conflict Studies Research Centre Occasional Paper No 102, 3 February 2004.

41. Kate Hudson 'A pattern of aggression. Iraq was not the first illegal US-led attack on a sovereign state in recent times. The precedent was set in 1999 in Yugoslavia', *The Guardian*, 14 August 2003.

42. Vladimir Putin, 'Seichas mwi uzhe slishim drug druga', *Mezhdunarodnaya Zhizn'*, 31 October 2003, pp. 3–9.

43. Andrew Monaghan, 'Does Europe exist as an entity for military cooperation?: Evolving Russian perspectives 1991–2004', *The Quarterly Journal*, 3:2 (2004), pp. 47–62.

44. Paul Fritch, 'Building hope on experience', *NATO Review*, Autumn 2003.

45. Simon Saradzhyan, 'Kremlin struggles with Ukraine-NATO relations', *ISN Security Watch* 16 December 2005 (http://www.isn.ethz.ch/news).

46. Andrei Kelin, *'Rossiya-NATO: k novomu etapu sotrudnichestva?' Mezhdunarodnaya Zhizn*, 31 December 2004, pp. 79–90. Kelin is the Deputy Director of the European Cooperation Department of the Ministry of Foreign Affairs.

47. Nikolai Poroskov, 'Chetire bukvwi khorosho, a vosem' luchshche', *Vremya Novostei*, 12 May 2005.

48. Yuri Morozov, *Joint Peacekeeping in the Eurasian region: structures and pro*spects, Conflict Studies Research Centre, Russian Series Paper No 04/31 October 2004.

49. V.I. Ostankov, 'Problemi voprosi nauchno-metodologicheskovo obespecheniya voennoi bezopasnosti Rossiskou Federatsii', *Voennaia Mysl*, 28 February 2005, pp. 13–6.

50. See for example John Kriendler, *NATO Headquarters Transformation: Getting Ahead of the Power Curve* Conflict Studies Research Centre Special Series Paper 05/29 June 2005.

51. Kelin, op cit.

10

GERMAN-RUSSIAN BILATERAL RELATIONS AND EU POLICY ON RUSSIA: RECONCILING THE TWO-LEVEL GAME?

Graham Timmins

Introduction: The Common Foreign and Security Policy and Russia

The election of Vladimir Putin as Russian President in March 2000 presented the European Union (EU) with a window of opportunity to develop its relations with the 'New Russia'. Whereas the Yeltsin regime had pursued a policy of benign neglect towards the EU throughout the 1990s and had focussed its attention more on North Atlantic Treaty Organization (NATO) and US relations, Putin had quickly recognized the potential that Russia's relations with the EU presented in supporting the domestic priority of economic modernization. Yet when the Commission report on relations with Russia was published in February 2004 and acknowledged that motivations for cooperation between the EU and Russia existed in a wide range of areas, it was noted that relations had come under 'increasing strain' on sensitive issues. The response, it was argued, was for the Commission and the member states to 'concert their positions and speak with one voice' in order to project a coherent and consistent policy line in negotiations with the Russian government.[1] The report highlighted two interconnected sets of concerns; the first being the institutional shortcomings of the EU's Common Foreign and Security Policy (CFSP) in general terms and the second specifically focused on the emerging 'two-level game' influencing the internal dynamics of EU policymaking on Russia.

The first of these two concerns relates to the incremental fashion in which EU foreign policymaking has developed since the end of the Cold War and the establishment of the CFSP in 1992. As Forster and Wallace have argued, the CFSP was to a great extent driven by the Balkan experience in the 1990s which exposed the EU's continuing dependency on US military power as a guarantee for European stability and accelerated the American agenda for burden sharing.[2] The CFSP was not, however, indicative of a shared European desire for a collective foreign and security policy. As Peterson and Bomberg have argued, the CFSP represented the bullish attitude of some member states that the 'Monnet method' of gradual integration which had been so successful in generating economic cooperation could be applied to foreign policy in equal measure.[3] Although it is possible to be overly critical of the CFSP given the relative short period of its existence, there has been widespread discussion of its failings in addressing what Hill referred to in 1991 as being the 'capabilities-expectations gap' in European foreign policy.[4] The Common Strategy on Russia launched in June 1999 was the first output emanating from an agreement reached at the Amsterdam European Council summit in June 1997 to use common strategies to more effectively coordinate member state positions on key foreign policy areas. But although the Commission was expected to implement the Common Strategy on Russia in order to strengthen the objectives contained in the Partnership and Cooperation Agreement (PCA) signed with Russia in June 1994, it was also decided in June 1999 to create a High Representative for the CFSP who would coordinate EU foreign policy from within the Council Secretariat. There was, therefore, an inevitable institutional tension between the supranational and intergovernmental executive bodies. The creation of a CFSP 'Troika' intended to comprise the CFSP High Representative, the Council Presidency and the Commissioner for External Affairs but which later included the Commission President was intended to provide a bridge between the Commission and the Council but was never going to be more than a 'muddling through' solution to a complex problem of how best to coordinate EU foreign policy short of creating a fully federalized decision-making mechanism.

The second concern relates to the bilateral interaction between the larger member states and Russia and the impact these relationships were having on EU policy. Although the intention to formulate a common EU position on Russia remains firmly in place, the Russian government under Vladimir Putin has on the whole preferred to do business through bilateral channels. Given the high degree of reliance on Russian energy exports shared by many member states and the trade and investment opportunities afforded by the developing Russian economy, the larger member states have to a great extent reciprocated this preference. But this parallel process of EU and bilateral relations, it is argued, has resulted in a two-level game where the larger member states have used the EU level to talk tough on the normative agenda and to criticize Putin on his track record on democratic reform whilst deploying the bilateral relationship for a more pragmatic agenda on economic cooperation. The internal division on EU-Russian relations became highly apparent in November 2003 when Silvio Berlusconi used the Italian Presidency of the European Council to call for a reassessment of the EU's attitude towards Russian military action in Chechnya at the EU-Russia summit in Rome. It was not so much what Berlusconi had said. France, Germany and the UK as well as Italy had for some time been seeking to develop close bilateral relations with Russia and had moderated their criticism of Putin's domestic policies.[5] Rather, it was that the statement had been made within an EU capacity which had caused most controversy and had led directly to calls for the Commission report to be produced. The suggestion made from within the Commission and by smaller EU member states, the latter arguably having more to gain from a cohesive European foreign policy than the larger states, is that the 'pragmatic bilateral level' has effectively undermined the 'normative multilateral level' by reducing the authority of the Commission's 'European voice' in its dealings with Russia.

The purpose of this chapter will be to examine the development of the 'two-level game' from the perspective of German-Russian relations under the Social Democratic (SPD) chancellorship of Gerhard Schröder during the period 1998–2005. German-Russian relations are seen as being pivotal to the EU-Russia relationship and Schröder was quick following the election of the Social Democratic-led 'Red-Green coalition' with the Green Party in 1998 to place Germany at the centre of EU policy development on Russia. This is not too surprising given the geopolitical context of German-Russian relations together with the extensive economic links that existed between the two countries. Moreover, the 'Europeanisation' of the German foreign policy agenda towards Russia is by no means unique to Schröder. Willy Brandt had been successful in Europeanising the West German state's Ostpolitik (eastern policy) in the 1970s via the creation of European Political Cooperation (EPC), a mechanism designed to coordinate European Community (EC) member state foreign policy positions and which had contributed to the creation of the CSCE in 1975. Helmut Kohl had also been quick after the collapse of the (East) German Democratic Republic (GDR) in 1989 to assimilate German unification into an acceleration of the European integration process as a means of reducing any fears its eastern or, in addition, its western neighbours had regarding Germany's international position at the end of the Cold War. However, the German-Russian relationship developed added significance under the Red-Green coalition given Schröder's unwillingness to publicly criticize Putin on human rights, civil liberties and political reform issues at a time when international concern regarding the direction of Russian domestic policy was growing and prompted accusations that Germany was pursuing a *Realpolitik* which favoured economic interests to the neglect of promoting (western) political norms and values. Given this pivotal nature of Germany's relations with Russia, it is somewhat contradictory that Germany would be viewed as the EU member state doing most to damage EU policy.

The Red-Green Coalition's Agenda on Russia

There has been considerable continuity in the policy line adopted by German chancellors in their dealings with both the Soviet Union during the Cold War and Russia in the contemporary context and Schröder in this respect was no exception. All have favoured the articulation of the German foreign policy agenda through multilateral organizations and have adopted a soft power approach of attempting to promote economic partnership as a means of developing stable political relationships.

This policy of 'constructive engagement' could be seen in the position taken by the Kohl chancellorship towards Russia soon after the end of the Cold War. In advocating the need to sign a PCA with Russia, the intention had been to establish a legal basis for the EU's relations with Russia and to link economic and technical assistance with a 'structured' political dialogue. Chancellor Kohl had also been the first western leader in 1997 to raise the prospect of a common economic area between the EU and Russia. The Christian Democratic Union's (CDU) thinking on Russia in the developing post-Cold War agenda can be traced back to the Schäuble-Lamers paper, *Reflections on European Policy*, produced as an internal discussion in September 1994 during the German incumbency of the EU Council Presidency where it was argued that the EU would need to develop a policy which would 'give Russia the certainty that, alongside the EU, it is acknowledged as the other centre of the political order in Europe'.[6] The significance of this statement was that it was the first occasion that any of the EU member states had turned their attention towards Russia in such an explicit and forthright manner. The CDU were at this time focused on the political project of extending the EU's institutional order eastwards and had already made the connection that enlarging the EU to the East would require a policy on Russia which would ameliorate the perception of enlargement as a threat within the Russian leadership.

The SPD in the main shared the CDU's eastern agenda throughout the 1990s albeit with sharp criticism of Kohl's willingness to make extensive financial loans to the Yeltsin Administration without, it was argued, adequate control mechanisms that the funds were being used appropriately or were likely to be repaid given the precarious state of the Russian economy at the time. The SPD was also critical of Kohl's relationship with Boris Yeltsin which had prompted accusations of 'sauna friendship' (Saunfreundschaft) during the 1998 German election campaign on the basis that Kohl had invested too much political capital in the Yeltsin regime to the neglect of democratic reform and the development of civil society in Russia.[7] It is, therefore, somewhat ironic that the new German Chancellor, Angela Merkel, has lodged many similar accusations against Schröder regarding his personal friendship with Putin which has stretched as far as private invitations to each other's birthday celebrations.

In addition to articulating its concerns regarding Germany's bilateral relations with Russia, the SPD had become equally forthright in voicing its growing frustrations with the shortcomings of EU foreign policy during the course of the 1990s. The Srebrenica massacre in July 1995 had prompted a fundamental transformation in German thinking on the CFSP and Germany's military participation in international peacekeeping operations not just in the SPD but across the party spectrum and within society as a whole and added a new emphasis which would lead to the creation of the European Security and Defence Policy (ESDP) during the German Council Presidency in the first part of 1999. But many members of the SPD were equally concerned by Russian military action in Chechnya and the inability of the EU to influence Russian behaviour. Hostilities had commenced soon after the signing of the PCA in 1994 and had led to ratification of the treaty being postponed until December 1997 following the negotiation of a ceasefire. Reports of human rights infringements and war atrocities in Chechnya had once again served to underline the need for a more effective European foreign policymaking process in the minds of SPD officials. But it was not just Chechnya that had prompted the SPD's concerns on Russia. Domestic economic trends which were to lead to the collapse of the rouble in August 1998 had heightened concerns that Russia was in danger of growing political instability. Boris Yeltsin had developed an increasingly erratic style of leadership and there were growing signs that authoritarian factions, of which Vladimir Zhirinovsky was arguably the most dangerous, were starting to gain in electoral popularity ahead of the Duma elections in 1999 and Presidential elections in 2000.

The emerging view inside the SPD was that concerted action among the EU member states was required to address the course of domestic reform in Russia and to persuade the Russian leadership down a route that would contribute to the creation of a stable European political order. But, in addition to pushing the political stabilization of Russia as a foreign policy priority for the EU, there was also an element of economic self-interest driving the newly elected SPD's policy on Russia. Schröder had pledged during the 1998 election campaign to make combating unemployment in Germany his highest political priority. Much as in the early 1960s when West Germany had been facing its first major economic recession in the post-war period and Willy Brandt's eastern policy (Ostpolitik) had been motivated as much by the need to open up new markets into the east as it had been by a desire for the humanitarian gains of reduced tension in east-west relations, Schröder looked to Russia to assist in alleviating Germany's economic difficulties. By the late 1990s Germany had become Russia's largest single trading and financial partner accounting for 17.5 per cent of total foreign trade turnover, 32 per cent of accumulated foreign investment and with over 2,000 Russian-German joint ventures operating in Russia.[8] The motivation to grow the Russian market where there remained considerable investment and export opportunities was not difficult to understand and the establishment of stable bilateral relations with the New Russia rapidly gravitated towards the top of Schröder's list of foreign policy priorities.

In the run up to the 1998 federal elections in Germany the SPD had produced an internal discussion paper which had stressed the need to take a more pragmatic approach towards its relations with Russia and one which would broaden political dialogue. This more pragmatic line would be integrated into a common strategy on Russia and the German Council Presidency in the first part of 1999 was used to complete negotiations. The subsequent *EU Common Strategy on Russia* was launched at the Cologne European Council summit in June 1999 and represented the first manifestation of the EU's desire to strengthen its foreign policy profile and was set within the EU's evolving concept of 'strategic partnership' with Russia with the central objectives being measures which would foster 'a stable, open and pluralistic democracy in Russia, governed by the rule of law and underpinning a prosperous market economy benefiting alike all the people of Russia and of the European Union' and which would assist in 'maintaining European stability, promoting global security and responding to the common challenges of the continent through intensified cooperation with Russia'.[9]

But much as had happened with the PCA in 1994, implementation of the Common Strategy was hampered by the resumption of military hostilities in Chechnya and it was not until the middle of 2000 that any tangible progress could be made in developing relations. But if the EU Common strategy had failed to make the positive impact intended by the EU member states, Germany's bilateral relations with Russian under Putin had got off to the worst possible beginning following Putin's appointment as Prime Minister in September 1999. Already having met with Yeltsin in February and Prime Minister Sergei Stepashin in June, Schröder declined to meet what was Russia's fifth Prime Minister in the space of just eighteen months. Although Putin was relatively unknown and many observers shared Schröder's view that Putin was unlikely to be little more than an interim appointment, the size of the tactical mistake became clear once Yeltsin had announced that Putin was his preferred candidate to succeed him as President at the elections in March 2000. Both Tony Blair and Jacques Chirac moved quickly to arrange meetings with Putin and this put

Germany on the back foot in terms of establishing diplomatic relations with the new Russian Administration. It was not until June 2000, shortly before the Feira European Council Summit, that Putin travelled to Berlin for his first meeting with Schröder and despite Schröder doing his best to play catch up by talking up the summit as the start of 'a new strategic partnership between the two nations', Putin delivered his own snub by first meeting with Helmut Kohl and then caused diplomatic embarrassment by referring to Schröder in passing as the *Fuehrer*.[10] It was not until December 2000, one year on from Putin's appointment as President, that Schröder made his first visit to Moscow and had the opportunity to establish good relations with the new Russian leader.

But despite these personal difficulties, Putin's election had opened a window of opportunity for Germany. Putin had set out an agenda which highlighted economic modernization as the top priority in a wider process of normalization (see Chapter 2). Russia had also started to wake up to the implications that the EU's eastern and central European enlargement would have for the Russian economy and was attracted to the ESDP as an alternative to what it perceived in the Middle-Term Strategy as 'NATO-centrism' in Europe.[11] The growing importance of the EU on the Russian foreign policy agenda was acknowledged in the new Russian Foreign Policy Concept published in June 2000. Whereas the 1993 Foreign Policy Concept had made no direct reference to the EU, it was stated in the new document that 'the Russian Federation views the EU as one of its main political and economic partners and will strive to develop with it an intensive, stable and long-term cooperation devoid of expediency fluctuations'.[12] But the willingness of the new Russian Administration to develop a relationship with the EU exposed the shortcomings of the Common Strategy. Despite the ambitious rhetoric of the Commission President, Romano Prodi, who argued at the May 2000 EU-Russia summit that the EU and Russia were moving towards the 'creation of a wider European area of peace, stability and prosperity, a new European order, a pax Europea between equal partners'[13], the reality of the situation was that the EU was far from having a common policy on Russia and the Common Strategy was heavily criticized for its declaratory nature and prompted discussion regarding whether it could be asserted that the EU had a Russia policy in any meaningful sense.[14]

Divergence in the EU and German Relationships with Russia

The period 2000–5 will undoubtedly be recorded as having been something of a 'golden period' in German-Russian relations as far as the deepening of the economic and political relationship between the two states is concerned. But the same period will also be remembered for its contentious nature given the stark contrast between the positive state of German-Russian relations and the disappointment encountered in the EU's political relationship with Russia which reached its lowest point in late 2004 following the Beslan school massacre and the allegation of Moscow's attempts to influence the Ukrainian elections. Above all else, this period most clearly represents the emergence of the EU 'two-level' game on Russia.

Both Germany and Russia, albeit for quite different reasons, had been disappointed by the Common Strategy on Russia. Schröder had been frustrated by the dilution of Germany's original agenda of generating political stability through the development of economic relations into a set of declaratory intentions which placed the normative agenda at the centre of the relationship. Whereas Schröder's intention had been to replicate Brandt's policy towards the GDR and Eastern Europe in the 1960s of 'liberalisation through stability', the Commission and several of the member states had seen the success in exporting the 'western model' into the Central and Eastern European applicant states during the accession negotiations as evidence of what Ian Manners has referred to as the EU's 'normative power'.[15] What many observers had failed to fully appreciate was that the EU's ability to influence the reform programmes in Central and Eastern Europe (CEE) had been due to the anticipation of membership. As Russia did not seek to become a member of the EU, this particular lever lacked credibility and considerably reduced the ability of the EU to influence Putin's domestic reform programme. Putin was also disappointed by what he perceived to be the absence in the Common Strategy of any attempt to extend a genuine offer of partnership to Russia and had reacted in irritated fashion to the Common Strategy on the grounds that the concept of strategic partnership, it was argued, would have held greater credibility had it been an agreed document with Russia rather than a unilateral document on Russia. The view from Moscow was that Russia continued to be seen from Brussels as an object of EU foreign policy in the Common Strategy rather than being given what it considered to be its rightful place at the European table as a European 'Great Power'. The response from the Russian leadership was the Medium-Term Strategy towards the EU which Putin presented at the EU-Russia summit in Helsinki in October 1999.[16]

It was against this mutual disappointment that the June 2000 German-Russian bilateral summit in Berlin took place and provided an opportunity to restore good personal relations between Schröder and Putin and to develop substance around the concept of strategic partnership. The SPD talked up the summit by anticipating a 'results-oriented' meeting which would foster Germany's economic relationship with Russia. It was also noticeable that public criticism of Russian military action in Chechnya and the arrest of the Russian media tycoon, Vladimir Gusinsky, were played down and human rights issues in general were conspicuous for their absence in German press statements. Putin in turn, described Germany as 'Russia's leading partner in Europe and the world' and attempted to utilize the meeting to exploit European concerns over the US missile defence plans and to call for an alternative European missile defence initiative which would include Russia.[17] What this summit did most of all is reveal the shifting trend in the SPD's thinking on Russia. The criticism that Germany had neglected to foster democratic reform in Russia lodged against Kohl prior to the 1998 election had vanished and Schröder was now happy to praise Putin for his commitment to 'the European community of values' whilst seeking to capitalize on the economic opportunities, in the oil and gas sectors in particular, using an agenda of pragmatism and constructive engagement with Russia. The following year later Schröder took the unusual step of publishing a policy statement on Russia in the German daily newspaper, Die Zeit, in April 2001. In the statement, *German Russian Policy - European Eastern Policy*, it was argued that Russia was the main priority for the EU and that Germany, 'given its location and history was the main initiator and motor of the European Union's policy towards Russia' and called for a broad dialogue that would create 'a new normality in relations between the two states – which would be without illusions and sentimentality, open and trusting but determined and interest-based'.[18] This position was consistent with the SPD's rhetoric signalling a new pragmatism in German foreign policy and was indicative of the generational change which had taken place within the German political class following the 1998 elections. The statement had been purposely timed to coincide with the German-Russian summit in St Petersburg where a bilateral governmental consultation process including strategic working groups at ministerial level on economic and financial relations was agreed and the 'Petersburg Dialogue' was launched as a means of facilitating discussion between politicians, diplomats and specialists on issues of common interest and was seen as a means by which civil society could be fostered in Russia.[19] The Putin-Schröder relationship flourished in the period following the summit in April 2001. With the energy dialogue between the EU and Russia in its infancy and with Germany dependent on energy imports and desperate for new contracts which would create employment opportunities at home, Schröder's motivation to put Berlin in the foreground of the EU's relations with Russia is not difficult to understand. Putin, in turn, was keen to develop close bilateral relationships with the larger EU member states in the assumption that they would provide a means by which the Commission could be circumnavigated where the need arose and were more fitting partners for Russia which began to assert its claim to Great Power status with growing conviction.

From the Russian perspective, Putin saw an advantage in cultivating bilateral relations with Germany for two key reasons. Firstly, western investment and technical support were crucial to Putin's desire for economic modernization. Although Schröder had been unable to arrest the slowdown in the German domestic economy, the large heavy industrial giants were posting record profits as a consequence of foreign investments and by 2005 Germany had become the world leader in the export of manufactured goods. If closer economic cooperation with Europe was the immediate objective for the Russian leadership, Germany was viewed to be the most appropriate partner with whom relations inside the EU could be developed. Secondly, the growing view from Moscow was that the Commission lacked the political authority to engineer a coherent European foreign policy line and that EU-Russia summits were little more than exercises in symbolic posturing where Russia would be berated on its track record on democratic reform. The attack on the World Trade Centre in September 2001 and Russia's willingness to participate in the 'war on terror', not least because it opened up greater scope for manoeuvre in Chechnya, had generated improved relations with the US following the deterioration which had followed the NATO-intervention into Kosovo in 1999 and had reduced the foreign policy importance of the EU in political terms to Russia. In terms of Russia's projection of its interests on to the international stage, it was becoming more beneficial to work with the US than the EU and Putin could afford to be more selective in deciding with which EU member states he chose to work.

In an article produced for *Die Zeit* in April 2002, one year on from Schröder's piece claiming Germany to be the motor for EU policy on Russia and on the eve of the German-Russian Governmental Consultation in Wiemar, Putin pronounced that 'Russia believes in a great future for its partnership with Germany' and pointed to the intensification of the political relationship between the two countries since the launch of their strategic partnership in St Petersburg the previous year.[20] The pay-off for the German diplomatic offensive came at the German-Russian bilateral summit in Yekaterinburg in October 2003 where a raft of political and economic agreements were reached and prompted Schröder to claim that 'Russian-German relations are so good that they cannot get any better'.[21] A combined investment of one billion Euro to fund a range of construction projects and a six billion contract to build the Baltic Sea gas pipeline placed Germany clearly in front as the leading foreign investor in Russia with the combined investment of eight billion Euro by Siemens the largest single investor at the time. When in July 2004 Schröder and Putin presided over the signing of a contract between the German and Russian energy concerns, E.on and Gazprom and which represented the single largest German investment since the Siberian Gas Pipeline deal in the late 1970s, Der Spiegel's headline 'The Hour of the Strategists', summed up the view that German-Russian relations were now driven by economic interests in general and the energy partnership specifically.[22] On the political front, an agreement on transit access across Russia for German military deployment to Afghanistan for the UN peacekeeping operation made Germany the first NATO member to receive such a deal.[23] What Russia in return was seeking was an ally within the western community. Speaking at the press conference after the end of the summit, Putin expressed Russia's new found confidence in stating that 'Russia's arms are getting stronger and stronger and it will hardly prove possible to twist them, even for such a powerful partner of ours as the European Union'.[24]

But if German-Russian relations were enjoying their highest point under Schröder, criticism of German policy towards Russia was mounting in Europe. Schröder's attitude towards German-Russian bilateral relations and the impact it was having on EU-Russian relations had attracted disquiet in Brussels from 2001 onwards when, following the attack on the World Trade Centre in September 2001, he had been the first western statesman to call for a reassessment of Russian military policy in Chechnya.[25] The Commission was highly concerned regarding the potential damage that Putin's preference for strong bilateral relations with the larger member states could have on EU policy should it be reciprocated in western capitals. Moreover, as EU-Russian relations began to move up the political agenda, the smaller member states to the north and east began to push for a more consistent policy on Russia and raised their concerns regarding what they perceived to be the lack of strategic direction towards Russia in Brussels. Alleged human rights violations in Chechnya had been a recurrent irritant in the EU-Russian relationship but western protests at what was perceived to be the growing authoritarianism of Putin's Administration increased following the arrest of Mikhail Khordokovsky in October 2003 and were exacerbated still further in the Organization for Security and Cooperation in Europe (OSCE) report on the Duma elections in December 2003.[26] The consistent refusal by Schröder to criticize Putin in public and his preference to raise what concerns Germany had in private, it was argued, was having a detrimental impact on EU policy

Schröder's policy line on Russia also began to provoke extensive discussion within the political class in Germany and in November 2003 was the subject of a parliamentary debate in which opposition parties lined up to criticize the policy line adopted by Schröder. With the SPD-led coalition looking unlikely to win the federal elections due in 2006, the Christian Democratic Union (CDU) began to articulate the direction in which it would take German policy. As Friedbert Pflüger, the CDU's main spokesman on Russia, argued, although the CDU recognized Germany's interests in a stable Russia and one with which Berlin had close relations, 'partnership [with Russia] requires straight talking from the German government and the EU when in Russia the rule of law is abused and human rights are contravened'.[27] The message that was slowly emerging was that a CDU-led government would follow a similar policy line in terms of the energy dialogue and international cooperation on tackling terrorism but not at the expense of ignoring failings in democratic reform. The Schröder policy line was also putting the Red-Green coalition under pressure. Green party representatives had also spoken out against Schröder in the parliamentary debate in November 2003 and in September 2004 the head of the Green party, Reinhard Bütikofer, joined over 100 international politicians in signing an open letter criticizing the failings of the West's policy on Russia.[28]

Conclusion: Evaluating the Schröder Legacy

The Schröder chancellorship began in 1998 amidst promises that German European and foreign policy would be driven by a pragmatic agenda with addressing the domestic economic situation the government's top priority. By the end of his period in office in late 2005 the German domestic economy had shown little sign of improvement and unemployment had increased. Europe was entering a period of political turbulence following the failure of the Constitutional Treaty and Germany had been unable to broker the financial deal with the UK which it most desired in order to shift a proportion of the budgetary burden carried by Germany. Schröder could look to the Bundeswehr's leadership of the UN peacekeeping operation in Afghanistan as evidence of Germany's growing maturity as an international actor but its traditionally close relations with the US lay in tatters following the Iraq War of 2003. Russia was the one success that Schröder could claim for his own.

Yet growing criticism both within Germany and from outside of his unwillingness to speak out on the democratic shortcomings of the Putin Administration were viewed as an example of realpolitik rather than constructive engagement which effectively undermined EU policy on Russia. Furthermore, when Schröder was appointed to the board of the Russian energy company, Gazprom, and became chairman of the consortium overseeing the construction of the Baltic Sea pipeline from Russia to Germany in December 2005, a project he had helped broker shortly before the German elections in September, he did little to enhance his personal reputation. The deal had angered the Polish government and provoked accusations of a new Rapallo as the pipeline skirted around Polish territory. The fear expressed by Polish observers was the prospect that Russia could use energy as a political weapon to stifle Polish demands for a more assertive EU policy towards Russia in much the same manner as it had been used to punish the Ukraine and other former Soviet republics who had taken a pro-western line or voiced criticism of the Putin Administration.[29]

Schröder was also heavily criticized inside Germany where his decision to accept the appointment had provoked calls for a code of conduct on private-sector involvement of former senior politicians.[30] Despite this almost universal condemnation of the German foreign policy line on Russia, Schröder consistently defended his position on Russia and in an interview with the Suddeutsche Zeitung in October 2004 argued that 'he had no intention of changing governmental policy' on the basis that the state was the only guarantee of stability in Russia and that to criticize Putin's strategy was to misunderstand the nature of the challenge confronting the Russian leader in his attempt to push through reform in Russia but would also run the risk of destabilizing the country to the detriment not just of Russia but also to the European continent.[31]

This response provides an important insight into Schröder's thinking on Russia and rejects the notion that Germany had moved away from its traditional patterns of foreign policy projection during the Red-Green Coalition. Rather than undermining EU policy, it can be argued that the pragmatic approach taken in the development of German-Russian bilateral relations under Schröder filled an important policy vacuum which the unrealistic and declaratory nature of the Common Strategy had created after 1999. The establishment of the Four Common Spaces initiative at the St Petersburg EU-Russia summit in May 2003 and agreement on a 'road maps' approach at the London summit in Autumn 2005 suggests a subtle but important shift towards an 'interests-driven' approach in EU-Russian relations which in the words of the former German commissioner, Gunter Verheugen, will lead to action rather than action plans.

Although German-Russian bilateral relations have been viewed as an obstacle to the creation of a coherent EU policy line on Russia by some observers within the Commission and elsewhere within the EU, the very opposite may turn out to be the case. Germany has been at the heart of the Four Spaces initiative and it was a key Franco-German discussion paper that set out the road maps proposal in the course of 2004. Rather than obstructing EU policy, German-Russian relations have acted as an example of how constructive engagement can be successfully deployed in dealings with the Putin Administration and provide a more pragmatic model for EU policy on Russia. The divergence between EU and German relations with Russia may, given a longer-term perspective, be seen to have acted as a catalyst for change and the development of a more realistic policy approach towards Russia at the EU level.

The interim conclusion where this discussion is concerned is that it is probably too early to fully evaluate the legacy that Schröder will leave behind in terms of the evolution of EU-Russian relations. It will be instructive to see how Schröder's successor, Angela Merkel, takes German policy forward both at the German bilateral level and the European multilateral level. Merkel had announced during the 2005 election campaign that she would take a tougher line towards Russia in terms of democratic reform and respect for human rights and civil liberties and suggested that she would be 'willing to endure "less comfortable" ties with the Russian leader'.[32] During Merkel's first visit to Moscow for the German-Russian bilateral summit in January 2006 she did take the high profile route of meeting with Russian human rights organizations and stated in the press conference following the summit that 'the situation in Chechnya and the Northern Caucasus [were] subjects on which a mutual understanding was not immediately reached'.[33] However, Merkel was keen to reaffirm the new German government's commitment to the Baltic gas pipeline and stressed that her visit marked the commencement of a 'new strategic partnership' with Russia which would go 'far beyond the economic and energy issues' favoured by her predecessor.[34]

Merkel's foreign policy has so far received a positive reception and it is recognized that a Grand Coalition with the SPD is not the best political constellation in which she can distance the CDU from the legacy of the Red-Green Coalition.[35] The coalition agreement between the CDU and SPD was noticeable for the lack of detail on foreign policy and, in particular, the absence of a clear line on Russia. It would, however, be incorrect to argue that this situation reveals a space within which German foreign policy is likely to take a new turn. The Merkel chancellorship during the election campaign and beyond has displayed the typical patterns of German foreign policymaking which will continue to emphasize soft power and the European dimension. Schröder too had started his chancellorship in Autumn 1998 with tough talk on Russia and Merkel may find her agenda is increasingly driven by the economic agenda requiring her to play the same two-level game unless EU policy can be nudged further towards an interests-based process.

Notes and References

1. *Communication from the Commission to the Council and the European Parliament on relations with Russia*, COM(2004) 106, 09 February 2004.
2. Anthony Forster and William Wallace 'Common Foreign and Security Policy: From Shadow to Substance' in Helen Wallace and William Wallace (eds.), *Policy-Making in the European Union*, 4th Edition (Oxford: University Press, 2000), pp. 461–91.
3. John Peterson and Elizabeth Bomberg, *Decision-Making in the European Union* (London: Macmillan-Palgrave, 1999), p. 232.
4. Christopher Hill, 'The Capability-Expectations Gap, or Conceptualizing Europe's International Role, *Journal of Common Market Studies*, 31:3 (1993).
5. It should, however, be noted that the UK is in a different position to France, Germany and Italy in that it is not reliant upon Russian energy exports. See Graham Timmins 'Bilateral Relations in the Russia-EU Partnership: The British View' in Hanna Smith (ed.), *The Two-Level Game: Russia's Relations with Great Britain, Finland and the European Union*,

(Helsinki: Aleksanteri Institute/Kikimora Publishers, 2006). The UK has, nevertheless, been equally reluctant on occasions to criticize Putin but this is due in the main to the viewpoint that such criticism is unlikely to be useful in developing constructive relations rather than being a consequence of energy reliance.

6. Karl Lamers, *A German Agenda for the European Union* (London: Federal Trust for Education and Research/Konrad Adenauer Foundation, 1994), p. 24.

7. Christoph Neßhöver, 'Russlandpolitik: Neue Bescheidenheit' in Hanns W. Maull et al (eds.), *Vier Monate Rot-Grüne Aussenpolitik*, (University of Trier: Arbeitspapiere zur internationalen Politik, 1999), No. 1.

8. Economic Relations of Russia in 1997–2000: Germany, Moscow: Russian Business Press Agency, http://www.bpress.ru/free/er/germany.htm.

9. European Commission, *The Common Strategy of the European Union on Russia*, June 1999, http://www.eur.ru/en/p_244.htm.

10. A mistake which can be less easily explained if it is realized that Vladimir Putin is a fluent speaker of German.

11. *Ibid.*

12. *Foreign Policy Concept of the Russian Federation*, http://www.bits.de/EURA/EURAMAIN.htm#Rfpoldoc..

13. Romano Prodi, http://europa.eu.int/comm/external_relations/russia/summit_29_05_00/prodi_speech_29_05_00.htm.

14. See William Wallace 'Does the EU have an Ostpolitik?' in Anatol Lieven and Dmitri Trenin (eds.), *Ambivalent Neighbours: The EU, NATO and the Price of Membership*, (Washington DC: Carnegie Endowment for International Peace, 2003).

15. See Timothy Garton Ash, *In Europe's Name: Germany and the Divided Continent*, (London: Vintage, 1994), p. 176 and Ian Manners, 'Normative Power Europe: A Contradiction in Terms?', *Journal of Common Market Studies*, 40:2 (2002).

16. *Russian Middle-Term Strategy towards the EU (2000–2010)*, http://www.delrus.cec.eu.int/en/p_245.htm.

17. Angelo Codevilla, 'Europe's Dangerous Dalliance with the Bear', Wall Street Journal Europe (7 June 2001) cited in *Johnson's Russia List*, http://www.cdi.org/russia/Johnson/5287.html.

18. *Die Zeit* (5 April 2001). The article has since been reproduced at: http://www.bundesregierung.de/interview,-35312/Bundeskanzler-Schroeder-Deutsc.htm.

19. See Christian Meier, '*Deutsch-Russische Beziehungen auf dem Prüfstand: der Petersburger Dialog 2001–2003*', (Berlin: Stiftung Wissenschaft und Politik-Studie, 2003) No.10 for a detailed examination of the Petersburg Dialogue.

20. Vladimir Putin, *Die Zeit* (10 April 2002).

21. *Moscow Times* (16 October 2003).

22. *Der Spiegel* (12 July 2004).

23. *Guardian* (16 October 2003).

24. *Ibid.*

25. See Gerhard Shröder's response to Vladimir Putin's speech to the German Parliament on 25 September 2001. Full text available in German at: http://www.bundestag.de/parlament/geschiechte/gastredner/putin/putin_wort.html.

26. OSCE/Office for Democratic Institutions and Human Rights, Russian Federation: *Election to the the State Duma 7 December 2003, OSCE/ODIHR Election Observation Mission Report* (27 January 2004), http://www.osce.org/documents/odihr/2004/01/1947_en.pdf# search='osce%20duma%20elections'.

27. Deutscher Bundestag, Stenografischer Bericht, 75. Sitzung, berlin: Donnersatg, den 13. November 2003 (Plenarprotokoll 15/75), p. 6447.

28. *Stern Magazin* (7 October 2004). The letter 'An Open Letter to the Heads of State and Government of the European Union and NATO' can be found at Johnson's Russia List, http://www.cdi.org/russia/johnson/8385-24.cfm.

29. See Claus Christian Malzahhn, 'Taking Stock of Gerhard Schröder', *Der Spiegel* (14 October 2005), http://www.spiegel.de/international/0,1518,379600,00.html.

30. *Financial Times*, 'Poles angry as Schröder takes pipeline job' (12 December 2005), *Deutsche Welle*, 'Schröder Undoing his own legacy', (13 December 2005) at http://www.dw-world.de/popup_printcontent/0,,1814599,00.html and *The Independent*, 'Schröder on defensive over job with Russian gas company' (14 December 2005).

31. *Sueddeutsche Zeitung* (1 October 2004).

32. *Financial Times* (16 July 2005).

33. Dmitry Babich, 'Merkel in Moscow', *Russia Profile.org*, http://www.russiaprofile.org/international/2006/1/17/3063.wbp.

34. *International Herald Tribune* 'Plain Talk from Merkel to Putin', http://www.iht.com/bin/print_ipub.php?file=/articles/2006/01/16/news/merkel.php.

35. See Marco Overhaus (ed.), *The Foreign Policy of Germany's Grand Coalition: Base Line and First Assessment at the Beginning of Merkel's Term*, (University of Trier: Foreign Policy in Dialogue, 2006) 6:18, http://www.deutsche-aussenpolitik.de/newsletter/issue18.pdf.

11

SHORTCUT TO GREAT POWER: FRANCE AND RUSSIA IN PURSUIT OF MULTIPOLARITY

Julie M. Newton

Introduction[1]

No developed countries embrace the concept of multipolarity as much as France and Russia do. Using fulsome language on frequent occasions, both sides go to great pains to emphasize their mutual goals to replace the current US-dominated unipolar system with a multipolar world order. 'France and Russia', hailed Jacques Chirac, 'have a common vision of the future…, a certain vision of a multipolar world that takes fully into account the end of the Cold War and the process of reunification of the European continent.'[2] This is not mere diplomatic pomp. These two countries genuinely see each other as like-minded pioneers in the struggle for multipolarity.[3] Each views itself as a vanguard power, indeed a great power, with a universal mission to help erect a new, multipolar system of international relations. Each envisions this future system as one in which emerging poles of power – including the European Union (EU) (inspired by France), Eurasia (Russia), China, India and Latin America (Brazil) – would join the highest ranks of the international stage within a multilateral, law-based framework, putting an end to 'unjust' and 'unequal' American unipolarity.[4] Moreover, their multipolar quest even lies at the heart of their bilateral relationship.

None of this is surprising – even though it may seem particularly odd to link France (an established democracy and the seventh largest capitalist economy in the world)[5] and Russia (a 'bureaucratic authoritarian' polity with an emerging, state-capitalist economy)[6] in any serious way. But France and Russia are comparable in highly specific ways that concern contemporary international relations, despite the huge and obvious differences between them at all other levels – political, economic, social and normative.

Comparing France and Russia's pursuits of multipolarity from the mid 1990s to the present day – and especially, explaining the sources of those pursuits – is the subject of this chapter. What are the underlying sources driving France and Russia to embrace foreign policies aimed at erecting multipolarity? Put another way, what informs contemporary French and Russian foreign policy orientations? Are their multipolar visions as similar as they appear? And if not, what might their differences suggest for the future of Franco-Russian relations – and indeed for EU-Russian relations, in general?

Answering these questions, this chapter posits that French and Russian multipolar pursuits are driven by the interaction of at least three crucial sources. The first source is material, flowing from the struggle for power that ensued after changes in the international structure in 1989–91: Russia and France have suffered from parallel geopolitical realities of relative decline on the international stage. The second is ideational: deep in the inner store-chests of French and Russian national identities, they share comparable 'great power' mentalities. And the third source is institutional: the Presidents in both countries (from Chirac to Yeltsin to Putin) show strong preferences for multipolar policies and both countries grant their Presidents unusually great constitutional authority to chart their nation's foreign policy orientation.

Material Sources of Multipolarity: Decline as Catalyst for Change

Any analysis of multipolarity – or the drive to erect a multipolar system of international relations – must begin with the geopolitical structure acting as a catalyst for change. At the most basic level, France and Russia's multipolar pursuits are the predictable geopolitical reactions of two diminished powers to the unipolar order dominating the international system since the bipolar order collapsed in 1989/91. That collapse pitted France and Russia together as the industrial world's 'two great losers'.

Take France first. German reunification issued Paris an immediate international demotion. With Germany reunited, forgiven and physically dominant, France lost its superior post-war rank as the European Community's (EC's) political leader and international spokesman. Moreover, the Union of Soviet Socialist Republics (USSR)'s collapse eliminated France's grand Cold War role as the East-West interlocutor. Those combined events kicked the power-pedestal out from under Paris, leaving the French belittled on the world stage ever since. No longer capable of even aspiring to be the unique broker between East and West, France has grimly faced its new reality of becoming a mere medium-sized power of diminishing economic rank. While France fell to seventh place in the world economies by 2003[7] – down from fourth at the beginning of the 1990s – this downward trend looks far worse when measured on the 'Growth Competitive Index' (GCI), a gauge of a country's ability to sustain economic growth over the medium term. In 2004, the GCI ranked France only twenty-eighth in the world (largely due to structural economic problems), behind the UK (thirteenth), Germany (fourteenth) and Spain (twenty-fourth).[8] This declining reality, combined with growing social discontent, exemplified by French people's rejection of the EU Constitution in May 2005, unprecedented race riots in the suburbs in autumn 2005, and French youths' overturning of labour reforms in the spring 2006, has deepened France's 'nostalgic melancholy',[9] le 'mal français', its sense of 'decline'[10] or, as former Foreign Minister Michel Barnier put it, France's persistent case of 'rheumatism'.[11] The situation appears so glum that a new word has come into French fashion: *déclinologues*.[12]

For Russia, of course, the consequences of 1989/91 were even more staggering with three fundamental collapses. First, the collapse of the Berlin Wall and German reunification quickly snuffed out Russia's outer empire. Second, Russia lost huge portions of its age-old inner empire practically overnight when the USSR imploded. The memorable phrase by Russian President Vladimir Putin – that 'the collapse of the Soviet Union was a major geopolitical disaster of the century'[13] – reveals the traumatic extent of that psychological loss for many Russians.[14] Third, the Soviet economy disintegrated into crisis at the end of the 1980s, as a result of dismantling the Communist system.[15] In combination, this triple collapse left Russia more diminished politically, economically, demographically, territorially and psychologically than at any other time in Russian history, even including Russia's humiliating situation after the Crimean War.

The contrast between Russia and France's sudden, precipitous declines and America's post-Cold War power-surge left Moscow and Paris uneasy. What worried them most is that 'a world dominated by the United States would be one in which their values and interests would be served only at American sufferance.'[16] They feared the growing 'inequality between states', which inflates America's political power on the world stage beyond measure, and rued their own lack of economic or material capacity to correct that political inequality.[17]

In response, both France and Russia turned to foreign policy as their instrument for change. In the mid 1990s, they both actively seized upon the political goal of hastening the shift from the current unipolar system to a multipolar one as their best, if not only, short-term means of improving their international lots. Such a new, more fluid system, they believed, would allow them to exert influence and promote their interests.[18] It would 'diminish, as least partially, the position of geopolitical dominance currently held by the United

States'.[19] As former French Foreign Minister Hubert Védrine explained, there are 'counterproductive' and 'unsatisfactory' consequences of American 'hyperpower' that must be overcome.[20] 'Here is the reason for our desire to work towards a multipolar world.'[21] And to realize that desire, the first step had to be erecting *Europe-puissance* (power-pole). After all, wrote an American observer, 'the European Union is the only likely sponsor of an alternative to Washington's project of a permanent pax-Americana'.[22] Russian Foreign Minister Sergei Lavrov would no doubt agree, although he would probably add Russia as another 'likely sponsor' of the project to overcome *pax-Americana*. To this end, Lavrov claimed, 'A multipole diplomacy has no alternative'.[23]

But was there no alternative? As we will see, it is debatable whether 'multipole diplomacy' was the best, most rational choice for rebuilding French and Russian long-term power or even for generating short-term leverage. Domestic politics aside, additional forces beyond material decline exist to explain their choice of 'multipole diplomacy'.

Ideational Sources of Franco-Russian Multipolar Pursuits: Great Power Mentalities

If geopolitical decline provided the catalysts for French and Russian foreign policy change, it was the ideational factor of a great power mentality that aimed the direction of change squarely towards multipolarity. Citing Dmitri Trenin, Hanna Smith wrote, 'Russian foreign policy is geared to the fundamental goal of redoing Russia as a great power in modern conditions [said Trenin]' *This aspiration informs the Russian predilection for multipolarity*, and this is a theme that appears in all forms of multipolarity in Russian foreign policy arguments from Kozyrev to Primakov, and Ivanov til Lavrov.'[24] France is similar: 'The only myth [among the French] that seems to have survived intact whatever the vagaries of collective experience is that of French *grandeur*.'[25] That is because, as Charles de Gaulle preached, 'France cannot be France without *grandeur*.'[26] In fact, France is even doomed to *grandeur*. As de Gaulle eloquently put it, 'France, because she can, because everything invites her to do so, because *she is France*, must carry out in the world policies that are on world scale.'[27] It is this myth that feeds France's preference for multipolarity today, just as it has done since the Gaullist era.

Such ideational sources of foreign policy behaviour are frequently dismissed as secondary, epiphenomenal, or mere 'window dressing' for material imperatives.[28] But trying to rank sources in this way can be misleading, causing us to underestimate the importance of national identity as a crucial source of foreign policy behaviour. While identity is mutable, manifold and complex, it acts as a national glue made from collective myths and memory by which a nation's people come together in consensus.[29] National identity, as part of the nation's collective unconscious based partly on memory, informs a nation about who and where it is, in what direction it points and where it seeks to wind up. [30] It is a nation's '*compass*'[31], or in modern terms, its Global Positioning System, which not only informs the country where to go, but also indicates what it perceives are the best routes to get there. In this way, national identity influences the way national interests are conceived *and* pursued.[32] It shapes how countries interpret the fast-changing material world around them, and, in turn, affects the way they react in terms of foreign policy behaviour.[33]

For both Russia and France, the myth of greatness is a profound part of their national identities. Both countries perceive themselves as 'great powers' as a result of historical precedent, civilizational contribution or geopolitical stature, and each seeks recognition as such on the contemporary world stage. If 'the Russian mentality is a great power mentality'[34], Vladimir Putin's great power assertions are not just 'spin', but indications of ambition and instructions for action: 'Russia was and will remain a great power. It is preconditioned by the inseparable characteristics of its geopolitical, economic and cultural existence.'[35] In fact, whatever its reality, Russia 'is doomed' or 'predestined' to great powerdom, Andrei Kozyrev once said. 'It remained as such for centuries despite repeated internal upheavals.' Today is no different, and policy flows from that 'destiny'.[36]

'France', too, 'has constructed a national political culture based on notions of greatness, honour and her rank in the league-table of nation.'[37] It is a myth of *la grande nation*, often bearing little resemblance to reality, and is as cultural as material.[38] Permanently lodged in the French collective memory, this myth endures even when objective grounds for it have disappeared. French glory is 'continuous', and 'found whatever the régime in power.'[39] More important still, national catastrophe or material decline actually nourishes the cult of French greatness. 'Far from being undermined by repeated national catastrophe [1870, 1914, 1940, 1961 (Algeria)], [this cult] fed off … disaster to reach fruition.'[40]

This is, however, more about *memory* of 'inherent' greatness than *reality* of present glory. As Jan-Werner Müller writes, '…It is of particular interest how countries which so far have emerged as relative losers of the post-Cold War world – such as France and Russia – are recasting their memories of the twentieth century, and reorienting their policies on the basis of particular "lessons from the past". Often this recasting has taken a radical turn, and memory has become shorthand for a glorious national past that needs to be regained in the near future (and the "near abroad").'[41]

Whatever the memory of greatness, since 1991, myth and reality in both countries have been so out of sync that both nations have suffered identity crises. Post-Soviet Russia's identity crisis caused Moscow's foreign policy to shift and vacillate[42] until President Putin's second term when Russian policy congealed into a coherent 'Doctrine', aimed at rebuilding Russian greatness atop objective pillars of energy-fuelled strength.[43]

For France, that identity crisis manifests itself in a national malaise, a polarized, adrift and 'worried country',[44] threatened by globalization which holds up a merciless mirror reflecting the disparity between France's declining reality and myths of glory. Today, this disparity poses a serious threat to France's traditional model, *le modèle français*, at political, social, economic and foreign-policy levels. So important, this threat even challenges the Fifth Republic. 'Vive la VIme République!' echoes from influential French corridors.[45]

In other ways, too, France's enduring self-identification with *grandeur* (as *la grande nation*) parallels Russia's age-old 'great power' (*velikaya derzhava*) mentality. First, for both, greatness includes a universal role as missionary to lead other states and peoples. Russia, for example, deemed itself during the twentieth century as the vanguard of a new Communist world order based on Marxist-Leninism. Later in that century, Gorbachev baptized Russia as the pioneer of a new Kantian international order based on soft power and inspired by 'New Thinking'.[46] After 11 September 2001, Putin's Russia declared itself the vanguard of a new 'global antiterrorist coalition', 'directed at solving concrete problems', and 'one of the elements of a new global security system in the twenty-first century.'[47]

As for France, it too sees itself as a civilizing missionary, spreading its ideas and voice beyond its borders.[48] This is as true today as it was during the French Revolution. 'We have acquired the conviction of our vocation, our duty, to carry a particular, original voice, a voice that reverberates and is heard across the world...To be French means to take into consideration the world beyond France,' opines Prime Minister de Villepin.[49] President Chirac incarnates this perception. He nurtures a 'vision of a grand and glorious France with a unique leadership mission in the world'.[50]

Second, while both see themselves as great powers with missions, they historically struggle to be recognized as such by their peers. Peer-recognition is hard-going, though, given the myth-reality disconnect. Moreover, it is more elusive for Russia (perhaps even 'superpowered' Soviet Russia) than for France, which until recently ranked near the top of the world economic and military powers (as Mitterrand proudly noted: 'fourth, fifth or sixth economic force, third military power and cultural role 'without equal'[51]). Even so, ever since France's humiliating defeat by Prussia in 1870, the French 'collective mind' has focused on 'the gulf between the glorious past and the prosaic present in which France seemed so insignificant'.[52] This gulf became still more acute after losing the last important piece of the French empire, Algeria.[53] De Gaulle's attempts to repair that gulf by making France the vanguard of an independent

Europe (*Europe Européene*) and a European confederation (*Europe des nations*), the East-West conduit and the trailblazer of a quasi-multipolar bipolarity, were instantly rendered obsolete when Germany reunited. Afterwards, France struggled to find a new platform for exerting global influence. By 1992, that platform became Europe's political union, explaining why France led the charge towards Maastricht. But herein lies France's greatest dilemma ever since: more Europe through political union means less France. France cannot consistently lead Europe if enmeshed inside it – especially now that it is but one of 25 members. France's European path to renewed – and internationally recognized – greatness remains strewn with obstacles.

For Russia, being recognized as a great power is an historical *idée-fixe*. Ever since the seventeenth century, Russia has struggled to overcome enormous obstacles (economic, political, administration, education, transportation and technology) in order to be considered great by its European rivals.[54] 'There is a line to be drawn,' Iver Neumann concludes, 'from Ivan III's 500-year-old campaign to be recognized as the peer of the Holy Roman Emperor to Putin's ongoing campaign to be recognized as the peer of Chancellor Gerhard Schröder and President Jacques Chirac.'[55]

The problem for both France and Russia here is not just that sustained decline in rank or unparalleled loss of greatness is psychologically painful. Rather, losing greatness poses potentially serious political and social troubles, since great powerdom provides sources of social and political cohesion, national stability and political legitimacy for autocratic governments in Russia, faced with Russia's far-flung regions and interests across Eurasia, and a strong, *dirigiste* state in France, whose Fifth Republic upholds a *certaine idée* of the *modèle français* including strongly Presidential political institutions.

As a result of their great-power dilemmas, one possible solution is to *invent* necessary greatness through 'social creativity', as explained by 'social identity theory' (SIT).[56] Here we get closer to the ideational sources of Franco-Russian multipolar pursuits.

According to social identity theory, disadvantaged groups (such as, pre-revolutionary Russia, the former USSR, post-Soviet Russia, or post-imperial France) struggle to attain (or re-attain) superior positioning for their group, even if the material costs are high.[57] When their group has no immediate hope of successfully competing, they find a unique, third way to frame themselves as superior to others; they use deficits to their advantage. In other words, they take 'shortcuts to greatness'.[58] The Soviet experiment was just that: a 'shortcut to greatness' vis-à-vis the West by reframing Russia as the world's unique pioneer of a new Communist order. The same was true of Gorbachev's 'new thinking': Gorbachev recast the USSR as the world's unique soft-power pioneer whose leadership in forging a Kantian world order would lift Moscow to the leagues of post-modern greatness.[59]

Yeltsin's Russia by mid 1990s veered away from Gorbachev's Kantian vision, taking a different kind of 'shortcut to greatness': multipolarity. As a pioneer of a multipolar world order, Yeltsin's Russia would manoeuvre within the American unipolar world to erect new poles of power forming a more egalitarian international system. It employed 'Gorchakovian' tactics, taken from Russian Foreign Minister Prince Gorchakov from 1867–82, who after Russia's defeat in the Crimean War stressed multivectored foreign policies to allow Russia to leverage its power on the world stage[60] – not unlike de Gaulle after both World War II and Algeria.

Putin continues to rely on multipolarity as a 'shortcut to greatness', but has added new means: hard-power economics or geo-economics are emphasized over 'Gorchakovian' politics as a surer way of erecting a Russian great-power pole.[61] But Gorchakovian or Gaullian tactics *à tous azimuths* remain irresistible for Putin; his 2003 alignment with France and Germany against America on Iraq, aimed at transforming the EU and post-Soviet Russia into weighty actors capable of affecting genuine influence, is but one example. Not by accident, Putin, who expresses great respect for de Gaulle, has been called a Russian Gaullist or 'Neo-Gaullist'.[62]

For France's Fifth Republic, multipolarity has also been the preferred shortcut to *grandeur*. General de Gaulle, like Prince Gorchakov, employed diplomatic savvy to enable a weakened France, having just lost the last vestiges of its empire, to 'punch above its weight' and carve out a greater role for itself on the world stage. French *grandeur*, of course, allowed France to pursue regional and global interests more freely, but more importantly, it provided a rare element of national consensus for a country commonly called ungovernable. ('How can you govern a nation that has more cheeses than days of the year?', de Gaulle once quipped.[63]) But, like Russia, France lacked the material means to ensure cohesion at home and protect national interests abroad. So for 45 years, Paris has pursued the shortcut solution of multipolarity (or before 1989 multipolar-bipolarity) via *Europe Européene* and a French-led European-Soviet entente during the Cold War, and the EU after the Cold War. This is why former Minister of European affairs, Pierre Moscovici, embraces *federal* Europe: '[France] knows that she is today a 'power of world influence', but also that she cannot be a truly world power except via a politically united Europe.'[64]

In short, great power mentalities encouraged France and Russia to look for shortcuts to compensate for their material declines, and the *seemingly* fastest, most irresistible route lay beyond their own borders. They sought to resolve their own internal problems, in large part, by trying to hem in the US (especially after the unilateralist-minded George W Bush Administration came to power), by tying it down, like an encumbered Gulliver, in a multipolar world order with enforceable laws and multilateral constraints. None of this is to pass judgment on the merits, demerits or prospects for a multipolar international system; it is merely to point out that Paris and Moscow sought to hasten its arrival for their own internal needs.

Institutional Sources of Multipolarity: Presidential Authority over Foreign Policy

But what if different presidential leadership had existed in France or Russia in the early twenty-first century? Had another leader – unmoved by the appeal of a multipolarity-shortcut and set on an alternative solution to material decline – come to power, then perhaps Russian and French foreign policies would be substantively different today. Leadership preferences matter, for political leaders are not only directed by material considerations when defining state interests, nor are they only motivated by domestic political forces, they are also guided by their own values, perceptions and beliefs.[65] But leadership preferences *especially* matter in France and Russia, because these two countries grant their Presidents unusual institutional powers to dominate foreign policy.[66] For Russia, the President remains the single most important political institution in Russia. Super-presidential powers were institutionalized in the 1993 Constitution, and Putin has enhanced them in practice through administrative reshuffling.[67] President Putin, by concentrating so much power in his own hands through 'the power vertical'[68], has enhanced the considerable constitutional powers bequeathed to him as President. He is the undisputed master of foreign policy,[69] and is considered responsible for the decision to cut gas supplies to Ukraine in January 2006.[70] This situation accords well with Russian political culture, since Russian foreign policy is historically *tsarskoe delo* [a Tsarist matter].[71] In short, Putin prefers multipolarity as a quicker means of enhancing Russia's claim to 'great powerdom' for the sake of state. He is different from Mikhail Gorbachev, who sought great powerdom for the sake of the people, not the state, and for whom multipole diplomacy was not an option, since it decouples foreign policy from domestic reform and compensates for lack of domestic reform with foreign policy-generated leverage.

For France, the 1958 Constitution, revised in 1962, also gives the French President great authority in foreign policy. One Russia specialist at the Quai d'Orsay said, 'it doesn't really matter what we think over here'.[72] Chirac has his *own* policy towards Russia and considers himself *his* own advisor on Russia, since he translated Russian literature and considers himself an expert on Russia, he said. 'French policy towards Russia is mostly made by Chirac himself'.[73]

This is also true of French foreign policy generally, especially during periods of cohabitation when the President 'jealously guards his prerogative'.[74] Even if

France had strong Foreign Ministers in Védrine and de Villepin, they are known to hold ideas commensurate with those of Chirac.[75] And if de Gaulle said foreign policy is *the* primary policy, Chirac employs multipolar foreign policy *as compensation* for economic decline and the difficulty of achieving domestic economic reform. Not all contenders for French leadership (namely, Nicholas Sarkozy) espouse multipolar pursuits with such alacrity.

In sum, the combination of all three comparable sources – parallel geopolitical decline, similarly frustrated 'great power'/ *'grandeur'* mentalities and multipolarity-minded leaders – impels both France and Russia towards foreign policy doctrines for multipolarity that are complementary and mutually supportive. Below, we explain these parallel Chirac and Putin doctrines, and then turn to contemporary Franco-Russian bilateral relations that organically flow from those two multipolar visions.

The Chirac Doctrine for Multipolarity

According to the 'Chirac Doctrine', multipolarity is 'ineluctable',[76] as Chirac puts it; but it must be set into motion by proactive diplomacy. That catalysing job falls to the EU, which must don state-like features, including military sovereignty, necessary to create a counterweight to America and usher in multipolarity. The proactive diplomatic job falls to Gaullian France – a job that Chirac takes seriously. In January 2006, when Chirac upgraded French nuclear deterrence, he pleaded with Europeans to look to French nuclear forces as 'a core element' in the 'ambitious idea of concerted deterrence of the European continent', as the basis of a 'common defence…, with a view to a strong Europe responsible for its own security'.[77]

France is the EU's political leader, but not only France. As Chirac sees it, for Europe to become such a power pole, it has to be built around a Franco-German core, just as Charles de Gaulle believed (though Chirac's rivals disagree[78]). The two countries must form what Chirac calls a 'pioneer group'.[79] Former Minister Védrine calls this duo as 'the voluntary inspirers', the 'trainers' for Europe-puissance.[80] Prime Minister de Villepin goes further: Europe needs 'nothing less than to move towards a "Franco-German union", to put in place "Françallemagne"'.[81] In 2003, the late Jacques Derrida and Jürgen Habermas hailed France and Germany as 'avant-gardist core Europe' and 'locomotives' for this new 'pole'.[82] For all the above, the goal is to create a 'EuroGaullist' Europe, defined as a Europe *vis-à-vis* America, rather than *alongside* it as a would-be-equal *partner*.[83] Given that EuroGaullist EU is the federalist heir of de Gaulle's confederal *Europe Européene*, Ralf Dahrendorf and Timothy Garton Ash were right to point out a 'renaissance of Gaullism' in the early twenty-first century.[84]

Regarding Russia's role in Chirac's neo-Gaullist doctrine, Moscow has a supporting role as a 'major pillar' of the future international order.[85] But Russia cannot be integrated into a Gaullist EU pole. By definition, Russia cannot be part of an EU conceived in EuroGaullist terms for geopolitical reasons: including a country as large as Russia would dilute Europe's capacity to become a cohesive and powerful counterweight to America. 'Russia cannot, must not, be a member of the European Union, not tomorrow or even after tomorrow – in fact, not ever, if this word [union] is to have any meaning. She must remain our external frontier....Instead, it is necessary to build with Russia a privileged partnership, much wider than that which exists today.'[86]

Even so, Chirac considers Russia as France's crucial polar-partner. He continues the Gaullist tradition of maintaining close relations with Moscow to lend further leverage to the Franco-German motor, ensure a stable backyard for the EU while Brussels concentrates on European construction, and guarantee that Bush's America and Putin's Russia do not forge any 'condominium' over European heads.[87] These three objectives guarantee French warmth towards Putin's Moscow, despite Putin's increasing authoritarianism. In the beginning (2000), when Franco-Russian relations chilled in keeping with EU criticism of Russia's new war in Chechnya, it was Chirac who continued to invite Putin to France, and it was Putin who continued to resist until October 2000.[88] President Chirac was also the leading supporter, along with Gerhard Schröder, of Russia's G8 Presidency.[89] From 2005 onwards, as Western criticism of Putin's authoritarian-leaning tendencies mounted and as Germany hardened somewhat under new leadership,[90] Chirac's France insisted that Franco-Russian relations were 'particularly strong' with no criticism publicly mentioned.[91] Indeed the 'Chirac Doctrine' rests on close relations with Russia by definition – explaining one French official's private view that as long as Chirac remains President, Paris will resist stiffening its Russia policy.[92]

The Putin Doctrine for Multipolarity

The 'Putin Doctrine' for a Great Russia in a multipolar world begins with Putin's strategy to rebuild a strong Russian state. A recentralized Russian state can then lead the charge to consolidate Russian authority across the CIS in order to form a Russian- dominated Eurasian power-pole, which would in turn join the nascent, multipolar world order as a great power. Three main features characterize this Doctrine.

First, at home, this Doctrine resembles aspects of the Soviet state.[93] An authoritarian-oriented administration substitutes 'politics with so-called political technology' and 'laws and values with decisions and instructions'.[94] The regime has marginalized liberal-democratic, Western-oriented political parties and civil society development. Moreover, with Russia's new energy wealth (from 1998 to 2005, Russia had seven straight years of growth, averaging 6.4 per cent annually)[95], Russia is more confident to reclaim its title of great power and become the centre of a twenty-first century Eurasian power-pole.

Second, as part of Putin's drive to erect that pole, the Putin Doctrine requires Russia to reconsolidate authority in the CIS. Not only does Putin seek to consolidate Russian power across much of the former USSR, some say that he aims to transform the region into a 'bastion of Russian influence', as 'Russia-plus'.[96] To do this, Moscow puts primary focus on geo-economics, but since 2004, Putin has increasingly resorted to political threats and military pressure. In January 2006, for example, Deputy Prime/Defence Minister Sergei Ivanov warned against those 'trying to change the geopolitical reality in a region of Russia's strategic interest'. Ivanov even compared the threat to Russia posed by this 'interference in Russia's internal affairs by foreign states' to terrorist attempts to 'gain access to weapons of mass destruction.' He saluted recent Russian military upgrades, including the principle of unilateral preventive strikes (using the term 'pre-emptive'), in order to protect Russian security in the region.[97] Given that Russian authority across the Commonwealth of Independent States (CIS) is a prerequisite for restoring traditional great powerdom to Russia, Ivanov's toughness is hardly surprising.

Third, to generate international leverage for this great-power project, Putin asserts an emphatic multivectored foreign policy that boldly points in all directions without favouring any single area or region. His policies are neither pro-Western, nor pro-Asian. Rather, they are Russian, aimed at building the Eurasian power-pole and multipolarity. Putin does not want to integrate Russia formally into the EU or North Atlantic Treaty Organization (NATO) – goals that both Gorbachev and Yeltsin implicitly and/or explicitly sought – since Western membership would frustrate Putin's project. Worse, Putin sees the EU as a troublesome constraint and dangerous contagion (since the EU preaches values such as pluralist democracy, pooled sovereignty, and soft power influence over hard-power arm-twisting – so much of which is alien to Putin's traditional model for Russian renewal.) But neither does the Putin leadership seek entangling alliances with China in the East, India in the South, or America in the West. While it seeks tactical, pragmatic partnerships with all the above, the 'Putin Doctrine' embraces none as a strategic choice. Putin's choice is Russia as an independent power-pole.

Fourth, the EU remains crucial to Putin's project. Besides being Russia's most important trading partner, the EU is also Russia's main political and security collaborator for erecting multipolarity. In 2005, after Europe's vague talk about obligations to embrace Ukraine quieted down when the Constitution failed, a relieved Putin said the EU and Russia should now turn, as equal partners, to *deepening* and *defining* European security – an impossibility, he stressed, if the EU continued to swallow up Russian interests via expansion.[98]

And inside the EU, France is Putin's key partner for political and security questions. Russia views France as the EU's 'political spokesman' and 'unarguable leader' of 'Old Europe'.[99] When the European Security and Defence Policy (ESDP) gained momentum in the early 2000s, Paris, as a leader of ESDP, became even more important to Moscow. As a Russian Embassy official in France said, ESDP was just one example giving hope for a strong new EU in partnership with a great Russia that could better balance America's unipolar power.[100] (Russia's sanguine view of ESDP has lessened over time, however, as EU-Russian discord grows over Ukraine, Moldova, Georgia and Belarus.) Nevertheless, Franco-Russian relations remain Moscow's traditional bilateral bridge towards its multilateral goals.

Franco-Russian Bilateral Relations since 2002

For France, of course, the same is true. The two sides are propelled together by parallel multipolarity visions that are rooted in and explained by mutual material decline, analogous great power/grandeur identities and similar presidential preferences for multipolarity. Their comparable self-identification as great powers charged by history to erect two poles of power explains why Paris and Moscow so greatly value their political relations, despite less impressive economic ties.[101] All this explains why Paris and Moscow declare 'strategic partnership'[102] at remarkably numerous official meetings since 2002, even if Germany remains Russia's greatest interest in Europe. It is why Chirac invited Putin to Paris on a rare *state* visit (Feb. 2003), and why they initiated pioneering bilateral cooperation in the security and defence field. Chirac and Putin (in 2002 at Sochi) established a unique Franco-Russian Cooperation Council on security questions (CCQS) to discuss their mutual concerns and joint visions for all-European security. The idea is to implement those ideas at the multilateral EU-Russia level via the bilateral level first.[103] In 2003, that Council planned and executed joint Russia-French naval exercises, which Putin acclaimed as the first 'step towards building security based on a multipolar world.'[104]

All this culminated in early 2003, when Putin joined arms with Chirac and Schröder to fend off America's invasion of Iraq. Though the move was politically dangerous for Moscow – since it risked hard-won political capital with the US – it represented an unusual chance to corral America's unbridled power through the combined strength of 'old Europe', or what de Gaulle would have called *Europe Européene* 'from the Atlantic to the Urals'. If it had worked, it would have breathed life into the twenty-first century concept of multipolarity, and that might have been the start of something new in the post Cold-War world.

But it failed. For both Russia and France, the lessons were bitter. In a decidedly unipolar world, it was no use to try and punch above your strategic weight. The failure to stop the Iraqi invasion proved that influencing Washington was and is impossible without adequate hard-power, particularly economic. In the summer of 2003, Putin redoubled his efforts to acquire economic might for Russia. He declared a 'new strategic partnership' with the US, fundamental to setting conditions necessary to Russia's economic recovery.

But focusing on America hardly meant reducing Russia's strategic emphasis on the EU – Russia's greatest energy customer and the Western keystone to Putin's emerging project to build a rent-fuelled energy superpower. In the fall 2003, after signing pipeline and technology deals with its priority partner, Germany,[105] and then returning from Rome, the nominal EU centre during the EU-Russia summit, Putin rushed back to Paris for an Elysée meeting Moscow had requested. Putin wanted to reassure Chirac that *in Russian eyes*, France is *the* 'political and security spokesman' for the EU.[106] Putin took pains to assure Chirac that Russia remains loyal to the Paris-Berlin-Moscow troika, viewed as the motor towards a multipolar future featuring both European *and* Russian super poles. In this context, Franco-Russian relations have been celebrated with high-flying symbolic gestures ever since.

In April 2004, Putin even ushered the French President to Russia's top-secret control centre for all Russian intelligence satellites in Krasnoznamensk. Chirac was the *first and only* foreigner ever to be shown this classified security establishment.[107] Chirac returned the honour in March 2005 when he invited Putin to the French Air Force Command at Taverny, one of the main decision centres of French defence.[108] Upon the two leaders' return to Paris, Schröder and Zapatero were waiting for them. The troika had now expanded to a quartet to include Zapatero's Spain. This was followed by yet another troika meeting in Kaliningrad in July.

More recently, as Putin's relations with the West have deteriorated as a result of the Kremlin's increasing authoritarianism, and as France continues to weaken after its rejection of the EU Constitution and mounting domestic woes, Franco-Russian relations are even more important (particularly to France) as lifelines to keep their respective great power/multipolarity projects afloat. On February 13–14, 2006, Prime Minister de Villepin met with Putin to 'speak in unison, *now as never before*, in the international arena', to strengthen the two countries' interaction, and to add new substance to their '*real* strategic partnership', through more economic, technology, energy transfers, space and nuclear-fuel cooperation.[109] 'Our cooperation is not interrupted for a second,' stressed de Villepin.[110] Indeed not: the two sides are co-dependent as a result of interlocking multipolarity visions.[111]

In short, those visions explain why France and Russia, together with the German economic heavyweight, have led the way to institutionalizing broad EU-Russian political and security ties that are now more extensive than those between the EU and the US.[112]

Conclusions: Poles Apart?

But if France and Russia are linked by their joint multipolarity projects, their strategic partnership remains more symbolic than substantive. De Villepin even felt compelled to stress that their 'strategic partnership' is *'real'*. Paradoxically, Franco-Russian relations remain strategically and tactically unfulfilled, no matter how high-flying the rhetoric and frequent the visits. Not only does Franco-Russian trade lag behind Russia's trade with Germany, but also Britain, Italy and the US.[113]

There are two answers to this riddle. The first one has to do with Germany: the geopolitical keystone of Europe. Both claim weighty Germany, and not the other, as their first strategic partner in the pursuit of multipolarity and renewed national greatness. The primacy of Germany reduces the Franco-Russian partnership to supporting status for both sides, whatever the stated goals.

But geopolitics, as always, is hardly sufficient to explain the Franco-Russian lack of deeper substance. Ultimately, that explanation also has to do with divergent normative values between France and Russia. These two countries part ways at the most crucial level – that of aspired normative values, underpinning their political institutions, inspiring their leaderships and affecting the character of their foreign policies. Their respective conceptualizations of 'greatness' are thus irreconcilable. For France, greatness is associated with liberal democratic, EU-style, soft-power qualities of a post-modern power for which sovereignty is relative and negotiated. For Putin's Russia, 'greatness' is conceived in more traditional terms of hard power and total sovereignty, smacking of the nineteenth century. As a result, French and Russian normative visions for a multipolar world order diverge, meaning that Russia and France are, in the final analysis, poles apart. The trouble is this divergence in aspired values also separates Russia from the EU, with troubling implications for the future of Russia's relationship with the entire West.

One last question remains: will the multipolar 'shortcut to greatness' pay off for either side? As for France, perhaps not – at least, not so far. With sluggish economic growth, France's reliance on politics is hardly enough to allow Paris to 'punch above its weight' (or rather, 'wrestle above its weight', given Jacques Chirac's passion for sumo-wrestling) in today's global arena of unprecedented economic competition. Worse, Chirac's Doctrine, combining multipole diplomacy with a EuroGaullist identity-building approach to the European project, has done more to divide the EU than unite it so far. Timothy Garton Ash put it best: 'The neo-Gaullist vision of a unipolar Europe in a multipolar world is a multipolar Europe in a still unipolar world.'[114] Old Europe pitted itself against New Europe (led by Poland, UK, Spain and Italy) over Iraq in 2003. As *Le Monde* editor Colombani lamented, 'Personally, the error I feel the current French leaders have made is to consider that European identity can *only* be forged by opposing the United States.' This attitude, informing Paris's foreign policy generally, has 'weakened the French position and especially its capacity to further French goals'.[115] It is 'a dream as illusive as non-alignment was in the 1960s', he concluded.[116] More worryingly, by focusing 'narcissistically' on the differences between the two brethren Western halves, the Chirac Doctrine is one of the reasons hindering the emergence of a 'post-West' (including 'free countries on both sides of the Atlantic, but ....[not] confined to them'), united to meet the real threats of the twenty-first century – those from global poverty to global warming.[117]

As for Russia, multipole politics have also brought Russia little; witness the failure of the Franco-German-Russian peace camp in 2003. What *has* brought dividends, however, has been Putin's Doctrine to transform Russia into an energy pole of power so it could compete as an economic/political heavy weight on a future multipolar international stage. Will the Putin Doctrine for a Great Russia in a multipolar world turn out to be the successful 'short-cut' for resurrecting Russia as a great power? Judging from the Russian growth statistics of almost 7 per cent, we are inclined to say maybe. But whether this power-pole can be politically stable over the medium to long term, and whether it is about power for the sake of Russian citizens, is far less certain. This Russian power-pole increasingly appears to be '*in* Europe, but not *of* Europe'[118]. It is in European economic space, but outside Europe's normative aspirations based on pluralist democracy, rule of law as a 'causeway' not a weapon,[119] mitigated sovereignty, and soft-power and multilateralism as preferred diplomatic tools. Can this rather nineteenth century vision of the Russian power-pole be competitive or even sustainable in the twenty-first century world? And that makes us wonder whether Putin's shortcut to great power via the multipolar pathway might ultimately lead to a dead-end for the Russian people.

Notes and References

1. 'Shortcut to great power' inspired by: Deborah Welch Larson and Alexei Shevchenko, 'Shortcut to Greatness: The New Thinking and the Revolution in Soviet Foreign Policy' *International Organization*, 57:1 (2003), pp. 77–109.
2. 'Conference de Presse Conjointe de M. Jacques Chirac…et de M. Vladimir Poutine…,' Kremlin, Moscou (2 July 2001), http://www.elysee.fr.

3. Jaques Chirac, Interview to Presse Xin Hua (7 October 2004), http://www.elysee.fr.

4. Hanna Smith, 'What can Multipolarity and Multilateralism tell us about Russian Foreign Policy Interests', in Hanna Smith, (ed.), *Russia and its Foreign Policy: Influences, Interest and Issues* (Helsinki: Kikimora Publications, 2005), p. 36 and Hubert Védrine, *Les Cartes de la France à l'heure de la Mondialisation* Dialogue avec Dominique Moïsi (Paris: Fayard, 2000).

5. Statistics based on Purchasing Power Parity (PPP) calculations of GDP: http://www.cia.gov/cia/publications/factbook/rankorder.

6. Lilia Shevtsova, *Putin's Russia*, (Washington, DC: Carnegie Endowment, 2005), pp. 324–27.

7. CIA *World Factbook*: http://www.geoplace.com/hottopics/CIAwfb/factbook/rankorder/2001rank.html.

8. GCI measures: 'the quality of macroeconomic environment, the state of the country's public institutions and, given the...importance of technology in the development process, a country's technological readiness.' Based on UN/OECD data : http://www.nationmaster.com/index.php.

9. Védrine, *Les Cartes, op. cit.*, p. 63.

10. Jean-Louis Andréani, 'L'antienne libérale du «mal français» *Le Monde* (27 October 2005), http://www.lemonde.fr.

11. Michel Barnier, 'Etats-Unis – Europe : vers une nouvelle alliance ?', Speech, The American University of Paris, (24 January 2006).

12. De Villepin: John Thornhill, 'Fear and Self-loathing in Paris', *Financial Times*, (27 Jan. 2006), p. 8.

13. Vladimir Putin, 'Address to the Federal Assembly of the Russian Federation', (25 April 2005), http://www.kremlin.ru/eng/text/speeches/2005/04/25/2031_type70029_87086.shtml.

14. Almost half, 45 per cent, of Russians still identified with the USSR in 2003: Stephen Whitefield, ed., *Political Culture and Post-Communism* (Basingstoke: Palgrave, 2005), p. 132.

15. See Archie Brown, 'Mikhail Gorbachev: Systemic Transformer' in Martin Westlake,ed., *Leaders in Transition* (Macmillan, London: 2000), p. 15 and Robert English, 'The Sociology of New Thinking', *Journal of Cold War Studies*, 7:2 (2005), p. 70–71.

16. Robert Jervis, 'Understanding the Bush Doctrine', *Political Science Quarterly*, 118:3 (2003), p. 384.

17. Kenneth Waltz, 'Globalization and Governance: 1999 James Madison Lecture, Columbia University', *PS: Political Science and Politics* (December 1999), p. 8–9. Also available at: http://www.apsanet.org.

18. Yevgeny Bendersky, 'Russia's Future Foreign Policy: Pragmatism in Motion', *PINR, Power and Interest News Report*, (4 May 2005) in *JRL*, 4 May 2005.

19. *Ibid.*, p. 2.

20. Védrine, Les *Carte, op. cit.*, p. 9.

21. Hubert Védrine, *Face à l'Hyperpuissance: Textes et Discours, 1995–2004*, (Paris: Fayard, 2003), p. 163.

22. Richard Rorty, 'Humiliation or Solidarity?' in Daniel Levy, Max Pensky, John Torpey, ed., *Old Europe, New Europe, Core Europe: Transatlantic Relations after the Iraq War* (New York: Verso, 2005), p. 37.

23. Sergei Lavrov, 'Forget the Inferiority Complex' *Argumenty I Facty* (April 13, 2005), *JRL*, April 13, 2005. Also available at: http://www.cdi.org.

24. Dmitri Trenin in Smith, (ed.), *op. cit.*, p. 39. (Emphasis added.)

25. Robert Gildea, 'Myth, Memory and Policy in France since 1945' in Jan-Werner Müller, ed., *Memory and Power in Post-War Europe* (Cambridge: Cambridge University Press, 2002), p. 75.
26. Charles de Gaulle, *Mémoires de Guerre I, 1940–1942* (Paris: Plon, 1954), p. 1.
27. Jean Lacouture, *De Gaulle: The Ruler, 1945–1970* (London, Harvill, 1991), p. 393.
28. See Jonathan Haslam, *No Virtue like Necessity: Realist Thought from Machiavelli to the Present* (Cambridge: Cambridge University Press, 2002) and William Wohlforth, 'The End of the Cold War as a Hard Case for Ideas', *Journal of Cold War Studies*, 7:2 (2005), p. 165–73.
29. Jan-Werner Müller, 'Introduction: the power of memory, the memory of power and the power over memory', in Müller, *op. cit.*, p. 18.
30. Thomas Berger, 'The power of memory and memories of power: the cultural parameters of German foreign policy making since 1945', in Müller, *op. cit.*, p. 78–83.
31. English, *op. cit.*, p. 74.
32. J.Newton, Talk at 'ForumduFuture', French National Assembly, (23 June 2005).
33. English, *op. cit.*, p. 74.
34. Evgeni Bazhanov in Smith, *op. cit.*, p. 47.
35. Vladimir Putin, *First Person*, 214; Elin Hellum, 'Identity and Russian Foreign Policy: An Analysis of the Official Discourse, 1992–2004,' MPhil Thesis, St. Antony's College, Oxford (April 2005), p. 36.
36. Andrei Kozyrev, 'Rossiya I Ssha: Partnerstvo ne prezhdevremenno, a zapazdyvayet', *Izvestiya*, 11 March 1994, 3; Kozyrev, 'The Lagging Partnership', *Foreign Affairs*, 73:3 (1994), p. 62–3 and Hellum, *op. cit.*, 27–8.
37. Robert Gildea, *The Past in French History* (New Haven: Yale University Press, 1994), p. 112.
38. *Ibid.*, p. 113.
39. *Ibid.*, p. 115.
40. *Ibid.*, p. 165.
41. Müller in Müller, *op. cit.*, p. 8.
42. Margot Light, 'Post-Soviet Russian Foreign Policy: The First Decade' in Archie Brown, ed., *Contemporary Russian Politics: A Reader*, (Oxford: Oxford University Press, 2003), pp. 422–23.
43. See Andrei Grachev, 'Putin's Foreign Policy Choices', in *Leading Russia: Putin in Perspective*, Alex Pravda, ed. (Oxford: OUP, 2005), pp. 262–3 and Vladimir Putin, 'Interv'yu frantsuzskomu telekanalu TF1' (11 Feb. 2003), http://kremlin.ru/appears/2003/02/11/2356_type63379_29773.shtml.
44. Dominique de Villepin, *Le Requin et la Mouette* (Paris: Plon, 2004), p. 247.
45. Michel-Edouard Leclerc, Interview, Radio Classique, Paris (May 2005); Jacques Lang in: Robert Graham, 'Fears of Change and the Fifth Republic: Why French Reforms must start at the top', *Financial Times*, (1 September 2004), p. 11.
46. Larson and Shevchenko, *op. cit.*
47. Igor Ivanov, 'Nel'zya siloy navyazyvat' demokraticheskiye tsennosti' *Kommersant-Daily* (5 March 2003), 10: Hellum, *op. cit.*, p. 63.
48. Sophie Meunier, 'The French Exception' *Foreign Affairs*, pp. 104–16; Gildea, 'Myth…', *op. cit.*, p. 70
49. De Villepin, *Le Requin…*, *op. cit.*, pp. 250–1.
50. Elaine Sciolino, 'Chirac Clings to his Vision for France', *New York Times* (June 1, 2005). www.newyorktimes.com.
51. Mitterrand's ranking in Gildea, '…Past…', *op. cit.*, p. 112.

52. *Ibid.*, pp. 102–3.
53. Gildea, 'Myth...', *op. cit.,* pp. 70–4.
54. Larson and Shevchenko, *op. cit.,* p. 91.
55. Iver Neumann, 'Russia as a Great Power', in J. Hedenskog, V. Konnander, B. Nygren, I. Oldbert, C. Pursiainen, ed., *Russia as a Great Power* (Abingdon: Routledge, 2005), p. 25.
56. Larson and Shevchenko, *op. cit.,* pp. 77–109.
57. *Ibid.*, p. 90.
58. *Ibid.*, pp. 77–109.
59. *Ibid.*
60. 'Roundtable Discussion – Russian Foreign Policy: Amidst the Economic Crisis' no 1 (1999), *International Affairs* (Moscow), p. 59.
61. Bobo Lo, *Vladimir Putin and the Evolution of Russian Foreign Policy* (Oxford: Blackwell, 2003), pp. 65–6.
62. Vladimir Putin, *First Person*, transl. K. Fitzpatrick (London: Hutchinson, 2000), p. 194. Vyacheslav Nikonov, 'Russian Gaullism: Putin's Foreign Policy Doctrine', *Russia Watch*, no 5 Harvard University (March 2001).
63. French folklore: http://www.dicocitations.com/resultat.php?id=1205.
64. Pierre Moscovici, *Les Dix Questions qui Fâchent les Européens*, (Paris: Perrin, 2004), p. 25.
65. Jeffrey Checkel, *Ideas and International Political Change* (New Haven: Yale University Press, 1997), p. 8 and in *Hellum, op. cit.,* p. 9.
66. On Russian super-presidential powers: Eugene Huskey, 'Democracy and Institutional Design in Russia' in Brown, ed., *Contemporary Russian Politics,* pp. 29–45; On French presidentialism: Ezra N. Suleiman, 'Presidentialism and Political Stability in France', in Juan Linz, Arturo Valenzuela, ed., *The Failure of Presidential Democracy*, (Baltimore: Johns Hopkins Press, 1994), pp. 148–50, pp. 152–7; Nicolas Jabko 'Comment la France définit ses intérêts dans l'Union européene' *Revue Française de Science Politique*, 55:2 (April 2005), p. 227 and pp. 238–39.
67. On Putin's strengthening of powers: Alex Pravda, 'Introduction: Putin in Perspective' in Pravda, ed, 23–36; Archie Brown, 'Vladimir Putin and the Reaffirmation of Central State Power, *Post-Soviet Affairs*, 17: 1 (2001), pp. 45–55.
68. Richard Sakwa, *Putin: Russia's Choice* (London: Routledge, 2004) p. 129, pp. 159–60.
69. Andrei Grachev, 'Putin's Foreign Policy Choices, *op. cit.,* pp. 262.
70. Noted in: Vladimir Frolov, 'Weekly Experts' Panel: Gazprom's gambit or blunder?' *Russia Profile* (6 January 2006), JRL, #7, http://www.cdi.org.
71. Dmitri Trenin, Bobo Lo 'The Landscape of Russian Foreign Policy Decision-Making (Moscow: Carnegie Moscow Centre, 2005), www.cargenie.ru, p. 9.
72. Charles Dernier, Guillaume Narjollet, conversations with author, Quai d'Orsay, Paris, (May, June 2005).
73. *Ibid.*
74. Jabko, *op. cit.,* p. 238.
75. J-M Colombani and Walter Wells, *Dangerous De-Liaisons*, (NJ: Melville House, 2004), p. 66.
76. Chirac in: Védrine, *Face...*, *op. cit.,* p. 19.
77. Jacques Chirac, Speech to Strategic Forces, Brest, 19 January 2006, http://www.diplomatie.gouv.fr.
78. Moscovici, *op. cit.,* p. 91 and p. 219. Moscovici claims this duo is too exclusive for an enlarged Europe. Better to have 'variable geometries' with different leadership associations according to the project.
79. Moscovici, *op. cit.,* p. 91.

80. Védrine, *Face...*, *op. cit.*, p. 347.
81. Moscovici, p. 86 ; as 'bedrock' : D. de Villepin, Visit to Germany, 'Speech at Humboldt University, (Berlin, 18 January 2006), http://www.diplmatie.gouv.fr.
82. Levy, et al., *op. cit.*, p. 6.
83. The opposite of EuroGaullism is EuroAtlanticism, which envisions the EU as global actor in balanced partnership with America: Timothy Garton Ash, *Free World* (London: Allen Lane, 2004), pp. 82–91 and pp. 64–8.
84. Timothy Garton Ash, Ralf Dahrendorf, 'The Renewal of Europe: Response to Habermas,' in Levy, et al., *op. cit.*, p. 141.
85. 'France and the Centres of Power in the Contemporary World', Ministère des Affaires Etrangères, (August 12, 2005), http://www.diplomatie.gouv.fr.
86. Moscovici, op. cit., p. 63 and Védrine, op. cit., *Face...*, *op. cit.*, p. 166.
87. Colombani and Wells, op. cit., p. 128; French 'condominium' fears date to 1970s détente: Julie Newton, *Russia, France, and the Idea of Europe*, (Basingstoke: Palgrave-Macmillan, 2003), p. 86.
88. Newton, *op. cit.*, p. 243.
89. Madeleine Vatel, 'M. Poutine, prochain president contesté du G8, obtient le soutient de Chirac et Schröder' *Le Monde* (5 July 2005), http://www.lemonde.fr.
90. Natalie Nougaryrède, 'La France toujours concilainte avec la Russie malgré les critiques allemandes envers Moscou', *Le Monde* (20 Jan. 2006), http://www.lemonde.fr.
91. See 'Political Relations: France-Russie', Ministère des Affaires Etrangères, Paris, 19 Jan. 2006, www://http. diplomatie.gouv.fr and Michel Barnier, 'Etats-Unis–Europe...', *op. cit.*
92. Dernier, Narjollet, Conversations with author.
93. Grachev, 'Putin's Foreign Policy Choices', *op. cit.*, p. 263.
94. Yuri Levada, Conference: 'Russia: Today, Tomorrow – and in 2008', American Enterprise Institute (14 Oct. 2005), available at: http://www.aei.org/events/event ID.1119,filter.all/transcript.asp.
95. http://www.cia.gov/cia/publications/factbook/geos/rs.html#Econ.
96. Lilia Shevtsova at Conference, 'Russia: Today, Tomorrow – and in 2008', *op. cit.*
97. Sergei Ivanov, 'Russia must be strong', *Wall Street Journal*, (11 Jan. 2006), *JRL*, http://www.cdi.org.
98. *Rossiskaya Gazeta* (2 June 2005) in Nina Bachkatov, 'Russia and the CIS', *Inside Russia and Eurasia* (25 September 2005), www.russia-eurasia.net.
99. Andrei Grachev, interview with author, Paris (2 December 2003). See also Andrei Grachev, 'Mezhdu 'Evrodruz'yami' I 'evrobyupokratami' *Novoe Vremya* no 46 (16 Nov 2003), novoevremya.com.
100. Sergei Parsinov, Porte Parole, Ambassade Russe, telephone conversation, Russian Embassy, Paris, (1 July 2003).
101. 2005 trade volume with Russia: French: seven billion, versus German: 26 billion euros. Laure Mandeville, 'German chancellor sets new tone in talks with Putin', *Le Figaro* (17 January 2006), http://www.lefigaro.fr.
102. 'Russia, France Said Developing Stronger Strategic Partnership', Moscow ITAR-TASS (7 Nov. 2003), http://www.toolkit.dialog.com.
103. French Defence Minister Mme. Alliot-Marie likened it to Russian matrioshkas: the bilateral Council, the smallest doll, fits inside the largest doll, representing Russia's eventual inclusion in European security architecture. The middle dolls represent increasing degrees of defence and political cooperation.

104. Vladimir Putin, 'Interfax Presidential Bulletin Report for July 8, 2003', Interfax (8 July 2003), http://toolkit.dialog.com; 'Russian Foreign Ministry: French naval exercise step to European security system' Intar-TASS (July 16 2003), http://toolkit.dialog.com.

105. 'Russia's Putin, Germany's Schroeder in Yekaterinburg for Consultations', INTAR-TASS (8 October 2003), http://toolkit.dialog.com.

106. Andrei Grachev, interview with author, Paris (June 2003).

107. 'Putin, Chirac Krasnozamensk Visit shows 'Transparency of Russian Space Program', *Izvestiya*, (6 April 2004), http://toolkit.dialogue.com.

108. Isabelle Lasserre, 'Putin in Paris Seeks Europeans' Support', *Le Monde* (18 March 2005).

109. 'France, Russia lInkiede by Real Strategic Partnership' *ITAR-TASS*, (13 Feb. 2006), http://toolkit.dialog.com.

110. 'Dominik de Vilpen: Vysokie Tekhnologii v politike', *Rossiiskaya Gazeta*, (13 Feb. 2006), available at : http://www.rg.ru/2006/02/13/vilpen.html.

111. *Ibid.*

112. Dov Lynch, Conference, 'Russian Security Policy: Evolving Trends and Prospects', Fondation pour la Recherche Stratégique (17 June 2005).

113. *Russia: Import-Export*, http://www.users.globalnet.co.uk/~chegeo/.

114. Ash, *Free World, op. cit.*, p. 94.

115. Colombani and Wells, *op. cit.*, p. 93.

116. *Ibid.*, p. 137.

117. Ash, *Free World, op. cit.*, pp. 182–95.

118. Neumann, *op. cit.*, p. 25.

119. Jeff Kahn, 'The Search for the Rule of Law in Russia', Conference Paper, 'Political Leadership, Political Institutions and Political Culture in the USSR and Russia', St. Antony's College, Oxford, (24–26 June 2005).

12

A EUROPE DIVIDED BY RUSSIA? THE NEW EASTERN MEMBER STATES AND THE EU'S POLICY TOWARDS THE EAST[1]

Kristi Raik

Introduction

Nowhere else is the impact of the Eastern enlargement on the European Union (EU)'s foreign and security policy felt as strongly as in relations with Russia and the other Eastern neighbours of the Union. On the eve of enlargement, it was the Atlanticism of the incoming member states that caused most concern among many old EU countries. However, the fear that the new member states would act as 'Trojan horses of the US' and put a brake on the development of the European foreign, security and defence policy seems to have been unfounded. The same cannot be said about another major concern of the old member states: they were right to assume that the new Eastern members were going to complicate relations between the EU and Russia by bringing the burden of history and their own problems in relations with the Eastern neighbour to the Union's table. The new member states on their behalf were hoping that EU membership would have a positive impact on their relations with Russia. They had also been expecting the EU to move towards a more unified and consistent Russia policy. Yet neither Russia nor the EU have lived up to their expectations: during the first one-and-a-half years of EU membership, (the time covered by this chapter), their relations with Russia developed in a negative rather than positive direction, and the EU still lacks a coherent policy towards Russia that would help to address the concerns of its Eastern members.

The main argument put forward in this chapter is that relations with and attitudes towards Russia distinguish the new Eastern member states from the old and create a division that is likely to be one of the most profound and long lasting ones in the field of EU foreign and security policy. It should be stressed, however, that although the relationship with Russia does distinguish the new member states from the old, there are also important differences among the new members in this regard. The eight Central and Eastern European countries (CEECs) that joined the EU in 2004 are still to a certain extent united by their recent past and geographical location, but they do not constitute a uniform group on most policy issues, and they are mostly not eager to act or to be seen as a distinct group.

Simplifying matters slightly, one can say that the further East a country is situated, the more dominant and problematic the role of Russia is in its foreign policy. The most complicated cases are Estonia and Latvia, and relations with Russia are also a highly important and sensitive issue for Lithuania and Poland. This chapter primarily focuses on these four countries, but the arguments developed below apply to a lesser degree to the other new Eastern members as well. In the foreign policy of the Czech Republic, Slovakia and Hungary, the importance of Russia has somewhat declined. This is explained above all by geography – these countries are located in Central Europe, at some distance from the Russian border, and the Czech Republic does not even have a common border with the Commonwealth of Independent States (CIS) area. Poland, by contrast, shares the border with Ukraine, Belarus and the Russian enclave of Kaliningrad, and hence the development of Russia and other Eastern neighbours has great significance for its security and stability. Finally, Slovenia differs from the other CEECs when it comes to both history and geography: having been part of the former Yugoslavia, it was never directly subject to Moscow's control and its foreign policy and contribution to the EU's external relations are oriented more towards the Balkans and Mediterranean area than the CIS.

Keeping these differences between the new EU countries in mind, the division between the new and old member states is first and foremost explained by the fact that the dividing line between East and West continues to hold an important place in the identity and foreign policy of the former. Having been part of the former Eastern bloc, it is an existential matter for these countries that they have now secured their place in the West. The new EU members are worried about the future direction of Russia and continue to see the Eastern neighbour as a possible threat to their security. Such views distinguish the new member states from the old and especially from the large EU countries. The latter tend to assess the current situation and future prospects of Russia in more positive terms, and do not share the threat perception of the new members. The suspicions of the new EU members towards Russia, combined with the differences between the new and old member states in this regard, account for the strong Atlanticism of the former. Nonetheless, their Atlanticism is by no means directed against the EU; their relationship with Russia also makes these countries strong advocates of a common EU foreign policy, since it is vital for them to receive support from the EU in their Eastern relations.

One of the main goals of the new EU members – especially Poland and the Baltic States – is therefore to influence the EU's policy towards Russia and its other Eastern neighbours. However, for several reasons examined below, it has been and will be very difficult for the new members to achieve much with respect to the EU's relations with Russia. Compared with their awkward, one might even say handicapped position in EU-Russia relations, they have much better preconditions for taking an active part in the EU's policy towards its new Eastern neighbours: Ukraine, Moldova, Belarus and the South Caucasus countries. Through both the EU and bilateral relations, they have indeed been actively engaged in supporting political and economic reform and integration into the EU of the countries situated between the EU and Russia. As we know, this inevitably creates tensions in EU-Russia relations, because Russia and also the new EU countries tend to view the situation as a struggle over spheres of influence. Furthermore, the activeness of the new members in relation to other Eastern EU neighbours has to be seen not only as a policy towards the respective countries, but at least as importantly, as an indirect Russia policy. It is aimed at reducing the threat of Russia by shifting the EU's border – and thus the border between East and West – further to the East. It is one of the hugest challenges of the new members to avoid sharpening the confrontation between the EU and Russia over their common neighbours.

The chapter will begin with a brief discussion of the historical background to the current division between the new and old EU countries with respect to Russia and will then explore the division from the Eastern member states' perspective. The third section of the chapter analyses the EU's relations with Russia, focusing on the positions of the new member states. The fourth section examines the problematic relations of the Baltic countries with Russia in the context of EU enlargement and the common policy on Russia. Finally, the difficult issue of the common neighbours of the EU and Russia will be considered, looking at the aims and interests of the new member states in this field.

The Shadows of History

The painful experience of communist rule will overshadow the new EU countries' relations with Russia and their position in the EU policy towards Russia for years to come. The celebration of the end of World War II held in Moscow on 9 May 2005 made the tensions inherited from recent history surface more strongly than ever since the collapse of the Soviet bloc. The conflict between the perceptions of history held by Russia and the new EU members could hardly be sharper: the victory and liberation of May 1945 celebrated by the former marks one of the darkest points in the history of the latter; whereas the collapse of the Soviet Union, characterized by President Putin as 'the greatest geopolitical catastrophe of the twentieth century', was the happiest dream-come-true for most people in the CEECs. The unwillingness of Russia critically to reassess the Soviet period became apparent in the discussions prior to the celebration. The visible rehabilitation of Soviet history that took place in the Russian domestic arena did not encourage hope of a reconciliation to take place in the near future. As long as Russia refuses to acknowledge the occupation and repression of Central and Eastern Europe (CEE) by the Soviet Union for more than 40 years, relations are bound to remain tense.

In spite of their shared experience of communist dictatorship, there are notable differences between the new EU members when it comes to the impact of the burden of history on their current relations with Russia. Moscow's iron grip was felt most painfully by the Baltic States, which were annexed to the Soviet Union in 1940. The Soviet occupation wiped the Baltic States off the map for half a century until they succeeded in restoring their independence in 1991. Since then, their relations with Russia have been plagued by many problems, which will be examined in more detail below. The Visegrad countries – Poland, Hungary and at that time Czechoslovakia – formally retained their independence during the Cold War, but in practice their experiences of the totalitarian Soviet system were almost as traumatic as those of the Baltic States. As far back as the late 1980s, however, Moscow began to adopt a more compliant attitude towards the withdrawal of these countries from its sphere of influence. Thus their integration into the West has not required overcoming the same degree of Russian resistance as was encountered by the Baltic States.

Poland has been taught by history to distrust not only Russia, but also other European great powers. Squeezed between its two large neighbours, Russia and Germany, Poland has over the centuries repeatedly been forced to submit to one or the other, or has been divided between them. It is from these bitter historical memories that Poland's current opposition to the strengthening of the Franco-German axis within the EU arises. The reverse side of this position is Poland's Atlanticism which is somewhat stronger than that of the other CEECs. The suspicious attitude of Poland towards Franco-German leadership in the EU is to a large extent shared by the other new Eastern member states, most strongly by the Baltic countries. The historical mistrust has been reinforced by the warm relations of France and Germany with Russia, and the willingness of the three countries to join forces in order to counterbalance the hegemony of the United States in world politics.[2] The latter was expressed most strongly during the Iraq crisis in early 2003, when the leaders of the three European great powers together expressed strong criticism of US policy.[3]

The new EU countries are deeply worried about the tendency of large member states to determine EU policy towards Russia at the expense of smaller countries' interests or to water down a common EU policy by their bilateral relations with Russia. In recent years there have been many examples of the large member states' tendency to show more understanding for Russian views than for those of its small neighbours, and to prioritize bilateral relations with Russia over EU policy. In the negotiations held in 2002 and 2003, the large EU members were willing to make concessions to Russia on the transit of Kaliningrad residents through Lithuania.[4] In February 2004, the French President Jacques Chirac paid a visit to Hungary with the purpose of trying to repair relationships with the applicant countries which had been damaged during the Iraq crisis and to demonstrate his support for enlargement. However, his statements (yet again) caused strong irritation in Eastern Europe: according to Chirac, the EU should show more respect for Russia's national interests and take into account its concern about the situation of the Russian minority in the Baltics.[5] In May 2004, France and Germany published a draft document on the future development of relations between the EU and Russia, which again increased the concern of the new member states. Among other things, the Franco-German document proposed a gradual transition towards visa-free travel and suggested increased Russian participation in decision-making on European defence.[6] In September 2005, Germany and Russia bilaterally agreed to build a new gas pipeline under the Baltic Sea. The Baltic countries and Poland were not consulted about the plan which they fear will weaken their geopolitical position.

What worries the Eastern EU countries most is not necessarily the content of negotiations between the large EU countries and Russia, but rather the way in which great powers negotiate among themselves about matters which may be vital for the smaller states situated between them and yet without involving them. In order to ensure that the historical deals between the European great powers, which have caused suffering to smaller nations in CEE, would not be renewed in future, it is of utmost importance to the latter that the EU should speak with one voice in relation to Russia and deliver a message which all the member states have had an opportunity to influence. To some extent, the disagreements among EU countries reflect their different views on Russia's position in Europe: are we dealing with one of Europe's historical great powers which, as a matter of course, has a place at European negotiating tables, or the heir to the Soviet Union, which shoulders the blame for the horrors of totalitarianism? The Baltic States and Poland in particular have made efforts to gain support for the latter view from their Western partners. For example, they used the 9 May 2005 celebration in Moscow as an opportunity to make their historical experience better known to the outside world. On the initiative of several new member states' delegates, the European Parliament (EP) adopted a resolution on 12 May 2005 that commemorates the victims of Nazism, fascism as well as Soviet tyranny.[7] It was also of huge symbolic importance for the CEECs that the 9 May anniversary prompted statements from EU leaders calling for Russia to admit the wrongdoings of the Soviet Union.[8]

The East-West Divide in a New Form

In light of their historical experience, it is understandable that the new Eastern EU members have striven to become part of the 'West' in order to free themselves from the Russian sphere of influence. Membership of the EU and NATO has given them confidence that they are now situated on the Western side of the East-West border, but this does not in their eyes diminish the importance of that border. For them, the East-West divide continues to play an important part in defining their identity and foreign policy. From their perspective, the 'West' continues to be defined essentially through its relationship with the 'East'. The West represents freedom, stability and prosperity, and it safeguards the functioning of democracy, the rule of law and the market economy. To a large degree, the level to which these values are implemented continues to define the EU's Eastern border and divide Europe, although the 'East' is no longer attempting to construct a rival model of society and no longer constitutes a direct threat to the 'West'. Huntington's controversial view of the world divided into civilizations supports this understanding of today's Europe, especially since the border drawn by Huntington corresponds fairly closely to the Union's present Eastern border.[9] The new member states consider this dividing line more important than the old members do.

The transatlanticism of the CEECs is a logical component of this thinking. The unity of the West is crucial for these countries because they believe it strengthens their own belonging to the Western community. The cooperation between the old European great powers, on the contrary, threatens Western unity and creates uncertainty about the position of the countries situated on the East-West border. The Iraq war created a situation where the East Europeans could not avoid choosing their side in the confrontation that split the West, but it is very much in their interest that a similar situation should not occur again in future. If it were to happen, however, the strength or weakness of the EU's policy towards Russia plays an important role in the considerations of the new EU members: the more unified and effective the EU's Eastern policy is, the more important it becomes for the Eastern member states not to do anything that would undermine this policy.

The new member states are particularly active in promoting a stronger EU policy towards the new Eastern neighbours (Ukraine, Belarus, Moldova and the South Caucasus countries). By their activity in this area they wish to prevent the EU's Eastern border from becoming a new velvet or even iron curtain dividing Europe. Thus, the emphasis they place on the continuing importance of the Eastern border does not mean that the CEECs wish to preserve this dividing line; on the contrary, it is more important for them than for the old member states to promote the commitment to Western values and European integration of the EU's Eastern neighbours.

The best guarantee to the stability and security of Eastern EU countries would be the inclusion of Russia in the European integration project on the basis of Western values. However, the CEECs have little faith in this prospect. As is well known, their attitudes towards Russia are more critical and negative than those of the old member states. Russia's turn towards a more authoritarian leadership under Putin, the increase in limitations on political freedom, human rights violations and the situation in Chechnya are arousing more concern and criticism in the Eastern EU countries than further to the West. Although the new member states do not perceive Russia as a military threat at the moment or in the near future, uncertainty about Russia's future development keeps the big Eastern neighbour on their list of potential threats. The official rhetoric of the CEECs has been brought into line with that of the West: Russia is an important partner and is not regarded as a threat. However, the partnership conceals serious concerns about Russia's great power ambitions. Among other things, President Putin's attempt to manipulate the presidential elections in Ukraine, and the nostalgia expressed by Russians towards the Soviet Union in recent discussions of history have strengthened their concern about Russia's imperialist tendencies.

The old EU countries have often viewed the East Europeans' critical stance and fear of Russia as an unfortunate burden of history and have reproached these countries for anti-Russian attitudes and even paranoia. For their part, the new Eastern EU members have regarded their own view of Russia as more realistic. The optimistic belief of Western countries in the development of Russia towards a liberal Western democracy has appeared naive and dangerous in the eyes of the former Eastern bloc countries.[10] In recent years critical voices have gained ground in the West as well, but many Western Europeans still either believe in Putin's commitment to lead his country gradually towards the Western model of democracy, or do not consider this issue to be that important. The US has been more critical than the EU towards the state of democracy, human rights and the rule of law in Russia, and it has more visibly brought these issues up in official meetings between the two states. The Americans have also been more supportive of the former Eastern bloc countries in the historical debate over the Soviet occupation and totalitarianism.[11] This obviously reinforces the Atlanticist orientation of the new EU members. However, it should also be stressed that relations with and attitudes towards Russia distinguish the new EU countries not only from the old member states but also from the US. Although the latter is more critical in the questions of democracy and human rights, it does consider Russia a strategic partner in the fight against terrorism. The East-West border that is still perceived as vital by the Eastern EU members has nowadays little relevance for their most important transatlantic ally.

How do the New Members Deal With the Values-Interests Dilemma?

The EU's relations with Russia are dominated by two closely related dilemmas: between the protection of stability and the promotion of democracy, and between economic interests and political values. These tensions are now greater than ever before since the collapse of the Soviet bloc due to the watering down of value-based cooperation as a result of developments in Russia in recent years, and the increase of mutual economic dependency between the EU and Russia after enlargement. So far it is not clear how the new member states will deal with these dilemmas and find a balance between these conflicting goals in their relations with Russia.

The EU, as we know, stresses the central role of common values in its relations with Russia. By contrast, Russia emphasizes practical benefits of the strategic partnership, expecting relations with the EU to support its political and economic goals. Determined to defend its sovereignty, it does not accept EU intervention in its internal development and decision-making. It is a fundamental impediment to EU-Russia relations that these are two very different kinds of actors: the sharing of sovereignty, which is one of the most characteristic features of the EU, is strongly rejected by Russia.[12] The talk of common values by the EU has not led to their consistent promotion. On the other hand, the strategic partnership and practical cooperation have also remained thin.[13]

The need to reform relations with Russia has been acknowledged in the EU for several years. According to a rather critical Communication issued by the Commission in February 2004, the EU's relations with Russia needed a new approach which should be 'effective, realistic, balanced and consistent' and create a 'genuine strategic partnership' to replace previous political declarations and an ad hoc agenda.[14] The Communication repeats the earlier emphasis on common values as the starting point for relations and expresses concern that Russia's commitment to these values has weakened. It also mentions several issues that concern specifically the new member states (then candidates) and were causing tensions in cooperation between the EU and Russia. These issues included a 'more assertive stance' adopted by Russia towards a number of acceding states and CIS countries, disagreements concerning the extension of the Partnership and Cooperation Agreement (PCA) to cover the new member states, as well as broader treaties with Latvia and Estonia which Russia has not ratified (see more on these below).

The critical approach of the Commission was welcomed by the new member states who had also been demanding from the EU a stricter and more realistic policy towards Russia. The strictness that they still call for means above all a clear definition of the EU's policy and consistent adherence to it by the Union and all the member states. The CEECs have accused the EU of spinelessness and of adopting an overly compliant attitude towards Russian demands. On many occasions they have also expressed their indignation over double standards of the EU: the criteria for democracy and minority rights demanded of smaller Eastern European countries have not been applied to Russia, which for its part has harshly criticised the minority situation in the Baltic States, appealing to Western norms. Instead of double standards and naïve optimism, the new members have demanded of the EU a more honest and critical assessment of the state of democracy and human rights in Russia.

Yet the new member states are also sceptical of the ability of the EU (or any other external actor, for that matter) to promote democracy in Russia. At least at present, there is insufficient will among Russians themselves to build a Western-style democracy.[15] The promotion of democracy may thus be futile or counterproductive, bringing about instability. Hence one could argue that supporting stability in Russia should now be a more important goal for its Western neighbours than the promotion of democracy. On the other hand, the democratisation of Russia would be the best and most enduring guarantee of security and stability of its neighbours in the longer perspective, which is why the new member states keep stressing the importance of common values in EU-Russia relations.

However, their economic interests suggest that they might be inclined to turn a blind eye to the value questions and prioritise pragmatic cooperation with Russia. The share of Russia in their foreign trade is below 10 per cent in most cases, but it is expected to rise in the future. The new member states' exports to Russia are even smaller than their imports, but they hope to take advantage of Russia's current economic growth and raise the level of exports. Even more importantly, the CEECs are dependent on imports of energy, especially natural gas, from the east. Looking for ways to reduce their energy dependency on Russia (for example, through a possible new oil-pipeline from the Caspian Sea through Ukraine to Poland) is a high priority for these countries, but any new solutions are bound to be slow and costly. Hence, to the extent that there is a trade-off between political values and economic interests, it may be rational for the CEECs to keep the two issues separate from each other and focus on the latter.

The new member states have announced (even before accession) their willingness to participate actively in the formulation of the EU's Russia policy. They consider their own familiarity with Russia to be an important resource which can benefit the EU as a whole. After all, it is one of the problems of EU-Russia relations that the parties do not 'speak the same language' and do not always understand each other's way of thinking. The Eastern EU countries are undoubtedly better equipped to speak the same language with the Russians, and not just because of their linguistic skills. However, there are many factors limiting their ability and their opportunities to influence the EU's relations with Russia. The most important obstacle remains the willingness of the large EU countries, most notably Germany and France, to maintain their special relations with Russia and to prioritise bilateral cooperation over common EU policy. From their viewpoint, the new members are a burden rather than a resource for the EU's relations with Russia – a view which is not uncommon in EU institutions and among the old member states in general. Secondly, the new member states themselves have not (yet) formulated a vision of the development of EU-Russia relations, which could be applied as a common EU policy. Their demands of unity and consistency are justified, but they should also make a greater effort to develop constructive ideas. Thirdly, an obvious hindrance is their own bilateral relationships with Russia, which are characterised by prejudice and negative attitudes on both sides, and particularly in the case of the Baltic States, by unresolved disputes. Finally, it is worth pointing out that during the first years of membership, the activities of all newcomers in the EU are limited by their lack of experience concerning the common institutions and procedures.

No matter what the contribution of the new members will be, their accession has increased the pressure to develop the EU's policy towards Russia, since there is no denying the growing importance of Russia to the EU. A positive aspect is that the new member states stress the need for a uniform policy towards Russia and are themselves willing to conduct their own relations with Moscow to a large extent via Brussels. Furthermore, as the newcomers gain experience in the Union, their ability to utilise their knowledge of Russia to the advantage of the common EU policy will gradually improve.

Russia's Shrinking Sphere of Influence: the Baltic Countries as a Sore Point

A large number of the problems (feared and actual) caused by enlargement for the EU's relations with Russia concern the Baltic States, especially Estonia and Latvia. The Baltic countries have been seen as the 'troublemakers' in EU-Russia relations, as they have brought issues such as their large Russian minorities[16] and the lack of agreement on border treaties on the EU's agenda.

Since the collapse of the Soviet Union, it has been one of Russia's foreign policy goals to maintain its influence in the 'near abroad', primarily in the area of the former Soviet Union. The detachment of the Baltic States from its sphere of influence has been a bitter indication for Russia of its weakened international status. For many years, the protection of Russia's strategic interests in its neighbouring areas included rigorous opposition to the Baltic States' membership of NATO. EU enlargement was never opposed by Russia in the same way, but despite accepting it in principle, Russia did in practice place many obstacles in the way of the Baltic countries' accession. Russia's 'assertive attitude' towards candidate countries, noted in the above-mentioned Communication by the Commission, has been primarily aimed at Estonia and Latvia. The main target of criticism from Moscow has been the situation of the Russian minority in the two countries, which has been used by Russia as an instrument for maintaining its influence in the Baltics. Before enlargement, Russia constantly called into question Estonia's and Latvia's EU accession, appealing to violations of human rights in these countries. However, the EU and other international observers have confirmed that the two countries satisfy international norms and the criteria for EU accession in this field (which is not to deny that Estonia and Latvia still face a huge challenge in integrating the Russian-speaking minorities better into their societies).

A particularly sharp dispute between the EU and Russia broke out in early 2004, on the eve of enlargement, when Russia refused to extend the PCA to cover all the new member states. As a condition for the extension of the agreement, Russia presented a list of demands which would protect its special interests against the possible negative effects of enlargement. The EU agreed to most of Russia's demands, the majority of which concerned trade, and these were recorded in a separate protocol that was appended to the PCA. One of the most difficult issues in the prolonged negotiations was the Russian proposal to include in the protocol a specific reference to the protection of Russian minorities in the new member states. The dispute aroused a minor political storm in Estonia and Latvia where it was seen as a test of their ability to defend their interests in the EU, and of the EU's readiness to show solidarity towards its small border states and to protect them from Russian assaults. In Estonian and Latvian public debate, a possible agreement between the EU and Russia on the protection of the Russian minorities was even compared to the secret protocol of the Molotov-Ribbentrop Pact of 1939 which defined the division of the spheres of influence between Germany and the Soviet Union. It was a bittersweet victory for Estonia and Latvia that the EU did not eventually accept the inclusion of this matter in the protocol. A contrary result would have placed them in a strange position in the Union, almost as if they were to be kept in an observation class.

To the disappointment of the Estonians and Latvians, EU membership did not bring an end to Russian criticism – on the contrary, during the first year of membership, the 'attacks' were more frequent than in previous years. For example, in a speech given by the Russian Defence Minister Igor Ivanov in London in July 2004, he defined Estonia and Latvia as 'sources of danger' which were not adhering to the norms of democracy and human rights and instigated military and political tension. Russia has also repeatedly stressed the need to protect the rights of Russians in the CIS countries and the Baltics. In Estonia and Latvia the Russian statements have been seen as part of an intensified propaganda war through which Russia aims to damage their international reputation and position. In the future, the Russian minorities are likely to remain an important tool in Russia's attempts to increase its influence in the neighbouring areas. The Baltic States are also concerned about Russia's influence on their domestic politics. This appeared most strongly in the spring of 2004 when the Lithuanian President Rolandas Paksas had to step down, after being impeached among other things for connections with the Russian mafia.[17]

Estonia's and Latvia's relations with Russia have also been soured by border disputes. The treaties were initialled in the late 1990s, after Estonia and Latvia had given up demands with respect to their former territories that were annexed to Russia during the Soviet occupation. Since then, the border disputes have, strangely enough, no longer been about the location of borders. Russia continued to postpone the signing of the treaties, trying to link this issue to a political declaration including a reference to the Russian-speaking minority, which could not be accepted by Estonia and Latvia. EU accession gave new hopes that the treaties would finally be concluded, as this became an issue of not just bilateral relations, but relations between Russia and the EU, and a possible hindrance to Russia's relations with the whole Union. Estonia and Russia did indeed sign the treaty in May 2005 and it was ratified by the Estonian Parliament in June, and Latvia and Russia came close to signing their agreement. However, the process was stalled by unilateral declarations that Estonia and Latvia attached to the treaty. The declarations made a reference to the Soviet occupation (indirectly in the case of Estonia) and the legal continuity of the two countries going back to the pre-occupation period. Unsurprisingly, they caused a fierce reaction from Russia. Conflicting perceptions of history thus remain the main obstacle to the solution of the border disputes.

The Victory Day celebration in Moscow on 9 May 2005 refreshed the historical memories and revived anti-Russian sentiments among the Baltic population. Along with tens of other heads of states, their leaders received an invitation in late 2004 to join the 9 May celebration in Moscow. Understandably the invitation to celebrate with their former occupier the historical event that for them marked the start of totalitarian rule aroused bitter reactions in these countries. Domestic opinion was divided between 'pragmatists' who favoured participation and 'hardliners' taking a more emotional, nationalist position and demanding a rejection of the invitation. In the end, the Estonian and Lithuanian presidents did not attend the event, but it is worth stressing that their decision was not based on domestic consensus. The Latvian president Vaira Vike-Freiberga, by contrast, chose to join the world leaders in Moscow to celebrate Europe's victory over Nazism, but whenever speaking about this event, she also reminded her audience about the darkest points in Latvia's recent history.

It is unfortunate for the Baltic countries themselves that they failed to take a common position on this highly sensitive and internationally visible issue. The failure indicates a lack of common vision concerning relations with Russia and weakens their ability to promote their shared interests in the EU's policy towards Russia. The domestic debate in each country remains divided between pragmatists and hardliners. The foreign policy leaders tend to favour a pragmatic approach that aims to avoid the escalation of problems and heated reactions to Russian statements, and to normalize relations. They have kept relatively quiet in the EU about their problems with Russia, since this would be likely to harm their position and reputation in the EU. On the other hand, membership of the EU and NATO has encouraged them to make more critical and aggressive statements towards Russia. In the public debate in Estonia and Latvia, several voices have called for a more active pursuit of the border treaties via the EU and demanded compensation from Russia for the damage caused by the Soviet occupation. The EU has not, however, wished to take an active role in these disputes, but has confined itself to stating that it hopes the border treaties will be concluded soon.

Estonia and Latvia still hope for support from the EU in improving their relations with Russia and for protection from pressure and groundless accusations from Moscow. Relations with Russia are for them the most important issue on the EU's foreign policy agenda. The Latvian president Vike-Freiberga even called the ability of the EU to formulate a common policy towards Russia a 'litmus test' of common foreign policy, failure of which would allow Russia to 'divide and rule' aimed at maximizing its own benefit.[18] At least in the near future, the EU is not likely to pass this test, as the member states are unable or unwilling to agree on a common policy that would address the concerns of new members. In the light of the problems causing friction in relations between the Baltic States and Russia, one has to say that although these countries have perhaps the most experience and expertise of all the EU countries regarding their Eastern neighbour, they also have the worst preconditions for utilizing their expertise in the EU's Russia policy.

The Common Neighbours: the EU and Russia on a Collision Course?

Russia's aim of remaining a regional great power distinct from the EU has become more explicit during President Putin's period in office.[19] Having lost its grip on the countries of east central Europe and the Baltics, Russia has attempted to strengthen its ties with the CIS countries.[20] The boundary of Russia's sphere of influence has not, however, stabilized. As shown by the recent revolutions in Georgia and Ukraine and the 'European turn' made by Moldova, a growing number of CIS countries have chosen a Western orientation and aim to become members of the EU. Russian attempts to control these countries have proved to be counterproductive. Since Russia perceives such developments as a further shrinking of its sphere of influence, they inevitably create tensions in its relations with the EU.

As a result of enlargement, the fate of the Western CIS countries and South Caucasus has become increasingly important for the EU. The European Neighbourhood Policy (ENP), which currently creates the framework for the EU's relations with all neighbouring countries, covers six CIS countries: Ukraine, Moldova, Belarus and the Southern Caucasus countries Georgia, Armenia, and Azerbaijan. The EU's relations with these new Eastern neighbours have been a source of friction not only in relations with Russia, but to some extent also within the EU itself, reinforcing the tendency for its Eastern policy to create a division between the new and old, Eastern and Western member states. The new direction of Ukraine and Georgia has been warmly welcomed and supported by the new Eastern EU countries, whereas many old member states are quite reluctant to increase the EU's engagement in the area.

The most active advocate of a specific ENP has for a long time been Poland.[21] The then foreign minister Bronislaw Geremek first suggested the creation of an Eastern Dimension policy of the EU in 1998 in his speech inaugurating Poland's membership negotiations. Poland was critical of the Union's decision to lump all the neighbouring countries together under the ENP, a policy that does not respond to the European aspirations of some Eastern neighbours and does not provide sufficient incentives for them to reform. Poland's – and also Lithuania's – special role in the EU's relations with the new Eastern neighbours was evidenced most strongly during Ukraine's Orange Revolution when the two countries played an active role in negotiating a solution to the crisis in late 2004. After the Orange Revolution, Poland and Lithuania, with the support of many other new member states, called for the EU to offer Ukraine a clear prospect of membership. The Union is not, however, willing to accept any new candidate countries for the time being. The primary reasons are internal: in the aftermath of the 'big bang' enlargement and the French and Dutch 'no' to the Constitutional Treaty there is serious concern that the Union would not be able to function with an ever growing number of member states. In the case of its Eastern neighbours, there is also an important external reason for caution, shared in particular by the old large member states: they do not wish to irritate Russia or to let the European aspirations of some CIS countries harm relations with the largest Eastern neighbour of the EU.

For Poland, Ukraine's integration into the EU is primarily a security matter: Ukraine is regarded as a buffer against Russia, and hence, if it were to reject the 'European option' and strengthen its bonds with Russia, Poland's security would be considerably weakened. The EU's role is regarded as indispensable – quoting a Polish expert, 'The execution of Poland's security interests /.../ will be either executed as a part of EU Eastern policy developed with Poland's participation or will not be executed at all'.[22] The Polish view is more or less shared by the other new member states. They see the integration into the EU of Ukraine, Moldova, Georgia and possibly other Eastern neighbours as a way to promote security, stability and democracy in Europe. One of the main reasons for their position is uncertainty over the future course of Russia – thus, their policy towards the forenamed countries is just as much a policy towards Russia. The promotion of European values and norms in the EU's new Eastern neighbour states is seen as a way to put pressure on Russia to move in the same direction and to abandon its imperialist tendencies. The European integration of Ukraine in particular is a determining factor for the development of Russia – as Zbigniew Brzezinski has put it, Russia can remain a Eurasian empire only if it is able to maintain control over Ukraine.[23] If Russia nevertheless continues to move in an authoritarian direction, the Eastern EU members hope that the countries in between will constitute a buffer against it.

The eagerness of the new members to support the European orientation of the CIS countries is thus essentially linked to the formation of spheres of influence in Europe. From their perspective, the EU should aim to weaken Russia's control over the countries in between, for which the EU and the CIS are mutually exclusive and competing options. This corresponds with the Russian understanding of a zero-sum game being played with the EU. The EU, by contrast, does not formulate its foreign policy in terms of geopolitical realism and refuses to see its relations with Ukraine as a matter of competing spheres of power. In this issue too the new EU countries appear to be closer to the US than to the old member states: it is a geopolitical interest and strategic goal of the US to prevent the supremacy of Russia in the CIS region (although the official position of the US holds that the CIS countries' good relations with Russia and their integration into the Euro-Atlantic structures are not mutually exclusive options).[24]

The tension between the EU and Russia is certainly not eased by the fact that the most vigorous advocates of the new Eastern neighbours within the EU are themselves former Eastern bloc countries. For the latter, this issue involves a strong symbolism and solidarity among nations that have been suppressed by Russia, dating back to the Soviet time and beyond. Having detached themselves from the Russian sphere of influence and successfully completed the transition to democracy and the market economy, the new EU countries are now eager to pass on their knowledge and experience to other former Eastern bloc countries that are still struggling with similar problems. In addition to pushing the EU to become more engaged, they have active bilateral relations with their Eastern neighbours, aiming to spread European norms and values further to the East. It is worth stressing here that the new member states view Russia differently from the other Eastern neighbours: while the EU's chances of promoting democracy in the former are considered slim, there is considerably more optimism with regards to the latter.

Even though the new member states have not been able to persuade the EU to offer membership to countries such as Ukraine, they have definitely made a considerable difference to the EU's policy in this area. The Union has become more aware of and interested in specific problems in the East. It has increased support to the European-oriented reforms of Ukraine, Georgia and Moldova and adopted some new measures (although far from sufficient in the new members states' opinion) against the authoritarian regime in Belarus. Perhaps most importantly, the EU no longer approaches the CIS countries mostly through Moscow as it used to do before. In other words, its policy towards Ukraine and the other new neighbours is becoming more and more distinct from its policy towards Russia. Even though some member states are resolutely against further enlargement and would not mind leaving the new Eastern neighbours to the Russian sphere of influence, no one in the EU can object to enhanced support for political and economic reforms in the neighbourhood. If the neighbours themselves are successful in implementing reforms, the question of their membership or at least closer association will inevitably come onto the EU's agenda in future. In that case the new member states will in themselves be a strong case for their argument: the EU has to remain open to all European countries that share its values, and enlargement is the most effective means for the Union to promote stability and well-being on this continent.

Conclusion: any Common Policy is Better than no Common Policy

The division between the old and new member states over the EU's relations with Russia is unlikely to disappear in the foreseeable future. There are considerable differences between the views of the old and new members not only with respect to the desirable scope, tone and content of the EU's policy towards Russia, but also the history, current situation and future prospects of the Eastern neighbour. The two dividing lines in EU-Russia relations – first, between the new and old EU countries, and second, between the new EU members and Russia – are reinforced by attitudes of mistrust and prejudice which have long historical roots. The EU's policy towards Russia will continue to be plagued by these divisions and suspicions. The tensions are enhanced by the European aspirations of a growing number of countries situated between the EU and Russia, and by the eagerness of the new Eastern members to support this development.

Given the problems and tensions resulting from enlargement, a common EU voice and consistent policy towards Russia is now even more necessary than before. The political and economic significance of Russia pushes the member states towards a common approach, even though they at the same time wish to preserve their bilateral relations with Russia. The new member states need EU foreign and security policy first and foremost to receive support in their relations with Russia and other CIS countries. From their viewpoint, the EU should aim to balance the regional power ambitions of Russia, which are primarily directed at the CIS region, but are also reflected in Russia's policy towards the Eastern EU members, especially the Baltic countries. At the same time, it is necessary for the EU to work against a zero-sum game of competing spheres of influence that tends to evolve in current EU-Russia relations. Because of both their political and economic ties with Russia, it should be in the interest of the Eastern EU countries even more than the Western to avoid increased confrontation. However, the new member states also have a stronger interest in requiring Russia to adhere to European norms and values. Given the present authoritarian tendencies in Russia, it is obviously difficult to reconcile these aims. As argued above, the new members have yet to develop their vision of how to combine their contradictory goals in relations with Russia and how to promote them through the EU.

Finally, it is worth noting that in spite of the huge importance of Russia for the EU, the strength or weakness of the EU's policy towards Russia should not be seen as an indicator of the development of the Common Foreign and Security Policy (CFSP) on the whole. Rather than being a litmus test for the CFSP, relations with Russia constitute one of its most difficult puzzles, but they do not prevent the EU from moving forward in other areas of CFSP. For the new member states, the wish to promote a stronger EU policy towards Russia and the new Eastern neighbours is one of the main reasons for supporting the CFSP and even European integration in general. Thus, it is not in their interest to put a brake on further integration in the field of foreign and security policy. After all, when it comes to relations with Russia, the existence of any common EU policy is better for the Eastern member states than no common policy at all, since a common policy by definition means that there is a possibility to protect their crucial interests.

Notes and References

1. The chapter is a revised and extended version of the section 'Eastern members distinguish new members from old' in Kristi Raik and Teemu Palosaari, 'It's the Taking Part that Counts: The new member states adapt to EU foreign and security policy', FIIA Report 10/2004, The Finnish Institute of International Affairs, Helsinki.
2. See for example Jacek Rostowski, 'Spain and Poland should stand firm on voting', *Financial Times*, 26 May 2004.
3. *Euobserver*, 14 April 2003.
4. The EU-Russia summit held in November 2002 agreed on a simplified procedure (Facilitated Transit Document) for travelling between mainland Russia and Kaliningrad. Subsequently, heated negotiations were held on the details of implementing the agreement, with Lithuania defending its right to control transit through its territory. The issue was finally settled to the satisfaction of all parties; the agreement came into force in July 2003 and has worked satisfactorily.
5. *Helsingin Sanomat*, 25 February 2004, 'Chirac hyvitteli Venäjää'.
6. *Euobserver*, 15 March 2004, 'Franco-German plan sees visa free travel for Russians'.
7. EP resolution on the sixtieth anniversary of the end of World War II in Europe on 8 May 1945 (P6_TA(2005)0180).
8. For example, Günther Verheugen on 2 May 2005, *Financial Times*, 3 May 2005.
9. See Samuel P. Huntington, *The Clash of Civilizations and the Remaking of World Order* (New York, Simon & Schuster, 1996), pp. 26–7. Toomas Hendrik Ilves, Member of the European Parliament and former Foreign Minister of Estonia, refers to Huntington's dividing line when justifying the need for a new EU neighbourhood policy; see T. H. Ilves 'The Grand Enlargement and the Great Wall of Europe', *The Estonian Foreign Policy Yearbook 2003*, pp. 181–200, p. 182.
10. For example, according to Robert Cooper (Director General for External and Politico-Military Affairs, Council of the European Union), 'Russia has largely given up its empire, joining the rest of Europe as a post-imperial state. /.../ Russia seems to have abandoned its imperialist gains and its imperialist ambitions.' Robert Cooper *The Breaking of Nations. Order and Chaos in the Twenty-First Century* (London, Atlantic Books 2003), p. 54.
11. One concrete expression of support, highly valued by the Baltic countries, was a declaration by nine US Congressmen issued in April 2005 (importantly, prior to the 9 May celebration in Moscow) that called for Russia to acknowledge the occupation of the Baltic countries.

12. Dov Lynch, 'Russia's Strategic Partnership with Europe', *Washington Quarterly* 27:2 (2004): 99–118, p. 112.

13. See Hiski Haukkala, 'A Problematic Strategic Partnership' in Dov Lynch (ed.), *EU-Russian security dimensions* (Paris: EU ISS Occasional Paper 46, July 2003).

14. *Communication from the Commission to the Council and the European Parliament on relations with Russia*, COM(2004) 106, 9 February 2004. http://europa.eu.int/comm/external_relations/russia/russia_docs/com04_106_en.pdf

15. This view is supported by public opinion surveys. See Richard Pipes, 'Flight from Freedom: What Russians Think and Want', *Foreign Affairs* 83:3 (2004) pp. 9–15.

16. The Russian minority is largest in Latvia, where it constitutes approximately 29 per cent of the population. The proportion of ethnic Latvians in the population is only 59 per cent; other important minority groups are Belorussians, Ukrainians and Poles. Of the population of Estonia, approximately 26 per cent are Russians and 68 per cent ethnic Estonians. By the end of 2005 nearly half of the Russian population of Estonia and Latvia had been granted citizenship of their country of residence, almost the same number are stateless, and the rest are Russian citizens. In Lithuania the minority situation has not caused problems: Russian speakers account for only 7 per cent of the population, and most of them are Lithuanian citizens.

17. Paksas was charged with violating the Constitution and breaking his oath of office. The presidential election held in June 2004 was won by Valdas Adamkus, who was president of the country also in 1998–2002. The fact that the presidential crisis was dealt with in accordance with the constitution is a notable indication of the viability of Lithuania's democracy and the rule of law.

18. *Dagens Nyheter*, 2 April 2005, 'Lettland kräver enig Rysslandspolitik i EU'.

19. Dmitri Trenin, 'Russia and Global Security Norms', *Washington Quarterly* 27:2(2004): 63–77, p. 77.

20. Lynch, 'Russia's Strategic Partnership with Europe', p. 104.

21. Polish views on the Eastern policy of the EU are outlined in more detail e.g. in the 'non-paper' published in 2003 by the Foreign Ministry of Poland.

22. Andrzej Harasimowicz and Przemyslaw Zurawski vel Grajewski, 'Costs and Benefits of Poland's Accession to the EU in the Area of the Common Foreign and Security Policy and the European Security and Defence Policy', in *Costs and Benefits of Poland's Membership in the European Union*, (several authors), (Natolin European Centre: Warsaw, 2003), pp. 204–17, p. 215.

23. Zbigniew Brzezinski, *The Grand Chessboard: American Primacy and Its Geo-strategic Imperatives*, (New York, Basic Books, 1997).

24. See Michael Baun, 'EU Neighbourhood Policy and Transatlantic Relations: Focus on "Wider Europe"', in Andreas Maurer, Kai-Olaf Lang and Eugene Whitlock (eds.) *New Stimulus or Integration Backlash? EU Enlargement and Transatlantic Relations* (Berlin, German Institute for International and Security Affairs 2004), pp. 63–70.

PART 3

PARTNERSHIP IN PRACTICE

13

EU-RUSSIA POLITICAL RELATIONS: NEGOTIATING THE COMMON SPACES

Thomas Frellesen and Clelia Rontoyanni

Introduction

It has been suggested that relations between the European Union (EU) and Russia can be seen as that between an elephant (being the EU) and a bear (being Russia) in the sense that there are few commonalities, few meeting points, and little common understanding.[1] From this perspective, Russia is stuck in the nineteenth century geopolitical state-to-state thinking, while the EU approaches the external world from a unique, postmodern standpoint. The scope for misunderstanding would thus appear to be very significant.

The EU's policy towards Russia is sometimes criticized as a failure. Some commentators argue that in fact there has not been much of a common policy at all. Member states often seem to pursue their own interests with Russia, led mainly by trade and energy considerations, to the detriment of common EU positions. While there may be elements of truth in both assertions, we will argue that EU-Russia relations have advanced significantly over the past years. Extreme scepticism is misplaced.

In the past two years, the EU and Russia have agreed to work towards increasingly close cooperation (possibly containing elements of convergence and integration in selected areas) in four broad domains that encompass nearly the whole range of the EU's multifaceted relations with Russia. These broad areas are now known as the 'four common spaces', which were initially agreed at the St Petersburg summit of May 2003: a Common Economic Space (CES); a Common Space of Freedom, Security and Justice; a Common Space of External Security; and a Common Space of Research and Education.

This chapter will aim to give a broad overview of the main directions of the EU's political relations with Russia – especially dialogue and cooperation in the areas of internal and external security (the second and third common spaces) and place it in the context of the evolving EU foreign policy. It will seek to address some of the main arguments and criticisms, including those pointing to a lack of unity and consistency on the part of the EU. Finally, the chapter will attempt to shed some light on the debate over the so-called 'values gap' dividing the EU and Russia with reference to the issue of Chechnya.

Russia in the Overall EU Foreign Policy Context

The EU is not a state and therefore it cannot be seen as a foreign policy actor in the traditional sense. Many EU specialists have pointed out that the EU's economic weight is not matched by proportionate political clout. There can be little doubt that the EU's capacity to define and pursue foreign policy objectives lags behind that of the US, despite the comparable size of the two economies. The EU has more limited instruments and resources and, most importantly, EU member states have not yet fully committed to developing a single EU foreign policy and speaking consistently with one voice. To an extent, the EU's 'Common' Foreign and Security Policy (CFSP) still remains aspirational. Common foreign policy positions tend to concern specific areas, leaving ample scope for member states to pursue their bilateral policies in parallel.

The EU Constitution, which was put on hold by the negative referenda in France and the Netherlands in spring 2005, could have done much to strengthen the EU foreign policy machinery. In particular, the adoption of the Constitution would introduce the post of an EU Foreign Minister and abolish the system of half-yearly rotating Presidencies by EU member states, which undermines policy continuity and has proved rather confusing and irritating to third countries.

Nevertheless, if one looks at EU external relations and the development of the CFSP over the past decade one cannot but be struck by what has been achieved in a relatively short time-span. The EU had conducted an external relations policy for decades prior to the introduction of CFSP in 1992 via its traditional Community instruments of trade and development assistance (managed by the Commission). The CFSP added a new political focus and the explicit intention to act in a more deliberate and concerted manner in relation to third countries and international issues than had hitherto been the case. The addition of a European Security and Defence Policy (ESDP) as part of CFSP in the late 1990s has led to previously unthinkable activities for those who saw the EU primarily as a glorified trading bloc. For example, the EU has taken over police and military missions from the UN and North Atlantic Treaty Organization (NATO) in the Balkans and led its own military mission in Africa.[2]

Perhaps most importantly, the EU's eastward enlargement, which will eventually include 11 Central European countries – former allies or republics of the Soviet Union[3] – could in itself be seen as arguably the EU's greatest foreign policy achievement in terms of projecting stability and prosperity beyond the Union's borders. The EU has also launched a European Neighbourhood Policy (ENP) to reinforce relations with those countries surrounding the EU, which are unlikely to join the EU in the foreseeable future.

There can be little doubt that Russia is by far the EU's most important neighbour. On the other hand, relations with Russia have posed some of the most difficult challenges for EU foreign policy. Compared to its other neighbours, the EU's leverage in relation to Russia is much more limited. To a large extent, this is due to Russia's aloofness from EU-centric integration processes. Russia's size and its perception as 'different' from the rest of Europe, which still seems quite prevalent both in the EU and – most importantly – in Russia's self-image, make it a rather unlikely volunteer for EU membership even in the longer term. In the case of Russia, the EU's policy toolkit lacks the instrument of accession, which has proved such a powerful stimulus for the political and economic reform processes pursued by Russia's Central European neighbours.[4] As a result, Russia seems rather immune to the 'transformational effect' of an EU gravitational pull. In addition, member states do not always agree on the best approach to take with regard to Russia, whose diplomacy has at times skilfully capitalized on occasional differences in the priorities of EU member states to bolster its demands *vis-à-vis* the Union as a whole. This can be seen for example in Russia's pursuit of visa facilitation arrangements.[5]

However, internal EU disagreements on Russia should not be exaggerated. There is a consensus about the need for strong partnership with a democratic, liberal Russia. At times member states may differ about how best to achieve such a partnership, and what degree of 'firmness' or 'friendliness' should be applied, especially when approaching the sensitive issue of Russia's adherence to the 'common values' of democracy and human rights. The existence of a broad EU consensus on relations with Russia explains why there was such uproar in the Council and the European Parliament after the Rome EU-Russia Summit of November 2003, when Prime Minister Berlusconi violated the common line by expressing his own views on Chechnya and the Yukos affair. Partly in response to this, in February 2004 the Commission issued a *Communication* on relations with Russia, which inter alia recommended that the EU should improve the coherence of its policy towards Russia, including by agreeing a set of priorities and common positions at the beginning of each Presidency. An implicit intention was to guard against the risk of other EU leaders violating the 'gentlemen's agreement' that requires the Presidency to speak on behalf of the EU as a whole. The Commission *Communication* also stressed the need for shared values as well as common interests as the basis of a genuine strategic partnership with Russia and called for a frank dialogue with Russia on common values, notably democracy and human rights.[6] The General Affairs and External Relations Council endorsed the Commission's recommendations in its session of 24 February 2004.

EU-Russia Relations Reviewed

It is beyond the scope of this chapter to review the entirety of EU-Russia relations. It is however worth noting that these relations have intensified dramatically over the past years. The trade figures provide a good illustration: after the latest EU enlargement the EU is the destination of more than half of Russia's exports. While Russia's share is comparatively smaller in the EU's external trade, it has nevertheless become the EU's fourth largest trade partner and the key supplier of its energy.

On the other hand, EU-Russia relations are about much more than trade and energy. The EU's technical assistance programme, Technical Assistance for the Commonwealth of Independent States (TACIS), which has supported Russia's reform efforts for more than a decade, is currently being transformed into a bilateral cooperation programme to reflect the equal basis of the EU-Russia relationship. In line with Russia's growing prosperity and consolidation of internal reform processes, a review of TACIS is oriented towards progressively supporting EU-Russia interaction under the four common spaces and towards co-financing of joint projects by the EU and Russia. In addition, Russia now participates in the EU's research programmes and Russian students participate in the Erasmus programme. Millions of Russians visit the EU as tourists annually, making Russia the most important new source of income for the European tourist industry.

The EU and Russia now share more than 2000 kilometres of common borders, making issues of border management and security mutual priorities for cooperation. The fact that we now share such a long common border illustrates how interdependent the EU and Russia have become: joint approaches will be necessary if the EU and Russia are to tackle shared challenges and threats such as illegal migration, pollution, or cross-border crime effectively.

As the EU is developing its own CFSP, cooperation with Russia on foreign policy issues is expanding beyond issues where cooperation has traditionally been good, such as the Middle East Peace Process, to include other issues of mutual concern such as the 'frozen conflicts' (in Transdniestria in Moldova, Abkhazia, South Ossetia and Nagorno-Karabakh in the South Caucasus) in what the EU likes to call 'our common neighbourhood'.

The functional expansion of EU-Russia relations is in fact the foremost reason for revisiting the contractual framework for relations, the Partnership and Cooperation Agreement (PCA), which is due for renewal in 2007. The PCA has provided a good and solid framework for relations over the past decade (with structured dialogue mechanisms and legally binding provisions for settling issues such as trade disputes). However, in the 12 years that have followed the conclusion of the PCA, much has changed in Russia and within the EU as well as in the breadth and content of bilateral relations. It is therefore widely acknowledged that the agreement no longer fully reflects the reality of the relationship and will need to be updated and adapted. A relevant discussion was ongoing at the time of writing, so it would be somewhat premature to speculate on the eventual outcome of the review of the framework of EU-Russia relations. Nevertheless, a new framework for bilateral relations can be expected to emerge from these discussions.

Negotiating the Common Spaces

Meanwhile the common midterm agenda has been fleshed out in the road maps for the four common spaces agreed at the Moscow EU-Russia Summit in May 2005.[7] The origin of the 'common spaces' can be traced back to the idea of former Commission President Prodi for the establishment of a Common European Economic Space (CEES) between the EU and Russia in 2001 to promote greater interaction and convergence between the economies and societies of the two sides, including through a free trade area. Work on this concept continued for two years and formed part of what was to become the first common space.[8] These efforts will be given a further boost by Russia's expected accession to the World Trade Organization (WTO).

Efforts to provide new impetus to EU-Russia relations in spring 2003, when relations were tense over Kaliningrad transit and other issues related to the EU's coming enlargement, gave rise to the idea of extending the concept of the economic space to cover other areas in the relationship. It is difficult to pinpoint the specific origin of the four spaces initiative. A small group of EU ambassadors in Moscow also played an active role in pushing the idea from a sense that it would be a good way to create a positive agenda and find a way out of the rather negative atmosphere that the enlargement-related issues (Russian concerns over potential loss of trade, new visa barriers, difficulties in transit between Kaliningrad and mainland Russia) had created.

The four spaces in their very nature mirrored the kind of action plans that had been developed in previous EU partnerships, such as the New

Transatlantic Agreement (NTA) that guided EU-US relations. The documents guiding EU-Russia relations, the PCA, the EU's Common Strategy and Russia's own 'Mid-term Strategy' of 1999 for relations with the EU, were outdated and did not provide concrete short and medium term action-oriented goals that encompassed the whole range of bilateral relations. The four spaces thus filled a conceptual and programmatic gap. The concept of 'common' spaces was attractive in the sense that it coincided with the positive notion of breaking down barriers, avoiding new dividing lines and moving towards the vision of a common European home.

The idea of working towards the four spaces was endorsed by the St Petersburg Summit of May 2003. However, at that stage the content of each of the spaces was not clearly defined. Relevant negotiations on four road maps, one for each of the four spaces, went on for two years after the St Petersburg Summit. The road maps were to operationalize the content of the four spaces by specifying concrete, mutually agreed priority actions to advance their aims in the medium term.

Negotiations of the road maps were held in separate expert groups, with Foreign Ministers regularly reviewing the state of play. On the EU side the Commission led the negotiations on the first, second and fourth spaces, supported at times by the Presidency. The negotiations on the third space (external security) were led by the Presidency and were mainly held in the regular meetings of the Russian Ambassador with the EU's Political and Security Committee (PSC) in Brussels. Talks on the other spaces alternated between Moscow and Brussels.

The Russian preference for high-level negotiations was reflected in the nomination of four senior interlocutors to lead negotiations on the Russian side, with Foreign Minister Lavrov being in charge of the third space himself as well as overseeing the overall management. Industry and Energy Minister Khristenko was responsible for negotiations on the first space (the CES). Presidential aide Viktor Ivanov was designated as Russia's chief negotiator for the second space (freedom, security and justice) while Presidential aide Sergei Yastrzhembsky was in charge of the fourth space (research and development), which proved to be the least controversial. Talks on the first space, which included trade and economic cooperation as well as transport, energy and environment, were not free of controversial points (most notably the old irritant of the charge Russia imposes on EU airlines for Siberian overflight). To some extent, the talks were affected by the bilateral negotiations on the terms of Russia's accession to the WTO, which were completed in April 2004. As a result, basic agreement on the road maps for the first and fourth spaces emerged earlier than in the second and third spaces, where some sticky points complicated progress.

For example, the EU's insistence on the simultaneous finalization and entering into force of the readmission and visa facilitation agreements was hard for Russia to accept in the course of negotiations on a road map for the second space. In the third space the issue of cooperation in what the EU likes to call 'our common neighbourhood' was a major hurdle. Russian negotiators disliked the term 'common neighbourhood' which they perceived as a cover for EU attempts to expand its influence at Russia's expense in the Commonwealth of Independent States (CIS) region.[9] Russian officials used the discussion to express irritation with the EU's ENP, in which Russia had refused to participate. The search for politically neutral language on this point demanded some creativity. The somewhat linguistically clumsy compromise formula 'regions adjacent to the EU and Russia' helped finalize the agreement on the road map for the third space.

The issue of common values spanned both the second and third spaces. While reaching agreement on common principles was not easy, it proved perhaps less difficult than one would have imagined. Some critics may argue that, in view of the apparently widening 'values gap' separating Russia from the EU, the exact formulations used in the text of the spaces are rhetoric of relatively little consequence. However, such a sceptical view would risk underestimating the continuity of the principles underlying the relationship, including for setting the agenda and future priorities in bilateral relations.

Despite the difficulties encountered during the negotiation process, the discussions were useful in themselves because they helped the two sides gain a better understanding of each other's perspectives and clear up some misperceptions, especially in the more political second and third spaces. In addition, the negotiations on the road maps involved many government agencies and officials on both sides, many of whom had not previously been so directly engaged in EU-Russia relations (for example, the Russian Federal Service for Drugs Control). To a considerable extent, these new contacts reflected the expansion in the breadth and content of EU-Russia relations, which had come to touch upon ever more areas of society on both sides. The first space, the CES, is discussed in greater detail by Marco Fantini in Chapter 14. This chapter will focus on the more political second and third spaces.

The Second Space – Freedom, Security and Justice

The expansion in new functional areas and institutional contacts was particularly characteristic of the area of Freedom, Security and Justice (FSJ) which makes up the second space.[10] It represents a key growth area in EU-Russia relations because the issues it covers, such as terrorism, border security, drug trafficking and forged travel documents, have become priority items for both sides.

Within the EU itself, FSJ has become one of the fastest-moving areas for internal policy development in the EU because it touches many problems (for example, cross-border crime, terrorism, illegal migration) that can be more effectively addressed at EU level. The emergence of terrorism as a key international security threat has added momentum to this pre-existing trend. As is true for other EU policy areas, in FSJ as the EU's own internal policy developments intensify, so does the scope for cooperation with third countries. EU-Russia cooperation in the second space is a good example of this.

EU-Russia cooperation in this field dates back to the late 1990s, when the two sides began to coordinate efforts to combat transnational organized crime. The EU also provided support for Russia's efforts in the area of legal and judicial reform, notably through the TACIS programme. Similarly, the EU has supported projects carried out by the Council of Europe to strengthen Russia's own financial monitoring mechanisms to enable the Russian authorities to combat money-laundering effectively. These efforts contributed to Russia's accession to the international anti-money laundering body, the Financial Action Task Force (FATF). Such cooperation efforts will continue and expand with the implementation of the second space. One of the lesser-known examples of practical EU-Russia cooperation in the FSJ area is the creation of a training centre, operated by the Russian Interior Ministry, for law enforcement officials at Domodedovo airport outside Moscow, which provides specialized training in combating drug trafficking. The centre also provides training for law enforcement officials from other CIS countries, which reflects the cross-border nature of the drug threat.

At the London Summit of October 2005, the EU and Russia announced that agreement had been reached on two major issues coming under the second space: a readmission agreement and a visa facilitation agreement. Negotiations on these agreements had been going on for several years. In fact, the EU had proposed a draft readmission agreement to the Russian side almost five years earlier. The conclusion of both agreements was a significant achievement, especially bearing in mind that these were the first two agreements of this type that the EU has concluded with a third country.

A readmission agreement – essentially an agreement that establishes agreed rules for the prompt return of illegal migrants – had been high on the EU agenda for a long time. Readmission agreements are seen as important instruments for combating illegal migration and, to some extent, also trafficking in human beings – insofar as the quick return of illegal immigrants can be expected to act as a deterrent for potential illegal migrants, who often fall victims to criminal networks of people-smugglers or traffickers of human beings.

Russia had concluded a readmission agreement – the first of its kind – with Lithuania in 2003 as part of the agreement with the EU on the transit of people between mainland Russia and Kaliningrad after EU enlargement. The agreement in many ways served as a kind of insurance, in case of abuse of the eased transit system that did not require visas. The same logic underlay the

EU's request for a readmission agreement together with a visa facilitation agreement: in cases where visa facilitation was abused, a readmission agreement would ensure that people overstaying their visas would be speedily returned. The EU-Russia readmission agreement went further in also including third country nationals. This was important for the EU, as many illegal migrants reach the EU via Russia.

Russian officials were at first not keen on the idea of a readmission agreement for fear that Russia would be receiving thousands of people, including third country nationals, who could not be easily returned to their home countries. But EU-Russia discussions contributed to an internal Russian reflection process, which led to the recognition that illegal migration was a problem shared by Russia and the EU. Russia itself is estimated to be hosting between five and ten million illegal migrants from southern CIS countries and elsewhere. The utility of readmission agreements became a joint realization and Russia soon launched its own negotiations with neighbouring countries with a view to concluding similar agreements.

Nevertheless, there were concerns in Russia that the conclusion of a readmission agreement with the EU, prior to Russia's own conclusion of similar agreements with neighbouring countries, would lead to the need to accommodate thousands of returned third country citizens in Russia. The agreement between the EU and Russia therefore included a transition clause concerning third country nationals, which stipulated that the agreement would only come into force for nationals of those countries with which Russia had a readmission agreement of its own – or at the latest three years after the conclusion of the agreement. This compromise was not ideal for the EU, but it was the necessary price to pay for concluding an important agreement, which will significantly strengthen the scope for cooperation between the EU and Russia in combating illegal migration and trafficking in human beings in the medium to long term.

The agreement on visa facilitation was no less of an achievement. The issue of easing visa arrangements was crucial to Russia and President Putin gave it his personal attention. The rather technical question of visa facilitation took on a special political symbolism in the Russian context due to the still fresh memories of Soviet restrictions on foreign travel. The accession into the EU of former Eastern-bloc members required their preparation for applying Schengen rules for visa regulations with third countries and stricter border controls. From Moscow's perspective, however, these implications of former allies' accession to the EU gave the impression of a new 'paper wall' being built. This perception was hardly surprising: in the 1990s, Russian citizens had just begun to benefit from the newly-won freedom of travel, especially to Central European countries, with which Russia enjoyed either visa-free travel or relatively liberal visa arrangements. New visa requirements introduced in the context of EU enlargement gave Russians the impression that their freedom to travel was being curtailed.

To some extent, this perception was exaggerated. While visa requirements can be a rather irritating bureaucratic obstacle, the issuing of visas at consulates of EU member states in Russia is a relatively speedy affair and refusal rates are low. It is true that for Russian citizens living in regions without any EU member state consulates, obtaining a Schengen visa can be more complicated. However, problems exist on both sides. The difficulties experienced by EU citizens travelling to Russia are little known to the Russian public: getting a Russian visa can often involve much hassle – and certainly higher expense than the other way around.

In fact, the easing of travel restrictions was genuinely a mutual interest. Most of the consulates of EU member states in Russia had difficulties coping with the sheer number of visa applications (about two million visas are issued each year). At the same time, European business associations were beginning to lobby for a more relaxed approach that would make it easier for European business people to travel to Russia to take advantage of emerging trading and investment opportunities. So a new, more flexible visa arrangement made sense for both sides. As EU and Russian societies grew closer, business links expanded and more people were keen to travel for various purposes in both directions so the facilitation of visa arrangements was a logical step.

The EU-Russia Summit of 2003 recognized the idea of a visa-free arrangement, proposed by President Putin, as a long-term goal. A more ambitious formulation was not possible at the time, as the multitude and complexity of issues to be addressed before a visa-free arrangement could be put in place (for example, security of travel documents, standards of border protection) made any specific time frame unrealistic. Meanwhile, a visa facilitation arrangement was a more workable way of making visas easier and cheaper to obtain for people with demonstrable reasons to travel frequently. The facilitations eventually agreed concern mainly businesspeople, members of sporting and cultural delegations, journalists, students, researchers, officials and diplomats. Visa fees on both sides were set at 35 euros. It was also agreed that multiple-entry visas for the above groups would be issued in greater numbers and for longer periods of validity, thus reducing the inconvenience and expense of frequent visa renewals.

The visa facilitation agreement was an important first step in EU-Russia visa discussions and it was the first time the EU had concluded an agreement of this type with any third country. There may have been some disappointment among the broader public that most people, who usually travel as tourists, would benefit from the agreement only in terms of lower visa fees. However, to minimise the risk of abuses, it had been agreed from the outset that facilitated arrangements should at this initial stage aim to make life easier for people who travelled frequently and were in real need of facilitations. At the same time, it is clear that this first agreement is not intended to be the last – barring unforeseen problems during the implementation phase. As the number of travellers increases, pressure for wider-ranging facilitation arrangements is likely to lead to further agreements in this area. The discussion on long-term visa free arrangements will continue and may well lead to the consideration of broader facilitation measures in due course.

The Third Space – External Security

Cooperation between the EU and Russia in the area of external security is also a relatively recent growth area. Ever since the EU began to develop a CFSP in the early 1990s, Russia expressed greater interest in closer cooperation. Russia seems to proceed from the rationale that, whatever would come out of EU efforts, it was better for Russia to be involved as closely as possible in order to ensure that it had a chance to influence developments. This has over the years led to the recurrent situation that Russia appears to be keener on closer cooperation with the EU in the area of the CFSP/ESDP than the EU might be ready for. From the EU standpoint, the priority remains to develop cooperation internally, especially in the area of the ESDP. Cooperation with third countries naturally takes second place and focuses mainly on various degrees of third-country association with EU-led peacekeeping and other operations. A recurrent theme in EU-Russia discussions has been Russia's strong wish to be more closely involved in the planning of operations and for the EU and Russia to cooperate as equals rather than Russia simply contributing to EU operations, in whose preparation it has had little input.

On foreign policy issues more generally, the EU-Russia dialogue has progressed to the extent that it is now the most regular and extensive such dialogue that the EU has with any third party. Still, there is much potential for more effective coordination. On some issues views converge to a great extent. An example is the Middle East Peace Process, where both the EU and Russia form part of the Quartet with the US and the UN. Although neither the EU nor Russia has the lead on this important international issue, it can on occasion make a significant difference in discussions when the two argue along similar lines. The same can be said for discussions on non-proliferation and disarmament, where EU and Russian views on strengthening the multilateral framework for cooperation in general have tended to coincide in recent years.

As EU actions in the world are gradually gaining coherence and are starting to have a more tangible impact, especially as far as the EU's neighbourhood is concerned, Russia's interest in dialogue and cooperation with the EU in this area appears to be growing. The EU enlargement of 2004 was in many ways a wake-up call for Russia's foreign policy establishment, which had initially focused mainly on the anticipated 'geopolitical losses' resulting from the earlier eastward enlargement of NATO. Eventually, geopolitically-minded Russian officials and opinion formers came to see the gradual 'expansion' of the EU into what they consider Russia's sphere of interests in its immediate periphery as a largely unwelcome challenge to its influence and interests.

The 2004 enlargement, into what was previously part of the Soviet Union, was bound to cause resentment – at least on the part of the Russian policy establishment. To this extent, some negative fallout on the overall climate of the EU's relations with Russia could be considered more or less inevitable. On the other hand, it could not be denied that EU enlargement had some potentially very concrete implications on specific Russian interests, for example on visa arrangements or on economic and trade relations. The agreement on the facilitated transit of Russian citizens between Kaliningrad and mainland Russia through Lithuania, which came into force in July 2003, was the first example of a successful compromise reached in the context of EU enlargement. The understanding on the implications of enlargement that was reached in April 2004, which led to the extension of the PCA to all new EU accession countries, was another such example, which testified to the ability of the EU and Russia to find pragmatic, mutually satisfactory solutions to common problems.[11]

Values vs Interests: the Example of Chechnya

It is often argued that the 'values gap' dividing the EU and Russia may be too deep to allow for meaningful efforts to build a genuine strategic partnership based on common principles. The argument that refers to Russia's perceived 'democratic backsliding' has become more prevalent after a series of moves and political reforms by President Putin, which resulted in a centralization of power in the hands of the federal executive (and the President in particular) as well as an overall reduction of political pluralism.[12]

Some experts explain Russia's 'failure' to comply with Western expectations with regard to democracy and individual rights in terms of Russia being a different kind of political entity from today's 'post-modern' Western states. Russia is a geopolitically-minded state whose attitudes to its own citizens and to the external world resemble those of great powers in the nineteenth century.[13] The EU, on the other hand, is a Union based on shared values of democracy, respect for human rights and minorities, which strongly colour its attitude to the external world.

According to such an interpretation, the EU's criticism of Russia's record on democracy and human rights and Russia's irritated response to external criticism would seem to be two incompatible policy lines – existing in parallel without much potential for meaningful dialogue and interaction. Some expert Russia-watchers even argue that it makes little sense for the EU to seek to promote Russia's adherence to liberal values and democratic norms; instead, the EU should focus on concrete interests, especially in the economic and energy sectors, which are intelligible and interesting to Russian decision-makers.[14]

Chechnya stands out as the most persistent and high-profile contentious issue in the EU's political relations with Russia in the past decade. Of all points of controversy that have emerged on the bilateral agenda, Chechnya has arguably had the greatest part in souring the overall political climate and undermining mutual confidence in EU-Russia relations. More broadly, it has coloured European perceptions of Russia and – to some extent – dampened enthusiasm for a closer partnership with Russia in EU policy circles. Many European politicians, officials and ordinary citizens see the Russian authorities' conduct in Chechnya as a test of the country's professed adherence to European values of human rights and democracy.

The first Chechen conflict of 1994–6 did much to damage the reputation of President Boris Yeltsin as a democrat and was arguably a factor in delaying the development of the EU's relations with Russia. Already during the first conflict, the EU became actively involved on the ground as the largest provider of humanitarian aid to the conflict's civilian victims – a humanitarian effort that continues to this day.

The second Chechen conflict, which began in the second half of 1999, had arguably a stronger impact on the EU's perception of Russia. The EU has always proceeded from the premise of Russia's territorial integrity and did not at any point raise the issue of the Chechens' self-determination. Russia's right to resort to armed force to suppress separatism, especially after the rebels' armed incursion into the republic of Dagestan, was therefore never questioned by the EU. The focus of EU criticism was on the humanitarian consequences and serious human rights abuses, which accompanied the Russian authorities' handling of the conflict and the subsequent counter-terrorist operations in the republic.

Russia for long resisted the inclusion of Chechnya on the agenda of bilateral meetings with the EU. Russian officials dismissed EU concerns over human rights abuses in the course of 'counter-terrorist operations' and reacted with indignation to EU calls to engage in talks with Chechen separatists with a view to finding a peaceful solution. Chechnya became a recurrent point of controversy in successive EU-Russia summits, most clearly at the one in November 2002, which had to be moved from Copenhagen to Brussels due to Russian anger at the perceived tolerance by the Danish Presidency of Chechen separatists.[15] At the same time the EU came under fire from human rights advocates for muting its criticism on Chechnya. They argued that the EU had turned a blind eye to human rights abuses in Chechnya and the broader North Caucasus from concern not to jeopardize European economic interests. Some human rights advocates argued that more consistent and firmer EU criticism was needed, a policy of 'shaming Russia'.

The EU has not shied away from raising Chechnya, including at the UN Commission on Human Rights, where the EU sponsored draft resolutions on Chechnya in 2000–2 and again in 2004. However, the draft resolutions were defeated in 2002 and 2004, largely due to the composition of this UN forum, which included many countries keen to avoid criticism of human rights abuses in the context of internal conflicts. More broadly, it could be argued that EU resolutions – whether unilateral or in a multilateral context – did not prove a very effective instrument in fostering a constructive dialogue with Russia with a view to achieving positive change on the ground in terms of the restoration of peace and the rule of law, protection of human rights and return to a normal life in the republic.

As a result, the EU began to search for a new approach to promote a more fruitful engagement with Russia on this issue. A change in the EU approach on Chechnya became visible in 2004, when the EU seized the opportunity opened up by President Putin's invitation to Russia's international partners to contribute to the rehabilitation of Chechnya. At the EU-Russia summit in November 2004, which took place in The Hague, President Putin welcomed the proposal made by Commission President Barroso and German Chancellor Schröder for an EU contribution to the rehabilitation of the Chechen republic. Such a contribution would build on the EU's humanitarian assistance to the region, which increasingly needed to be complemented by more sustainable inputs towards the republic's longer-term recovery. In this context, in September 2005 the EU allocated 25 million euros to a special programme for the rehabilitation of schools, hospitals and income-generation projects in Chechnya and also in the neighbouring republics of Ingushetia, North Ossetia and Dagestan.

At the same time Russia agreed to open regular human rights consultations with the EU and to discuss Chechnya in this context. The first such meeting was held in Luxembourg on 1 March 2005 at Directors' level on both sides. The consultations allowed each side to raise issues of concern. Chechnya continued to be a key preoccupation for the EU, while Russia used the consultations to voice its concerns mainly about the situation of Russian minorities in Latvia and Estonia. It may still be too early to evaluate the effectiveness of the consultations after only three rounds. It has certainly been useful to have a dedicated venue for discussing human rights-related concerns in much more depth than was hitherto possible. Improving mutual understanding and making concrete progress on human rights issues is likely to take time and a long-term engagement. Russia's readiness to enter into such a dialogue was in any case laudable and has contributed to an improved, more open atmosphere for discussions, which should in time help encourage improvements on the ground.

Conclusions

The EU's relations with Russia have a very recent history. Regular official contacts began only eight years ago, but have grown impressively to encompass a very wide range of policy areas, departments and levels of the two administrations as well as parliamentary links. Economic interaction has also expanded significantly. It is true that so far the EU and Russia have devoted much of their attention to rather short-term trouble-shooting to deal with urgent matters as these arose, especially in the run up to the EU's eastward enlargement. It was no mean feat that problems such as the one of transit of persons to Kaliningrad were dealt with in a timely, constructive and mutually satisfactory manner.

The four common spaces represent a move to a positive agenda that sets goals to guide and structure the development of future cooperation. The road maps for the four spaces are the result of the first effort to set jointly defined priorities. The effort invested in them reflects both sides' wish to build a multifaceted, solid partnership, not just at the level of official institutions but with deep roots in links between their societies. The common spaces therefore demonstrate the growing ambitions that both the EU and Russia have come to harbour for the still emerging partnership.

It may be too early to predict the eventual outcome of the common spaces initiative. It might be somewhat unrealistic to expect the four road maps to be implemented in their entirety. They are jointly agreed work plans, meant to facilitate cooperation by guiding energies on both sides. During the course of their implementation, it cannot be ruled out that priorities may evolve further. Various elements of the spaces will probably be implemented at an uneven pace, though at present it seems hard to assess which ones are likely to progress the fastest.

The economic space will no doubt remain in focus and gain additional momentum from Russia's WTO accession. Russia and the EU have already launched several new sectoral dialogues within the first space to help strengthen economic interaction by linking up transport and energy networks, seeking approximation in product standards and investment conditions. The fourth space is very promising, as both sides recognize the expansion of people-to-people contacts as the most important element for the consolidation of their relations in the longer term. A very concrete achievement here was the establishment of the Russian-European Studies Institute in Moscow, which, as of 2006, will train young Russian officials and students on EU affairs, thus contributing to a better understanding in Russia of the complex workings of the EU.

The second space, a recent growth area in bilateral relations, contains many legally complex or sensitive issues from the political or security points of view, which inevitably complicates efforts to agree upon new initiatives. The conclusion of the visa facilitation and readmission agreements was an important achievement in this space so far. These agreements, once implemented, are likely to provide momentum for intensified cooperation in other areas where ties are already growing, including border cooperation, document security, and cooperation in combating illegal activities, notably illegal migration and trafficking of human beings and drugs.

The third space is perhaps where expectations should be somewhat more modest. On many issues such as the Middle East the EU and Russia will continue to cooperate productively. From the EU point of view, Russia and the EU could work together in concrete ways to help find durable settlements to the frozen conflicts in the South Caucasus and Eastern Europe, where together they could make a real difference. However, fruitful cooperation on these and other 'common neighbourhood' issues will be dependent on overcoming residual suspicions and zero-sum thinking. Confidence-building in this area may be a rather slow process, especially in view of Russian sensitivities to the involvement of 'external' actors, including the EU, in what is commonly referred to in Russian parlance as the 'post-Soviet space'.

The development of mutual trust remains for the time being an unknown variable, which will however be crucial for the success of the common spaces and the consolidation of a genuine and durable partnership, worthy of the term 'strategic'. To a significant extent, increased contacts, frank dialogue and cooperation in specific issues will be the way to build this trust. At this stage, however, neither side has a clear vision of the long-term endpoint of the relationship. For the time being, Russian membership of the EU appears outlandish both in EU and in Russian mainstream policy circles. Existing models of association with the EU may not correspond to the needs and preferences of Russia. A unique kind of partnership may have to emerge to reflect the evolving self-perceptions of the EU and Russia, particularly when it comes to their mutual roles on our continent and in the world.

The discussion on a new framework for EU-Russia relations to replace the existing PCA, whose initial period of validity runs out in 2007, is already under way and is likely to be the next step in the gradual process of defining the 'strategic endpoint' of the relationship. Whatever replaces the PCA will no doubt draw heavily on the common goals enshrined in the four spaces, but might well build on the experience accumulated in the meantime to go further in exploring new possibilities for the longer-term future.

The issue of mutual trust cannot be separated from the thorny question of values. No genuine partnership is possible without a profound understanding on shared fundamental principles that bind the partners together. It is such a durable basis that allows short-term disputes and tensions, which will inevitably arise even in the closest of partnerships, to be overcome without weakening the foundations of the relationship. It is perhaps with this rationale that many voices in the EU have lamented what is seen as the erosion of democracy in Russia in recent years and castigated the lack of a clear and determined EU effort to promote democracy and democratic forces in Russia. Such views tend to overestimate the potential impact of any EU (or that of any other external actor for that matter) policy towards Russia on the development of democracy in that country. While the Russian political scene has become less pluralistic under President Putin, this does not warrant either idealist depictions of Russian democracy under Yeltsin or pessimism about Russia's democratic prospects in the future.

To some extent the EU can and should try to encourage the development of liberal values and democratic principles in Russia. However, in the authors' opinion, the most promising way of fostering these principles in Russia is by increasing interaction with Russian society to give more Russian citizens the opportunity to see for themselves how European societies are run and make up their own minds to which principles their own country should adhere. We can do this through political dialogue with Russia, but more importantly by gradually opening our borders, schools and universities, especially to the younger generation. Only Russians themselves can ultimately make the choice in which direction Russia will go and on which values Russian society should be based. Neither the EU nor any other external actor has the right or the ability to make this choice on their behalf.

At the same time, it does not necessarily follow that the EU should focus only on its economic interests in relations with Russia and ignore values. While the EU has limited influence over developments in Russia, it is inconceivable for the EU to put aside issues of human rights and democracy in its relationship with Russia. The EU shares more than 2000 km of borders with Russia and it is in the interest of the EU to help promote real democracy in its largest neighbour as the best guarantee for long-term stability in the immediate vicinity to the east of the EU. Russia's unquestionable adherence to democratic norms would have a significant impact on developments in Belarus, the Caucasus and Central Asia and thus also help address EU security concerns arising from these regions.

Notes and References

1. M. Emerson et al., *The Elephant and the Bear: The European Union, Russia and their Near Abroads* (Brussels, Centre for European Policy Studies, 2001).
2. The EU's first operation under the ESDP was the EU Police Mission in Bosnia-Herzegovina, which followed up on the UN police mission in January 2003. Later in 2003, the EU followed up on NATO's operation 'Essential Harvest' in the Former Yugoslav Republic of Macedonia with the military operation 'Concordia' and police mission 'Proxima'. In December 2004, the EU launched its largest military operation in Bosnia-Herzegovina (EUFOR 'Althea'), which took over from the NATO-led SFOR. The EU launched its first military operation in Africa, operation 'Artemis' in the Democratic Republic of Congo, in June 2003.
3. The Czech Republic, Estonia, Hungary, Latvia, Lithuania, Poland, Slovakia and Slovenia joined the EU in May 2004. Bulgaria and Romania are expected to do so in 2007. Accession negotiations with Croatia began in October 2005.
4. See for example Heather Grabbe, 'The Implications of EU Enlargement' in S. White, P. Lewis and J. Batt (eds.), *Developments in Central and Eastern European Politics 3* (London, Palgrave, 2003).
5. Russia first sought to conclude visa facilitation agreements with Germany, France and Italy. The agreement with Germany was signed in December 2003 and those with France and Italy in June 2004. These three bilateral agreements created pressure for a comparable EU-Russia agreement, which was signed in spring 2006.
6. European Commission, *Communication from the Commission to the Council and the European Parliament on relations with Russia*, COM (2004) 106, 9 February 2004.
7. The texts of the road maps may be found on the *Europa* website: http://europa.eu.int/comm/external_relations/russia/summit_05_05/finalroadmaps.pdf#ces
8. The Concept Paper for a CEES, which was prepared by a High Level Group of experts from both sides, was approved at the Rome Summit of November 2003. The paper is available on the Europa website: http://europa.eu.int/comm/external_relations/russia/summit11_03/1concl.pdf
9. For an explanation of this zero-sum logic, see for example Vladimir Degoyev, 'Wider Europe's Horizons in the Caucasus', *Russia in Global Affairs*, No. 4, October–December 2004.
10. This policy area was previously referred to as Justice and Home Affairs.
11. *Joint Statement on EU Enlargement and EU-Russia Relations*, Brussels 27 April 2004. The text can be found on the Europa website: http://europa.eu.int/comm/external_relations/russia/russia_docs/js_elarg_270404.htm
12. Lilya Shevtsova, 'The Logic of Backsliding', *New Europe Review*, 2:3 (2005).
13. Dmitry Trenin, *Reading Russia Right*, Moscow Carnegie Centre Policy Brief No. 42, 2005.
14. Katinka Barysch, *The EU and Russia: Strategic Partners or Squabbling Neighbours?* (London, Centre for European Reform, 2004).
15. In November 2002, Denmark turned down Russia's request for the extradition of Akhmed Zakaev, the envoy of Chechen separatist leader Aslan Maskhadov, on the grounds of insufficient evidence to prove the Russian authorities' claim that Zakaev was guilty of armed insurgency or terrorism.

14

THE ECONOMIC RELATIONSHIP BETWEEN RUSSIA AND THE EU: HISTORY AND PROSPECTS

Marco Fantini[1]

The Legacy of the Soviet Period on Russia's International Trade Structure

Russia's Communist experience resulted not only in political, but also in economic isolation from the West. Trade and financial transactions with the non-Communist world were not ruled out *per se* – indeed the Soviet authorities carefully nurtured a reputation for being reliable debtors and were not averse to tapping foreign financial markets when needed. Nevertheless, the doctrine of economic self-sufficiency (autarky) and the country's adversarial relationship with the West quickly reduced economic contacts to a minimum. The situation did not change radically after the victory in World War II; indeed, the extension of Soviet power over central Europe allowed the Union of Soviet Socialist Republics (USSR) access to supplies of advanced mechanical equipment (notably from Eastern Germany or the Czech Republic) and to agricultural produce, giving new life to the system. The USSR did not join any of the major international economic institutions (such as International Monetary Fund (IMF) and the World Bank), and prevented its satellites from participating in the Marshall Plan and in the organisation that ran it, which later developed into the Organization for Economic Cooperation and Development (OECD). Soviet-bloc countries instead joined the Council of Mutual Economic Assistance (Comecon), whose transferable rouble system offered the Soviet Union the opportunity to base trade with its satellites on a favourable monetary regime, unconnected to world prices and not dependent on hard currency.

The demise of the Eastern bloc brought the restrictions to international trade to an end. First to go was the transferable rouble system, followed by the break-up of the Soviet Union and the decision to introduce national currencies in each of the 15 new republics. This resulted in rapid changes in the patterns of trade throughout the former Soviet bloc with a substantial reorientation of trade away from traditional partners and towards other countries, particularly the European Union (EU). In Russia the share of exports directed at other Commonwealth of Independent States (CIS) members fell from 64 per cent to 18.5 per cent between 1990 and 1995 while exports to former Comecon members declined from 15.5 per cent to 11 per cent in the same period, exports to the other trade partners, primarily the EU, US and China, grew from 20.5 per cent to 70.5 per cent.[2] Although the bulk of the geographical readjustment of trade had already taken place by 1995, the fact that the CIS trade share continued to decline in Russia at least until 2003 testifies to the slowness of the readjustment.

The greater part of the gains in trade have concerned the EU (and to a lesser extent the Far East). This result appears natural in light of the so-called gravity theory of international trade, which states that the intensity of trade ties between countries is largely determined by the product of their Gross Domestic Products (GDPs) and the square of distance. This has an important consequence: despite the fact that Asia and the US have been growing faster than the EU in the last decade, the role distance plays in trade implies that Europe is bound to remain Russia's main trade partner for the foreseeable future.[3] The geographical distribution of Russia's population, 78 per cent of which lives in the European part of Russia, and its transport infrastructure, which is Moscow-centric and less developed in the Asian part of the country, further reinforces this tendency.

A striking feature of Russian foreign trade is its high degree of specialization on a narrow range of products. The country exports mainly primary goods; over 60 per cent of its exports are hydrocarbons (Russia is the world's largest gas exporter and second largest oil exporter after Saudi Arabia). The remainder of exports is dominated by other products of the extraction industry or at any rate by goods which have undergone a limited amount of processing, such as ferrous and non-ferrous metals, base chemicals, forestry products, precious metals or gems, and the like. In these products, as well as in goods requiring a high input of energy, which is comparatively cheap in the country, Russian companies are competitive, but exports are often held up by partners' trade barriers. Amongst manufactures, one of the main exports are arms, which indeed represent almost the only conspicuous (in terms of size) example of high-tech exports; however, bearing in mind that arms exports are heavily influenced by political factors, this highlights the fact that by and large Russian manufacturing industry still remains uncompetitive on world markets.

Contrary to popular belief, economists have gradually come to believe that a large endowment with natural resources can be more of a curse than a blessing. Comparative research has shown that countries rich in resources often tend to live off their wealth, neglecting to nurture a favourable breeding ground for non-resource based businesses.[4] This surprising result is explained by many factors: the focus of politics tends to be dominated by clashes over the distribution of the income from the natural resources, rather than establishing the right conditions for growth; in good times, windfall receipts from the taxing of resource extraction lead to weak budget constraints, generating wasteful spending programmes, while the volatility of prices for many commodities periodically results in severe downturns which governments are ill-equipped to counteract. Perhaps the most insidious danger, however, is the so-called *Dutch disease*. The term refers to the detrimental effect that the discovery of bountiful natural resources has on a country's manufacturing sector: the resulting real appreciation of the currency may make industry uncompetitive.

Russia is usually considered to be suffering from Dutch disease. Largely because of a strong increase in oil prices, the rouble has appreciated strongly since 1999. Although non-extractive industrial output and labour productivity have risen, industry is under pressure from foreign imports. Russian manufacturers have been by and large unable to gain market share abroad, as highlighted by the composition of exports, in which the share of manufactures is shrinking. Studies of customs data have indicated that Russian industries are not upgrading the quality of their products but rather tend to remain concentrated on lower-value added productions.[5]

The Russian government has long been aware of the dualism between a prosperous natural resource-exporting sector and a struggling manufacturing sector; the ways in which it has sought to counter it, however, have varied. Russian policymakers had four weapons at their disposal to try to support domestic industry. One was industrial policy, which could imply either direct government involvement in production or a more sophisticated strategy of 'picking the winning sectors', to be supported through incentives of various kinds or directly through subsidies. Another was an 'activist' trade policy, in which strategic industrial sectors are protected through restrictions on imports. A third consisted of increasing windfall taxation on the resource sector, in order to limit the appreciation of the currency. Finally, a fourth one, which to some extent is in contradiction with the second, consisted of trying to support industry by seeking integration with trade partners, increasing economic growth and reducing barriers to exports. Russia has tried, with variable results, all of these strategies, sometimes simultaneously. However, the fact that some of these strategies were, in the final analysis, incompatible, has affected relations with the EU and indeed, with most trade partners. The history of Russia's foreign economic relations since the 1990s has been shaped by the way in which these strategies have been successively applied.

Russia's Rapprochement with the EU

Historically, the Soviet Union's policy had been to maintain a cold stance towards the EU in a mirror image of the US's traditionally favourable attitude towards European integration. Bilateral EU-Russian relations only really took off at the beginning of the 1990s when Russia began to receive substantial funding from the EU's vast programme of Technical Assistance for the CIS (TACIS) as well as food aid. During the mid-1990s, Russia sought greater integration with its big neighbour, the EU. It had already signed a Trade and Cooperation Agreement but felt the need for a more substantive relationship. Following long negotiations, the EU and Russia signed a ten-year Partnership and Cooperation Agreement (PCA) at the Corfu summit in 1994, which finally came into force in December 1997 (see Chapter 7). Although the immediate impact of the PCA on the trade regime was limited, its long-term economic aims were very ambitious with a specific commitment to establish a Free Trade Area (FTA), when conditions allowed it. Such an FTA would be the largest in existence in terms of the population involved. Although the FTA clause is non-binding, it should be noted that it was absent in the PCA agreements signed later with the non-European CIS countries. It is also remarkable that this aim was mentioned so early, given that Russia was not even considered to have a market economy until 2003.

The PCA was also significant because it gave additional momentum to TACIS, which since its 1991 inception has allocated more than 2.6 billion euros to Russia. During the 1990s Russia was engulfed in a very deep recession and the lack of experience with the workings of the market economy led the Russians – at least initially – to seek expert advice abroad, so that for several years Western experts were prominently employed as economic advisers, directly or through programmes run by international organizations. At the time of the design of the TACIS programme, therefore, one of the main needs for the Russian economy was to acquire Western know-how in institutional design. Given the bad public finance situation of the time, the Russian authorities faced severe budgetary constraints which seriously hampered their ability to obtain such know-how on the required scale. TACIS, whose sister programme Economic Reconstruction Assistance for Poland and Hungary (PHARE) was to prove effective in preparing the Central European countries to make the transition to the market economy and eventual EU accession, therefore provided an ideal answer to this need. TACIS also offered an additional advantage from the EU viewpoint: the funds would not directly flow to the Russian budget, but the EU would retain control over all expenditure. Given the doubts about the effectiveness and reliability of the Russian administration existing at the time, and the deteriorating federal budget situation, this point was not negligible.

In the second half of the 1990s, Russia's circumstances continued to worsen. The political situation seemed more and more unstable. Although Boris Yeltsin succeeded in winning re-election after a difficult electoral campaign, this did not result in policy continuity: his policies became increasingly erratic and towards the end of his second mandate, he dismissed six prime ministers in little more than 18 months. The economic situation was hardly more encouraging: apart from a single year (1997) in which minimal growth was recorded, output continued to contract steadily; the economy was largely demonetarized, as many transactions took place in barter form. By 1998, GDP had fallen by around 40 per cent from 1991 levels. In August of that year, a severe financial crisis bankrupted the banking system and led to a default on domestic federal debt (much of it held by foreigners).

The worsening economic situation unsurprisingly dimmed EU enthusiasm for deepening relations with its big Eastern neighbour. Although the EU generally looked with sympathy at President Yeltsin, perceived as the leader who would consolidate democracy in Russia, the persistent recession and the apparent incoherence and unsustainability of Russian economic policies induced the EU to maintain a cautious stance, even though some of its member states (notably Germany and Italy) were big bilateral creditors of the Russian government. In particular, any move towards an FTA, which the Russians were initially quite keen on, was quietly put off the agenda; it was decided that bilateral progress would at any rate have to await Russia's World Trade Organization (WTO) accession. This, however, has been a very slow process: although Russia started negotiations with the international trade body in 1993, no final date for accession has yet been clearly established.

The situation began to change after the election of Vladimir Putin to the Russian presidency in 2000. Several factors contributed to a renewal of interest in bilateral relations. The EU side was encouraged by a series of promising developments in Russia. First, boosted by higher oil prices and the positive effects of the rouble devaluation, the economy recovered strongly: real GDP increased at an average annual 6.8 per cent rate from 1999 to 2004. Second, particularly during Putin's first mandate, the government contributed to the recovery by following prudent macroeconomic policies, defusing the federal debt problem completely within a few years, remonetizing the economy and gradually reducing inflation to still high, but manageable levels *(see Table 1)*. Furthermore, the president appointed liberal reformers – often with a strong technical background – to the key economic ministries. German Gref, the respected Minister for Economic Development and Trade, was charged with elaborating a long-term development programme for Russia. In line with presidential recommendations, the Gref plan did not aim at an old-style protectionist defence of struggling industrial behemoths, but rather at transforming the economy along Western models. Although implementation of the plan was somewhat uneven, proceeding in fits and starts, the first Putin administration achieved important successes not only in macroeconomic stabilization but also in pushing through a series of key structural reforms, such as the reform of the tax code, of the pension system, of the labour code, and that of federal-regional fiscal relations. The orthodox free-market approach of the government and the spectacular consolidation of public finances, as well as the rapid expansion of EU trade with Russia gradually won over many sceptics including in the EU.

Table 1: **Russia: Key Macroeconomic Indicators**

	1996	1997	1998	1999	2000	2001	2002	2003	2004	2005*	* as of
GDP, real % change on year	-3.6	1.4	-5.3	6.4	10.0	5.1	4.7	7.3	7.2	6.2	1–9/05
Industrial production, % change on year	-4.5	2.0	-5.2	11.0	11.9	2.9	3.1	8.9	7.3	4.0	1–11/05
Gross Fixed Capital Formation, % change on year	-18.0	-5.0	-12.0	5.3	17.4	10.0	2.6	12.5	10.9	10.2	1–11/05
Unemployment, % (end of period)	9.3	9.0	13.2	12.4	9.9	8.7	9.0	8.7	7.6	7.8	11/05
Exports of goods, $ billion	89.7	86.9	74.4	75.6	105.0	101.9	107.3	135.9	183.5	220.1	1–11/05
Imports of goods, $ billion	68.1	72.0	58.0	39.5	44.9	53.8	61.0	76.1	96.3	111.1	1–11/05
Current account, $ billion	10.8	-0.1	0.2	24.6	46.8	33.9	29.1	35.4	58.6	62.9	1–9/05

1) New methodology from 1.1.2005, figures for 2001–2004 revised, not comparable with previous years.

Source: Bank of Finland Institute for Economies in Transition (BOFIT).

On the Russian side, too, circumstances seemed ripe for a renewal of ties with the EU. Vladimir Putin does not share his predecessor's fascination with the US and is more drawn to Europe, particularly Germany where he had worked as a young State Security Committee (KGB) officer. Economics, too, seemed to dictate a stronger relationship with the EU: as the Russian public finance situation improved greatly, the IMF and the World Bank, where American influence is strong, lost a lot of its leverage. In the meantime, trade with the EU ballooned: by 2000, it had nearly doubled from 1995 levels. Trade was especially strong with Germany and Italy, countries with whose political leadership Putin also established warm ties. Trade and investment statistics reaffirmed that US companies, with only a few exceptions in the oil and gas sector, continued to play a subordinate role in the country compared to the Europeans. Finally, only the EU held the key to the solution of several headaches, such as communications with Kaliningrad, a Russian exclave that by the time of the EU accession of Poland and Lithuania was to be surrounded entirely by EU territory, and the hoped-for waiver of strict visa requirements which most countries had imposed on Russian citizens and which were perceived as somewhat humiliating. In recognition of the growing importance of the EU to the country's political and economic objectives, the Russian foreign ministry over time substantially beefed up its permanent representation in Brussels, not only in terms of the staff but also through the nomination of high-level personalities to the post of Representative.[6]

One area which received much attention from both sides was the energy sector. Such interest, quite natural in light of the fact that the majority of Russian exports to the EU relate to energy products, was rekindled by a number of concomitant developments. At a *global level*, from 2000 onwards oil and gas prices started increasing steadily from the lows of the late 1990s, bringing back memories of the oil shocks of the 1970s and 1980s. In Asia, energy-hungry China and Japan started actively seeking new long-term sources of fossil fuels and urged Russia to reorient its export capacity towards the Far East. In the EU, the gradual exhaustion of North Sea gas fields and the lagging development of nuclear energy implied that dependence on fossil fuel imports was bound to grow significantly over the coming decades[7] and therefore secure sources of supply to fill the gap had to be found and developed. Furthermore, the bloc was set on revamping its energy policy in order to introduce a number of internal market principles to a market that had remained to some extent compartmentalised and segmented along national lines. One consequence of this had a direct bearing on Russia: the destination clauses which prevented buyers of Russian gas from reselling it to companies located in other EU member states and which were in force in contracts with Italian, German and Austrian companies, were incompatible with the development of the single market.

Russia for its part had several objectives; first, it was anxious to attract funding for the large-scale investments required to maintain its decaying energy infrastructure and satisfy new export needs (the capital requirements have been quantified at a staggering 715 billion euros from 2003 to 2030); second, given the EU's legislative activity, it feared that reforms would put long-term gas supply contracts at risk, which were felt to be an essential precondition to obtaining long-term finance for developing new gas and oil fields; and finally, the impending enlargement of the EU to the Central and Eastern European region made it urgent to find solutions to a number of problem issues linked especially to transit and to the situation of the Russian Kaliningrad exclave, which depends on energy imports from Russia and was destined to be entirely surrounded by EU territory.

This convergence of interests led to the establishment of the EU-Russia Energy Dialogue in 2000, with the aim of addressing all problems relating to trade in energy, in particular by contributing to the development of (especially the Russian) energy sector, enhancing supply security and reducing its environmental impact, notably by reducing the transport risks but also at the source, by introducing conservation measures in Russia (the traditionally low domestic prices of gas – up to five-six times below the price of gas sold to the EU[8] – had always provided a disincentive for investment in conservation). It is notable that the structure of the Energy Dialogue differed from that of the PCA in its more informal nature, in its involving the private sector in a prominent way and in a more streamlined structure, even though the PCA subcommittee on energy has continued to exist alongside the Dialogue. The Dialogue is organized around four thematic groups and chaired by the Commissioner for Energy on the EU side and the Minister for Industry and Energy on the Russian side.

While EU-Russia relations were never completely problem-free, the highest point was probably reached around 2002–3. Following the establishment of the Energy Dialogue, the EU granted Russia market economy status[9] in 2002, a solution to ease transport to and from Kaliningrad was found and steel and textiles agreements were signed. The potentially most important step, however, was the decision taken at the St. Petersburg summit in May 2003 to establish in the future four EU-Russia 'common spaces': a common economic space (CES); a common space of freedom, security and justice; a space of cooperation in the field of external security; and a space of research and education.[10] The name chosen for the economic section of the agreement, 'Common European Economic Space', is in itself very significant, as it directly recalls the European Economic Area (EEA). Although not well known by the general public, the European Economic Area agreement of 1994 represented an important landmark in the history of the EU, as it introduced two important and novel principles: first, it extends internal market legislation to a group of non-EU members;[11] second, the non-EU signatories have undertaken to introduce all new EU internal market regulations almost automatically into their legislation. In exchange for that, EEA countries enjoy unfettered and tariff-free access to the EU internal market. This means that in practice EEA members have joined, if not the EU, the internal market. The name chosen therefore suggested an ambition to realize something similar for Russia.

To anyone contemplating how to integrate the still rather insular Russian economy with the remainder of Europe, an EEA-like formula looks indeed like a visionary concept for the future. It would avoid the difficult political challenges – first of all, in terms of size and voting power – that eventual Russian membership in the EU would bring, while at the same time implicitly recognizing an essential ingredient of any attempt to integrate Russia's economy with the EU's, that is the primacy of EU regulations – an essential element because the EU will never be willing to adapt its regulations to any significant extent for the sake of Russia. In practice, the EEA formula looked too ambitious for the short-term, so the parties agreed to work on developing a workable concept within a high-level reflection group.

Roughly starting from the beginning of Vladimir Putin's second presidential mandate, however, EU-Russian relations started to deteriorate as a result of several factors.[12] The general deterioration in the political climate certainly played an important role; specifically, concerns about an unchecked growth in the power of the presidential administration, the reduced role of free, independent media, and the perceived brutality of the repression of the Chechen insurgency rekindled longstanding European suspicion about Russia's commitment to democracy. In the economic domain, the trial of oil magnate Mikhail Khodorkovsky for tax evasion and other charges, seemed unduly harsh to EU eyes, while its result, the bankruptcy of a company that only one year earlier had been considered Russia's most prosperous, reinforced doubts about the risks of investing in Russia. Furthermore, on the EU side there was considerable frustration at the lack in progress, year after year, in solving a number of trade irritants.[13] Russia in turn was irked by the suspicion that the European Neighbourhood Policy (ENP), unveiled in 2003, marked a step back from a privileged relationship as it treated Russia on a par with all other neighbours, including the less developed South Mediterranean countries. Eventually, Moscow refused to participate in the ENP.[14] In addition, in September 2003 Russia signed an agreement with Ukraine, Kazakhstan and Belarus establishing the Single Economic Space (SES), a new trade bloc which the EU fears may create obstacles to its own plans for deepening trade relations with the area.[15]

The growing European frustration with Russia manifested itself visibly after the Rome EU-Russia summit in November 2003. At the summit, the rift within the EU on Russia policy had come to the forefront, notably as Italian premier Silvio Berlusconi broke ranks to express openly his support for President Putin. Following the summit, a reassessment of the EU policy towards Russia took place, which was formalized in a Commission Communication of February

2004 which described in quite sombre tones the state of relations.[16] However, some progress continued to be made: the EU signed an agreement with Russia on the country's World Trade Organization (WTO) accession in May 2004, while Russia agreed to ratify the Kyoto Protocol, an objective which had long proven elusive. Nevertheless, in the following year EU-Russian relations remained choppy and in the run-up to the May 2005 summit, it was not taken for granted that the two sides would be able to come to a comprehensive agreement on the four common spaces, which had eluded them for over a year. It is significant that attention focused on producing 'road maps' for the common spaces, which would serve as pragmatic short-term working documents, rather than on developing the still somewhat vague final objectives of the Common European Economic Space (CEES).[17]

The text, approved at the May 2005 summit, is broad in scope and foresees actions in many domains; it also identifies priority sectors. Most of the measures, however, are limited to establishing or reinforcing bilateral dialogue and do not introduce binding commitments. Among the most significant aspects are the following:

- *reinforcement of regulatory dialogue*, which shows Russian openness on convergence of their industrial standards and regulations to the EU ones, particularly in a number of priority sectors (the term 'harmonization' is employed for the auto industry and textiles, 'approximation' for pharmaceuticals).
- *establishment of a dialogue on protection of intellectual property rights*, a key concern of the EU given the low level of protection now existing in Russia, and envisage gradual harmonization of legislation in this area.
- *approximation of competition policy*; although Russia has adopted antitrust legislation, its economy is highly concentrated and its competition framework has so far failed to prevent the increase in market dominance by a few large groups.

The text also cautiously foresees the possibility of an agreement on investment related issues, a hot topic following the Yukos case. Harmonization is also evoked, amongst other solutions, in the area of customs facilitation, an important issue given the current burdensome transit regime, and in the related chapter on transport which foresees several joint actions, including Russia's participation in the Galileo project. The Energy Chapter foresees *inter alia* initiatives in the area of nuclear energy (where Russia has long complained about EU restrictions to imports of fissile materials), and foresees a feasibility study on interconnection of the electricity grid, which would facilitate Russian exports of electricity to the EU.

Current Problems and Future Prospects

At the beginning of 2006 neither of the two sides seems to be entirely satisfied with the state of bilateral relations. This section ventures to analyse the reasons for the mutual frustration.

On the EU side, it seems clear that internal political developments in Russia have created a negative climate. Although Russia has been able to count on some sympathy from a number of EU countries, the EU has generally been fairly steadfast in its rejection of the alleged authoritarian bent of President Putin's second term. The 2004 accession of eight Central and East European countries (CEECs) seems to have, on balance, reinforced distrust of Russia despite the fact that they maintain important trade links with Moscow. The political elements of the relationship have also proven to be an important problem for the Russian side. Moscow has long complained of the Baltic states' treatment of their large ethnic Russian minorities. It perceives the EU's frequent references to the situation in Chechnya as meddling in its internal affairs and does not comprehend the EU's reluctance to view it as a purely law-and-order issue. The political legitimization given to separatist Chechen leaders is seen as support for terrorism.

Distrust inevitably has claimed its toll. The EU side has also been alienated by the Russian negotiating style, which was seen as excessively Machiavellian, bent on so-called 'cherry-picking' to limit cooperation only to a selected number of proposals without attempting to build a wide relationship[18] and on constant attempts to split the EU into several camps. The slow progress on long-standing trade irritants led to scepticism on the chances for ambitious policy visions and to a focus on 'deliverables'.

One might think – and it sometimes seems to be believed in Moscow – that the focus on 'common values' so typical of the EU (see Chapter 8) need not inevitably result in a weakening of purely economic relations – *pecunia non olet*: hence a certain Russian lack of understanding of the EU's insistence on linking the economic to the ethical. This attitude, however, betrays a simplistic view of modern international economic relations. In the current complex regulatory environment, much of what can be done to deepen international economic integration requires a climate of collaboration between administrations and *bona fide* implementation of agreements and political undertakings. Principles such as harmonization or mutual recognition demand a high degree of trust between the parties, usually ensured only by common membership in the EU but even more limited trade-related concessions require some degree of confidence. It is no coincidence that the Commission's department dealing with the international aspects of the internal market put a considerable emphasis on the reliability of counterpart authorities in the context of, for instance, the ENP.[19]

Another area where the 'values gap' is holding up economic integration is the dearth of foreign direct investment (FDI) in Russia. Compared with neighbouring transition economies, and corrected for its size, Russia attracts relatively little inward investment while being an important source of outward FDI, an indication of lack of confidence by investors. While in 2003 over 10 per cent of gross fixed capital formation in the Czech Republic, Poland or Hungary were financed by inward FDI, the corresponding figure was only 1.5 per cent for Russia (see Table 2). In today's world, FDI is a key driver of growth and development, not so much because it makes capital available but especially because it fuels trade integration and the transfer of key technological and managerial know-how. The persistently poor performance of Russia in attracting foreign investment, despite strong GDP growth in the last five years, is not only due to macroeconomic fundamentals or the Communist past – many of Europe's best performers in this area share similar handicaps – but rather to the perception that there is in Russia a less developed societal sensitivity for the basic tenets of economic liberalism, such as the right of individuals to be defended from State abuse.[20] The Yukos case has, unfortunately for Russia, provided a justification for the continued reluctance of many investors – Western but also Russian – to invest in the country.[21] Given the long memory of international investors in the field of political risk, the Yukos case may well display detrimental effects in the long term.

Table 2: FDI flows in Russia and in selected neighbouring countries (millions of dollars and percentages)

FDI, mill US$	1985–1995 annual ave.	2000	2002	2003
Russia - inward	424	2714	3461	1144
Russia –outward	*94*	*3177*	*3533*	*4133*
Czech. Rep. - inward	541	4984	8483	2583
Czech. Rep. - outward	*24*	*43*	*206*	*232*
Hungary – inward	1096	2764	2845	2470
Hungary – outward	*13*	*620*	*275*	*1581*
Poland – inward	761	9341	4131	4225
Poland – outward	*17*	*17*	*230*	*386*
Inward FDI as a percentage of gross capital formation				
Russia	1.6	6.2	5.6	1.5
Czech Republic	8.5	32.7	44.5	11.6
Hungary	15.2	24.5	19.1	13.5
Poland	4.2	23.8	11.4	11.1
Central and Eastern European average	2.8	18.3	16.8	9.5
World average	3.9	19.8	10.1	7.5

Source: UNCTAD, World Investment Report 2004, Country fact sheet Russian Federation

Apart from values, the complementarity of the structure of trade has probably contributed to the difficulties in the relationship. Paradoxically, this complementarity, while promising significant medium-term gains from international division of labour, has probably led to a stiffening of protectionist tendencies in both the EU and in Russia. The potential for intra-industry trade, which usually readily finds political supporters, is scant in the short-term. Conversely, some industrial branches have much to fear from competition from the other partner; for example, the EU fertilizer or aluminium industry seems to fear Russian competition, while Russian automakers have lobbied for higher import duties on cars.

Another area of cooperation which has perhaps not lived up fully to initial expectations is the energy sector. There have been some notable successes: the removal of destination clauses, the attraction of EU investments into Russia, increased cooperation between EU and Russian companies, the launching of negotiations on the trade in nuclear materials, a study on the integration of electricity markets and the introduction of stricter controls on maritime safety for tanker traffic (reducing the risk of spills is a high-priority topic for EU member states along the shores of the Baltic sea). In addition, the two sides have opened a joint technology centre in Moscow and have solved the most pressing problems linked with the enlargement of the EU. However, while both the EU and Russia want to preserve the Energy Dialogue, it is clear that six years after it started, several of the objectives defined in the first of the annual Progress Reports on the Energy Dialogue have been only partially achieved and the agreements that have been reached are usually of a technical nature, rather than representing significant political breakthroughs.

Several explanations can be put forward for the long lead time required for reaching agreements in this area. Apart from the general fact that EU-Russia agreements have, as a rule, never been reached easily and quickly, the energy sector is in many ways more sensitive than others. First, the fact that over 60 per cent of exports and, according to some estimates, up to 25 per cent of Russian GDP depend on it make the Russians understandably wary of making concessions, particularly given that world demand for energy is increasing rapidly and that the EU is increasingly dependent on imports. One example of this is that Russia has, over time, clearly cooled to the idea of utilizing production-sharing agreements, an instrument that protects investors from the risk of changes in state policies, to encourage development of new oil and gas fields in remote areas, considering that it was conceding too much. Second, the EU side has been wary of becoming excessively dependent on energy supplies from Russia, reflecting a belief that Europe should not put itself in a situation where it could be pressured by any one supplier; this doctrine – usually expressed by the catchword 'supply security' – notably finds expression in the EU limits on imports of nuclear fuel, which Russia suspects of being essentially due to protectionist pressure from EU producers and has been fighting hard to lift. And last but not least, the Energy Dialogue, besides public sector players, brings together private-sector representatives of a diverse and essentially oligopolistic sector which do not necessarily have converging interests.

No doubt, the Russian trend towards greater, and more direct, state control of the energy sector, which has been apparent during the second Putin administration, is adding to Europeans' fears. State ownership of most of the gas sector, the creeping renationalization of the until recently largely private oil sector, and most of all an ideological climate that appears to promote the utilization of natural resources as instruments of state power inevitably heighten these anxieties. Such worries cannot be readily dismissed: on at least one occasion, the Yukos case, the Russian authorities have been ready to accept a clearly negative impact on foreign investors and some disruption in oil output as a 'necessary evil'; more recently, in the case of the January 2006 cuts in gas supplies to Ukraine, it has been noted that the request by Gazprom for an instant quadrupling of the prices for its supplies to that country and to Moldova, which *per se* may well be justified in commercial terms, has not been extended to Belarus, which can lead one to suspect that the timing and approach are at least partly linked to geopolitical considerations.[22]

The worst fears of 'energy blackmail' from Russia may well be exaggerated: the mirror image of the EU's dependency from Russia as a supplier is Russia's dependency on the EU as a market, given that the transport network would allow only minimal reorientation, and Russia could hardly afford jeopardizing in the short run 60 per cent of its exports and in the long run its reputation as a reliable supplier. Nevertheless, it seems clear that at present the fundamental energy policy choices of the two sides run opposite to each other: Russia is intent on expanding the state role in the energy sector, while the EU wants to introduce as much market competition in its energy markets as possible, which is largely incompatible with having to depend on a state supplier operating as a de facto monopoly. Therefore, it seems difficult to expect much dynamism from this area in the short term. It is probably indicative that, although Russia and Ukraine quickly came to an agreement and the gas cuts were lifted in a matter of days, most comments in the EU focused on European vulnerability and the need to diversify the energy supply, concerns which were reflected in the Green Paper on energy policy published in March 2006. This may also have repercussions on EU-Russia cooperation not only in the gas field but also in the areas of nuclear fuel and electricity, where security is, if possible, even more of an issue.[23]

As for the wider trade picture, in recent years the slowness of Russia's WTO accession negotiations has come to interfere considerably with the development of bilateral trade relations. Both sides have come to view WTO accession as a necessary precondition to any significant bilateral agreements, as these must rest on the bedrock of the international trade rules contained in the WTO agreement. This factor has also affected the talks on the CEES.

The PCA structures, too, have been blamed, particularly by the Russians, for not being conducive to cooperation. Although the sectoral Energy Dialogue seems to find support on both sides, Moscow authorities have criticized the PCA on several occasions, saying it is too 'bureaucratic' and slow to deliver results. The EU has tended to attribute the slowness of the dialogue to the difficulty in obtaining a coordinated position from the Russian line ministries. The different cultures of the EU and the Russian administration have contributed to the problem: the Russian administration tends to rely on political guidance for issues that the EU prefers to solve at technical level, so that decisions are often deferred to summits, where, however, the negotiating mandate of the EU representatives is sharply limited by the need to refer to the member states for any important decision.

An important though undeclared motive of Russian dissatisfaction with the PCA is linked to the view that the agreement, having been negotiated in a period of relative Russian weakness, contains a number of obligations, for example on financial services, with which Moscow is now uncomfortable. The EU remains attached to the PCA framework but the fact that the PCA agreement will expire in 2007 allows Moscow to demand a comprehensive overhaul of the cooperation framework; in addition, upon WTO accession, the rules of the trade organisation will de facto replace those agreed in the PCA. This opens the question of what could be the structure of any new cooperation framework. One issue which might be debated is whether, once Russia joins the WTO, a comprehensive agreement on cooperation like the PCA is needed at all. EU relations with the US or Japan, for instance, are not regulated by a PCA-type agreement, which regulates all aspects of cooperation, but take place on an ad hoc basis. This solution would probably be most appreciated by those Russians who wish the country to retain a free hand in its economic policies and avoid binding international engagements, while the EU has shown a preference for maintaining a framework agreement, essentially for the opposite reason.

The parallel with the US may however not be entirely appropriate for various reasons. First, because Russia is not yet in the WTO, hence there is a greater need for a satisfactory bilateral framework; second, because a strong bilateral EU-Russia framework would be unlikely to undermine the WTO, as would be feared in the case of a bilateral EU-US agreement; third, because of the value of such an agreement in particular as far as standards and technical regulations are concerned, given the interest in harmonising Russian standards and regulations with the EU, which is not a realistic expectation in the case of the

US. Finally, given the poor problem-solving record, there is a need for an effective dispute settlement mechanism in such an agreement.

The main question, however, is not so much the architecture of the relationship but whether, in light of the difficulties encountered in the last years, it can be expected to deepen and how. Overall, both sides seem to be conscious of its importance, despite the long-standing and mutual ambivalence. Moscow has a strong economic interest – which it is conscious of – in fostering good trade relations with the EU, which is bound to remain the country's top trade partner for the foreseeable future. If Russia wants to succeed in diversifying its exports, its manufacturers must be able to penetrate the EU market. Furthermore, the EU can provide both the technical know-how that Russia needs in order to modernize its industry, and capital to rebuild the country's rundown capital stock and infrastructure.

The EU too has a growing interest in trade with Russia. The 2004 enlargement has moved the EU's centre of gravity to the East; the bloc now shares a long border with Russia, and, despite the trade reorientation, the new EU member states still have important trade links with Moscow. The strong economic growth recorded by Russia in the last few years (between 1999 and 2004, GDP increased at an average 6.8 per cent annual rate) offers interesting market opportunities to EU firms, most of which have been confronted with sluggish domestic demand in the EU for much of the first half of the decade. The EU and Russia are also likely to grow more interdependent over the next years: as the North Sea gas fields are gradually depleted, the EU will have to import more and more of its gas from abroad, and Russia is home to the world's largest gas reserves. In the longer term, Russia offers EU companies not only a large market next door, but also access to a skilled and inexpensive labour force; if Russia succeeded in improving its investment climate, it could prove a precious production base for high-labour cost Europe.

The approval of the road maps on the four common spaces at the May 2005 summit was a step forward, but it remains to be seen whether the largely non-binding commitments they contain will translate into significant changes. How then can Russia and the EU relaunch the trade relationship and encourage the integration of their economies? In the medium to long term, analyses conducted with international trade models indicate that the technically most promising avenue is not to focus on tariff barriers, but rather on the so-called non-tariff barriers to trade (NTBs), namely the regulatory barriers. Estimates show that their elimination would result in large welfare gains, particularly for Russia, equivalent to a multiple of what can be achieved from simple trade liberalisation.[24] What would be required to effectively neutralise the existing NTBs, however, would go beyond both WTO rules and what is foreseen currently for the CEES. It would require moving towards a 'deep integration' preferential agreement combining free trade in goods and services with significant regulatory convergence in a range of key areas. Regulatory convergence would have to cover, at a minimum, industrial standards, customs, competition law, and matters related to investment. A degree of convergence on the environment, energy, telecommunications and transport also seems indispensable in light of the importance of these sectors for the EU internal market and for bilateral links.[25]

The scenario of a deep FTA makes sense in theory, but what obstacles might it encounter in practice? On the EU side, growing worries on the democratic nature of Russian institutions will remain an important concern, if not a political precondition for closer links with Russia (although the imperfect nature of democracy in several partners, for example in the Mediterranean and the Persian Gulf, has not prevented the EU from negotiating free trade agreements with them). From a technical viewpoint, a key factor will be to what extent Russia can generate more trust in its willingness to abide by commitments, particularly in the immediate aftermath of WTO accession; one closely watched issue will be the development of energy prices for industrial users, which Russia has pledged to double within ten years in its WTO accession agreement with the EU. Given low EU tariff barriers, it should be possible to overcome resistance to an FTA with Russia if the conditions are right.

As for Russia, the obstacles are somewhat different. The level of Russian tariffs is currently significantly higher than in the EU,[26] therefore an FTA with the EU would have a measurable budgetary effect (customs duties make up 7.3 per cent of total tax revenue; it is likely that over half of them are levied on imports from the EU[27]); this problem should however not be insurmountable per se in light of the currently comfortable budgetary position. However, the current Russian tariff structure offers significant protection to some industries which are likely to resist the reform.[28] But, apart from the issue of protectionism, Russia has long shown reluctance to commit to wide-ranging alignment to the EU *acquis*, as the members of the EEA have done. While the country is prepared to adopt technical standards and, in some areas, EU regulation, it wishes to retain national control of most regulatory activity.[29] In this sense, Russia differs from Ukraine, which is open to wide-ranging regulatory alignment as a step towards EU membership.

Conclusion

Russia's long and painful transition from the planned to the market economy has often provided an unfavourable backdrop for the development of economic ties with the EU, largely by encouraging protectionist and inward looking policies. Hence, tariff and regulatory barriers continue to slow the country's economic integration with the EU, as highlighted by the structure of trade and the low level of FDI. The EU for its part has remained cautious without reaching an internal consensus on an ambitious 'vision' for Russia.[30] Russia's long WTO accession process, too, has resulted in slowing down the development of bilateral ties. At present, the two partners seem to be at a crossroads between the status quo and advancement to a next level, which would have to be a FTA with substantial, although selective, regulatory convergence. On the Russian side, assuming that WTO accession is realized as planned, the main obstacle to this development seems to be the recent trend towards strong state intervention in the economy, which is largely incompatible with EU market rules. The EU will also have to take care to show tact and flexibility on Kaliningrad, given that fears abound that 'foreign forces' seek its independence from Russia and that the current arrangements remain not fully satisfactory for Moscow. As for the EU side, the obstacles seem to lie primarily in lingering distrust of the Russian willingness and ability to conform to agreements and, generally, to rules-based systems. In general, the history of the economic relationship between the EU and Russia persuasively shows that political factors have had an important bearing even on technical choices; the further integration of the two economies is therefore likely to depend largely on finding a clear – and shared – political vision of Russia's place in Europe. This vision will, most probably, also depend on the choices made in Ukraine and other former Soviet republics.

Notes and References

1. Until December 2004, the author was Desk Officer for Russia in the European Commission's Directorate-General for Economic and Financial Affairs. The views expressed here reflect his personal opinion only and do not necessarily coincide with the Commission's position. The author wishes to thank Jean-Pierre De Laet, Lutz Güllner, Hiddo Houben, Antonio Parenti, Jeffery Piper, Vladimir Mau, Andreas Papadopoulos, and an anonymous Russian referee for their support and their insightful comments. Responsibility for any remaining errors is however entirely his own.
2. See B. Lissovolik and Y. Lissovolik, *Russia and the WTO: The Gravity of Outsider Status*, IMF Working Paper (2004).
3. See V. Arora and A. Vamvakidis, *How Much Do Trading Partners Matter for Economic Growth?*, IMF Staff Papers, 52:1(Washington, 2005) on the high degree of stability in the relative importance of a country's trading partners over time.
4. See, for instance, J. Sachs, A. Warner and M. Warner, 'Natural Resource Intensity and Economic Growth', in J. Mayer, B. Chambers and A. Farooq (eds.), *Development Policies in Natural Resource Economies* (Northampton, MA and Cheltenham, Edgar Elgar, 1999).
5. See K. A. Soos, E. Ivleva and I. Levina, 'Russian Manufacturing Industry in the Mirror of its Exports to the European Union', *Russian Economic Trends*, 11:3 (2002), pp. 31–43(13).

More recent data seem to indicate that the situation may have improved somewhat, but it is unlikely to have changed radically.

6. A notable example is Mikhail Fradkov, who was nominated Permanent Representative to the EU in 2003. In addition to his duties as Permanent Representative in Brussels, Mr Fradkov had the rank of government minister, an unusual honour for an ambassador. Mr Fradkov went on to become Prime Minister of Russia in 2004.

7. Current EU Commission forecasts indicate that, by 2020, EU imports of oil will increase by one fifth from the 2000 level while those of natural gas will grow by some 140 per cent.

8. See D. Tarr and P. Thompson, 'The Merits of Dual Pricing of Russian Natural Gas', The World Bank, July 2003.

9. In addition to the political significance of the decision, which was taken largely as a political gesture without a concrete *quid pro quo*, the recognition of market economy status makes it more difficult to challenge Russian companies on the basis of anti-dumping regulations.

10. The decision on the four common spaces confirmed and extended a decision taken at the May 2001 summit to begin work on a 'Common Economic Space'.

11. There were seven original non-EU signatories to the EEA. Over the course of time three of them have joined the EU while one, Switzerland, never ratified the agreement. The three remaining EEA members are Norway, Iceland and Liechtenstein.

12. See F. Lyukanov, 'Autarky's Eternal Values', commentary in *Gazeta.ru*, 8 September 2004.

13. A good example is the issue of the Siberian over-flight charges. Some fifteen years after the break-up of the Soviet Union, foreign airlines are still being charged substantial fees for over-flying Siberia.

14. See M. Dodini and M. Fantini 'The European Neighbourhood Policy: Implications for Economic Growth and Stability', *Journal of Common Market Studies* 44.3 (2006).

15. The main fear is that creation of the SES might make bilateral trade negotiations more complex, thereby slowing their progress. See European Commission *Communication from the Commission to the European Parliament on relations with Russia*, COM(2004) 106, 9 February 2004, p. 2. This fear seemed especially relevant for Ukraine, given that the signing of the pact had been interpreted by some as a signal of disillusionment with the EU. The election of Viktor Yushchenko to the presidency, however, has been marked by repeated indications that deepening of relations with the EU is a primary objective. The implications of this for the viability of the SES remain to be seen.

16. See European Commission, *Communication* (2004). Note that strictly speaking this represented the position of the European Commission, not the European Council. The two organs often show subtle differences in approach, given their different roles and composition.

17. See D. Danilov, 'Russia-EU Summit: Gloomy Forecasts Ahead of Jubilee Festivities', *OANA*, 22 April 2005.

18. To this, Russians reply that the Europeans too resort to cherry-picking when it suits them. This is alleged, for example, on the Russian demand for visa-free travel.

19. See Dodini and Fantini, 'The European Neighbourhood Policy'.

20. A respondent in a 2005 survey of CEOs carried out for Russia's Foreign Investment Advisory Council significantly stated: 'The decision to invest in Russia has as much to do with trust, transparency and consistency by the Government as it does with assessments of risk and return.' See *Russia: Investment Destination, A Survey of 158 Foreign Investors*, Foreign Investment Advisory Council (FIAC), Moscow, 2005, available at http://www.pbnco.com/

21. The FIAC *Russia: Investment Destination* survey reports that 'The Yukos affair and subsequent claims against Russian businesses for back taxes have shaken investors' confidence in Russia'.

22. Vladimir Putin is generally considered to be hostile to the pro-EU, westernising course of Ukrainian President Victor Yushchenko. During the 2004 presidential elections, he openly supported his opponent Viktor Yanukovitch.
23. For several years RAO UES, the Russian electricity company, has been trying to export electricity to the EU. To do this on a significant scale, however, would require synchronous connection of the two electricity networks, a move with important safety implications as problems in one area would be immediately propagated to the other. Furthermore, in the case of electricity, dependence on foreign suppliers cannot be addressed by holding reserve stocks as is done for oil.
24. The limited gains from simple tariff cuts derive largely from the fact that (except for processed foods, vehicles and clothing), the EU imposes low tariffs on imports from Russia (about 2 per cent in trade-weighted terms), owing not least to the zero import duty on oil and gas. On this point, see M. Manchin, *The Economic Effects of a Russia-EU FTA*, Tinbergen Institute Discussion Paper T1 2004- 131/2, Rotterdam, 2004, which also includes a discussion of previous studies on the same topic.
25. For instance, the EU will only seriously envisage free trade in energy-intensive goods, or in goods whose production entails significant costs for environmental protection, if Russian firms are subjected to broadly comparable conditions as EU ones.
26. According to WTO data, tariff levels amount to 4.2 per cent in the EU (simple average of *ad valorem* MFN tariffs, 2004 data) compared to 9.9 per cent in Russia (2001 data). Source: WTO, Russian Federation Statistical Profile, EU Statistical profile, April 2005 (available from http://stat.wto.org). Data from Manchin, *The Economic Effects*, show a similar picture. WTO accession might however significantly modify the picture.
27. Data refer to the 1999–2001 average. Source: WTO, *ibidem.*
28. See Table 3 in Manchin, *The Economic Effects*, for evidence of significant levels of protection (tariffs higher than 10 per cent in several sectors: processed food, textiles, clothing, some metals, vehicles, other manufactures, chemicals, etc).
29. V. Mau gives a good summary of the Russian position: 'we need standards developed in Russia and for Russia. There can be no question of parameters being developed under control of European entities. The idea is that Russia should determine its own targets and goals rather than formalise its desire to join the EU.' See V. Mau, *Problems and Prospects of Relations between Russia and the EU*, Academy of the National Economy under the Governance of the Russian Federation, Moscow, July 2002.
30. On the current lack of a clear long-term vision in the relationship, see S. Karaganov *et al*, 'Evropeiskaia strategiya Rossii: novyi start', *Rossia v globalnom politike, tom 3, No.2, Moscow, March–April 2005*. (2005).

15

RUSSIA AND THE EUROPEAN SECURITY GOVERNANCE DEBATE

Mark Webber

Introduction: The Evolution of European Security Governance

Security governance can be defined as the coordinated management of issues by multiple and separate authorities. As applied to Europe, its most obvious formal characteristic is the development of dense patterns of multilateralism and institutionalization. This feature does not negate the continuing relevance of the state-as-actor but it clearly suggests that this actor is, to an important degree, subordinated to institutional imperatives and processes of cooperation, as well as subject to a normative discourse on the appropriate principles of order. Governance of this type was not absent in Europe during the Cold War, however, since the late 1980s it has both 'widened' and 'deepened'. Security governance has come to acquire a pan-continental (rather than a bipolar) quality that involves overlapping interactions among a range of state, institutional and private actors in multiple security-relevant issue areas. At both analytical and policy levels the conceptualization and operationalization of security governance can be disputed; however, what seems eminently clear is that European order is now as much about institutions and norms as it is state-centric concerts, balances of power, and the conduct and settlement of war.[1]

The development of Europe's security governance has occurred against a backdrop of policy-driven controversies concerning the appropriate roles and hierarchy of security institutions. For two to three crucial years after 1989 this came in the guise of the so-called 'architecture' debate concerning the relative merits of NATO, the then Conference (now Organization) on Security and Cooperation in Europe (CSCE/OSCE) and the post-Maastricht European Union (EU). Complicating this debate was the collapse of the Warsaw Pact and the

Soviet Union, and the emergence of the Soviet successor states (Russia included) in tandem with the Commonwealth of Independent States (CIS). Through the course of the 1990s, these debates ebbed and flowed against the tumult of Yugoslavia's collapse, the westward reorientation of the Baltic region and former Warsaw Pact states, and processes of Cold War military reorientation.

At the same time, there was a seeming disconnection between continental Europe and the former Soviet Union (FSU). In the former, security governance had followed a curious evolution. An assumption that the North Atlantic Treaty Organization (NATO) would wither away after the Cold War proved mistaken. Under American guidance, the Alliance had asserted itself against a CSCE alternative (variously supported by the Soviet Union, and the West German and Czech foreign ministries) during 1990 and in the following two years a French preference for a European defence structure oriented around the European Union/Western European Union (WEU) was effectively stalled by American and British opposition. The possibility of 'a common defence policy' noted in the Maastricht Treaty on European Union was politically significant but did nothing at this point to materially detract from the Alliance. The nascent European Security and Defence Identity (ESDI) was, in fact, to develop within NATO rather than autonomous of it. On this basis, one analyst was able to claim that by 1995, 'European security was once again dominated by the NATO alliance and US leadership, perhaps to a greater extent than even in the last years of the Cold War.'[2] During the remainder of the decade, however, the security identity of the EU came more and more into focus as a consequence of the development of the Common Foreign and Security Policy (CFSP), 'third pillar' activities under Justice and Home Affairs (JHA) and, crucially, from 1999, the European Security and Defence Policy (ESDP). Thereafter, in terms of military security a division of labour has emerged between NATO and the EU. This has not been without its problems, but powerful factors have provided it with an inexorable logic. These include: an emergent consensus among EU and NATO member states (post-Bosnia and post-Kosovo) on the need for a specifically European intervention capacity, shifts in US foreign policy after '9/11' which have downgraded American willingness to underwrite NATO intervention in Europe, and the adaptation of the Alliance such that cooperation with the EU is both possible logistically and plausible politically.[3]

On this last point, NATO's adaptation has to be seen as a broad and ongoing project. It was undertaken in the post-Cold War period as a response to the loss of the traditional Soviet adversary and came subsequently to embrace an agenda that encompassed the stabilization of the Balkans, enlargement, and partnership with non-allies. This agenda was encapsulated in the 1999 new *Strategic Concept*, but had to be refashioned anew in response to first 9/11 and then the 2002–3 Iraq crisis. These two events challenged the notion of American commitment to NATO and elevated issues of counter-terrorism and proliferation to centre stage, in part precisely to meet American demands that the Alliance remain relevant to 'new' security challenges. Yet NATO's 'old' agenda did not disappear. The enlargement of 2004 brought in seven new members (including the three Baltic states which had once formed part of the Soviet Union) to add to the three states (the Czech Republic, Hungary and Poland) who had entered in 1999. At the same time, NATO revamped its various partnerships. This included the launch in 2002 of the NATO-Russia Council (NRC)(see below), and on the basis of decisions at the Prague and Istanbul summits (in 2002 and 2004 respectively) a greater attention to Central Asia, the south Caucasus (Armenia, Azerbaijan and Georgia), the Middle East and the southern Mediterranean. By 2005, therefore, the case could still be made that despite the divisions over Iraq, NATO remained very much in business even if its business now meant that military operations had become 'an adjunct to its political and diplomatic functions', a kind of OSCE 'in camouflage' 'embracing the widest possible number of states across the range of security issues'.[4]

A parallel process had also been going on within the EU. The Iraq crisis had undoubtedly damaged the credibility of CFSP, but the takeover by the EU of NATO peacekeeping operations in Macedonia and Bosnia in 2003 and 2004 respectively demonstrated the continuing vitality of ESDP. An increase in the EU's membership from 15 to 25 states in 2004, meanwhile, indicated an even more profound contribution. Enlargement, to quote Antonio Missiroli, is 'a security policy by other means [... by] extending the Union's norms, rules, opportunities and constraints to successive applicants [the EU] has made instability and conflict on the Continent decreasingly likely'.[5] Finally, the launch in 2003 of the European Neighbourhood Policy (ENP) embracing inter alia political dialogue and security cooperation with states in an arc from Moldova and Ukraine, through the south Caucasus, the Middle East and down to North Africa, suggested an EU responsibility well beyond the parameters of enlargement.

All of these initiatives should not be taken at face value. Official EU and NATO documentation certainly talk them up,[6] but close analysis reveals that both organizations remain plagued by internal dispute, and that the initiatives detailed above remain subject to questions concerning resources and political will. Yet this qualification notwithstanding, European security governance has come to be defined by the enlargement of the EU and NATO, on the one hand, and the multiplication and deepening of security functions within these two organizations, on the other. Crucially, these processes have since the early 2000s partly blurred the disconnection noted above between continental Europe and the FSU.

Russia and European Security Governance

Security governance has not developed against Russia. This may be a controversial claim to those Russians who perceive NATO and EU enlargement as threatening (see below). However, both organizations have been the sites of a network of ties aimed at embedding relations with Moscow. There are many reasons for this that reflect calculations relating to Russia's geo-economic importance as a major provider of fossil fuels, and the potential diplomatic, military and intelligence benefits of practical cooperation in dealing with common challenges to security. In these respects, Russia is an unavoidable interlocutor given its position in the UN Security Council (UNSC), its expert knowledge on proliferation, terrorism and defence industries, and its regional influence in non-EU/NATO Europe as well as in trouble spots outside of Europe such as Central Asia and Afghanistan. The fact that Russia is itself the source of certain security problems – notably the safety of Russia's military and civilian nuclear infrastructure (nuclear-powered submarines, power-stations etc.), the status of its biological and chemical weapons capabilities, and the prevalence of a variety of 'soft' security threats ranging from arms and drugs smuggling, people trafficking and money laundering, to the spread of HIV/AIDS and environmental degradation – only adds to the need for engagement.

Cooperation has, in fact, been a leitmotif of the pronouncements of European and American governments as well as of NATO and EU documentation (see below). It is a theme, moreover, that persists as the majority view despite the entry into these two bodies of neighbouring states (the Baltics and Poland, for instance) with an engrained scepticism of Russian intentions.

True, there remain plentiful areas of disagreement. On the implementation of the CFE Treaty regime, Russian policy toward Belarus, Moldova and Georgia, and the conduct of the war in Chechnya, to take just a few examples, Russian policy has been at odds with a general consensus among EU and NATO member states. Yet this state of affairs is itself offset by cross-cutting cleavages. On a range of issues – the Iraq crisis, the Kyoto Protocol, and ballistic missile defence – disagreements have occurred as much within and between the EU and NATO as they have with Russia.

One might also question the commitment to cooperation in Russia itself. Here, official thinking, it could be argued, continues to be characterized by a suspicious, threat-based security culture. Keynote texts (namely the *National Security Concept*, the *Military Doctrine* and the *Foreign Policy Concept* adopted in 2000, and the 2003 *Defence White Paper*) as well as the pronouncements of certain leading officials (most obviously, the Defence Minister, Sergei Ivanov, but also on occasion President Vladimir Putin) emphasise military instruments as a route to security, exhibit a distrust of actions and organizations of which Russia is not a part, and are informed by an inescapable feeling of beleaguerment and danger.[7] This outlook is in some senses readily understandable, the result of Russia's troubled emergence from the Soviet Union, the loss of influence in eastern Europe and parts of the FSU, and an exposure to terrorism and regional conflicts (both internally as in Dagestan and Chechnya, and near its external borders). Narrow security thinking of this type does, however, coexist with a much more nuanced outlook of security interdependence and exposure to multiple threats. Even Defence Minister Ivanov, an acknowledged 'hawk' has argued that the most pressing task of 'the global system of military-political relations [...] is to meet the challenges induced by the processes of globalisation [...] proliferation of weapons of mass destruction [...], international terrorism, demographic problems and ethnic instability [...] illicit drug trafficking and organised crime'.[8] This is a list not dissimilar to themes contained in the 2003 *European Security Strategy* of the EU and, for that matter NATO's 1999 *Strategic Concept* and subsequent Alliance statements.

Indeed, Russia's multiple security predicaments combined with its diminished diplomatic and military status and the needs of economic modernisation have resulted in a keen appreciation of the need to cooperate on security matters with centres of regional and world power, be these the US, China, India or, indeed, the EU, NATO and individual European states. Such reasoning was not absent during the Yeltsin period; however, the Putin leadership has introduced three important modifications. First, Putin grasped early on the dead end in which Yeltsin's foreign policy was parked – a policy characterized according to Bobo Lo by 'incoherence and disarray', one in which the 'limits of Russia's influence' had become evident 'in the Balkans, over NATO enlargement, in the Middle East, and even in its supposed backyard [the former Soviet Union]'.[9] One way out of this cul-de-sac was the altered security agenda provided by 9/11. This not only vindicated Russia's own long-held view that terrorism was a major international concern but also provided an upsurge of opportunities for Russia to prove its worth as a useful security partner.[10]

Second, Russia has toned down its opposition to enlargement. EU enlargement has never been opposed in principle, but NATO enlargement has. Yeltsin's tub-thumping admonitions failed to stop the process however. The 2004 enlargement and subsequent Ukrainian and Georgian aspirations to join the Alliance have certainly prompted public concern among Russian officials, particularly within the defence establishment.[11] Within the Putin leadership, however, the issue has increasingly been seen as less as a threat to Russia and more as an irrelevant distraction from the 'present-day threats and challenges' of 'terrorism [...], illegal migration, drug smuggling [and ...] the trade in humans and arms'.[12] According to Foreign Minister Sergei Lavrov, NATO enlargement also detracts from the need to build 'together, on a collective and equal basis [...] a united Europe without the longing for old dividing lines and without the malicious hopes of creating new ones'.[13] What such statements imply is a Russian concern at marginalization rather than a fear of NATO's military capabilities. A similar anxiety also applies to Russian views of the EU. Enlargement coupled with deepening integration and the imposition of Schengen barriers has had a profound effect on Russian thinking. Practical matters of trade diversion and visa regimes are prominent concerns here, but these sit within a broader context of feared Russian isolation.

The response in both cases has been to talk tough where specific Russian interests are at stake, but to accompany this with a realistic appreciation of the need to cooperate with the EU and NATO when necessary. The essence of this approach was spelled out by President Putin in a speech to the Russian Foreign Ministry in July 2004. Here he suggested that alongside the CIS, Russia's 'other traditional priority is, of course, Europe'. He continued

[t]he latest wave of EU and NATO expansion has created a new geopolitical situation on the continent, and the task now is not so much to adapt ourselves to it as, first, minimize the potential risks and damage to Russia's [...] interests and, second, to find here advantages for ourselves and turn them to good account. Here [...] there is no alternative approach but to build up equal cooperation with the European Union and the North Atlantic Treaty Organization [...][14]

Commensurate with this stance, the third innovation of the Putin period has been a move away from grandiose and fruitless schemes of European security premised on undermining NATO and EU dominance. During the Yeltsin period, these centred on elevating the OSCE to some form of pan-European coordinating body. Under Putin this is a position that has come to be recognised as both untenable and, given the OSCE's increasingly critical take on Russia's war in Chechnya and democratic deficiencies, as undesirable.[15] In their place, Russia has argued in favour of coordinated, pan-European efforts in security by a range of institutions – the OSCE, the Council of Europe, the CIS and the EU and NATO.[16] In practice, Russia has also supplemented this by a traditional attention to individual member states: the UK, the US, France, Italy and Germany.

In short, a sufficient basis has existed for Russia's involvement in European security governance, but it is an involvement that has its limitations. The underlying reasons for this are complex and relate to a host of factors, some (the nature of its security culture), have been alluded to above; others (the 'values-gap' between Russia and Europe, the nature of Russia's domestic politics etc.) are covered elsewhere in this volume. Here I want to concentrate on two further aspects, both direct consequences of the manner in which European security governance itself has developed since the end of the Cold War. The first refers to the nature of institutionalization and the second to geographic differentiation.

Russia and the Institutions of Security Governance

In one sense, security governance can be regarded as institutionally promiscuous; the 'governance' tag is intended to convey a picture of multiple and overlapping arrangements aimed at regulating security affairs. Here, Russian involvement is substantial. It has retained or assumed membership of bodies which have played a central or indirect role in European security, including the UNSC, the OSCE, the Council of Europe, the Group of Eight (G8), the Contact Group on the former Yugoslavia and the Collective Security Treaty Organisation (CSTO) of the CIS. Russia is also a party to the Treaty on Open Skies, the Chemical Weapons Convention, the Biological Weapons Convention, a host of nuclear disarmament and non-proliferation treaties and accounts for the largest holdings and the largest reductions under the 1990 Conventional Forces in Europe (CFE) Treaty.

However, in a system of security governance shaped to a significant degree by NATO and the EU what really matters is how far Russia is involved in mechanisms linking it to these two organizations. Russia is a member of neither and its leadership has shown no serious desire to pursue accession. However, in both cases Russia is involved in what, at first glance, appear well-developed partner relations.

The NATO-Russia Council

NATO-Russian cooperation can be traced back to December 1991 when Russia joined the nascent North Atlantic Cooperation Council (NACC). Entry into the Partnership for Peace (PfP) programme followed in 1995. Russian peacekeepers also took up station with the Implementation Force in Bosnia and Herzegovina (IFOR) in 1996 and with KFOR in Kosovo in 1999. The jewel in the crown of relations, however, was undoubtedly the NATO-Russia Founding Act of 1997, an initiative which seemed to presage a special and privileged relationship between the two sides. The Act, however, resulted in only a short-lived honeymoon. NATO's Operation Allied Force (OAF) and the 1999 enlargement were vehemently opposed by Moscow and led to an inevitable deterioration of relations.

The precise institutional configuration of these relations was not the source of the underlying problem, but it certainly did not help. The Permanent Joint Council (PJC) had, since its formation in 1997, laboured under several drawbacks. Some of these were purely procedural (how PJC meetings were chaired) but others were more substantive. In negotiations on the Founding Act, Russia had demanded that the PJC permit Russia the ability to 'block decisions [within NATO] that are unacceptable to it'.[17] This was expressly ruled out in the Founding Act itself and Russia, in President Bill Clinton's phrase, would only be permitted a 'voice in, but not a veto over, NATO's business'.[18] Despite this, Moscow continued to invest the PJC with an importance that was not shared among NATO members. It was particularly critical, for instance, of NATO's decision to launch OAF without any prior notification or discussion. Yet Russia itself often frustrated the work of the PJC. NATO officials bemoaned the tendency of Russian officials to adopt set positions, for creating procedural difficulties and for seeking to upset Alliance solidarity. Russia also refused to take up a liaison presence at NATO HQ in Brussels. NATO states, in turn, responded by adopting pre-cooked positions prior to meetings. The working of the PJC thus took on the unproductive format of the members of NATO on the one side and Russia on the other – '16 versus 1' ('19 versus 1' from March 1999).[19]

The May 2002 Rome declaration was a conscious effort to breathe new life into the relationship in view of these difficulties, but also to shift the agenda of cooperation. The declaration envisaged 'cooperative efforts' in crisis management, non-proliferation, arms control, search-and-rescue at sea, military reform, civil emergencies and so-called 'new threats and challenges'. Crucially, 'the struggle against terrorism' was also given far more prominence than the brief reference to it in the Founding Act, thereby reflecting its heightened importance both to NATO (the US particularly) and Russia. In order to pursue cooperation, the NRC was established to replace the PJC. Like its predecessor, the NRC afforded Russia no influence over internal NATO business but it would involve new methods of decision-making, moving away from '19 + 1' in favour of 'joint action at twenty' (or 27 following the 2004 enlargement). There would not, in other words, be a set NATO position presented to the NRC.[20] This initially aroused some concern at an increased possibility for the confounding of consensus not only with Russia but also among NATO's own members. Indeed, an informal principle of 'retrievability' by which any NATO ally could pull an item off the NRC agenda offered the additional problem that some of NATO's newer, more Russophobic members might condemn the NRC to paralysis. The more equitable formula also raised the question of how Russia would react to being just one of 27, having equal rights not just with major players like the US, France, Germany and the UK but also with Luxembourg, Iceland and the former Soviet Baltic states.

As of writing, the operation of the NRC has, in part, confounded such dire expectations. Deadlock has been avoided, retrievability has been rarely employed and in a major step forward from the PJC, the NRC has developed what two respected observers have referred to as 'a continual, quotidian interaction' among officials – a bureaucratic network involving a high-level preparatory committee, 17 sub-committees and sub-groups (as compared with the two attached to the PJC) as well as the regular ministerial and ambassadorial-level meetings of the NRC itself.[21] Within these formats, the NRC has managed to discuss the CFE Treaty and the situations in Iraq, Afghanistan, Georgia, Serbia and Montenegro, and Bosnia and Herzegovina. It has also provided a vehicle for practical cooperation. Early successes included civil emergency planning and rescue at sea. The Defence Ministers' meeting of the NRC in June 2005, meanwhile, was able to report the recent signing of a NATO-Russia status of forces agreement, the conclusion of an NRC Action Plan on Terrorism, preparations for Russian participation in NATO's Operation Active Endeavour in the Mediterranean, cooperation in defence reform, inter-operability, theatre missile defence, non-proliferation and data exchange. The cooperation plan for 2005 envisaged over 200 events including 50 joint exercises.[22]

These positives aside, the achievements of the NRC in other respects look much more modest. In many areas, including the politically significant ones of joint peacekeeping, theatre-missile defence, counter-terrorism, and non-proliferation, cooperation has amounted to consultations, seminars, exchanges of information, but has not entered what one Russian official has referred to as 'the next phase [of] effective cooperation'.[23] Further, NATO-Russia interaction has not kept pace with NATO's own internal transformation agenda. Issues of peacekeeping and expeditionary forces, defence modernization and standardization, and communications and surveillance might be construed as NATO's own business, however, if NATO and Russia are to work together at an operational level, their joint development is essential.[24] These areas have, of course, challenged NATO's own members and reflect the limitations of military capabilities as much as of institutional arrangements. The NRC framework has at least identified them as issues of attention, even if practical movement on them remains remote.[25]

A further limitation concerns the possible divergence of NATO and Russian priorities. This has tested the relationship since its inception in the early 1990s and is precisely one of the structural problems the NRC was created to address. The vast range of topics the NRC has addressed does suggest some overlap; however, there remain areas where either the possibilities for cooperation have yet to be realized (for instance, counter insurgency and action against drug trafficking in Afghanistan) or where Russian concerns (the continued stationing of US tactical nuclear weapons in NATO members states) have not been subject to consideration.[26]

The European Security and Defence Policy

As for the EU, here too Russia has enjoyed a special position. The broad institutional framework has been described in Chapter 7. With regard specifically to security, this was an area underdeveloped during much of the 1990s when relations were largely defined by economic issues of trade and technical assistance. A number of policy documents (the 1995 EU *Strategy for Future EU/Russia Relations* and the 1996 EU *Action Plan for Russia*) did envisage security cooperation, but it was not until the adoption by the EU of the Northern Dimension in 1997, and more so the *Common Strategy on Russia* in 1999 that this became concrete. At the EU-Russia summit of May 2003, relations were officially designated as falling within four 'common spaces': economic, freedom security and justice, external security, and research and education. The summit of May 2005 adopted 'road maps' for cooperation in all four. Within the 'space' of freedom, security and justice, activities have included dialogue on the Schengen arrangement, special provisions concerning Kaliningrad, an Action Plan on Organized Crime (agreed in 2000), an agreement (2003) between Russia and Europol and a joint statement (2002) 'on the fight against terrorism'. In the space of external security, the relevant road map notes existing initiatives and further intended cooperation under five headings: diplomatic dialogue and cooperation, combating terrorism, non-proliferation and disarmament, crisis management, and civil protection.[27]

There has thus been a clear development in the ambition and institutionalization of the EU-Russia relationship. Yet for all this, doubts remain as to its real significance. In early 2004, the Commission reported that on a host of issues (border agreements with Latvia and Estonia, cooperation with the EU Galileo satellite project, maritime and nuclear safety) the EU and Russia were in disagreement.[28] The EU External Relations Commissioner Chris Patten noted in a speech in February 2004 that 'five years of increasingly intensive cooperation' with Russia had given rise to less than positive results.[29] A May 2005 Report of the European Parliament (EP) noted 'Russia's potential as a special strategic partner for providing peace, stability and security, and fighting international terrorism and violent extremism, as well as addressing "soft security" issues such as environmental and nuclear hazards, drugs, arms and human trafficking and cross-border organised crime in the European neighbourhood'. The report went on to note, however, that progress in the two common spaces relating to security had lagged behind the others and that there was a need to do more than agree on the wording of texts and move toward 'real convergence on sensitive issues.'[30] Part of the blame here has been laid at the door of the EU itself, owing to what the EU's External Relations

Commissioner has referred to as 'a lack of coherence' on its part – an allusion to the sometimes incompatible positions held among member states on how to engage Russia. Others, however, have pointed to problems on the Russian side – a poor knowledge of EU procedures, an absence of proper coordination among ministries, and a lingering reluctance to regard the EU as such (as opposed to its important member states) as a worthy interlocutor. In short, according to one Russian observer, the EU-Russia dialogue has amounted more to 'a bureaucratic exercise than a vehicle for further integration'.[31]

Russian engagement with ESDP is illustrative of these sorts of problem. On the one hand, both sides have seen ESDP as a positive setting for cooperation. In Moscow, support for ESDP has been voiced in principle since its initiation in 1999. The fact that ESDP is potentially autonomous of both NATO and the US does make it attractive, but Russian statements on ESDP tend to view the initiative within a more nuanced (and arguably, more realistic) context. ESDP is not viewed as a device to undercut NATO and Russian commentary remains distinctly unimpressed by the EU's military capabilities. Rather, it is seen as indicative of the EU's broader geopolitical relevance, albeit (as noted above) as one institutional actor among several; engagement in some shape or form is consequently a *sine qua non* for Russia if it is to maintain its own claim to relevance as an important European actor.[32] Further, ESDP as a tool of crisis management offers practical opportunities for cooperative participation, given Russian experience in this field and its possession of useful military assets (heavy airlift, satellite reconnaissance etc.).[33]

Yet beyond a fairly constructive dialogue on possible avenues of engagement, on the ground Russian involvement in ESDP has been negligible. Russian personnel have participated in just one operation (four officers in the EU police mission in Bosnia). The section on crisis management in the 2005 EU-Russia 'Road Map for the Common Space of External Security' thus amounts to a list of unfulfilled desiderata: '*possible* cooperation in crisis management operations', '[c]onsideration of *possibilities* for co-operation in the field of long-haul air transport', '[c]ooperation in the field of training and exercises which *could* include observation and participation' etc.[34] This state of affairs has been bemoaned on both sides, yet it cannot simply be put down to technical or operational difficulties or indeed the innovative nature of ESDP as was once claimed by Russian officials. The initiative is now more than six years old, has given rise to nine separate missions and has involved non-EU states as diverse as Turkey, Ukraine, Switzerland, New Zealand, Canada, Brazil and Albania.

The problems are political as much as they are operational. Moscow has not been entirely satisfied with the institutional modalities. Reflecting the political and operational requirements of constructing broad, supportive coalitions for conflict management, the EU has developed a comprehensive set of arrangements under ESDP with other international organizations and 'third countries'. Russia falls within these general guidelines. It also has (in common with Ukraine and Canada) specifically designated 'arrangements for consultation and cooperation' on crisis management,[35] as well as access to regular liaison with the EU's Political and Security Committee. None of these, however, provide co-decision powers or indeed, even the semblance of equality that pertains in the NRC. Russia in this respect is treated no differently from any other non-EU member. Further, Russia has been unhappy at the seeming indifference of the EU to its detailed proposals for collaboration. The EU, for its part, has viewed Russian overtures as overly restrictive, almost a form of reverse conditionality whereby Moscow would like in some way to shape the agenda of ESDP or at least the particular terms of its participation, rather than the EU being the sole arbiter. And overarching all of this is a geopolitical issue. Russia, as detailed in Chapter 6, has executed a military withdrawal from the Balkans, hence, its lack of interest in the main site of ESDP action. Mooted ESDP deployments in trouble spots within the FSU (Moldova, Georgia), meanwhile, are viewed competitively rather than cooperatively given, as we shall see in the next section, Russia's own influence wielding in the region.

The Geography of Security Governance

The Russian Neighbourhood

The new 'neighbourhood' of the EU and NATO overlaps with Russia's own immediate geographic vicinity. This is an area which Moscow has routinely specified as the first priority of its foreign policy – for understandable reasons. Geographic proximity, lingering post-Soviet economic interdependence, and the presence of large Russian-speaking minorities all play a part here. Equally, there are important security considerations. The concerns noted at the outset of this chapter – what Defence Minister Ivanov has referred to as 'demographics, migration, drug trafficking [and] terrorism' – emanate most worryingly from the territory of the FSU.[36]

The priority attached to the region has not, however, made for a comfortable policy. During the Yeltsin period, Moscow soon abandoned the belief that the former Soviet republics would naturally gravitate toward Russia. An appreciation of the diversity of the region emerged accompanied by a range of foreign policy tools then aimed at the conscious preservation of Russian influence and interests. The principal multilateral vehicle for this was the CIS – a putative form of regional governance, supplemented by a network of formal bilateral arrangements and informal pressure. The latter included economic leverage stemming from Russia's gas, oil and electricity supplies as well as more traditional forms of political and military pressure. In Moldova and Georgia, Russia retained a military presence in the teeth of opposition from the host government as well as providing tacit support for separatist enclaves. In Ukraine, it established a political basis for the long-term headquartering of the Russian Black Sea Fleet. For all this, Yeltsin's policy essentially oversaw a retreat of Russian influence. Outside of Central Asia, only two successor states (Armenia and Belarus) could reliably be seen as oriented toward Russia, while the CIS was a less and less effective motor of post-Soviet integration.

Policy under Putin has adjusted to these dynamics with a more realistic appraisal of the limits of Russian influence and the utility of certain methods of pursuing Russian interests. Here, a number of features stand out. First, the CIS has become sidelined. Russian commentary on the organization tends to be derogatory and even Putin has argued that beyond performing 'a civilised divorce' of the former Soviet republics, the achievements of the CIS are 'insignificant'.[37] Second, and related, is an even greater affirmation of regional differentiation. The terms Russian 'near abroad' and 'post-Soviet space' have both fallen out of favour given their failure, according to Foreign Minister Lavrov, 'to reflect the existing realities' of regional integration and foreign policy orientation.[38] As the Russian leadership now recognizes, this 'space' has split into three directions: the Baltic states integrated with NATO and the EU; six states formally within the CIS but distant from it (four of whom – Georgia, Ukraine, Moldova and Azerbaijan have an increasingly Western orientation) and the remaining six (Armenia, Belarus, Kazakhstan, Kyrgyzstan, Tajikistan and Russia itself) who make up the 'core' of the CIS and are grouped together under the CSTO and thus represent the best hope of Russian-led integration.[39] The third, is what Fiona Hill has argued is a greater use of 'soft power' (trade, investment, Russian culture and consumer goods and, above all, energy resources) to pursue Russia's geopolitical position and 'to encourage neighbouring states to associate more closely with its regional policies'.[40] Certainly the military option has not been abandoned: in October 2003, Putin declared that Russia reserved the right to intervene militarily to settle regional conflicts. But as Defence Minister Ivanov has argued, more general foreign policy challenges – what he has referred to as unwelcome changes of 'policy on relations with Russia' among neighbouring states – are best dealt with 'from the standpoint of economic influence.'[41]

Despite these shifts of emphasis, it would be a mistake to regard policy under Putin as fully-formed. Certainly, it is a policy with some inconsistencies. Russia has entered the final stages of abandoning the Soviet military legacy in Georgia and Moldova – but retains in both countries a 'peacekeeping' presence.

Putin's downplaying of the CIS has been contradicted by leading ministers and even Putin himself has continued to talk up the organization, albeit in relatively modest terms as a forum of political solidarity and for spreading Russian culture and language.[42] These sorts of inconsistencies reflect, in part, poor policy coordination and, in part, the practical difficulties of policy adjustment – the need to construct what Putin has referred to as a 'comprehensive long-term strategy' – in the face of an ever-changing and continuingly-challenging landscape.[43] Over-arching all of this, however, has been a more deep-seated process of cognitive adjustment, one which remains incomplete. Both the Yeltsin and Putin leaderships have abandoned the Soviet method of, and rationale for, influence building, but both remain wedded to an assumption that Russia still has the potential for greatness and thus has a right, even a duty, to play the leading role among its neighbours.[44]

The Common Neighbourhood?

Russia's presumption of regional hegemony has occurred in an increasingly ill-disposed environment. In a much-cited article, Zbigniew Brzezinski noted in 1995 the emergence of 'geopolitical pluralism in the territory of the former Soviet Union'.[45] The focus of his attention at that point was Ukraine. Ten years later in response to the 'Orange' and 'Rose' revolutions in Ukraine and Georgia, Brzezinski wrote hopefully that a 'democratic geopolitical pluralism is beginning to surround Russia.'[46] Brezinski's assumption in both cases has been that regime change can be a motor of separation from Russia, unless that is Russia itself experiences democratization, in which case a process of voluntary integration might occur.

The view of many observers is that the latter condition has not been fulfilled and that forms of integration within the FSU remain weak. In the security context, James Sperling has noted the increasing differentiation but also the weakness of security governance in the FSU and Eurasia more broadly, whether this be under the auspices of the CIS and the OSCE or sub-regional fora such as the Shanghai Cooperation Organisation (SCO) or the GUUAM (Georgia, Ukraine, Uzbekistan, Azerbaijan, Moldova) grouping.[47] Only among the Baltic states has this condition of uncertainty been positively rectified, through accession to the EU and NATO. The Baltic route raises the question of how plausible elsewhere in the FSU are forms of governance centred on Brussels rather than Moscow?

Both the EU and NATO have, in fact, since the early 1990s developed overlapping layers of partnership and association which have extended institutional reach well beyond their core memberships. The altered post 9/11 security agenda and enlargement, in turn, have compelled both organizations to pay greater attention to their geographic peripheries. As noted above, the EU in 2003 launched the ENP, an initiative involving by mid 2005 individual Action Plans for cooperation with inter alia Ukraine and Moldova, and the prospect of similar plans with the three states of the southern Caucasus. The Action Plan agreed with Ukraine notes the possibilities for '[e]nhanced co-operation in our common neighbourhood and [on]regional security', and lists a range of detailed measures to address 'common security threats'.[48] An EU border assistance mission to Ukraine and Moldova was established in November 2005. Ukraine itself has participated in two ESDP missions in the Balkans and signed up in June 2005 to cooperate with the GALILEO European satellite navigation system.[49] Georgia has been the site of an EU rule of law mission (EUJUST Themis) since June 2004 – the first and so far only ESDP mission in the FSU. NATO, meanwhile, at its November 2002 summit in Prague decided to upgrade the EAPC and PfP mechanisms with a particular emphasis on 'the countries of the strategically important regions of the Caucasus and Central Asia'.[50] At the Istanbul summit of June 2004 'Individual Partnership Action Plans' were signed with Azerbaijan, Georgia and Uzbekistan. Georgia in March 2005 signed a transit agreement with the Alliance to support NATO operations in Afghanistan. Formally outside of NATO initiatives (but compatible with them), the US has also increased its bilateral military involvement in the southern Caucasus, pursuing from 2002 military assistance programmes with both Georgia and Azerbaijan. NATO's 'distinctive partnership' with Ukraine meanwhile dates back to 1997. A NATO-Ukraine Action Plan adopted in November 2002 was directed towards meeting Ukraine's 'aspirations towards full integration into Euro-Atlantic security structures'.[51] In April 2005, an 'Intensified Dialogue' was launched geared specifically to Ukraine's membership of NATO.

There remains a certain hesitancy to these processes, however. Despite the increasingly forthright case for membership made by Ukraine, Georgia and more recently Moldova, there is very little prospect of EU enlargement to these states in the short or medium term. Accession to NATO seems conceivable (especially in the case of Ukraine) but not yet probable. Similarly, despite repeated requests on the part of the Georgian and Moldovan authorities for greater involvement, the EU, under both ESDP and CFSP has played a growing but still negligible role in conflict resolution efforts.[52] Such hesitancy reflects a range a factors: the chronic nature of political problems in the region, the hostility of local separatist forces, the EU's inward turn following the 2005 constitutional crisis, and so on. But of equal import is sensitivity toward Russian interests.

Indeed, approaches toward the so-called western newly-independent states (Belarus, Ukraine, Moldova) and the south Caucasus have emerged as a test-case of cooperation between NATO and the EU on the one hand and Russia on the other. Here, progress has been qualified. NATO-Russia dialogue has not been absent. As noted earlier, Georgia and regional CFE issues have been considered by the NRC, but other strategic issues have been sidelined. NATO, for instance, has rebuffed Russian requests for formal contacts with the CSTO, seemingly on the grounds that this would imply recognition of a Russian sphere of influence. Enlargement, similarly, is off-limits. Ukraine's efforts to accede to the Alliance have already had a series of practical effects in loosening military ties with Russia and pose a major logistical problem in relation to the status of the Black Sea Fleet. These have been dealt with so far mainly between Kiev and Moscow; there is no public dialogue between Russia and NATO on the issue.[53] The whole matter, in any case remains subject to shifting attitudes on both sides. Steps taken towards Ukraine's practical integration in the Alliance have not, with the exception of Poland, been backed by any political enthusiasm among NATO members. The Russian attitude toward enlargement, meanwhile, as noted above, has moderated, but it remains far from favourable. Russian officials in public seem reconciled to the possibility of Ukrainian and Georgian membership. Yet while, on the one hand, recognizing NATO's post-Cold War strategic reorientation, continue, on the other, to regard the Alliance as having 'an offensive doctrine' which requires military counter-measures.[54]

The possibilities of EU-Russia regional dialogue are at least more explicitly expressed. The 2005 Road Map for the Common Space of External Security notes scope for dialogue on regional conflicts 'in regions adjacent to [...] EU and Russian borders'.[55] Russian officials have also claimed that Russia reserves no right of monopoly in the FSU and thus welcomes states of the region cooperating with the EU.[56] These are, however, only tentative steps forward. A residual distrust lingers in Moscow on international involvement. In the negotiations on the road maps, Russia insisted on the deletion of any reference to 'common neighbourhood', the term favoured in Brussels. Russia's undermining of the OSCE's role in Moldova and Georgia, moreover, hardly augers well for cooperation with the EU.[57] It also remains to be seen whether the EU itself is capable and willing to mobilize the instruments of CFSP and ESDP. In one telling case, in September 2005 a small EU team began work in advising and 'mentoring' the Georgian border guard, EU Foreign Ministers having failed to agree the previous April to a Georgian request to send a fuller force to replace an OSCE Border Monitoring Mission on the Georgian-Russian frontier.[58]

Conclusion

Since the end of the Cold War, the development of European security governance has involved Russia in what might be described as incorporation but not integration.[59] The centrality of the EU and NATO in security governance, but also the absence of a membership perspective on Russia's part (and, indeed, the reluctance to countenance let alone encourage a route to accession on the part of the US or European governments) means that this situation is likely to persist in the long-term. As such, it will mean a continuation of patterns of conditional cooperation through the pragmatic development of practical and increasingly institutionalized connections. These connections, productive in some senses, will however be by their very nature, self-limiting. To understand why, it is worth reprising the earlier discussion of institutions but here placing it in a somewhat broader analytical context.

According to Celeste Wallander, '[a]lthough institutions cannot force states to cooperate or act contrary to their interests, they [do] enable states to cooperate when it is difficult yet in their interests to do so'. Institutions, she continues, offer opportunities 'to solve different kinds of obstacles to security, such as the need for monitoring and sanctioning others' behaviour, coming to mutually acceptable agreements, increasing transparency about security interests and intentions, and creating incentives for cooperation when it is costly in the short term'.[60] By this logic, the fact that Russia and the member states of the EU and NATO share a modicum of interests mean that once institutional engagement is initiated, its positive effects ought eventually to be felt.

There are, however, limitations worth bearing in mind. First, even if we accept the benign consequences of institutions, Russia as a non-member of two core international organizations is, and will continue to be, semi-detached from the dense network that characterizes NATO and EU Europe. By comparison with the thirty European states who are members of either one or both organizations, Russia's situation is actually under-institutionalised. Its interactions have certainly increased, as detailed above, but it remains absent from the everyday, routine business of bargaining, influence-wielding and decision-making. Membership of the Council of Europe, the OSCE, the G8 or the UNSC is no substitute for this.

Second and related, the particular institutional forms which link Russia to NATO and the EU are weak. '[I]nstitutions', according to one definition are 'persistent and connected sets of rules, often affiliated with organizations, that operate across international boundaries. Institutions range from conventions [...] to regimes [...] to formal organizations.'[61] What counts here is that 'the relevant actors share an understanding of the rules that shape and constrain their interactions'.[62] The power of such 'rules' in the case under examination is, however, slight. By contrast with the rules which shape relations within NATO and the EU, those with Russia are premised on a less formal legal basis,[63] are less influenced by the linkage politics of myriad political, economic and social interconnections, and carry with them fewer disincentives to defect.

Third, even if we accept that institionalization involving Russia, while weak, nonetheless has a concrete form, it need not follow from this that a beneficial outcome is likely. As even their advocates point out '[w]e should […] beware of the easy fallacy of assuming that institutions have only positive effects'.[64] The limitations of resources, design and prerogative mean their achievements are often markedly beneath their declared objectives. Indeed, this mismatch may be a problem in its own right as the failure of good intentions shifts attention to the transaction costs of cooperation. In these circumstances, institutionalisation can, in fact, have paradoxical effects as the very procedures which are meant to enhance cooperation are called into question and become the site of divergent agendas. Such was the fate of the PJC, for instance. Further, institutions while usually originating in a conscious concern to facilitate cooperation (indeed, this is why states agree to form them) are often unequal in terms of outcome, precisely because their participants bring with them unequal resources of power.[65] Whatever the formalities in the working methods of Russia's relations with the EU and NATO, the imbalance of power continues to disadvantage the former. Practical and mutually beneficial cooperation can and has occurred but it has done so on the basis of two crucial assumptions which Russia has been required to accept: first, that the status of NATO and the EU is unquestioned; second, that Russia has no entrée into the inner workings and deliberations of either organization. What this ultimately means is that the debate on security governance has been carried out increasingly between and within the EU and NATO with less and less attention paid to the voice of Russia.

Notes and References

1. M. Webber, S. Croft, J. Howorth, T. Terriff and E. Krahmann, 'The Governance of European Security', *Review of International Studies*, 30:1 (2004), pp. 3–26.
2. K. Schake, 'NATO after the Cold War, 1991–1995: Institutional Competition and the Collapse of the French Alternative', *Contemporary European History*, 7:3 (1998), p. 381.
3. R. Whitman, 'NATO, the EU and ESDP: An Emerging Division of Labour?', *Contemporary Security Policy*, 25:3 (2004), pp. 440–8.
4. *Ibid*, pp. 440–1.
5. A Missiroli, 'The EU and Its Changing Neighbourhoods: Stabilisation, Integration and Partnership' in J. Batt et al., *Partners and Neighbours: A CFSP for a Wider Europe*, Chaillot Paper, 64 (Paris, EU Institute for Security Studies, 2003), p. 17.

6. See, for instance, NATO's 'Istanbul Summit Communiqué', 28 June 2004 at: http://www.nato.int/docu/pr/2004/p04-096e.htm [7 July 2005]; and the EU's 'A Secure Europe in a Better World – the European Security Strategy' 12 December 2003 at: http://ue.eu.int/cms3_fo/showPage.ASP?id=266&lang=EN&mode=g [7 July 2005].
7. For summaries and analysis of keynote Russian security texts see M. de Haas, *Putin's External and Internal Security Policy* (Camberley, Conflict Studies Research Centre), Russian Series, 05/05, February 2005.
8. S. Ivanov, 'The Armed Forces of Russia and Its Geopolitical Priorities', *Russia in Global Affairs*, January–February 2004 at: http://eng.globalaffairs.ru/numbers/6/506.html [accessed 7 July 2005].
9. B. Lo, *Vladimir Putin and the Evolution of Russian Foreign Policy* (London, Royal Institute of International affairs/Blackwell Publishing, 2003), pp. 14–5.
10. M.A. Smith, *Russian Perspectives on Terrorism* (Camberley, Conflict Studies Research Centre), publication C110, January 2004, pp. 9–10.
11. D. Alexeev, *NATO Enlargement: A Russian Outlook* (Camberley, Conflict Studies Research Centre), Russian Series, 04/33, November 2004, pp. 4–7.
12. O. Chernov (Deputy Secretary of the Russian Security Council), 'Russia-NATO-EU: Together Against New Threats to International Security', 12 September 2003 at: http://www.ln.mid.ru/brp_4.nsf/0/c10798d248db7578c3256ec9001cedc3?OpenDocument [7 July 2005].
13. Interview with the Polish newspaper *Trybuna*, 16 June 2005 carried in Documents and Materials of the Russian MFA, 17 June 2005, at: http://www.ln.mid.ru/bul_ns_en.nsf/kartaflat/en01 [7 July 2005].
14. 'Russian President Vladimir Putin's Address at the Plenary Session of the Russian Federation Ambassadors and Permanent Representatives Meeting, Moscow, Foreign Ministry, July 12, 2004', carried in Documents and Materials of the Russian MFA, 13 July 2005, at: http://www.ln.mid.ru/bul_ns_en.nsf/kartaflat/en01 [7 July 2005].
15. Russian disillusionment with the OSCE came to head at the end of 2004 when it vetoed the adoption of the organisation's budget.
16. 'Remarks by Russia's Deputy Minister of Foreign Affairs Vladimir Chizov at the Conference "Wider Europe: New Agenda"', (Bratislava, 19 March 2004), carried in Documents and Materials of the Russian MFA, 20 March 2005, at: http://www.ln.mid.ru/bul_ns_en.nsf/kartaflat/en01 [7 July 2005].
17. Yeltsin's foreign policy aide, Dmitri Ryurikov cited in *OMRI Daily Digest*, 3:62, 28 March 1997, at: http://archive.tol.cz/ublications/DD/RUS.html [3 December 2003].
18. http://www.cnn.com/ALLPOLITICS/1997/05/14/Clinton.nato/ [12 November 2003].
19. W. Matser, 'Towards a New Strategic Partnership', *NATO Review*, 49:4 (2001).
20. 'NATO-Russia Relations: A New Quality' (Declaration of Heads of State and Government of NATO and the Russian Federation), Rome, 28 May 2002, at: http://www.nato.int/docu/basictxt/b020528e.htm [7 July 2005].
21. In parallel, Russia agreed in April 2004 to send liaison officers to the two main NATO HQ at Mons, Belgium, and Norfolk, Virginia. See R.E. Hunter and S.M. Rogov, *Engaging Russia as Partner and Participant. The Next Stage of NATO-Russia Relations* (Santa Monica, RAND, 2004), p. 3, fn. 6 and p. 7.
22. 'Statement: Meeting of the NRC at the Level of Ministers of Defence', 9 June 2005, at: http://www.nato.int/docu/pr/2005/p050609-nrce.htm [7 July 2005].
23. N.N. Spasskiy (deputy secretary of the Russian Security Council), interviewed in *Yadernyy Kontrol*, 20 May 2005 accessed via World News Connection at: http://wnc.fedworld.gov/ [7 July 2005].

24. Hunter and Rogov, *Engaging Russia*, pp. 8–12.
25. Y. Grigoryeva, 'We Have Reached a Ceiling', *Izvestiya*, 11 February 2005 accessed via World News Connection at: http://wnc.fedworld.gov/ [7 July 2005].
26. 'Russia Pushing NATO, CSTO Cooperation', (RIA Novosti, 28 June 2005) at: http://en.rian.ru/analysis/20050628/40774407.html [7 July 2005].
27. http://europa.eu.int/comm/external_relations/russia/summit_05_05/finalroadmaps.pdf#fsj [7 July 2005].
28. *Communication from the Commission to the Council and the European Parliament on Relations with Russia*, COM (2004) 106, 9 February 2004, p. 5.
29. Speech to the European Parliament, 26 February 2004. at: http://europa.eu.int external_relations/news/patten/speech04_99.htm [7 July 2005].
30. C. Malmström (rapportuer), *Report on EU-Russia Relations*, Committee on Foreign Affairs, European Parliament, Session 2004–2009, document A6-0135/2005 (Final), 4 May 2005, paragraphs, 6–7.
31. S. Karaganov, 'Building Bridges with Brussels', *The Financial Times*, 19 May 2001.
32. Speech of Russian Deputy Minister of Foreign Affairs, V. Chizhov at the conference 'Russia and EU Common Foreign Policy: Aims and Challenges' (27 February 2004) at: http://www.russiaeu.org/pr13-04.htm [20 June 2005].
33. Y. Baluyevsky (First Deputy Chief of the Russian General Staff) as cited by RIA-Novosti, 8 July 2003 accessed via World News Connection at: http://wnc.fedworld.gov/ [7 July 2005].
34. http://europa.eu.int/comm/external_relations/russia/summit_05_05/finalroadmaps.pdf#fsj [7 July 2005].
35. Council of the European Union, 'Presidency Report on European Security and Defence Policy', document 10160/2/02, Brussels, 22 June 2002, Annexes, IV, V and VI at: http://register.consilium.eu.int/pdf/en/02/st10/10160-r2en2.pdf [7 July 2005].
36. Interviewed in *Profil*, 22, 13 June 2005 and carried on *Johnson's Russia List* at: http://www.cdiorg/ [30 June 2005].
37. As cited in F. Lukianov, 'Casting the Peelings Aside', *Vremya Novostei*, 28 March 2005 as carried in *Johnson's Russia List* at: http://www.cdiorg/ [30 June 2005].
38. Cited in V. Socor, 'From CIS to CSTO: Can A "Core" be Preserved?', *Eurasia Daily Monitor*, 28 June 2005 at: http://jamestown.org/edm/ [7 July 2005].
39. *Ibid.*
40. F. Hill, *Energy Empire: Oil, Gas and Russia's Revival* (London: The Foreign Policy Centre, September 2004), pp. 2–3.
41. Ivanov interview in *Profil* 13 June 2005.
42. V. Socor, 'Putin Obituary for CIS', *Eurasia Daily Monitor*, 31 March 2005 at: http://jamestown.org/edm/ [7 July 2005].
43. See 'Russian President Vladimir Putin's Address at the Plenary Session of the Russian Federation, Documents and Materials of the Russia MFA, 13 July 2005.
44. See, for instance, Putin's annual address to the Federal Assembly, 25 April 2005 at: http://president.kremlin.ru/eng/speeches/2005/04/25/2031_type70029_87086.shtml [7 July 2005].
45. Z. Brzezinski, 'A Plan for Europe', *Foreign Affairs*, 74:1 (1995), p. 31.
46. Z. Brzezinski, 'Russian Roulette', *Wall Street Journal*, 29 March 2005.
47. J. Sperling, 'Eurasian Security Governance: New Threats and Institutional Adaptations', in J. Sperling, S. Kay and S.V. Papacosma (eds.), *Limiting Institutions? The Challenge of Eurasian Security Governance* (Manchester: Manchester University Press, 2003), p. 13.
48. 'EU-Ukraine Action Plan', February 2005, pp. 2, 5–6. at: http://www.mfa.gov.ua/integration/ua-eu/doc/plan_ua_eu_eng.doc [7 July 2005].

49. China and Israel are the only other non-EU collaborators.
50. 'Prague Summit Declaration', 21 November 2002, paragraph.7 at: http://www.nato.int/docu/pr/2002/p02-127e.htm [7 July 2005].
51. 'NATO-Ukraine Action Plan', November 2002, at: http://www.nato.int/docu/basictxt/b021122a.htm [7 July 2005].
52. V. Socor, 'EU Policy Disarray in Georgia and Moldova', *Eurasia Daily Monitor*, 15 April 2005 at: http://jamestown.org/edm/ [7 July 2005]; N. Popescu, 'EU and Moldova: A Wind of Change', Moldova.org at: http://politicom.moldova.org/europa/eng/97/2/ [7 July 2005].
53. This is not to say that there is no dialogue at all. Ukrainian membership has undoubtedly been considered by Russia and NATO member states within closed diplomatic channels and in intelligence and military-to-military contacts. It has not, however, received the sort of substantive high-level political treatment which it deserves – akin, let's say to the way in which enlargement fed into talks leading to the Founding Act and the Rome Declaration.
54. Ivanov interview, *Profil*, 22, 13 June 2005; Russian Federation, Ministry of Defence, *Priority Tasks of the Development of the Armed Forces of the Russian Federation* (aka Defence 'White Paper') (2003), p. 42. at: http://www.mil.ru/articles/article5005.shtml [7 July 2005].
55. http://europa.eu.int/comm/external_relations/russia/summit_05_05/finalroadmaps.pdf#fsj [7 July 2005].
56. A. Yakovenko, Russian Foreign Ministry spokesperson, RIA news agency, 27 February 2005 as carried by World News Connection at: http://wnc.fedworld.gov/ [7 July 2005].
57. J. Löwenhardt, 'The OSCE, Moldova and Russian Diplomacy in 2003', *Journal of Communist Studies and Transition Politics*, 20:4 (2004); V. Socor, 'Russia Proves OSCE Irrelevance on Moldova at Year-End Meeting', *Eurasia Daily Monitor*, 14 December 2004 at: http://jamestown.org/edm/ [7 July 2005]; V-Y. Ghebali, 'The OSCE Mission to Georgia (1992–2004): The Failing Art of Half-Hearted Measures', *Helsinki Monitor*, 3, 2004; R. Egglestone, 'Georgia: OSCE to begin Training Georgian Border Guards Next Week', *Radio Free Europe/Radio Liberty* feature article, 15 April 2005 at: http://www.rferl.org/featuresarticle/2005/04/777d44c1-f845-457d-808d-c20ef8d91332.html [7 July 2005].
58. The Georgian request was backed by the UK and the three Baltic states, but opposed by France, Belgium, Italy, Spain, Greece and Germany. See V. Socor, 'France Leads the EU's Nyet to Georgia Border Monitoring', *Eurasia Daily Monitor*, 19 April 2005 at: http://jamestown.org/edm/ [7 July 2005].
59. O. Schuett, 'Russia and Europe: Balancing Cooperation with Integration', *Discussion Papers in German Studies* (Institute for German Studies, University of Birmingham) No.IGS98/1, 1998, p. 29.
60. C. Wallander, *Mortal Friends, Best Enemies: German-Russian Cooperation after the Cold War* (Ithaca and London, Cornell University Press, 1999), p. 5.
61. C.Wallander, H. Haftendorn and R.O. Keohane, 'Introduction' in H. Haftendorn et al., *Imperfect Unions: Security Institutions over Time and Space* (Oxford, Oxford University Press, 1999), pp. 1–2.
62. D.A. Lake, 'Beyond Anarchy. The Importance of Security Institutions', *International Security*, 26:1 (2001), p. 132.
63. Neither the NATO-Russia Founding Act nor the EU-Russia Partnership and Cooperation Agreement can be regarded as enjoying the same legal standing as the Treaty on European Union or the Washington Treaty of NATO.
64. Wallander et al., in Haftendorn et al., *Imperfect Unions* p. 10.
65. T.M. Moe, 'Power and Political Institutions', *Perspectives on Politics*, 3:2 (2005), pp. 215–33.

CONCLUSION

RUSSIA AND EUROPE: AN UNEASY PARTNERSHIP

Jackie Gower and Graham Timmins

Mutual Disappointment

One of the main objectives of the book was to examine the current state of Russia's relations with Europe from the perspective of both parties since the long-term prospects of any relationship must depend on meeting the needs of all those involved. What is particularly striking is the level of disappointment on all sides about what has actually been achieved over the past 15 years. There have certainly been a number of apparent breakthroughs in the development of a genuinely strategic partnership such as the NATO-Russia Founding Act in May 1997, the coming into force of the Partnership and Cooperation Agreement (PCA) in November 1997, the adoption of the European Union (EU)'s Common Strategy and Russia's Medium-Term Strategy in 1999, the establishment of the NATO-Russia Council (NRC) in 2002, the commitment to the four common spaces at St Petersburg in 2003 and the adoption of the road maps in 2005. However, the optimism and high expectations generated by such initiatives rapidly gave way to frustration at the slow progress being made in translating the ambitious goals into concrete achievements. It is clear that neither Russia nor Europe are satisfied with the current state of their partnership and both feel that the other has not lived up to their expectations.

From Russia's perspective, the West has provided only meagre aid to support its economic transition and been slow to open up its markets, either through the EU or the World Trade Organization (WTO). Enlargement of the EU and NATO went ahead with scant regard for the impact it would have either on Russia's geo-strategic interests or on the freedom of its citizens to travel and pursue their business interests in neighbouring states, or in the case of the Kaliningraders, their own state. While the establishment of the Russia-NATO

Council has been welcomed, the EU has refused to contemplate giving Russia even a symbolic seat at its decision-making table. Cooperation through the mechanisms agreed under the European Security and Defence Policy (ESDP) has been limited mainly to high-level dialogue and there has been very little in the way of Russian participation in actual missions. Russia's hope of acquiring 'an equal voice on major security developments in and around Europe'[1] has clearly not been realized either through the North Atlantic Treaty Organization (NATO) or the EU. In many respects the continent today as seen through the eyes of Russians seems once more to be divided into two halves, demarcated into 'insiders' and 'outsiders', with them firmly consigned to the wrong side of the fence. Although its Presidency of the Group of Eight (G8) and the Council of Europe in 2006 provided some satisfaction of its yearning for international status, there is still a strong feeling in Moscow that the rest of Europe is deliberately denying Russia its rightful place at the top table.

From Europe's perspective, the biggest disappointment has been that Russia clearly has not developed in the way that had been hoped – and on which Western policy since the end of the Cold War had been predicated. The issue of Chechnya has been a running sore in the relationship for over a decade and continues to arouse serious doubts about Russia's commitment to human rights. In recent years there has also been increasing concern that political and economic reform in Russia more generally is not only slowing down but actually going in the wrong direction. New controls over the media and Non-Governmental Organizations (NGOs) are seen as weakening an already overly 'managed' democracy, increased state ownership and controls compromise the market economy and there have been a number of high profile cases raising serious questions about respect for the rule of law.

Far from values in Russia and Europe converging, they seem to be diverging and how to deal with the widening 'values gap' has become one of the focal points in the discourse over future European policy towards Russia. There is a growing awareness that it may not just be a question of the Russian transition inevitably taking much longer than that of the former communist states in central and eastern Europe (CEE)[2] but rather that Russia may be pursuing a different trajectory towards a specifically Russian model. One conspicuous consequence of Russia's renewed self-confidence as an energy superpower is the refusal of its leaders to accept that the West has the exclusive right to define what constitutes a 'democracy'. At the G8 summit in July 2006 President Putin reportedly countered criticisms of domestic developments by arguing that Russia had different historical traditions and at the joint press conference, President Bush said 'I fully understand......that there will be a Russian-style democracy. I do not expect Russia to look like the United States'.[3] However, many people in Europe are unwilling to accept this view and continue to believe that unless

Russia conforms to the 'European model' it will be either impossible or morally wrong to develop a close partnership. A serious policy dilemma therefore inevitably arises because it is now recognized that as Russia is not seeking membership of either the EU or NATO, there is only quite limited scope for exercising leverage over her domestic developments. Therefore, it may well be that Europe has to accept that it will have to deal with Russia as it finds it rather than clinging to the false hope that it can somehow be moulded in the image of NATO and EU member states.

Continuing Commitment to the Partnership

Despite this mutual disappointment, there are clear signs that both parties are still committed to developing a more satisfactory partnership and indeed continue to describe it as 'strategic'. At the EU-Russia summit in Sochi in May 2006 the joint statement reported that they had agreed to extend the PCA to allow time for a new agreement to be negotiated 'which should provide a comprehensive and durable framework for the EU-Russia strategic partnership'.[4] President Putin in his Annual Address to the Federal Assembly the same month declared that 'Our biggest partner is the European Union......our joint work on implementing the concept 'of the common spaces is an important part of the development of Europe as a whole'.[5] NATO Secretary General Jaap de Hoop told Moscow University students at the end of a major public diplomacy event in Russia that 'the bridge is now built. We have that strategic partnership. And we are now taking steps to reinforce it, so it can bear more of the weight of international security.'[6]

The reason for the continued commitment to the partnership is recognition that it is in their mutual interest to do so: there is a significant degree of interdependence across several key policy areas. In the economic sphere the EU accounts for over 50 per cent of Russia's exports and Russia now ranks as the EU's fourth most important trading partner. The flow of FDI is increasing in both directions, with growing levels of private sector investment and the listing of a number of Russian companies on the London Stock Exchange.[7] Over ten million Russians now take holidays abroad each year, most of them to European destinations. Many European countries are heavily dependent on imports of Russian gas and oil but Russia is also dependent on European markets, especially for the sale of its gas.[8] So while the EU imports 30 per cent of its energy from Russia, it is also estimated that Russia gets 20 per cent of its total export earnings from the sale of gas to Europe.[9] Despite the threats to divert supplies to other buyers, such as China, in the short term at least the distribution network is fairly inflexible and it would take time and money to reorient Russia's trade in energy to new customers. In the security sphere there is also a high degree of interdependence between Russia and

Europe with a host of challenges that can be much more effectively met through constructive cooperation. These include the continuing problems of the frozen conflicts in Transdniestria and the southern Caucasus, environmental disasters, terrorism and soft security issues such as illegal immigration, people smuggling, drugs, money laundering and other forms of international crime.

Clearly therefore there are strong interests underpinning the EU-Russia relationship which will ensure that both will remain seriously engaged even when the going gets tough. There seems to be quite a broad consensus emerging that the best way forward is to concentrate on identifying specific areas where both Russia and Europe have a clear interest in making concrete progress, such as the visa facilitation and readmission agreements signed in May 2006. The road maps agreed with the EU in May 2005 provide a long list of potential areas for practical cooperation in the economic, environmental, security, police and judicial, regional, educational, cultural and research policy spheres. The NRC and its working groups also provide a good framework for increased technical and political cooperation on a wide range of practical issues. There is scope here for the steady development of an extensive network of active engagement involving not just the political leadership but also middle-ranking officials and members of civil society. The potential dividends in widening the network of people actively involved in aspects of the relationship are considerable with increased knowledge and understanding of each other, greater trust and also the transmission of values. So even a pragmatic, work-focused agenda does have the potential to lay the foundations for a deeper and stronger partnership. But it will almost certainly have its limitations if it is based simply on interest-bargaining and short term expediency without a common vision of the long-term European political order and their respective roles in it. In other words, it will fall short of being a 'strategic partnership' in any meaningful sense and 'uneasy' may more accurately reflect the way both parties come to view their relationship. The areas where this 'unease' is likely to be most evident are respect for democratic values, energy policy and the shared neighbourhood, compounded by the considerable uncertainty surrounding future developments in both Russia and Europe.

An Uneasy Balance Between Values and Interests

In the long-term it is almost certainly a false dilemma to debate whether interests should be allowed to trump values in shaping Europe's policy towards Russia since the quality of the partnership will depend on the extent to which it is based on shared values. Sometimes it is argued that Europe is managing to conduct a reasonably satisfactory relationship with China and the same would be possible with Russia, irrespective of the nature of its political regime. But in reality it is a false analogy since Europe has much wider ambitions for its partnership with Russia, which is after all itself a European country and a major player in all aspects of the continent's affairs. It is also an important difference that Russia, unlike China, does officially subscribe to democratic values and the market economy; the issue really is what should Europe do if there appears to be a gap between theory and practice.

This is a very difficult question and will almost certainly continue to be a source of underlying tension in the relationship. In Russia there is enormous resentment at what is widely regarded as the unwarranted interference in its domestic affairs and the tendency for other Europeans to presume to deliver 'lectures' on the alleged failings of its political and economic systems whenever representatives of the two sides meet. There are frequent complaints that Europe operates 'double standards' in condemning violations of human rights in Chechnya while turning a blind eye to the plight of the Russian-speaking minorities in Latvia and Estonia. Western support for the 'coloured' revolutions in a number of Russia's neighbours has also aroused suspicion about the intentions of outside agencies with their 'democracy' programmes operating within Russia itself. One of the main reasons given for the controversial new law on NGOs passed by the Duma in December 2005 was the suspicion that foreign-funded NGOs were hoping to engineer a similar 'revolution' in Russia.[10] But what seemed to the Russian authorities as an entirely justified move to protect the state was widely condemned throughout Europe as a serious threat to civil freedoms.[11] Inevitably, such vast differences in perception are going to cause tensions in the relationship.

It is also clear that one of the most evident results of Russia's self-confidence as a self-styled energy superpower, is that it is going to resist any attempt by its European partners to impose political conditionality into the joint programme for cooperation on matters of shared interest. However, there will be considerable 'unease' within Europe if it seems as if interests are being prioritized over values. In a resolution on the outcome of the Sochi EU-Russia summit, the European Parliament (EP) was critical of the partnership with Russia for being 'more pragmatic than strategic since it reflects in the first place common economic interests without achieving major results as regards human rights and the rule of law'.[12] There will be considerable pressure from many Members of the European Parliament (MEPs) and also some member states to impose political conditionality on the common spaces agenda, and also to ensure that the 'shared values' clauses of the current PCA are retained, and even strengthened, in any new agreement. There are almost inevitably some very difficult negotiations ahead both within the EU in agreeing its common position and then with Russia. The fact that the new member states are expected to be in the forefront of pressing the normative agenda will further antagonise Russia.

The interests versus values conundrum can be expected to be particularly difficult for the EU because it has constructed its international identity on the concept of normative power. Within NATO it may prove easier to adopt a more pragmatic approach and play down the significance of the normative agenda, particularly if that is the position of the US administration. But even here, there is a potential cost involved as in the long-term a common security culture can only be developed on the basis of shared values.

The Risk of Conflicts of Interest Over Energy

A further reason for concluding that the partnership between Russia and Europe will be an uneasy one is the expectation that in the two areas where it might at first sight have seemed that there is the strongest incentive for them to cooperate, there is also the greatest danger of hostile competitiveness, and even conflict. These two key areas are the common neighbourhood and energy.

In the case of energy, their interdependence as respective major supplier and consumer does not in itself guarantee a stress-free partnership even if it does provide a strong incentive to work to resolve issues constructively. Indeed commercial considerations alone would probably lead to periods of friction as the interests of buyers and sellers of any product may not always coincide. Even in the case of the gas supply crisis in January 2006, commercial factors were reportedly at the root of the problem although the extent to which it was subsequently politicized sent alarm bells ringing throughout Europe.[13]

There are a number of other areas where political and commercial issues combine to create a sense of unease on both sides and have the potential to escalate into full-scale crises. One very long-standing dispute concerns proposals to construct pipelines under the Caspian Sea to provide export routes to Europe from Kazakhstan, Turkmenistan and Uzbekistan. At the EU-Russia summit at Sochi in May 2006 Putin indicated that Russia would strongly oppose the construction of a gas pipeline from Kazakhstan to Azerbaijan which the EU Commission had been actively supporting.[14] He cited environmental reasons for Russia's position but it was suspected that his main motivation was to defend Russia's geo-strategic interests in the region and protect Gazprom from increased competition from other energy suppliers. Equally contentious have been decisions on the routing of pipelines in northern Europe where Russia is presumed to be deliberately trying to reduce the potential leverage of transit countries. The agreement between Russia and Germany to construct a pipeline under the Baltic Sea bypassing Poland was presented as a commercially-sound move to guarantee security of supply but was likened by the Polish Defence

Minister Radek Sikorski to the infamous Molotov-Ribbentrop Pact.[15] The political fall-out from the decision illustrates graphically the danger so-called 'pipeline diplomacy'[16] presents not just to good relations between Europe and Russia but also between fellow EU member states.

Russian companies have also reacted angrily to what they fear are attempts by European governments to block their acquisition of downstream distribution assets in European domestic markets on the grounds of energy security. Alexei Miller, Gazprom's chief executive, was reported to have warned EU ambassadors that 'attempts to limit Gazprom's activities in the European market and politicize questions of gas supply, which are in fact of an entirely economic nature, will not lead to good results' and went on to remind his audience that Gazprom was 'actively familiarising ourselves with new markets, such as North America and China'.[17] It was suggested that his scarcely concealed threat to reduce energy supplies to Europe had been prompted by rumours that the British government were exploring ways to block a bid from Gazprom to acquire a stake in Centrica, the UK's largest energy distribution company.[18] There have been frequent complaints from Russia that Gazprom's ambitions to acquire downstream energy assets in Europe are being thwarted by protectionism and Cold War prejudices. It is a good example of the way commercial and political considerations become entwined in the energy sector debate and easily lead to 'unease' about each other's motivations.

In Europe there is also the suspicion that Russia is deliberately trying to undermine attempts by the European Commission to develop a common energy policy by offering favourable bilateral deals. The agreement negotiated by Schröder and Putin on the North European pipeline has already been discussed but the fact that Italian Prime Minister Romano Prodi, a former President of the European Commission, was also willing to conclude a bilateral deal to open up the Italian and Russian energy markets to each other's companies was a blow to the hope that the EU would present a united front in negotiations with Russia on such issues.[19] One of the themes explored in the book has been the 'two-level game' in which European states conduct policy towards Russia both through bilateral channels and through the multilateral institutions of the EU and NATO. Energy is a particularly good example of this phenomenon and given the increasing pressure on governments to secure their energy supplies, it is likely to continue to be a source of tension in the relationship.

Inevitably therefore there will be a number of difficult issues and as Javier Solana observed 'to manage interdependence adroitly, you need partnership and trust'.[20] The problem is that despite many years of trying to build a strong partnership on energy through the Energy Charter Treaty (which Russia seems unlikely ever to ratify), the EU-Russia Energy Dialogue and the G8 very little has actually been achieved. Furthermore, it is clear that trust is in short supply with Europe increasingly nervous about the implications of Russia's self-proclaimed status of 'an energy superpower' and Russia fearing that Europe's quest for 'energy security' will involve reducing its dependence on Russian imports, with serious consequences for its economy.[21] So while energy will inevitably remain one of the most important issues on the shared agenda, it is likely to be the source of considerable unease in the relationship.

Competition for Influence Over the Shared Neighbourhood

The enlargements of NATO and the EU have inevitably had a huge impact on the geopolitics of the region that now lies between their eastern borders and Russia, transforming what had been largely accepted as Russia's 'near abroad' into a shared neighbourhood, with major incentives to cooperate but also significant risks of conflict. From Russia's perspective, the post-Soviet space is not just an area of vital geo-strategic importance to her national interests but also has strong historic and emotive ties and a large diaspora of Russian-speakers. The EU's initiative in 2003 to develop the European Neighbourhood Policy (ENP)[22] was inevitably going to unsettle its relationship with Russia given its obvious implication of a much more active engagement in countries traditionally regarded as not just close allies but 'part of the family'. As former EU Commission President Romano Prodi explained, the objective is to create a 'ring of friends' around the Union[23] and to use ENP Action Plans to encourage its neighbours to bring their political and economic systems in line with the EU model. Not surprisingly, this has been interpreted in Russia as a deliberate strategy by the EU to 'seduce' its neighbours into its civilizational orbit and weaken their ties with Russia. The 'rose revolution' in Georgia in November 2003 and the 'orange revolution' in Ukraine in December 2004 only reinforced the suspicion that Russia's traditional position as the hegemonic power in the region was at risk. Russia has responded with a charm offensive, trying to make the Single Economic Space (SES) concept more attractive and to reinvigorate the Collective Security Treaty Organisation (CSTO) to offer an alternative pole of attraction. Thus a distinctly competitive edge has been introduced into the politics of the region, especially as there is tension between the pro-Russian and pro-European factions in most of the countries concerned.

Although the ENP deliberately avoids making any commitment to future membership, as Karen Smith has observed, 'the ghost of enlargement haunts the EU's relations with its neighbours.'[24] Ukraine, Georgia and Moldova all have explicit aspirations for both EU and NATO membership and so enlargement will undoubtedly also haunt relations between both institutions and Russia for many years to come. In the EU's case, enlargement fatigue seems likely to keep it off the agenda for some years but Poland and some of the other new member states are determined that the EU's relationship with Russia should not be prioritized over the hopes of countries like Ukraine to achieve membership as soon as they fulfil the conditions. In the short to medium term, NATO enlargement is more likely to become a pressing issue as the member states are expected to reaffirm their 'open-door policy' at the Riga summit in November 2006 and give a positive 'signal' to Georgia and Ukraine, with some analysts suggesting 2010 might be a realistic date for both countries to aim for membership. [25] Although President Putin has publicly indicated that he is willing to acquiesce to further NATO enlargement[26], it is still likely to be a highly contentious issue, both in Russia itself and in the candidate countries themselves where there is substantial opposition to the idea. The appointment of pro-Russian Viktor Yanukovich as Ukraine's new Prime Minister in August 2006 raises the prospect of a difficult cohabitation with the pro-western President Yushchenko and uncertainty over the country's future political orientation. As was seen during the orange revolution, the battle for the heart and soul of Ukraine has the potential to bring Russia and Europe into open conflict and could prove to be the most serious risk to their partnership.

The other major potential flash-points in the shared neighbourhood are the 'frozen conflicts' in Transdniestria, Abkhazia, South Ossetia and Nagorno-Karabakh where Russia has strong interests and a military presence and the EU is becoming increasingly engaged at the behest of the Georgian and Moldovan governments.[27] Clearly the best chance of resolving these difficult disputes would be for Russia and the EU to work together to search for long-term solutions. However, so far there seems little prospect of Russia accepting that the EU has a legitimate role to play and may even see the status quo as best serving its interests as the unresolved conflicts would be an effective block on any of the states affected joining either the EU or NATO. The danger is that one or more of the conflicts will become 'unfrozen' and ignite into armed hostilities with Russia supporting the secessionists. The crisis in South Ossetia in summer 2006 came close to such a scenario, with the Georgian Parliament calling for the withdrawal of Russian troops and the Prime Minister suggesting the EU should take over their peacekeeping role in the region.[28] Such incidents have the potential to make Russia's partnership with Europe distinctly 'uneasy.'

Uncertainties Over the Future Development of Both Europe and Russia

A final reason for concluding that the Russia–Europe partnership will be 'uneasy' stems from the fact that there are considerable uncertainties about future

developments within Russia, the EU and NATO over the next decade. These
will make it more difficult for either party to feel confident that they know what
their erstwhile partner might be like in the coming decade. Trust and predictability
are essential in any successful partnership but in these circumstances they are
unlikely to be developed.

In the case of Russia, the Putin era has brought a period of welcome stability
after the often chaotic years under President Yeltsin. The early years of the
new millennium have seen something approaching an economic miracle with
the highest growth rates among the G8 states, rising standards of living for
most of the population, financial stability and the repayment of the country's
external debt. Admittedly, the economic boom owes a lot to high global energy
prices, but it is still an impressive achievement. In line with Putin's strategy, the
strong economy has provided the foundation for a much more self-confident
and assertive foreign policy and he rightly saw his chairing of the G8 summit
at St Petersburg in July 2006 as proof that Russia is now back as a global
power. The downside, as has been discussed in several chapters, is that state
power has been centralized and democratic controls weakened. As has already
been discussed, this does present dilemmas for European states and institutions
but at least in recent years it has been clear what Russia is, who is in charge and
what its policies are. This welcome stability and predictability, though, are
nearing their end with mounting speculation about what will happen after
Putin's final term of office ends in March 2008. The hope in European
policymaking circles is that his legacy will be the continuation of the
modernization course which necessitates greater cooperation with Europe on
a pragmatic, interest-driven basis. The fear is that his successor will turn his
back on the West, including Europe, and use Russia's strength as an energy
superpower to pursue an overtly nationalistic agenda. Equally disastrous would
be for Russia to disintegrate into chaos and crisis once its strong President is no
longer at the helm. This uncertainty is bound to cast a shadow over the
negotiations for a successor to the PCA and delay the development of enhanced
security cooperation within NATO and the ESDP frameworks.

The level of uncertainty about the future of the EU and NATO is less acute
but may still present some problems both internally and for Russia in terms of
feeling at ease with its partners. As has already been discussed, the possibility
and timing of any future enlargement of NATO and/or the EU will impact
heavily on the partnership and may also cause significant changes in both
institutions. The NATO summit at Riga may help to clarify the plans for further
transformation of its role and capabilities but the future of the transatlantic
alliance itself is likely to remain uncertain. For the EU the biggest issue is
whether the Constitutional Treaty will ever be adopted and may mean there is
a long period of introspection and institutional inertia. The future of the ESDP

and in particular how far the EU will move towards becoming a fully-fledged military actor has yet to be determined. There will also be some uncertainty in the bilateral relationships with President Chirac and Prime Minister Blair both gone and Angela Merkel's coalition distinctly fragile.

Conclusion: an Uneasy Partnership

In the Introduction the question was posed: what kind of partnership will develop between Russia and Europe? Three potential modes of cooperation were identified: strategic, normative and pragmatic. Clearly, at the present time there is an insufficient set of shared norms and values on which to build a normative partnership and there is little expectation that developments in Russia are likely to make it possible in the near future. Both Russia and Europe continue to express their commitment to the development of a strategic partnership. However, this would require a much deeper and more extensive agreement on the way in which common challenges should be met and the kind of European, and indeed world order, which they are hoping will be established. There are too many uncertainties and potential conflicts of interest and too little trust and predictability to expect a truly strategic partnership to be forged in the short to medium term. But that does not mean that in the longer term, such a goal might not be realizable.

It is in that context, that the pragmatic mode may not be such a disappointment in that by providing an agenda for intensified interaction and engagement, it is more likely that greater trust, understanding and mutual confidence will be developed over time. It is also likely to be the case that Europe has a better prospect of transferring its values through constructive engagement at all levels of Russian society than by imposing conditionality and delivering public rebukes. However, even a pragmatic relationship will be beset with tensions and uncertainties so for the foreseeable future 'uneasy' seems the most appropriate way to describe the partnership between Russia and Europe.

Notes and References

1. Dov Lynch, 'Misperceptions and Divergences', in Dov Lynch (ed.), *What Russia Sees*, Chaillot Paper No. 74 (Paris, Institute for Security Studies, January 2005, p. 9.
2. This is the view of Sir Roderic Lyne, former British Ambassador to Russia who said in a speech at Chatham House in London on 2 March 2006 that '(t)he Russian transition was bound to take a very long time and is still at an early stage.'
3. Neil Buckley, 'Confident Putin swats away criticisms from his G8 guests', *Financial Times*

17 July 2006.

4. 17th EU-Russia Summit, Sochi, 25th May 2006, available at http://www.eu2006.at/en/News/Press_Releases/May/2505Sochi.html

5. President Putin, 'Annual Address to the Federal Assembly of the Russian Federation', 10 May 2006, available at http://www.kremlin.ru/eng/sdocs/speeches.shtml?type=70029

6. See 'NATO-Russia Rally ends with call for dialogue', available at http://www.nato.int/docu/update/2006/05-may/e0526a.htm

7. Joanna Chung and Nikki Taitin, 'Rosneft raises $10bn in biggest Russian offering', *Financial Times* 15 July 2006. See also Mark Milner, 'Steel group joins Russian push to London' *The Guardian*, 2 August 2006.

8. 'Who's afraid of Gazprom?', *The Economist*, 4 May 2006.

9. Javier Solana, 'Why Europe must act collectively on energy', *Financial Times*, 8 March 2006.

10. Mary Dejevsky, 'Russia's NGO law: the wrong target', *Open Democracy* 15 December 2005, available at http://www.opendemocracy.net/content/articles/PDF/3123.pdf

11. Claire Bigg, 'Russia: NGOs say new bill threatens civil freedom', *Radio Free Europe/Radio Liberty* 23 November 2005.

12. European Parliament Resolution on the EU-Russia Summit held in Sochi on 25 May 2006, P6_TA-PROV(2006)0270.

13. Sacha Kumaria, 'Energy and the G8: Energetic Issues', *The World Today*, 62:1 (2006).

14. Andrew Beatty, 'Russia and EU head for pipeline battle', *European Voice*, 22–28 June 2006.

15. 'EU Criticizes Poland's Nazi Pipeline Comment', *Radio Free Europe/Radio Liberty*, 2 May 2006.

16. Vladimir Milov, 'The Use of Energy as a Political Tool', *The EU-Russia Review*, Issue One, May 2006, available at info@eu-russiacentre.org

17. Neil Buckley and Arkady Ostrovsky, 'Gazprom issues threat to EU gas supply', *Financial Times*, 19 April 2006.

18. Jean Eaglesham, 'Gazprom prompted rethink on UK merger rules', *Financial Times*, 16 April 2006.

19. 'Russia and Italy Agree to Open Energy Markets', *Radio Free Europe/Radio Liberty*, 20 June 2006.

20. Solana, 'Why Europe must act', op. cit.

21. Andrew Monaghan and Lucia Montanaro-Jankovski, *EU-Russia Energy Relations: the Need for Active Engagement*, European Policy Centre Issue Paper No.45, March 2006, p. 8.

22. Communication from the Commission to the Council and the European Parliament, 'Wider Europe – Neighbourhood: A New Framework for Relations with our Eastern and Southern Neighbours', COM(2003) Brussels, 11.3.2003.

23. Romano Prodi, 'A wider Europe: a proximity policy is the key to stability', speech to the Sixth ECSA-World Conference, Brusels 5–6 December 2002, SPEECH/02/619.

24. Karen Smith, 'The outsiders: the European Neighbourhood policy', *International Affairs* 81:4 2005, p. 767.

25. Liz Fuller, 'Georgia: Is Tbilsi Moving Toward NATO Membership?', *Radio Free Europe/Radio Liberty*, 2 June 2006.

26. Dmitri Trenin, 'Russia, the EU and the common neighbourhood', Centre for European Reform Essay, September 2005, p. 4, available at http://www.cer.org.uk/pdf/essay_russia_trenin_sept05.pdf

27. Simon Tisdall, 'Interests and aspirations clash in region of frozen conflicts', *The Guardian*, 8 February 2005

28. Andrew Beatty, 'EU cautious as Georgia and Russia stoke conflict', *European Voice*, 3 August 2006.

INDEX

Anthem Politics and International Relations

Brown, Kerry *Struggling Giant* (2007)
Ringmar, Erik *Why Europe Was First* (2007)
Nolan, Peter *Integrating China* (2007)
Rangaswamy, Vedavalli *Energy for Development* (2007)
Ellman, Michael (ed.) *Russia's Oil and Natural Gas* (2006)
Di Lellio, Janine (ed.) *The Case for Kosova* (2006)
Ringmar, Erik *Surviving Capitalism* (2005)
Ritzen, Jozef *A Chance for the World Bank* (2004)
Fullbrook, Edward (ed.) *A Guide to What's Wrong
with Economics* (2004)
Chang, Ha-Joon *Kicking Away the Ladder* (2003)